Reforming Transport Pricing in the European Union

TRANSPORT ECONOMICS, MANAGEMENT AND POLICY

General Editor: Kenneth Button, *Professor of Public Policy, School of Public Policy, George Mason University, USA*

Transport is a critical input for economic development and for optimizing social and political interaction. Recent years have seen significant new developments in the way that transport is perceived by private industry and governments, and in the way academics look at it.

The aim of this series is to provide original material and up-to-date synthesis of the state of modern transport analysis. The coverage embraces all conventional modes of transport but also includes contributions from important related fields such as urban and regional planning and telecommunications where they interface with transport. The books draw from many disciplines and some cross-disciplinary boundaries. They are concerned with economics, planning, sociology, geography, management science, psychology and public policy. They are intended to help improve the understanding of transport, the policy needs of the most economically advanced countries and the problems of resource-poor developing economies. The authors come from around the world and will represent some of the outstanding young scholars as well as established names.

Titles in the series include:

Air Transport Networks
Theory and Policy Implications
Kenneth Button and Roger Stough

Analytical Transport Economics
An International Perspective
Edited by Jacob B. Polak and Arnold Heertje

Intelligent Transport Systems
Cases and Policies
Edited by Roger Stough

Transport and Environment
In Search of Sustainable Solutions
Edited by Eran Feitelson and Erik T. Verhoef

Environmental Costs and Liberalization in European Air Transport
A Welfare Economic Analysis
Youdi Schipper

Reforming Transport Pricing in the European Union
A Modelling Approach
Edited by Bruno De Borger and Stef Proost

Reforming Transport Pricing in the European Union

A Modelling Approach

Edited by

Bruno De Borger

Professor of Economics, University of Antwerp and Catholic University of Leuven, Belgium

Stef Proost

Professor of Environmental and Transport Economics, Catholic University of Leuven, Belgium

TRANSPORT ECONOMICS, MANAGEMENT AND POLICY

Edward Elgar

Cheltenham, UK • Northampton, MA, USA

Published by
Edward Elgar Publishing Limited
Glensanda House
Montpellier Parade
Cheltenham
Glos GL50 1UA
UK

Edward Elgar Publishing, Inc.
136 West Street
Suite 202
Northampton
Massachusetts 01060
USA

A catalogue record for this book
is available from the British Library

Library of Congress Cataloguing in Publication Data
Reforming transport pricing in the European Union: a modelling approach / edited by Bruno De Borger, Stef Proost.
p. cm. – (Transport economics, management, and policy)
Includes bibliographical references and index.
1. Transportation–Prices–European Union countries–Econometric models. I. Borger, Bruno De. II. Proost, S. III. Series
HE242.A2 R43 2002
388′.049–dc21 2001033467

ISBN 1 84064 129 0

Printed and bound in Great Britain by MPG Books Ltd, Bodmin, Cornwall

Contents

Figures

Tables

Contributors

Bal, Frans, Economic and Social Institute, Vrije Universiteit Amsterdam, De Boelelaan 1105, 1081 HV Amsterdam, Nederland

Courcelle, Christoph, University of Antwerp, UFSIA, Prinsstraat 13, 2000 Antwerpen, Belgium

De Borger, Bruno, University of Antwerp, UFSIA, Prinsstraat 13, 2000 Antwerpen, Belgium
tel.: +32/3-220 40 57; fax: +32/3/220 40 26;
e-mail: bruno.deborger@ua.ac.be

Dickerson, Andrew, CERTE, Keynes College, University of Kent at Canterbury, Canterbury CT2 7NP, UK;
fax: +44/1 227 82 77 84

Gibbons, Edna, Trinity College, Civil, Structural and Environmental Engineering, Trinity College Dublin, Dublin 2, Ireland

Heaney, Quinten, Trinity College, Civil, Structural and Environmental Engineering, Trinity College Dublin, Dublin 2, Ireland

Kirwan, K.J., Trinity College, Civil, Structural and Environmental Engineering, Trinity College Dublin, Dublin 2, Ireland

Mayeres, Inge, CES, Naamsestraat 69, 3000 Leuven, Belgium
tel.:+32/16/32 66 55; fax:+32/16/32 69 10;
e-mail: inge.mayeres@econ.kuleuven.ac.be

O'Mahony, Margaret, Trinity College, Civil, Structural and Environmental Engineering, Trinity College Dublin, Dublin 2, Ireland,
tel.: +353/1/60 82 084; fax: +353/1/667 30 72;
e-mail: mmmahony@tcd.ie

Peirson, John, CERTE, Keynes College, University of Kent at Canterbury, Canterbury CT2 7NP, UK;
tel.: +44/1 227 82 33 28; fax: +44/1 227 82 77 84;
e-mail: j.d.peirson@ukc.ac.uk

Proost, Stef, CES, Naamsestraat 69, 3000 Leuven, Belgium,
tel.:+32/16/32 68 01; fax:+32/16/32 69 10;
e-mail: stef.proost@econ.kuleuven.ac.be

Sharp, Duncan, CERTE, Keynes College, University of Kent at Canterbury, Canterbury CT2 7NP, UK

Van Dender, Kurt, CES, Naamsestraat 69, 3000 Leuven, Belgium
tel.:+32/16/32 66 55; fax:+32/16/32 69 10;
e-mail: kurt.vandender@econ.kuleuven.ac.be

van den Bergh, Jeroen C.J.M., Economic and Social Institute, Vrije Universiteit Amsterdam, De Boelelaan 1105, 1081 HV Amsterdam, Nederland,
tel.: +31/20 444 60 97; fax: +31/20 444 60 05;
e-mail: jvdbergh@econ.vu.nl

Verhoef, Eric T., Economic and Social Institute, Vrije Universiteit Amsterdam, De Boelelaan 1105, 1081 HV Amsterdam, Nederland,
tel.: +31/20 444 60 97; fax: +31/20 444 60 05;
e-mail: everhoef@econ.vu.nlave

Vickerman, Roger, CERTE, Keynes College, University of Kent at Canterbury, Canterbury CT2 7NP, UK;
tel.: +44/1 227 82 34 95; fax: +44/1 227 82 77 84;
e-mail: r.w.vickerman@ukc.ac.uk

Introduction and a reader's guide

Bruno De Borger and Stef Proost

Nearly everyone is confronted with traffic problems today. We all know what it is like to be stuck in a traffic jam, many people feel dissatisfied with public transport services or complain about excessive pollution generated by traffic. Moreover, almost each of us has a relative, friend or acquaintance who has been injured or even killed in a traffic accident. The problem is a complex one and there are conflicting interests at stake. Not surprisingly, every interest group has advanced its own remedy.

The economic diagnosis of the transport problem is quite clear, however. Congestion, pollution and accident risks are typical examples of what economists call external costs. These costs are insufficiently captured in the prices paid for the different transport services, so that the users do not pay the full social cost of transport. In this sense, prices are 'wrong' from an economic viewpoint. The European Commission has, in its recent Green Paper on Fair and Efficient Pricing, underwritten this basic principle. Although the idea of marginal social cost pricing has been accepted in the economics profession for a long time, there have been very few attempts to study its implementation. This book is the result of a European research action that aims to fill part of the large gap between textbook prescriptions and real world policy.[1] It was the first to study, on a European scale, the difference between current transport prices and 'optimal' transport prices that correctly charge marginal external costs. In addition, the project analysed which pricing reforms are most needed for economic efficiency reasons, taking into account restrictions on pricing instruments that governments are facing. Economic efficiency is taken here in its broad sense, including concerns for excessive congestion and environmental and safety objectives.

Of course, there have been several previous evaluations of transport pricing reforms. However, the research project out of which this book grew was rather unique for at least three reasons. First, it systematically tried to compute the best pricing reform given the available pricing instruments, using numerical optimisation models especially designed for this purpose. This type of second-best optimisation may give challenging results, because the mathematical optimisation of pricing reforms balances many different objectives and constraints. Second, the analysis allowed for a very large number of transport markets and takes into account their interactions. Third, we used the same model to analyse optimal transport prices in many different European countries. This strongly improves the comparability of the different case studies.

STRUCTURE OF THE BOOK

The book is divided into four major parts. In the introductory chapters (Part I), we explain the principles underlying the models used and we discuss the various pricing policies that were analysed in the applications later in the book. Part II provides more details about the theoretical structure of the models used. The computation of all external and internal costs of the different transport services is dealt with in Part III. Finally, Part IV contains the case studies, applying the model to different European cities and regions.

A brief overview of the book is as follows. Part I consists of three chapters. In Chapter 1 (by De Borger and Proost) a simple graphical economic model is presented to explain the basic economic concepts used. It shows the motivation for marginal social cost pricing, and it compares pricing as a policy instrument with environmental regulations and investment in infrastructure. Chapter 2 (by De Borger, Peirson and Vickerman) surveys the different policy instruments – including pricing instruments – that can be used to correct for the external costs of transport services. A third chapter (by De Borger, Peirson and Vickerman) specifies the common pricing scenarios that are used in the different case studies later in the book. A certain commonality in the reform scenarios is necessary to be able to compare pricing reforms and their implications between different countries and cities.

The structure of the models used is detailed in Part II. Chapter 4 (by Proost and Van Dender) deals with the model used to study optimal pricing in an urban environment. This model has been calibrated to the local conditions in different European cities, and optimal pricing policies have been determined. Similarly, Chapter 5 (by De Borger) explains the working of the interregional model. The interregional and urban models have similar structures, but the interregional version includes an international dimension and places more emphasis on freight transport. Finally, Chapter 6 (by Verhoef, Bal and Van den Bergh) presents an experimental version of the urban model that has been used to compute optimal prices in a network representation of the urban area.

In order to make the pricing models operational, different types of data are needed. The data common to all case studies and the procedures used to estimate internal and external costs are discussed in the four chapters of Part III. Chapter 7 (by Mayeres and Van Dender) presents the computation of the different external costs that are included in the optimal pricing exercises. The chapter deals with external congestion costs, accident costs, air pollution and noise costs. The estimates put forward in this chapter are useful for other studies as well. In Chapter 8 Dickinson, Peirson and Vickerman consider in more detail the estimation of the relation between accident rates and the volume of traffic. The empirical study that is reported here is an important input in the estimation of the external accident cost. Chapter 9 (by Peirson and Vickerman) deals with the different problems in estimating the resource cost of different transport modes. Finally, in Chapter 10, O'Mahony and Kirwan discuss the speed–flow relationship used to estimate marginal external congestion costs. Moreover, they briefly explain some technical problems involved in road pricing.

Part IV consists of six chapters. It mainly contains the different case studies on optimal pricing in Europe. Importantly, the chapters are written in such a way that they can be read independently. Each chapter starts from the main transport problems that the city or region under consideration has been facing, and it examines how these problems will develop up to the year 2005 with unchanged policies. This is then the background to study different pricing alternatives for the year 2005, assuming different types of restrictions on the policy instruments (for example, is electronic road pricing feasible, can parking be appropriately priced, and so on).

The first four chapters deal with the urban case studies. In Chapter 11 Van Dender discusses the results of different transport pricing policies for Brussels. Similarly, Chapters 12 and 13 contain case studies for Amsterdam (by van den Bergh and Verhoef) and Dublin (by Gibbons and O'Mahony). Finally, Peirson, Sharp and Vickerman tackle transport pricing issues in London. The last two chapters in Part IV deal with non-urban transport. Chapter 15 (by De Borger) deals with optimal pricing of transport services in Belgium. Compared to the urban chapters, freight transport and the international coördination of freight pricing policies become important issues. In Chapter 16, Heaney, O'Mahony and Gibbons examine transport pricing in Ireland.

Finally, in the concluding Chapter 17 all results of this volume are summed up and compared. The chapter summarises the main findings and presents some caveats of our analysis. For example, since the analysis was the first of its kind it is obvious that more detailed models, using a similar methodology, are needed to confirm the results that are presented here. Moreover, the models used in this book are based on a number of assumptions, some of which may be relaxed in future work.

A READER'S GUIDE

This book is an edited volume that is not necessarily to be read from the beginning chapter straight through to the end. For example, professional transport economists with a good understanding of external transport costs and optimal pricing as applied to the sector may be most interested in the structure of the models used and in the empirical results. Other readers may be much more interested in the underlying theory and in the procedures to determine external costs. The following guide may therefore help the reader to decide which chapters are relevant to her interests:

- A non-economist without technical interest could start out by reading Chapters 1, 2 and 3 as well as the summarising Chapter 17. If there is an interest in urban applications she could pick in addition one or more of the chapters 11, 12, 13 or 14; if she is more interested in interurban transport problems she could instead look at Chapters 15 and 16.
- A non-economist with a more technical interest in the structure of the models will benefit from adding Chapters 4, 5, 6 and 10.
- A transport economist with little technical interest could drop Chapter 1 and may be especially interested in Chapters 2, 3, 7, 9 and 17, to which she can add some of the case studies.
- Transport economists with more technical interests may include the more technically challenging Chapters 4, 5 and 6.
- Readers specifically interested in the external costs of transport may benefit from reading Chapters 7 and 8.

ACKNOWLEDGMENTS

The idea for this book project originated in 1996 when we started our European research consortium TRENEN II STRAN. Quite a few researchers have been involved in both the research phase (1996–98) and the stages of updating, revising and editing the results. In Antwerp, Didier Swysen and especially Christophe Courcelle made large contributions to developing the interregional model discussed in Chapter 5. In Leuven, Sara Ochelen and consequently Kurt Van Dender have been the researchers on this project. Sara Ochelen helped to develop the first TRENEN models. We also thank Edward Calthrop for integrating parking issues into the urban model and Inge Mayeres for continuous support on external cost issues. Fortunately, we could count on secretarial support by Isabelle Benoit and, for the final editing work, on the help of several graduate students. Thanks is also due to Prof. Chris Nash from ITS Leeds, who managed the coordinating CAPRI consortium. He has been continuously encouraging our approach. Finally, a special word of thanks is due to Catharina Sikow, our scientific officer at the European Commission, who strongly supported our lines of research over the years.

The development of research ideas takes a long time. The two editors have benefited from research funds granted by the Transport Research Program of the Belgian Federal Science Policy Office and by the Flemish Fund for Scientific Research of Flanders since the early 1990s. They are grateful for having had the opportunity to pursue the research summarised in this book.

NOTE

1. TRENEN- II-STRAN (1996–1998) funded by the 4th research program on Transport of the European Communities, coordinated by CES-KULeuven (S. Proost and K. van Dender)

PART I

Principles

1. Transport problems: the economic diagnosis

Bruno De Borger and Stef Proost

1.1 INTRODUCTION

Conceptually, the economic diagnosis of the transport problems currently faced by many European countries is quite simple. Transport produces a number of negative side effects or externalities (such as congestion and air pollution) that users of the transport infrastructure either completely ignore, or insufficiently take into account in making their travel decisions. As a consequence, there is generally too much traffic. Moreover, the distribution of traffic between periods of the day and across transport modes is inefficient: too much traffic takes place at inconvenient times using socially undesirable modes. Under ideal circumstances the suggested economic solution to the externality problem is quite simple as well: users of all transport modes and services should be charged for the marginal social costs, including all external costs, they inflict on society. This induces users to take account of all social costs in making their decisions. Implementation of this first-best principle is in practice not trivial, however. It requires full knowledge of all social marginal costs and it has to correctly capture all the interactions between different transport markets. Moreover, the basic principle has to be adjusted in second-best situations where for technical or political reasons correctly pricing all transport services at their social marginal cost is not feasible.

In this chapter we provide a brief and fairly non-technical overview of the economic approach to the analysis of transport externalities that underlies much of the applied work that follows later in the book. A more complete treatment of the issues can be found in books on transport economics (see, for example, Button, 1992; Small, 1992).

The chapter is structured as follows. Section 1.2 starts from the simplest microeconomic model. We consider present volumes of traffic within a demand and supply model of the market for private passenger transport by road.[1] In Section 1.3 we give an illustration of the optimal tax which takes into account the external effects within this framework. We also clearly indicate which groups in society gain and which groups lose as a consequence of the introduction of the optimal taxes. In Section 1.4 we show that under realistic conditions a better solution can be obtained within the transport market by complementing tax policies with the use of other policy instruments. This relates to the difference between two types of external effect, that is effects linked almost exclusively to traffic volume (like congestion) and effects linked to other factors (like harmful exhaust emissions). To take account of these two different types of external effect it may be necessary to use different instruments. In Section 1.5 we show how the argument becomes more complex if different transport markets are simultaneously taken into account within a restricted range of policy instruments. We look at two concrete examples: first, we consider the interaction between the market for car traffic at peak periods and off-peak periods; second, the interaction between the markets for private car transport and public transport at the peak period is treated. Since the supply and demand model refers to a given transport infrastructure, Section 1.6 discusses the relation between optimal pricing policy and improvements to the transport infrastructure through investment. Finally, in Section 1.7 we briefly discuss a number of macroeconomic aspects which will only be briefly touched on below, namely, environmental policy, redistributional aspects, and the presence of other disequilibria elsewhere in the economy.

1.2 PRESENT ROAD TRAFFIC AS A MARKET EQUILIBRIUM WITH EXTERNALITIES

We shall begin with an analysis of one specific transport market. Let us take the concrete example of the market for car trips between Antwerp and Brussels (a 50 kilometre trip between two urban centres in Belgium) on a weekday in the morning peak between 7 and 9. Although there are, of course, a variety of different types of car, to keep things simple we assume that everyone uses the same type (for example a small car using petrol); moreover, by assumption each car has only one occupant.

In order to interpret present traffic as a market equilibrium, we need to consider the determinants of demand and supply on the transport market. The demand for transport will obviously depend on the 'price' of the trip. In transport economics this is usually expressed as a 'generalised' price (in EUR/vehicle-km.). It consists of several components. First, the traveller incurs a cost to pay for petrol, maintenance and repair, and so on. These costs consist in part of resource costs and in part of various taxes (for example VAT, excise duties). Second, apart from monetary expenditure, the generalised price also includes the value of the time spent on the journey.

Travelling by car takes time, and time is valuable ('time is money'). One expects that as the generalised price falls, more people will decide to make the journey by car. A fall in price might result from a drop in monetary expenditure (for example lower petrol prices) or from an increase in speed.

The following example will serve to illustrate the idea of a generalised price. Let us assume that the actual resource costs for the car journey (fuel costs, depreciation, maintenance excluding tax, and so on) amounts to 0.15 EUR/km and taxes to 0.1 EUR/km, giving a total expenditure of 0.25 EUR/km.[2] Let us further assume that with a low volume of traffic the average speed is 100 km/h. This means 0.6 minute per km. If we take the average time value to be 7.5 EUR/h, then one arrives at a time cost of 0.075 EUR/km. In other words the generalised price in low-density traffic will be 0.325 EUR/km.

On the supply side of the transport market, it is necessary to see how the costs of additional traffic depend on the traffic volume. The 'generalised' cost of transport also includes both monetary expenditures and a time cost. It is therefore immediately apparent that any additional traffic will cause the generalised cost for the motorist to rise as the volume of traffic on the road between Antwerp and Brussels increases. Indeed, average speed of the traffic flow will drop as more drivers come onto the road. In order to fully understand the relation between generalised costs and traffic volume it is worth looking in more detail at the various components of these costs as shown in Figure 1.1.

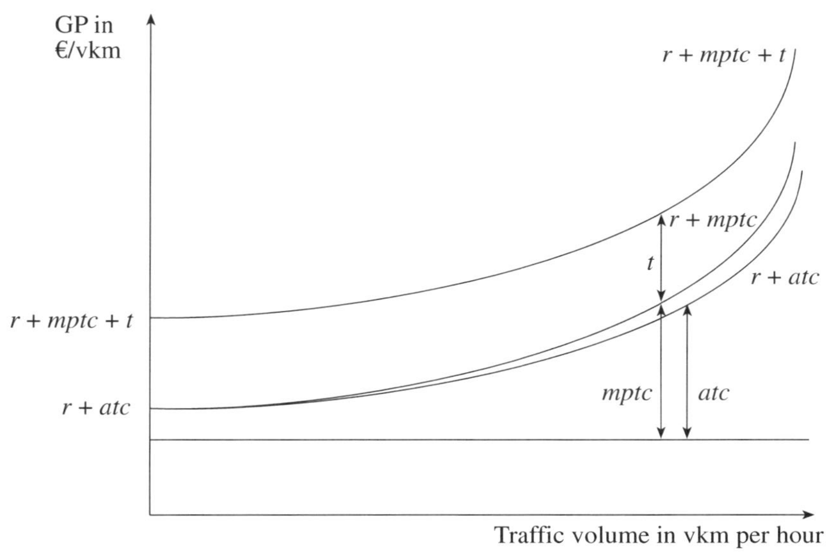

Figure 1.1 Private costs of car use

The first component the motorist takes into account is the actual resource cost. This is expressed per km and represented by *r*. To avoid making the graph unnecessarily complicated this is assumed to be constant, that is, independent of traffic volume. The second component is the time cost for the journey. We shall take it that any decision on the motorist's part will be influenced by the time costs he himself experiences. Thus, in deciding whether or not to go by car, he will not take into account the possible loss of time he causes others. In transport-economic terms, the only relevant time cost from the motorist's point of view is the *marginal private time cost*, that is what it costs him to drive on the motorway in a given volume of traffic. In theory the time cost for the motorist should consist of the average time cost for the actual flow of traffic, plus the increase in the average time cost which he himself causes. This follows from the fact that any additional vehicle increases the volume of traffic, thus causing a drop in the average speed. In practice the latter effect is in most cases so small that it can be ignored.[3] In this case the difference between the average and the marginal private time cost is virtually zero. It is only in very dense, slow-moving traffic that the effect of an additional vehicle will become noticeable. In Figure 1.1 we have drawn both the average time costs and the marginal private time costs as a function of the volume of traffic. They are represented respectively by *atc* and *mptc*.

The third component taken into account by the motorist is the tax he pays on fuel, maintenance, and so on. In Figure 1.1 this tax is expressed per km and represented by *t*; for the sake of simplicity it is assumed constant. The curve $(r + mptc + t)$ shows the private cost, including tax, from the motorist's point of view. This comprises all the monetary and time costs taken into account by the motorist.

The present equilibrium on the transport market 'Antwerp–Brussels' in the morning rush hour is shown graphically in Figure 1.2. The demand curve is represented by the downward sloping curve 'Demand'. It represents the volume of traffic (vehicles per hour) as a function of the generalised price. Alternatively, it expresses the willingness to pay for a trip (or value) of the motorist at varying traffic volumes. In the graph other determinants of demand, such as income and prices of alternative modes of transport (train, bus), have been kept constant. The curve shows that in the case of a very high generalised price, very few people will travel by car from Antwerp to Brussels in the given period. Only those willing to pay this high price will do so; for example, office workers without flexible working hours and with no suitable alternative mode of transport. As the price falls, more people will chose to go by car. Indeed, if the generalised price is very low, then drivers will include those who do not strictly speaking have to be in Brussels at that hour, like tourists interested in visiting museums, or shoppers.

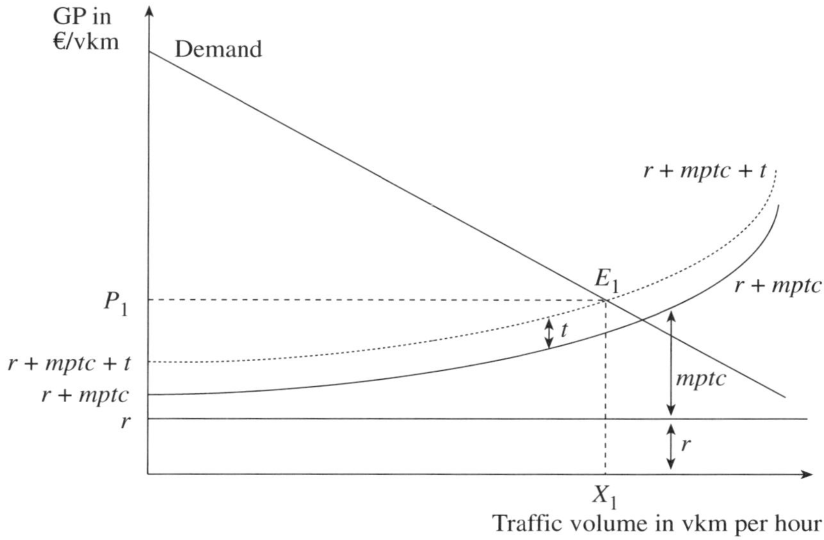

Figure 1.2 Equilibrium of car transport market

The present market equilibrium is E_1, the point at which the demand curve intersects the marginal private cost curve for the motorist.[4] The (generalised) equilibrium price is P_1. All drivers willing to 'pay' at least P_1 will use the car in the morning peak. Those who are not prepared to pay the cost of going by car will either forsake the trip or find another mode of transport to make it. However, it is obvious that the present equilibrium E_1 is economically undesirable, because it involves important remaining external effects: drivers do not pay for all social costs they impose on society. Many people make the trip without being willing to cover all marginal social costs it entails. By way of illustration, let us look at two external effects in more detail: congestion and air pollution.[5]

In equilibrium E_1 each motorist will already experience the effects of congestion: time costs per km are much higher than in free flowing traffic, since the speed of traffic under the given volume at E_1 is slower than in free flow. Assume that the average speed at the current equilibrium is 25 km/h. The motorist will certainly take into account the time loss he himself suffers as a result of this low average speed. What he will not take into account, however, is the time loss his road use imposes upon all other road users. Precisely how this time loss is to be calculated will be explained in Chapter 7; here we consider only a broad outline. Let us assume that at E_1 there are 3000 vehicles per hour travelling on the road from Antwerp to Brussels. Any additional traffic will slow down the average speed. For one single extra vehicle the drop in speed will of course be extremely small. Say that it amounts to something in the order of 0.04 km/h. Now in spite of this minute effect, the decision of an arbitrary motorist to go by car in the morning rush hour imposes a time loss on other road users which cannot be simply ignored. Indeed, the reduction in average speed implies for each of the other 3000 vehicles a time loss of 0.003846 min per km. Calculated at an average time cost of 7.5 EUR/h this means a total external congestion cost of approximately 1.45 EUR/km![6]

Each vehicle on the Antwerp–Brussels trajectory also contributes to air pollution, ozone formation, climate change, acid rain and harmful particulates. Motorists likewise fail to take into account this external environmental damage. Let us assume for the sake of argument that these environmental costs amount to 0.05 EUR/km.

The total marginal cost per km to the community for one additional car on the road will therefore be:

 0.15 EUR (actual resource costs)
+0.30 EUR (private time costs at an average speed of 25km/h)
+1.45 EUR (extra time costs for other road users)
+0.05 EUR (environmental costs for the rest of society)

Added up, this amounts to a total cost of 1.95 EUR per vehicle km. When we compare this with the prices charged at present, it becomes clear that road users pay far less than the real cost:[7] they are charged only 0.55 EUR/vehicle km (that is, resource cost (0.15), private time cost (0.30), current tax (0.10)). The difference lies in the marginal external congestion cost (1.45 EUR) and the marginal external environmental cost (0.05 EUR), which amount to much more than the tax paid (0.10 EUR).

It is important to emphasise once again that marginal external costs increase with the volume of traffic. This is especially the case for the marginal external congestion costs. As more traffic is using a road with given capacity, there will be more congestion. This means first, that additional traffic will have an increasing effect upon the average time cost and second, that any additional vehicle will cause a delay for a greater number of road users. Together these factors imply increased external congestion costs. To illustrate the issue we have represented the marginal external congestion costs (MECC) in Figure 1.3. The figure also contains the marginal external environmental costs (MEEC); for simplicity it is assumed that the latter remain constant per km.

As suggested before, equilibrium E_1 is socially unacceptable simply because it fails to incorporate these important external costs. It will be formally shown below why this is the case. To do so, it is useful to point out that, in order to measure total welfare at a particular equilibrium, economists con-

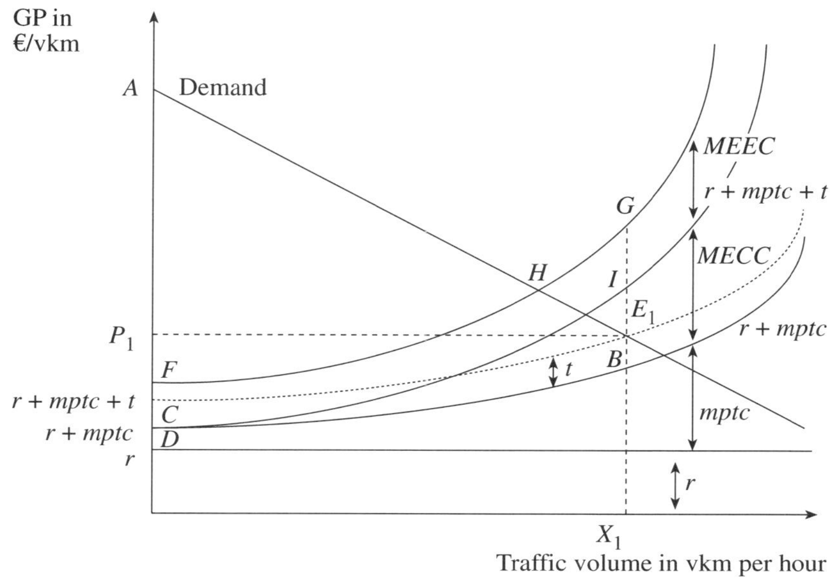

Figure 1.3 External costs of car use

sider the welfare of consumers and producers, tax income, and all external costs. To determine each of these components four *surplus concepts* are used, each expressed in monetary terms to allow a direct comparison. First, in the standard approach the direct welfare of the consumer in a market is measured via the consumer surplus. This measures the difference between what the consumer is willing to pay for the consumed quantity (reflected by the demand curve) and what he actually has to pay. In terms of Figure 1.3, consumer surplus is given by the area below the demand curve and above the market price. It expresses the fact that consumer welfare increases as the price falls. Second, producer surplus is used as a measure of producer welfare. It can be formally defined as the difference between what the producer actually receives for the quantity produced and the lowest price at which he was willing to supply this quantity. In a competitive market this boils down to the producers' profit. In graphical terms it can be represented as the area between producers' revenues and the marginal cost curve. Third, tax revenues are simply equal to the tax per unit times the quantity traded. Fourth, the final welfare component is the monetary value of the total external costs.

Importantly, typically the various surpluses will accrue to different groups. In the present case the consumer surplus goes to the motorist and the producer surplus goes to car suppliers, fuel suppliers, and so on.

Increased tax revenues benefit the government and imply a combination of one of the following three possibilities. Other taxes in the economy may be lowered, there may be an increase in public expenditure (for example education, health), or it may lead to a reduction in government deficit which itself lowers taxes for future generations. Finally, higher external environmental costs will largely be borne by non-motorists, for example by those with lung problems who are susceptible to the particulates and the ozone produced by traffic emissions.

A comparison of the welfare effects of different equilibria on the transport market differs slightly from the standard procedure in other markets. The reason is that the time costs make up an explicit component of the generalised costs. This must be taken into account in the interpretation of consumer and producer surpluses. Moreover, it is the case in a standard commodity market that the marginal resource cost refers to the production cost of one additional unit. A difference with other markets is that, on the transport market, the marginal private time costs due to an extra vehicle are experienced by all motorists on the road.[8] This involves a number of adjustments in the interpretation.

Specifically, the consumer surplus in equilibrium E_1 can be expressed as the area P_1AE_1 in Figure 1.3. Note that the time costs are included in the generalised cost. This means that the benefit from an increase in speed will show up as an increase in consumer surplus. With regard to the producer surplus, we need to distinguish two components. First, there is the surplus for the producer of the purchased goods, that is the profits for those who supply cars, tyres, petrol, and so on. In our present simplified example as shown in Figure 1.3, we assume perfect competition and constant resource costs r per km, so there is no economic profit. Hence this surplus is zero. The second component in the producer surplus comprises the time cost of the motorist, who in fact 'produces' vehicle-km by combining purchased goods (the car, fuel, and so on) with his own time. In their dual role of consumer and producer they 'pay' themselves as it were for the production of vehicle-kilometres. Note, however, that the surplus for the motorist as producer is likewise zero; after all, he pays exactly the average time cost, so that no surplus remains. The total surplus for the motorist as consumer and producer therefore amounts to the area P_1AE_1. Tax revenues in Figure 1.3 are shown as the area DCE_1B.

The final welfare component that needs to be considered is the monetary value of the total external costs, as expressed by the area *DFGB*. This area represents the sum of the marginal external costs from the first vehicle km to the last. It comprises the total external congestion costs *DIB* and the total environmental costs *DFGI*.[9]

In view of the above, total welfare is the sum of consumer and producer surplus, plus tax revenues, minus the total external costs. Given that the time costs form a component of the total production costs, this means that the total welfare at equilibrium E_1 can be expressed graphically as area P_1AE_1 plus DCE_1B, minus $DFGI$.[10] Interestingly, there is a second, and graphically much simpler, representation of total welfare which can be shown to be equivalent to the first one. It is the difference between the total willingness to pay and the total social costs. In graphical terms, welfare can then be represented by the difference between the area FAH and the area HGE_1.[11] We shall be using this simpler representation below.

1.3 A BETTER MARKET EQUILIBRIUM

The present equilibrium E_1 can of course be corrected. The purpose of the correction is to arrive at an equilibrium in which all motorists are confronted with the total marginal cost of their road use, including marginal external congestion and environmental costs.

The basic idea is simple enough, but it must be properly implemented. A first reflex (incorrect as it happens) might be to charge all motorists the marginal social cost at the *present* equilibrium E_1. This is shown in Figure 1.4. The present (too low) tax t would then be replaced by a tax BG which corresponds to the marginal external costs for car use at traffic volume X_1. This would be the wrong solution. Charging motorists tax BG raises the generalised price per vehicle km to $(r + mptc + BG)$. But, as can be immediately seen from the demand curve, imposing this tax would cause a drop in the volume of traffic to X_2 and the new equilibrium would be E_2. At that equilibrium the tax paid, shown graphically by the distance IE_2, is exactly equal to BG. Therefore, car users would in fact be paying much more than the additional external cost they are causing. What they pay is IE_2 while the marginal external cost is considerably less, namely IH. Charging the marginal external cost has caused a drop in car use and, as a consequence, in congestion. There is a reduction in the marginal external cost for two reasons. First, since the traffic volume is now further from capacity, any additional vehicle will cause less time loss. Second, the number of vehicles experiencing this time loss is now lower.

In social terms the volume of traffic is too low at E_2: even those who would have been willing to pay the marginal social cost are now priced off the road by the high tax. To avoid this situation and to arrive at the correct equilibrium, we need to set tax levels so that all motorists pay the marginal social cost that remains at the *optimal equilibrium*. We should be charging *'optimal' social costs*, not observed or current social costs. This is shown graphically in Figure 1.4. The optimal equilibrium E_3 is obtained at the intersection of the demand and marginal social cost curves. The correct tax is E_3J. Charging this tax will make everyone pay the marginal extra cost he or she causes at the optimal traffic volume X_3, that is, the traffic volume that remains after imposition of the tax.

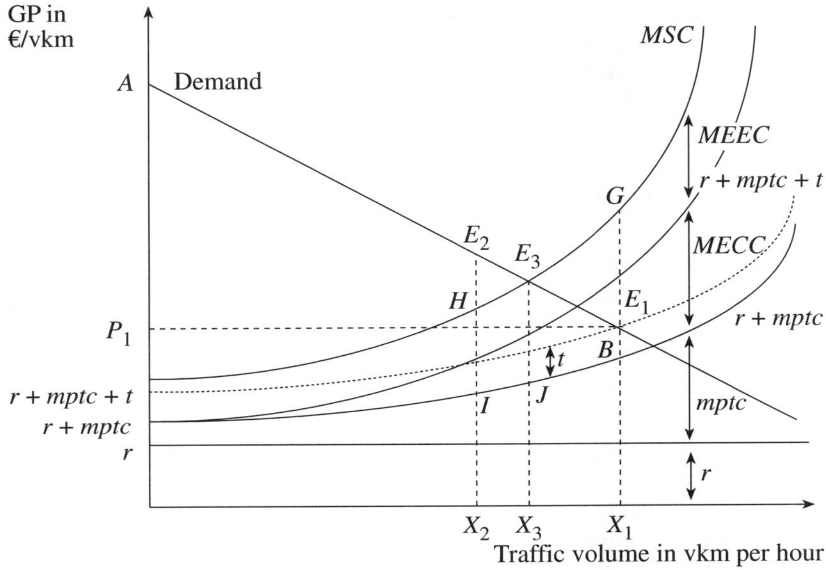

Figure 1.4 Optimal tax on car use

There can be a considerable difference between the external costs at present traffic volumes and those at optimal volumes. In the calculations presented later in the book we shall see that the marginal external cost in the best equilibrium may be as little as a third of the total marginal external cost in the initial equilibrium. This goes to show how important it is to take the marginal external costs in the optimal equilibrium, not the costs measured within the present transport market.

The switch from the present equilibrium E_1 to the 'optimal' equilibrium E_3 generates an *important welfare gain for society*. This can be seen by calculating the difference in total welfare in the two equilibria. Performing this exercise we see that the welfare gain corresponds to the area of the triangle E_3GE_1 in Figure 1.5. The interpretation of this area is straightforward: it represents the difference between the total willingness to pay by former road users who in the new equilibrium no longer use the road (due to the decrease in traffic volume from X_1 to X_3) and the high social costs for which they were responsible. This welfare gain is obvious. On the one hand, in social terms, there is a 'saving' of resource costs and of external environmental and congestion costs that the now eliminated traffic would have caused. On the other hand, there is the loss of 'benefits' this traffic would have enjoyed; the latter is measured by the demand curve, expressing car users' willingness to pay.

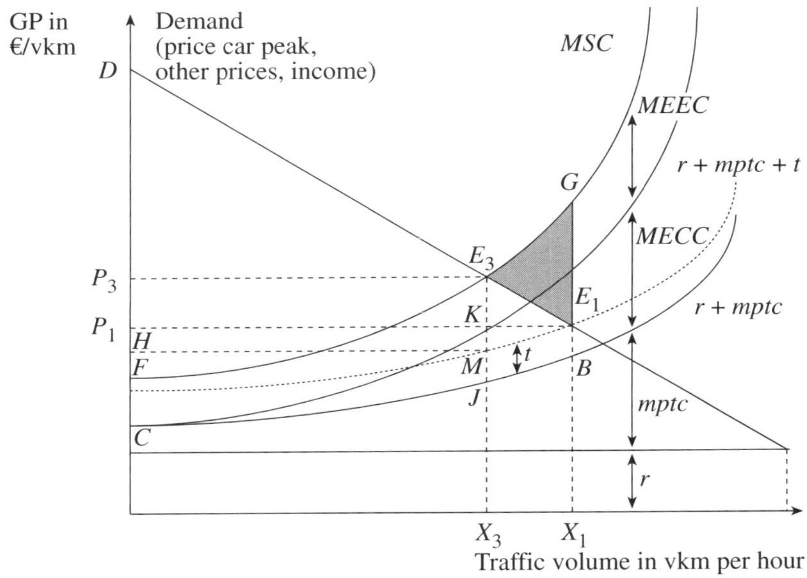

Figure 1.5 Welfare loss of inefficient pricing

Of course, the fact that a noticeable gain in welfare is generated does not mean that all parties are equally enthusiastic about the new equilibrium. This becomes apparent when we take a closer look at the welfare effects for car users, the shifts in external costs, and the changes in tax revenues. We illustrate the different changes in Figure 1.5.

Car users pay more than before: the generalised price is now P_3 instead of P_1. As a consequence the traffic volume decreases from X_1 to X_3. Those who give up the car will either have to opt for some alternative means of transport, or forfeit the journey altogether. They are worse off now than they were in the previous equilibrium E_1. Their loss in consumer surplus is shown as the triangle E_3E_1K. The remaining motorists also incur a loss in consumer surplus, namely the area $P_3E_3KP_1$, due to the increase in the generalised price from P_1 to P_3. The latter increase can be split into two components: the increase in tax per km (represented by ME_3) is partly compensated by a time gain per km equal to MK.

In view of the above, the shift in welfare for motorists as a group boils down to a net loss in surplus equal to the area $P_3E_3E_1P_1$. One thing is clear: if motorists do not get back part of the increased tax revenue under the form of a reduction in other taxes, they will be definitely worse off. One can therefore expect them to oppose a tax that incorporates the marginal external costs as long as there is no guarantee that other taxes will be reduced.

The decrease in traffic volume produces a decrease in the external costs caused by congestion and environmental damage. Both those who experienced the negative effects of congestion and those who suffered from environmental pollution are now better off. The monetary value of this decrease in external costs is shown as the area E_3GBJ. This area is the sum of decreases in average time costs for the remaining road users (equivalent to P_1KMH and also included in the change of consumer surplus) and the decrease in air pollution costs.

The government may win or lose in comparison with the previous equilibrium E_1. It loses the tax on people that decide no longer to use the car – a loss shown by the area E_1BJM. At the same time, it gains on the much higher tax on the remaining traffic; this extra revenue is given by the area P_3E_3MH. In theory, this extra tax revenue should allow other tax cuts to be made.[12]

Two conclusions can be drawn at this stage. First, optimal pricing will generate a total net increase in welfare. Second, not everyone stands to gain by the implementation of optimal prices. In particular, frequent car users will only gain if they somehow receive back a large part of the taxes they pay. In other words, the issue of redistribution of tax revenues will be crucial in determining the social acceptability of external cost pricing.

To conclude our analysis of equilibrium E_3 it needs to be pointed out that, in theory at least, this equilibrium can be reached by other means than through the tax system. In principle one can obtain a similar result by introducing a 'market' for peak-period traffic rights, where each motorist would receive a number of rights at, say, the beginning of the year. These will be required by anyone using the infrastructure at peak periods. Frequent peak car users can buy extra peak rights from motorists who have an excess supply of traffic rights, or who simply prefer to have the money rather than using the car. In theory such a market could be created. One can show that the equilibrium price for peak-period rights will be close to the optimal tax, provided the number of rights in circulation matches the optimal traffic volume. Such a system is difficult to operate, however, because transaction costs will be very high. Not only must peak rights be introduced for all roads where congestion is a problem, but there will be millions of motorists participating in the market. On the other hand, handing out negotiable peak rights to motorists is perhaps a politically more attractive option than having to create 'new taxes'. The same beneficial effects can, however, be achieved in a much more efficient manner by incorporating the external effects correctly in the pricing system and redistributing the surplus revenue among the population. As a solution, a system of optimal taxation seems far superior.

1.4 TOWARDS A MORE EFFECTIVE POLICY

So far our analysis has used a tax per vehicle km in the peak period to charge motorists for external congestion and environmental costs. This single policy instrument is meant to lessen congestion and get to grips with the environmental problem. In practice, however, it may be possible to attain an outcome even better than equilibrium E_3 by using other policy instruments apart from taxation. To support this argument it is instructive to distinguish between two types of external effects: those determined entirely by traffic volume (henceforth Type I) and those that are related to other factors as well (Type II). Congestion is a Type I externality. Air pollution is a typical Type II externality: the amount of air pollution depends not only on the volume of traffic, but also on engine efficiency and on the possible presence of a three-way catalytic converter.

The most suitable policy instrument will vary according to the type of external effect. The most direct way to tackle a Type I externality (for example congestion) is to reduce traffic volumes at peak periods. Assuming that the technical possibilities for implementing it are present, a peak-period tax per vehicle-km seems the right instrument, for it will produce the desired reduction in traffic. However, faced with an externality of Type II, and given present technologies, it is typically not optimal to rely solely on taxation instruments for at least two reasons. First, remember that the analysis of the previous section was based on the unrealistic assumption of one given car type. In reality, a large number of different types of vehicles exist. This would imply that, to implement perfect taxation of externalities, the emissions produced by each car would have to be monitored and taxed in function of the damage caused. The continuous monitoring and charging for emissions requires, however, an advanced system of measurement and a tax per km that varies from vehicle to vehicle in function of the pollutant level of the car. This does not look technically feasible in the near future.

Second, it was implicitly assumed in the previous section that the only way environmental costs could be reduced was through a reduction in vehicle-km travelled. Of course, this is not true in practice. Motorists do not necessarily have to reduce distances in order to cut environmental damage; other steps they might take include switching to a more environment-friendly car, or better engine maintenance.

In sum, perfectly taxing pollution is not feasible, and imposing a straightforward tax per km to account for environmental external costs is inefficient, given the existence of different types of vehicles and taking account of other possible alternatives to reduce emissions apart from reducing traffic volumes. It is more efficient to complement taxes with other instruments in order to tackle the environmental externality. Such possibilities exist. For example, one can reduce pollution levels from emissions of carbon monoxide (CO), nitrogen oxides (NO_x) and volatile organic compounds (VOC) by up to 80–90 per cent simply by fitting cars with a three-way catalyst. To get the same reduction in environmental impacts via a km tax, the level of a km tax would have to be sufficiently high to cut back traffic volumes by 80–90 per cent.[13] This is far from efficient. If one wants to reduce the external costs caused by air pollution, this should be done at the lowest cost to society. The social cost for compulsory fitting of a three-way catalyst is much less than the cost of reducing traffic volumes by 80–90 per cent, which would bring economic activity to a virtual standstill.

The best policy for Type II externalities seems therefore to be a combination of instruments. With our present technology it is not possible to reduce pollution from cars to an 'optimal' level simply by imposing taxes on the traffic volume (for example, a tax per km). One must therefore strive to achieve optimal levels by other means (for example compulsory catalysts, enforceable emission standards). Once these measures are in place, a tax per vehicle-km could then still be imposed to cover any eventual environmental damage remaining after cars have made the required modifications. This combination of instruments will produce the same environmental end result (for example 80 per cent reduction in emissions) at a much lower social cost than can be achieved by a tax on the volume of traffic alone.

The general principle is illustrated graphically in Figure 1.6. We assume that in the optimal equilibrium using only a km tax (E_3) none of the cars are fitted with a catalyst. The km tax charges motorists for both congestion and environmental costs. Given the present impossibility of a vehicle-specific tax on emissions, the environmental impact is based on the average emission. Under these circumstances it is clear that no motorist will be interested in having a catalyst installed: after all, he is taxed on the emission level of the average car independent of his efforts to reduce pollution. Let us now look at the effects of making the catalyst compulsory for all cars. The increase in purchase price implies in Figure 1.6 an increase in the actual resource cost r, indicated by dr. On the other hand, the immediate reduction in emissions will mean much lower marginal external environmental costs (they will fall by $dMEMC$). This will eventually yield an improved equilibrium E_4, which combines vehicle standards with a tax on car use. In this equilibrium the volume of traffic will increase slightly compared to E_3. The reason is that the compulsory catalyst limits the environmental damage, thus allowing a slight reduction in the km tax; consequently the demand for transport will increase slightly. The total increase in welfare compared to E_3 is equal to the area AE_3E_4B. This area comprises two components. The first relates to the initial traffic X_3 and is equivalent to the value of the reduced environmental damage and the cost of the catalyst. The second component concerns the difference between the willingness to pay and the social costs caused by the additional traffic ($X_4 - X_3$).

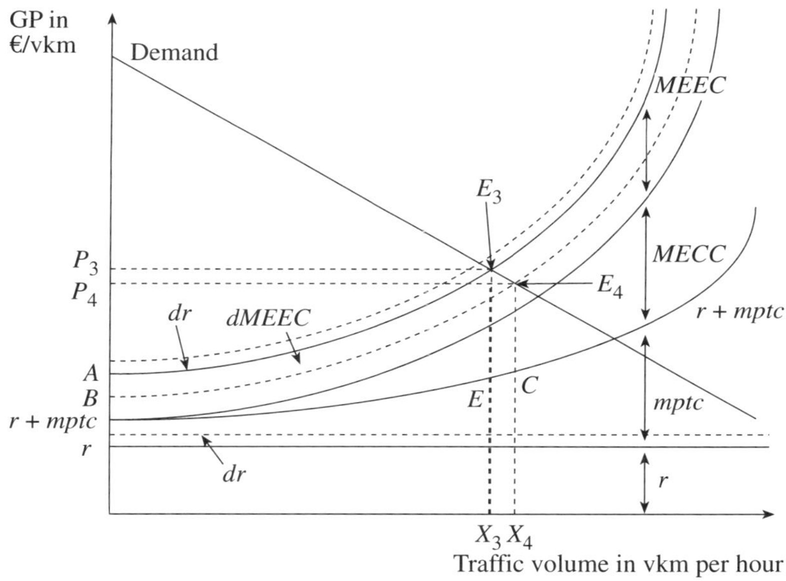

Figure 1.6 Emission regulation and pricing

In practice the purchase of the compulsory catalyst might be subsidised. Note, however, that in the future these sort of measures may no longer be necessary as soon as it becomes technologically possible to tax cars on the basis of their environmental efficiency.

The conclusion is clear enough. Whereas congestion can best be tackled via a peak tax per km, in the case of Type II externalities we need a combination of optimal pricing for the volume of traffic and environmental norms (or alternative measures) for cars (and drivers). This applies not only to air pollution, but also to noise damage and accident risks. A survey of possible pricing and regulatory instruments will be given below in Chapter 3.

1.5 THE RELATION BETWEEN DIFFERENT TRANSPORT MARKETS

So far the discussion has proceeded within a single given transport market, namely the market for peak-period car traffic between Antwerp and Brussels. In reality there are obviously many different transport markets, defined in function of place, time of day, transport mode, type of vehicle, and so on. For example, one might want to consider the market for car traffic with small diesel engines in the peak period within the Antwerp agglomeration, the market for bus transport in the off-peak period, the market for train traffic between Brussels and Antwerp in the rush hour, and so on. In theory the optimal taxes within different markets must be simultaneously investigated and calculated for at least three reasons. First, the demand within one market depends on the price on other markets. If there is a sharp increase in the price of a train ticket, the demand curve in the car market will shift to the right: whatever the generalised price there will be a higher demand for car use. The shift in the demand curve also implies a change in the optimal tax on car use. Second, the same infrastructure is used by different transport modes (like car and bus). If the price of car use is increased, the level of congestion will fall; consequently, the generalised price for buses declines since average bus speed will now be higher. Third, the interaction between transport markets can be of great importance when in practice it is impossible to set optimal prices for certain market segments. Unfortunately, this proves to be the rule rather than the exception due to technical limitations as well as political and social feasibility.

Two examples may perhaps serve to illustrate the importance of the interaction between market segments. The first concerns the impossibility of introducing a differential tax for peak and off-peak car use. In theory this is desirable to account for differences in congestion. Since peak-period congestion is much higher, the optimal tax on car use at these times should be correspondingly higher. Unfortunately the instruments to implement such a differentiated tax may not be available, and often the government resorts to a fuel tax instead.

Figure 1.7 presents simultaneously the transport market for car use between Antwerp and Brussels in the peak and off-peak periods. For the sake of convenience we make a number of assumptions. We start from a situation in which there is no tax on car use: this results in equilibrium E_1 for the peak period and E_2 for the off-peak period. We also assume that the demand for car use in the peak hours is not influenced by the pricing of car use in the off-peak hours and vice versa. Moreover we assume that congestion is the only external cost and that it is only feasible to impose a single tax for car use which applies to both peak and off-peak periods. If it were indeed possible to impose a differentiated tax, optimal taxes would equal marginal congestion cost in each particular period. But what level of taxation will have to be set if the government is limited to a single tax per km for both peak and off-peak periods?[14]

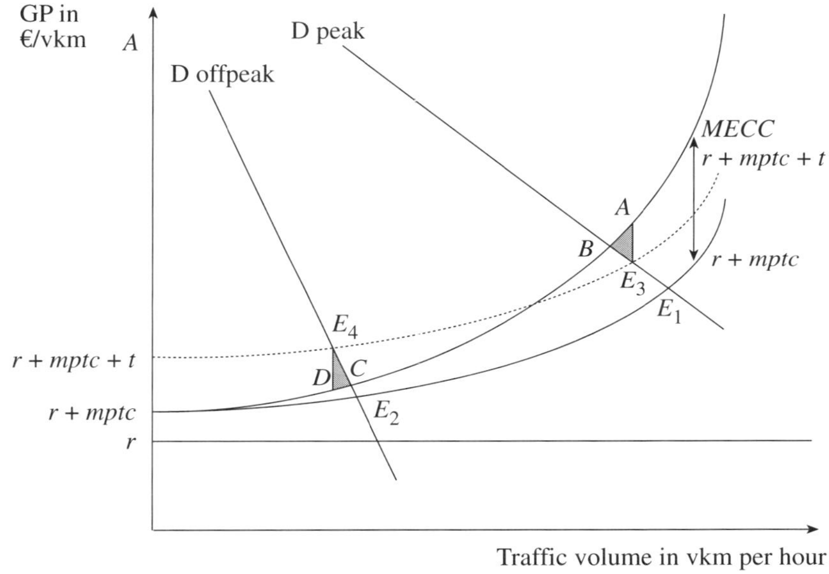

Figure 1.7 Optimal non-differentiated tax

In principle, one could start by charging the average marginal congestion cost. However, economic theory suggests that it might be advisable to take account of differences in the price elasticities of demand for car traffic in the peak and off-peak period. By definition these elasticities give the percentage change in the quantity demanded for a price rise of 1 per cent, that is they measure the price-sensitivity of demand. In Figure 1.7 the off-peak demand in equilibrium E_2 is less elastic than peak demand in equilibrium E_1. Economic theory suggests that it is better to impose an optimal tax closer to the external cost of car use in the peak period (compare De Borger et al., 1996). The reason is that, because of differences in price sensitivity, the same deviation between the generalised price and the marginal social cost (actual resource cost + marginal external cost) produces a larger demand distortion in the peak period (too much traffic) than in the off-peak period (too little traffic). By setting a tax level closer to the external cost at peak times one minimises the loss of surplus in comparison to the optimal tax raised if one were indeed able to differentiate between the two periods. The optimal undifferentiated tax produces the dotted marginal private cost curve, where the loss in surplus with respect to the differentiated prices is equal to AE_3B in the peak period and E_4CD in the off-peak period.

If one takes into account that each of the demand curves does depend on the prices in the two periods, then the computation of the optimal average tax becomes a lot more complex, for both demand curves will shift. Indeed, one will have to use a mathematical model to calculate the optimum.

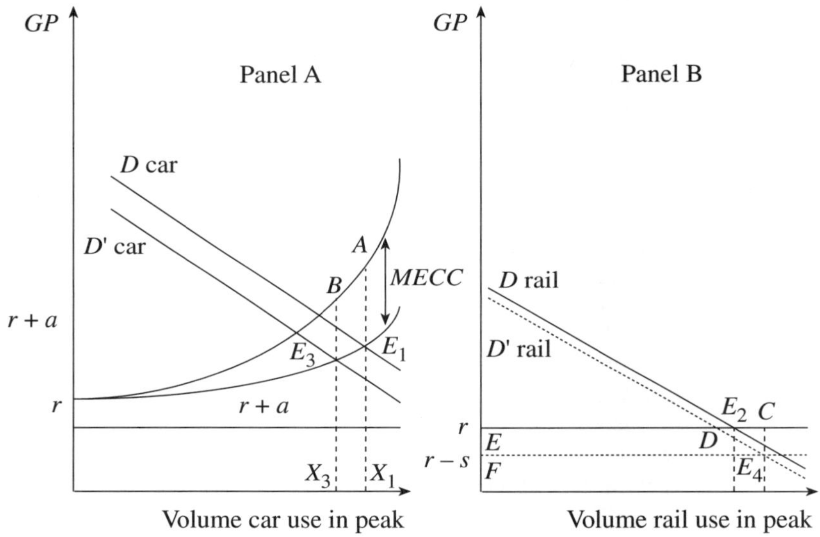

Figure 1.8 Pricing and interrelated transport markets

The second example concerns the relation between pricing of car and train travel in peak times, assuming that for social or political reasons car use is underpriced. Second-best theory argues that if prices are too low in one market, it is better to reduce prices below marginal social cost in the related market as well. This case is illustrated graphically in Figure 1.8, which shows car and train use at peak hours. To start with, let us assume that the price of a train ticket is equal to the marginal resource cost and that train traffic produces no external costs. This gives us equilibrium E_2 in Figure 1.8B. Let us further suppose that it is not feasible to impose any extra tax on peak car traffic, which gives us equilibrium E_1 in Figure 1.8A. Here of course the volume of car traffic is far too high, because there remains a significant external cost – represented by the distance AE_1 – for which car users are not charged. Given the assumption that peak car traffic cannot directly be taxed, another approach is to subsidise alternative modes of transport such as the train. That is what has frequently happened in the past in many European countries. Assume, then, that the train gets a subsidy s. This subsidy reduces the price of rail travel, with the result that the demand for peak car travel shifts to the left (from D to D' in Figure 1.8A). The 'substitute' has become more attractive, and whatever the generalised price for car traffic there will be slightly fewer cars. This gives us a new peak period equilibrium E_3 at traffic volume X_3. The reduced traffic volume will cause a slight increase in the average speed and hence a fall in the generalised price for private car use, in turn causing a slight shift to the left in the demand for train travel (from D to D' in Figure 1.8B). The final new equilibrium in the train transport market is E_4.

The graph shows how a subsidy to public transport can cause a shift in demand in a related market. On account of the diverse shifts in demand it is extremely difficult, without a mathematical model, to say whether such subsidies are justified or not, or how big they should be. The changes in consumer surplus are difficult to illustrate graphically. However, apart from consumer surplus changes, what can be shown is that the subsidy will produce three other important welfare effects. First, there is the saving on external costs through the reduction in car traffic. These external cost reductions correspond graphically to the area E_3BAE_1. Second, there is an undesirable negative effect, namely the 'excessive' use of the train, in the sense that train passengers are paying less than the marginal cost of the journey. The efficiency cost, that is the difference between the marginal cost and the willingness to pay, corresponds to the area E_4CD. Third, there is an important transfer of income from the government to train users. The total subsidy to the railways is ECE_4F in Figure 1.8B.

The question of public transport subsidies is a complex one and it is impossible to say a priori whether they are justified without a more thorough investigation. However, we can point at a number of factors that need to be taken into account in deciding whether public transport subsidies constitute an effective instrument for dealing with peak-period congestion. The first is the extent to which such subsidies make people decide to switch from private car to public transport. If this effect is small, that is, if the price elasticity of car transport demand with respect to the price of rail is small, then subsidies serve little purpose. Second, there is the price-sensitivity of current users of public transport. If there is a sharp rise in public transport ridership as a reaction to increased subsidies, then this will have an undesirable effect, namely their extra use of public transport costs more than what they themselves are willing to pay. Third, there is the danger that subsidies will cause a loss in productive efficiency. If public transport companies can always rely on subsidies, there is a risk that, unknowingly, inefficiency will start creeping into management and the workforce (so-called X-inefficiency).[15]

The two examples discussed in this section underline the interrelation between different markets and point to the necessity of determining optimal prices simultaneously for all transport markets. Moreover, they clearly show that the calculation of optimal taxes for different markets simultaneously is a highly complex matter; there is really no choice but to adopt a simultaneous model approach. This indeed provides the basis for the models used in the case studies in the second part of the present book.

1.6 THE RELATION BETWEEN PRICING POLICY AND INFRASTRUCTURE POLICY

Thus far the model developed in previous sections was based on a constant and given road capacity. The possibility of lessening congestion through extra investments (for example adding a lane to the Antwerp–Brussels motorway) has not yet been considered. The question is how to judge the desirability of additional investment in infrastructure, and what precisely is the relation between pricing policy and infrastructure policy? Does infrastructure policy make a pricing policy redundant, or does a correct pricing policy contribute to a better infrastructure policy?

Economists measure the desirability of new investment in infrastructure by comparing the total social cost (that is disadvantages) with the social benefits (that is advantages). If the benefits outweigh the costs, then the investment is economically desirable. Let us suppose, for instance, that one wants to increase the traffic capacity of a road. This can be done in a number of ways: by enlarging the road, by improving it, by investing in electronic traffic control (anything from, say, synchronised traffic lights to the more futuristic 'smart roads'), and so on. The first option involves additional space, the two others do not. The *total cost of an improvement in capacity* comprises the investment cost itself, the social cost of the extra environmental damage (impacts on open space, noise damage, and so on) and, if available land has to be sacrificed, the opportunity cost of the extra land use. The most important component among the *social advantages of a capacity improvement* is the discounted[16] sum of savings on congestion costs over the lifetime of the infrastructure. This means that any decent cost–benefit analysis will need to evaluate congestion costs from a social perspective: the full social costs must be accounted for, and not simply the private congestion costs to the individual motorist.

To see what effect correct pricing can have on infrastructure decisions, let us take the case of a proposed road improvement. We shall consider whether this investment is socially desirable first, when there is correct congestion pricing, and second, when external congestion costs have not been accounted for in prices. We shall see that road pricing has important repercussions when calculating the overall benefits of the investment. When there are high traffic volumes and congestion is not incorporated in the pricing system, the benefits will appear vastly greater than when road users are correctly charged for congestion. In other words, investments will be approved that would be totally unjustified in case of a good pricing policy; as a result there will be an overinvestment in infrastructure.

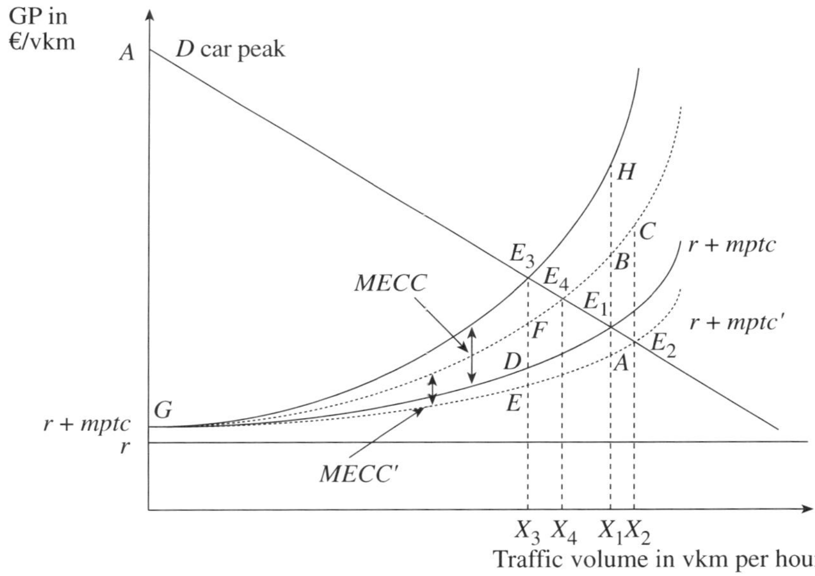

Figure 1.9 Optimal investment and pricing

We illustrate this idea in Figure 1.9. For convenience sake we assume that congestion is the only external cost. The benefits of the road extension are shown graphically for two different cases: first, when congestion costs are not captured in the pricing system; second, when there is optimal social pricing. When social costs are not incorporated[17] we have an initial equilibrium E_1. The road enlargement speeds up the flow of traffic and whatever the volume of traffic there will be an increase in the average speed. As a result of this there will be a fall in both private costs (from *mptc* to *mptc'*) and in marginal external costs (from *MECC* to *MECC'*), as indicated by the dotted lines. This produces a new equilibrium E_2, where there is both more traffic than before and a higher average speed. Both the average and external time costs are lower in E_2 than in E_1.

We now turn to the second case where correct social pricing policies are used. We start from equilibrium E_3 at the present road capacity. By the same reasoning as before, the road improvement produces a new equilibrium E_4. Here as well there is now more traffic ($X_4 < X_3$) and a higher average speed.

We first calculate the net benefits of the investment in the case of correct pricing. Here one must be careful to distinguish between the consequences for current traffic in the absence of the investment (X_3) and for the new traffic ($X_4 - X_3$) attracted by the higher road capacity. Existing traffic experiences lower time costs as a result of the increased speed. This is a social benefit that can be calculated by adding up the reduction in the marginal private costs and in external time costs for all traffic. In graphical terms, this benefit results in area GE_3F. With regard to the extra traffic, there is also a net social benefit, for the willingness to pay exceeds the costs generated. This benefit is measured through the difference between the willingness to pay and the social costs. In graphical terms it amounts to FE_3E_4. The total benefit from the investment in the case of correct pricing is therefore GE_3E_4.

Let us now turn to the other case, where congestion is not appropriately priced, so that the initial equilibrium is E_1. First consider the consequences for the existing traffic X_1. There is a saving on social (private plus external) congestion costs, represented graphically by *GHB*. Crucially, this benefit turns out to be much greater than in the case of correct pricing. After all, we are starting from a much higher level of congestion ($X_3 < X_1$), so the investment will have a correspondingly greater effect on time costs and more motorists will benefit from it. To determine the difference in benefit for existing traffic in the two cases, all we have to do is compare *GHB* with GE_3F. The difference is FE_3HB.

This sends out a clear message. By failing to charge for congestion in the pricing of existing traffic, the estimated benefits are far too high. Admittedly, there is a compensating second effect (usually much smaller) due to the welfare implications of the investment for the additional traffic generated by the road improvement. It is immediately apparent that by failing to charge for external congestion costs, any extra traffic entails a further cost to the community: because of incorrect pricing, the total willingness to pay of the additional traffic is less than the extra social costs it imposes. The net social cost of this extra traffic, that is the difference between the extra costs and the willingness to pay is represented by E_1BCE_2. In direct contrast to this, with correct pricing (as noted above) the additional traffic, far from imposing costs, actually generates an additional benefit equivalent to FE_3E_4.

Let us summarise briefly. Taking only present traffic into consideration, a capacity investment is more attractive when pricing does not appropriately capture congestion costs. Under these conditions there will be a greater readiness to invest in capacity and to regard it as 'necessary'. With correct pricing all new traffic constitutes a benefit for the community; with incorrect pricing the new traffic imposes a net cost on the community, in that it brings additional congestion costs for which it is not willing to pay. Given prevailing high levels of congestion, the effects on present traffic will typically weigh more heavily, and incorrect pricing will lead to overinvestment in infrastructure.[18] This is shown clearly in Figure 1.9 where the social benefits generated by incorrect pricing of present traffic are seen as more important than the extra costs of additional traffic.

So far we have been comparing the influence of investment for different pricing mechanisms, that is we have been examining the *relation between* pricing and investment. There is however another way of looking at Figure 1.9. In the face of high congestion at equilibrium E_1, one could interpret a revised and optimal pricing policy (leading to equilibrium E_3) and an increase in road capacity (leading to equilibrium E_2) as *alternative solutions* to the problem. Equilibrium E_3 (via correct pricing) produces less traffic, less congestion, less environmental damage and more welfare. In contrast, equilibrium E_2 (via investment) produces more traffic, continued congestion, and more environmental impacts. Added to this, in the latter case it is far from certain that investment will generate a gain in welfare; this all depends on whether the discounted time gain counterbalances the investment costs, including additional environmental damage. Whereas optimal pricing as an instrument for dealing with externalities like congestion brings a guaranteed welfare gain, this is much less certain in the case of additional road investment.[19]

Finally, we should add that some policymakers emphasise a further link between pricing policy and infrastructure policy. It is often claimed that the revenue from a congestion tax should be used to finance investment in road infrastructure; in this way optimal pricing might be said to generate more road infrastructure. Two questions arise. First, will optimal congestion taxes produce sufficient revenue to finance new investment in roads and to pay for their maintenance? Economic theory has shown that this depends very much on the technical and economic aspects of road construction and maintenance. Given an optimal investment and pricing policy, and if there are constant returns to scale in road construction, then in the long term the revenue from congestion taxes will exactly cover the cost[20] of road investment. If there are non-constant returns in road construction, then optimal taxes will generate either more or less revenue than the infrastructure costs.

The second question is more fundamental, namely whether it is desirable to directly allocate revenues from a congestion tax for investment in infrastructure? The answer is probably no. For a start, there is no clear economic justification to tie government investment (whether in education, transport, culture, and so on) to a particular type of revenue. This limits flexibility and leads to wrongly based investment decisions (for example 'the money is there to be spent' or 'the finances are not available'). Moreover, it is not desirable to link road investment and revenues from congestion taxes in the interim phase when such taxes are being introduced. As we have seen (see Figure 1.9), the need for new road infrastructure declines with the introduction of a congestion tax; both the volume of traffic and the marginal external congestion cost decrease with correct pricing. As a consequence, while there are increased government revenues, there is a less urgent need for investment. The revenue generated by a congestion tax can then be used for higher priority government investment, or for a reduction in taxes in other functional areas.

1.7 OTHER DIMENSIONS OF THE TRANSPORT PROBLEM

Up to this point the discussion has taken place within a much-simplified framework. In our treatment of the economics of externalities we have chosen to ignore a number of important additional aspects. In this section we briefly consider three of these: the problem of the redistribution of revenues, the relation with spatial planning, and the presence of other imperfections in the economy.

Internalising external effects via better pricing mechanisms will bring about major changes in income distribution. The high taxes levied on car users in peak periods will produce a shift of income away from car users to the government. Even if tax revenues are recycled back to the population in the form of tax reductions elsewhere, at the end of the day there will always be groups in the community who suffer a net loss. There is, after all, no concordance between those who pay the taxes, those who benefit from lower environmental damage, and those who receive the tax revenues.

The desirability and social acceptability of externality pricing through road pricing or other means will crucially depend on the redistribution of the tax revenues. Although the distributive effects of optimal pricing policies have been studied recently by, for example, Mayeres and Proost (1997), we have chosen to make very simple assumptions on the use of tax revenues in the case studies developed later in this book. Distributive motives that governments may have in determining optimal congestion taxes are ignored in most of the case studies, and it is simply assumed that tax revenues are redistributed lump sum to consumers. In those studies that take a different approach, the precise assumptions on the distributive process will be carefully explained.

Spatial planning is a major determinant in the long-term growth of mobility. In the present analysis the location of households and economic activity is taken as given and optimal location is not considered. In theory it could be, but it would substantially complicate the model. What are the implications of the present analysis for land use and locations? Two observations are in order here. First, the implementation of a congestion tax will help rather than obstruct optimal land use. To take one example, in the past, migration to the countryside was partly due to the failure to charge external congestion costs; the flight from the cities was both 'subsidised' and undesirable. Congestion pricing may in turn provide an incentive for commuters to return to the inner city. Probably one can expect optimal road pricing to lead to a greater reconcentration of household, school and work, as mobility at peak times becomes more and more expensive.[21] What the precise effects will be depends on the reaction to such a reconcentration. Conceptually it does not pose major problems, because optimal pricing can be seen as complementary to a well thought out land-use policy. Second, we need to consider what the effects are of not including location policy in our models. Endogenous location decisions will in our framework correspond to greater price elasticity in the demand curve for transport, since consumers get the opportunity to adapt to a new situation. That being the case, the equilibrium-congestion prices for peak periods that result from the models may be on the high side.

Economic theory clearly argues that pricing at marginal social cost in one sector can only be optimal if the same principle is applied in other sectors. But our economy is characterised by a number of *price distortions* and *market disequilibria*.

The most significant price distortions are those related to the labour market. The main culprit is perhaps the tax on labour income, for it tends to produce inefficient labour supply decisions. With a marginal tax rate of 50 per cent and an average VAT rate of 20 per cent on consumer goods, the total marginal tax on labour is 60 per cent. This means there is a significant distortion on the labour market between the marginal cost of labour and the demand for labour. This results in unofficial ('black') labour and a poor distribution of labour (too much 'do-it yourself' activities). It is difficult to see how the government can prevent this loss of efficiency, as it needs the labour taxes for its necessary redistribution policy. But more specifically, for our problem, the question is twofold. First, how can such distortions be taken into account when calculating optimal transport taxes; and second, does the presence of such distortions mean that the higher car tax should primarily serve to bring down the tax on labour? Analogous questions have in fact already been raised in connection with proposed environmental taxes. It has been argued that these generate a *double dividend*. In the case of a tax on externalities the first dividend would of course be a reduction in the externalities themselves (improved environment or less congestion); the second would be to reduce distortive taxes, in this case the tax on labour. The consensus in the environmental literature is that there is no such double dividend. In fact using environmental taxes increases the distortion on the labour market because the more expensive products (due to the additional tax) reduce the purchasing power of an hour of labour. Therefore the best that can be done is to use the revenue of the environmental tax to reduce existing labour taxes. This way one can limit but not fully eliminate the negative side effects on the labour market. This difficult issue is discussed more fully in Chapter 4 of this book.

1.8 CONCLUSION

In this chapter we have given a brief sketch of the theory of optimal transport pricing. The 'internalisation of marginal external costs' is a simple basic principle, but its implementation is complicated by two factors. First, it entails not only calculating or estimating the relevant external costs, but it also requires estimates of the reaction of transport users to the new pricing system. Second, since a perfect implementation of optimal prices is not usually feasible, an optimal departure from the basic principle may be necessary, not only for the transport market in question, but for all other markets. Precisely how this can be worked out in practice is the purpose of this book.

NOTES

1. We take private road transport as an example. In the empirical application the argument is applied analogously to other transport modes, including freight transport.
2. All figures used in the example are fictitious: the computation of the necessary external cost information is explained in detail in Chapter 7.
3. The effect of one additional vehicle on the average speed of the traffic flow is of course small, except in conditions of high congestion. Consequently its effect on the average time cost can be ignored relative to the average time cost itself. Assume for example that with a traffic volume of 3000 vehicles per hour the average speed is 25 km per hour. Given a time value of 7.5 EUR per hour, this means an average time cost of 0.3 EUR per km. Assume now that one additional vehicle causes a drop in speed of 0.04 km per hour. This means that the time cost would be increased by less than 0.0005 EUR per km. In comparison with the average time cost of 0.3 EUR this is almost negligible; it is less than 0.17 per cent. Often in the literature it is therefore assumed that the motorist ignores his own

influence on average time costs in taking decisions, so that the average time cost and the marginal private time cost are equal.

4. To keep the graphs as transparent as possible, and in view of the small difference between marginal private and average time cost, in the rest of this chapter we shall refrain from drawing in the average time cost.
5. Below attention will be given to accidents, noise damage and road depreciation as external costs. The estimates for these external costs are discussed in some detail in Chapter 7.
6. In other words the effect of a single additional vehicle on the time cost of the motorist himself are negligible, but the total effect on all other road users certainly is not.
7. We repeat that this is only an example. Below it will become apparent that the external costs, depending on the traffic flow (in turn dependent on location and time) and the type of vehicle, may not only far exceed the price for the consumer, but in some cases they may be lower.
8. The curve *mptc* gives the time cost valid for all km. This curve is therefore not the equivalent of the marginal cost (arrived at via the derivative of the total cost curve) in a classic market. The equivalent that is the derivative of the total costs (including the time costs) in relation to the traffic volume is represented by the sum $(r + mptk + MECC)$. This can be shown as follows. Let X be the traffic volume, then $TK(X) = (mptk + r)X$ gives the total cost. Consequently the marginal cost is

$$\frac{\partial mptk}{\partial X} X + mptk + r,$$

where the first term by definition represents the marginal external congestion cost.

9. In the literature the sum of the marginal private time cost and the marginal external congestion cost MECC is referred to as the marginal social congestion cost.
10. To arrive at the consumer surplus in our graph first calculate the total time cost in terms of resource cost and deduct it from the willingness to pay. The total time costs comprise both the private and the external costs. Thus the external time costs are already taken into account in the consumer surplus and should not be included again when calculating total welfare.
11. It is not difficult to show that the two indicators of total welfare in Figure 1.3 are indeed equal, but additional graphical constructions would be required to do so; these would make the diagram excessively complicated. To prove the equivalence of the two approaches it is essential to see that the total time costs can be measured graphically in two ways, namely as the sum of all private and marginal time costs, and as the product of the average time costs times the traffic volume.
12. Note that in the new equilibrium there is no reason to use the tax for additional investment in infrastructure, with the exception perhaps of the infrastructure needed to implement the new pricing mechanism (for example electronic toll systems).
13. When the place of the emission has no importance (as is the case with the greenhouse gas CO_2) we can ask ourselves whether it might not be more advisable to tackle them by measures outside the transport sector.
14. This is the case, for instance, if one uses a fuel tax instead of a direct km tax. Fuel taxes cannot vary according to the time of day.
15. The problem of subsidies needs looking into in more detail. Firstly, a fixed subsidy might be necessary to cover the fixed costs, thus yielding tariffs which approach the marginal cost. Secondly, subsidy structures could be worked out that provide a sufficient incentive to keep costs as low as possible (see Laffont and Tirole, 1993).
16. Discounted here means weighing the future benefits for the year t on the basis of a factor $1/[(1+i)]^t$ where i is the discount rate. After calculating this, the future benefits can be compared with present costs.
17. The example in the graph only takes into consideration the benefits at peak periods, since road capacity is responsible for most traffic limitations. This is a typical case of peak load pricing and investment.
18. For formal analysis of these issues see, for example, Wilson (1983) and d'Ouville and McDonald (1990).

19. We ignore the fact that optimal pricing can also require investment, for example electronic toll systems. In this sense our statement is a little too bold.
20. What we mean here is an annuity that covers both depreciation and interest charges.
21. This assumes the ability to change domicile without too much difficulty. It requires a transparent housing market and much lower registration fees when buying a house.

REFERENCES

Button, K. (1992), *Transport, the Environment and Economic Policy*, Aldershot: Edward Elgar

De Borger, B., Mayeres, I., Proost, S. and Wouters, S. (1996), 'Optimal pricing of urban passenger transport: a simulation exercise for Belgium', *Journal of Transport Economics and Policy*, January, 31–54.

D'Ouville, E.L. and McDonald, J.F. (1990), 'Optimal road capacity with a suboptimal Congestion toll', *Journal of Urban Economics*, **28**, 34–49.

Laffont, J.J. and Tirole, J. (1993), *A Theory of Incentives in Procurement and Regulation*, Cambridge, MA: MIT Press.

Mayeres, I. and Proost, S. (1997), 'Optimal tax rules and public investment rules for congestion type of externalities', *Scandinavian Journal of Economics*, **99**, 261–79.

Small, K. (1992), *Urban Transportation Economics*, Chur, Switzerland: Harwood Academic.

Wilson, J. (1983), 'Optimal road capacity in the presence of unpriced congestion', *Journal of Urban Economics*, **13**, 337–57.

2. An overview of policy instruments

Bruno De Borger, John Peirson and Roger Vickerman

2.1 INTRODUCTION

In the previous chapter it was argued that users of the transport system do not perceive the full marginal social cost of their travel decisions. This leads to traffic volumes in excess of what is socially desirable, and it implies a suboptimal distribution of transport flows over time and space. To tackle the various types of externality (congestion, noise, pollution, and so on) it was argued that a mix of price and non-price instruments would be required.

In this chapter we briefly review the types of policy instruments which can be used to deal with the various externalities. Although many instruments are applicable to all modes of transport we place somewhat more emphasis on road transport, because several instruments are specifically designed to deal with road congestion. Moreover, the purpose of the overview in this chapter is not completeness, but rather to provide the necessary information on economic policy instruments that is required to understand the choice of policy packages considered further in this book. For more details on price and non-price instruments in the transport sector we refer to standard textbooks in transport economics (for example, Button, 1992) or to recent policy documents at the European level (for example, EU Green Paper, 1996).

The structure of this chapter is the following. In Section 2.2 we consider various direct and indirect pricing instruments. Direct instruments charge the user for the transport service consumed, whereas indirect pricing measures involve the pricing of some related activity, for example off-street parking. The overview will make it very clear that most policy instruments that are currently used in many countries are not well suited to internalise external costs, and that new pricing instruments are urgently needed that allow temporal and spatial differentiation. Section 2.3 then briefly reviews non-price instruments. These are typically physical restrictions on the use of transport or on the level of the externality. Examples include licensing systems for the use of road space, reservation systems for public transport, emission restrictions, and so on. Conclusions are summarised in Section 2.4.

2.2 PRICE INSTRUMENTS

There exists a wide range of direct and indirect price instruments that can be implemented as part of a policy to ensure correct charging for transport. In this section, we present the most important instruments and assess their effectiveness in addressing the different types of externalities.

2.2.1 Taxes on Vehicle Purchases/Yearly Fixed Tax on Vehicles in Use

Taxes on vehicle ownership, either at purchase or on an annual basis, have an effect on the stock of vehicles. Of course, they indirectly affect overall car traffic volumes, and therefore congestion, noise, pollution and accident risks. It is clear, however, that they are very inefficient instruments to tackle congestion, since they are totally unrelated to vehicle use. For the same reason, they are not efficient to internalise the other externalities. In principle, annual vehicle taxes can be differentiated according to the level of noise, pollution or road damage (for example through vehicle age, power, or axle weight (for trucks)), and as such they do have some impact on external costs. For instance, higher purchase taxes on 'dirty' vehicles will cause a shift towards cleaner ones, thereby having a positive impact on air pollution. However, although annual vehicle taxes may play a minor role to correct for external cost differences between different types of vehicles (for example different classes of heavy goods vehicles), there are much more efficient instruments to achieve this objective, as discussed below. At the very best, if for some reason these more efficient instruments cannot be implemented, vehicle purchase taxes or annual vehicle taxes can be used as a very crude proxy for reflecting the external costs associated with different vehicle types. Of course, annual vehicle taxes are easy to implement and provide an easy source of fiscal revenue to governments.

2.2.2 Subsidies for Cleaner/More Fuel-Efficient Vehicles

A specific example of differentiation of annual vehicle taxes is the introduction of subsidies for cleaner or more fuel-efficient vehicles. They help to reduce the level of air pollution, and through altering the relative costs of transport they may have small effects on modal choice and on the overall volume of traffic. Although such subsidies are relatively easy to implement, the benefits are specific and limited. Moreover, the introduction of more fuel-efficient vehicles, without also increasing fuel prices, can have undesirable side effects. It clearly implies a price reduction for car users, which can lead to a higher demand for car usage, thereby worsening congestion, accident and noise problems.

2.2.3 Insurance Premiums

Drivers are currently not appropriately charged for the external accident costs (deaths and injuries, material damages, earning losses, and so on). To the extent that these costs are captured at all, this is typically done via vehicle or fuel tax revenues. If crude instruments such as vehicle taxes are used at all, they should take into account the safety characteristics of the vehicles.

Although difficult to implement in practice, a revision of insurance charges is probably the most efficient pricing instrument to internalise the external costs of accident risks. Implementation requires a careful distinction between costs that are private, and costs that must be considered external. It requires a sophisticated insurance structure based on full differentiation according to risk categories and incorporating all different variable accident cost components. It is unlikely that without an adaptation of liability regimes and compensation rules all external costs will be internalised.

2.2.4 Public Transport Subsidies

Public transport subsidies are often seen as a useful second-best policy in cases where private road transport for some reason cannot be priced at marginal social cost. However, it was shown in Chapter 1 that the desirability of public transport subsidies hinges upon a number of conditions. First, it must indeed be infeasible to correctly price private road transport. If in the future technology does allow external cost pricing for road transport, the first-best solution would be to have all modes internalise external costs, eliminating the need for public transport subsidies on these grounds. It is then socially desirable that public transport users also pay for the external costs they impose. Second, price effects must be such that subsidies succeed in shifting demand from car transport to public transport. However, the cross-price elasticities between private and public transport are in general quite low (see for example, Oum, Waters and Yong, 1992; and Goodwin, 1992) , which suggests that the efficiency of public transport subsidies in reducing congestion may be quite low. Third, the own price elasticity of demand for public transport must be limited, because otherwise the welfare cost of the subsidies themselves may become very high.

Given recent developments in pricing technologies for road traffic, it seems unlikely that there remains a strong efficiency case for public transport subsidies in the future. Of course, equity considerations may still justify lower prices for low-income population groups.

2.2.5 Parking Fees

Parking charges are a classic example of an indirect pricing measure. They are used in many cities across Europe to allocate scarce parking space and to generate revenues. Charging for the use of non-residential parking spaces affects travel decisions and clearly has side-effects on congestion and local pollution. However, compared with some other instruments to reduce these externalities they are quite inefficient since parking fees are not directly linked to external costs: they do not depend on the traffic volume or on distance travelled, and they are independent of the environmental characteristics of the vehicle. At best, if parking charges were differentiated according to location, length of stay and arrival/departure time, they can be seen as very crude proxies for external congestion costs for terminating traffic. It is clear, however, that traffic in transit through a congested area is not affected by parking fees at all.

Despite their inefficiencies parking charges are easy to apply and less costly than more sophisticated systems of pricing. Moreover, they probably do have an important role in future transport policies for a quite different reason, namely, that currently many car users do not pay the full resource cost of parking space. Making people pay the resource cost may have substantial positive welfare effects of which congestion and pollution reduction are important components. Note that parking charges also raise the issue as to the distribution of revenues. The proceeds may accrue to landowners (in the case of off-street parking) rather than to the public authorities.

2.2.6 Fuel Taxes

Fuel taxes are an important source of revenue in many countries. They are related to car use and do have some impact on overall traffic volumes and on modal choice. As they can be differentiated according to the fuel used (gasoline, diesel, and so on) and to its quality (leaded, unleaded, and so on) they may be efficient instruments to tackle certain types of emissions that are directly related to fuel consumption, such as CO_2. Of course, they are totally useless in internalising road damage, accident and noise costs. With respect to congestion, fuel taxes are very inefficient as well. It is sometimes argued that, to the extent that fuel consumption varies with vehicle speed and therefore congestion, a fuel tax is a very imperfect instrument for differentiating by space and time of day. This argument is not very convincing, however. First, fuel taxes are only very indirectly related to external congestion costs; they do not make the consumer pay an effectively differentiated price according to where and when travel occurs. Second, in small open economies high fuel taxes can, in some cases, be avoided by fuelling abroad. This restricts the efficiency of a fuel tax and it may give rise to tax competition. Third, over time high fuel taxes can also be avoided by switching to more fuel-efficient vehicles, which can cause dynamic inefficiencies in the sense of an excessive focus on fuel efficiency. This may have some beneficial effects for the environment, but at the cost of increased congestion. To tackle congestion, it is not fuel that has to be taxed, but car use in congested conditions.

2.2.7 Distance-Related Taxes: A Kilometre Tax

Recent proposals have focused on distance-related charges, for example in the form of a tax per kilometre, to correct for external costs. Although its implementation may pose some technical difficulties, experiments with trucks (for example, in Sweden) have shown the potential feasibility of a system of kilometre taxes. The efficiency of this instrument depends on how finely it can be differentiated. For example, it is clear that a kilometre tax differentiated by vehicle type, time of day (or even average speed) and location may to a substantial extent internalise congestion, pollution and noise externalities. Of course, it is unlikely that kilometre taxes can be sufficiently differentiated with respect to location or time of day in the near future, so that they may have only limited effects on the spatial or temporal distribution of traffic. In that case the tax remains a second-best instrument to tackle congestion and noise that, from the viewpoint of efficiency, is inferior to some systems of road pricing (see below). It does seem clear that, if the tax differentiation is based on the polluting and road damage characteristics of vehicles, a kilometre tax will be quite efficient as a way to price pollution and road damage. Finally, kilometre taxes may be useful in financing infrastructure costs.

2.2.8 Road Pricing

It has become customary to use the term 'road pricing' for a set of policy instruments that intend to charge vehicles the marginal external congestion costs they are causing at the time when and at the location where travel occurs. Few existing road pricing systems are currently operational in Europe (the Trondheim toll ring is an exception), although a large number of experiments in various countries are underway (see, for example, Johansson and Mattson, 1995, for more information).

Making abstraction of implementation costs, full road pricing is usually seen as the optimal policy on pure efficiency grounds. However, depending on the pricing technology one distinguishes several types of road pricing systems, ranging from simple area licensing to technologies allowing full electronic road pricing. Obviously, some of the less sophisticated systems are much less efficient than the first-best solution aimed at. The following systems are typically distinguished.

Area licensing/vignettes

Under this system, a licence is required to drive in certain areas and in some cases at certain times of the day. The system can be used in slightly different form in both urban and interregional environments. The urban version has been operating in, for example, Singapore. Highway vignettes for trucks, as considered in several European countries, can be interpreted as an example of interurban application of this system. In the latter case there is typically no time restriction. Since area licensing in urban areas is typically limited to highly congested zones it is more efficient than highway vignettes for trucks.

Of course, simple schemes such as area licensing and highway vignettes have the disadvantage that there is no specific charge for a specific journey. This limits the efficiency of this instrument in controlling congestion. However, if the system is applied in urban areas, and the distances travelled within the area are approximately constant, then it may come close to a tax per kilometre in the area considered. Still, there is insufficient differentiation with respect to congestion conditions.

Cordon pricing

The idea is to define a cordon and to charge all vehicles upon entering that area. The efficiency in terms of internalising congestion costs is obviously somewhat limited unless the fees charged are differentiated according to travel conditions (for example, peak versus off-peak). Cordon pricing has already been implemented in the town of Bergen (Norway) and on some French highways. It is relatively cheap and easy to implement on the condition that the area defined by the cordon is fairly homogeneous and has relatively few entrances. If toll collection is not done electronically an inconvenience is that the system itself causes some congestion. Electronic collection overcomes this problem.

Automatic vehicle identification (AVI)

This is the first of two systems of electronic road pricing. Automatic means are used to check on and register entrants to an area where charges are levied. Information about the car is registered at the time of passing by certain checking points. The required charges are billed to the user at regular intervals. Note that this system helps to overcome some of the disadvantages of the previous systems. Moreover, it allows in principle to vary the charges according to the degree of congestion (for example, a peak versus off-peak differentiation). However, it suffers from two obvious inconveniences. First, an individual faces some uncertainty with respect to the price he will have to pay. Second, as this system identifies the users, it is seen by many as an intrusion of people's right to privacy.

Smart cards

In the long run, this second technology to implement electronic road pricing probably comes closest to the first-best pricing solution for congestion. Moreover, it helps to solve the privacy problem for the user of the smart card. Registration and billing is effected via the card, and no identification of vehicles is necessary. Note that there is still a need for a back-up vehicle identification system to identify illegal users of a tolled road, but this can hardly be considered an obstacle to individual privacy. Of course, if the charge is made variable depending on traffic conditions then uncertainty about trip costs remains a problem. Finally, like for the other road pricing systems, smart card technology is mainly useful for pricing congestion externalities. It is difficult to differentiate between vehicles according to their age, size or overall pollution and noise characteristics. Other policy instruments must therefore accompany any system of road pricing.

2.2.9 Price Instruments: a Summary

We have identified a range of price instruments that go from basic vehicle ownership taxes to a full road pricing system which differentiates according to location, road traffic volumes and time of day so as to approximate full internalisation of the external costs of transport. This has demonstrated clearly that it is extremely difficult to find a single instrument that can address all of the concerns that society cares about. For example, fuel taxes are well suited to correct for external costs of CO_2, but they are totally inefficient in correcting for other externalities. As with most policy interventions, individual instruments are best suited to the solution of an individual problem; any attempt to use a single tool to solve a wider range of problems may introduce further inefficiencies.

Although it is difficult to summarise the desirability of using the different instruments to tackle the various externalities, we have tried to do so in Table 2.1. In interpreting the table it should be clearly understood that even the most sophisticated instruments would have to be accompanied by other policy instruments. Note in particular that full electronic road pricing,

Table 2.1 Price instruments and policy objectives

Policy instrument	Policy Objective					
	Congestion	Local air pollution	Overall pollution (CO_2)	Accidents	Noise	Infrastructure damage
Vehicle ownership taxes/charges	–	+ (if differentiated)	+ (if differentiated)	–	+ (if differentiated)	–
Fuel taxes	+	+	+++	–	–	+
Parking charges	+	+	–	–	–	–
Insurance	–	–	–	+++	–	–
Public transport subsidies	+	+	+	+	–	–
Kilometre tax	++ (if differentiated)	++ (if differentiated)	++ (if differentiated)	+	+	++
Highway vignette	–	–	–	–	+	+
Cordon pricing	++	++	–	–	+	–
Full electronic road pricing	+++	++	++	+	+	++

Notes:
– very limited or negative effect of the instrument on the externality
+,++,+++: positive effects in increasing order of desirability

although the closest to a first-best solution, is still a rather poor instrument to reduce environmental externalities if it cannot fully differentiate by vehicle type, by fuel efficiency and by other polluting characteristics.

The conclusions to be derived from the overview in this section can be summarised as follows. First, in principle a very fine system of road pricing that allows differentiation according to local conditions at all times (in terms of congestion, pollution, and so on) is probably the best price instrument to correct for external costs. Second, as such a system may not be available in the very near future, various second-best policies may help to reduce external costs. Reasonable policies include differentiation of vehicle registration taxes and Euro-vignettes according to externality characteristics of vehicles (pollution, noise, safety), differentiation of existing road tolls between peak and off-peak, introduction of new tolls where feasible, and the introduction of kilometre taxes for trucks. Finally, parking fees can be differentiated according to location and time of arrival/departure, and insurance regimes must be revised.

2.3 NON-PRICE INSTRUMENTS

Non-price measures are a very heterogeneous group of policy instruments, ranging from investment in transport capacity over emission norms on vehicles to various forms of traffic demand management. In this brief review we list some of the most important instruments, without any attempt at completeness.

2.3.1 Transport Capacity and Public Transport Supply

Policies determining the capacity of the transport system include direct investment in infrastructure, investment in public transport supply, investment in information and communication technology that improves the capacity of the system, and so on. In principle and in the short run, these measures have a direct impact on the traffic volume that can be accommodated. At the EU level considerable emphasis has been placed on capacity provision and efficiency of use (interconnectivity, interoperability and inter-modality). The importance of improving the interface between long distance systems and regional/urban networks has also been emphasised. This affects the extent to which different types of traffic, such as transit and local/regional traffic flows interact with one another.

Of course, improved infrastructure affects traffic volumes and therefore emissions, noise and congestion levels. However, there is sufficient empirical evidence that indicates that investment is in many cases not a very efficient instrument to reduce externalities. The existence of latent demand (see for example Small, 1992) implies the risk that traffic increases induced by the investment lead to small if any reductions in congestion in the long run. Moreover, the increase in aggregate traffic flows raises environmental costs. Finally, infrastructure construction itself can also have negative impacts on the environment. Not surprisingly, there has been a general move away from the use of a policy of 'predict and provide' for road traffic.

Investment in public transport infrastructure and supply may be a relevant policy to accompany pricing measures that internalise external costs. For example, road pricing is likely to shift users from the private car towards public transport so that additional investment in public supply may pass the cost–benefit test.

2.3.2 Safety Regulations

It is clear that safety is a vital concern. Policies aiming at reducing the probability and consequences of accidents include the development of common standards in the construction and design of transport infrastructure, regulations on the construction and safety features of vehicles, the imposition of speed limits, alcohol restrictions, the requirements for adequate training and testing of drivers, and so on.

Such policies are likely to be rather blunt in their operation, but clearly strongly affect external accident costs. As such they can be considered useful instruments to accompany revisions in insurance regimes and premium structures. It is to be expected in the future that improved use of telematics and real-time signalling systems will be able to relate safe driving conditions to changing traffic volumes more accurately. Since speed–flow relationships have a clear link both with congestion delays and accident rates this could then become an important non-price instrument.

2.3.3 Emission and Noise Regulations

A whole series of policy measures aims at directly regulating emissions (for example, emission norms) or noise. These policies can be quite effective relative to some pricing measures. The main reason is that pricing of pollution and noise is difficult in practice because current and expected future technologies probably do not allow sufficient fine-tuning of user charges according to the external pollution and noise costs generated. Moreover, emission norms or technology regulations are a more cost-effective way to reach pollution reductions than traffic reductions obtained via pricing measures. Some fairly simple measures (for example, requiring catalytic converters) have large effects on pollution. Obtaining the same impact through price increases only would require large price changes that drastically reduce traffic. The welfare reductions associated with these dramatic traffic reductions can easily be avoided by the direct regulation of technologies.

2.3.4 Demand Management Instruments

This type of regulation covers a range of possible measures aimed at controlling demand directly rather than by price. Instruments include the restriction of parking space, imposing car-free days, enabling vehicles with odd/even number plates to be allowed on odd/even days only, requiring a minimum level of occupancy of vehicles in certain designated areas or traffic lanes, designing the physical characteristics of road infrastructure to reduce speed, and speed limits. These latter two measures also affect safety considerations, but can be designed with different objectives to the fore.

Demand management instruments can be made quite specific in terms of where and when they operate. They can address both location-specific and time of day issues, and they can be made specific towards some types of users or vehicles (for example, trucks). Still, many of these instruments are very inefficient compared to other price and non-price instruments. In many cases they are easier to avoid (for instance, rescheduling with car-free Sundays), and produce unwarranted or even counterproductive side effects (such as increased driving around in search of a parking spot after a restriction in parking space supply). The overall efficiency of these instruments will usually be positively affected by the absence of tolling mechanisms. If appropriate pricing instruments are available they lose much of their attractiveness, except for the solution of very local problems.

2.3.5 Indirect Demand Management Instruments

The instruments discussed in the previous section are intended to operate directly on the user of a specific mode at the point of delivery. There are less direct measures that can be used. These include stimulation of alternative transport modes by improving service levels and quality (for example less noisy buses, inter-availability of ticketing systems between public transport operators), physical planning and other spatial economic policies, spreading and staggering of work, school and shopping hours, and stimulation of tele-activities (tele-commuting, home banking and home shopping). The importance of these latter instruments is the recognition that general changes in the organisation and location of activities can have profound impacts on the transport system.

These instruments are generally directed at reducing overall demand and

Table 2.2 Non-price instruments and policy objectives

	Policy objective					
Policy instrument	Congestion	Local air pollution	Overall pollution (CO_2)	Accidents	Noise	Infrastructure damage
Road Infrastructure	– (long run)	–	–	–	–	–
Public transport supply	+	–	–	–	–	–
Safety regulations	–	–	–	+++	–	–
Emission and noise regulation	–	+++	+++	–	+++	–
Direct demand management	+	+	–	+	+	+
Indirect demand management	+	+	+	–	+	–

Notes:
– very limited or negative effect of the instrument on the externality
+,++,+++: positive effects in increasing order of desirability

at the spreading and flattening of demand peaks. They are useful adjuncts to policies designed at educating transport users on the consequences of their activities, but it is clear that they are typically longer-term policies which will need to be used in conjunction with more direct acting policies.

2.3.6 Non-Price Instruments: a Summary

To summarise the effects of non-price instruments is difficult because they act generally in a much less direct way than pricing measures. Moreover, they are a much more heterogeneous group of policy instruments. An effort to present the desirability of the various groups of instruments is in Table 2.2. Admittedly, the impact on individual externalities is not as clear as in the case of price measures. However, the general picture is obvious. With the exception of very specific measures (for example, safety regulations, emission regulations) non-price instruments are likely to be less efficient, especially towards controlling the congestion externality. For congestion, pricing measures are by far to be preferred.

2.4 CONCLUSIONS

This chapter has identified the range of policy instruments from which we need to select policies for testing in the applications of the models described later in the book. As we have seen, there is no shortage of individual measures, but many of them have only limited impacts on some policy objectives. An important lesson of the overview in this chapter is, however, that non-price instruments can in some cases (for example, emission and safety regulations) be quite effective instruments, but that they completely fail to address the congestion externality. Moreover, it has become clear that in order to tackle congestion (and some of the other externalities) price instruments are required that allow differentiation in space and in time in order to more accurately reflect differences in external costs. In the next chapter we will therefore select a number of different policy packages which include specific instruments to tackle congestion, and compare their implications for welfare.

REFERENCES

Button, K. (1992), *Transport, the Environment and Economic Policy*, Aldershot: Edward Elgar.

EU Green Paper (1996), *Towards fair and Efficient Pricing in Transport*, Brussels.

Goodwin, P. (1992), 'Review of new demand elasticities', *Journal of Transport Economics and Policy*, **26**, 155–69.
Johansson, B. and L.-G. Mattson (1995), *Road Pricing: Theory, Empirical Assessment and Policy*, Boston: Kluwer.
Oum, T.H., Waters, W.G. and Yong, J.S. (1992), 'Concepts of price elasticities of transport demand', *Journal of Transport Economics and Policy*, **26**, 139–54.
Small, K. (1992), *Urban Transportation Economics*, Chur, Switzerland: Harwood Academic.

3. Policy reform packages

Bruno De Borger, John Peirson and Roger Vickerman

3.1 INTRODUCTION

The previous chapter resulted in two specific lessons for transport policy design. First, it suggested that there does not exist a single policy instrument that internalises all externalities simultaneously. Individual price and non-price instruments may be quite successful in internalising individual externalities (for example, insurance premiums to tackle accident risks, fuel taxes to correct for CO_2 emissions, direct emission regulation to reduce other air pollution), but a coherent transport policy necessitates a well-designed policy package, consisting of an appropriate combination of instruments. Second, the discussion made it clear that from an efficiency viewpoint an increasing reliance on pricing instruments is necessary. Moreover, internalising the congestion externality is difficult with the existing price instruments, so that new pricing tools will have to be introduced that allow differentiation of charges in time and space in function of local and temporal variations in congestion.

One of the main objectives of this book is to study the implications of various policy packages for transport demand and for overall welfare in a number of different European cities and countries, using a numerical optimisation model specifically designed for this purpose. In this chapter we present the policy packages that were selected for the empirical analysis reported on later in the book. The criteria for the selection of the policy packages were the following. First, they had to be consistent with a stronger emphasis on pricing instruments, as suggested by economic theory. Second, they had to be broadly in line with EU transport policy, as reflected in a number of recent documents. Third, a sufficiently wide variety of packages had to be considered in view of possible practical restrictions on policy instruments. Indeed, the 'optimal' combination of price and non-pricing instruments depends to a large extent on the possible existence of technical, social or political restrictions on the instruments. For example, it is clear that in some cities or regions electronic road pricing may be a very useful instrument to tackle congestion. However, whether it should actually be implemented depends on technical feasibility issues, on the degree of social acceptance and on implementation costs. We therefore analyse the implications of a fairly broad range of policy packages. They differ from one another in their assumptions with respect to the available policy instruments.

The structure of the chapter is as follows. We start out in Section 3.2 with a review of the transport policy debate as reflected in several EU-documents produced in the 1990s. In Section 3.3 we then turn to a precise definition and description of the policy packages to be implemented further in the book. Section 3.4 concludes.

3.2 RECENT DEVELOPMENTS IN TRANSPORT POLICY IN THE EU

The decade of the 1990s has seen considerable development in EU transport policy strategy. There has been a shift from the initial dominant concern with infrastructure and the Trans-European Networks (TEN) towards a more coherent set of policy instruments. To some extent this shift represents a return to the earlier priorities of the Common Transport Policy (CPT), but there are crucial differences. Whereas in earlier periods the CTP was more concerned with harmonisation and regulation, more recent documents show increased emphasis on deregulation and efficiently operating markets. In this section we briefly discuss three documents that show the movement towards increasing reliance on pricing instruments, the emphasis on new pricing instruments for internalising congestion costs, and the need to develop efficient alternatives for private road transport.[1]

3.2.1 White Paper 'The Future Development of the Common Transport Policy'

In the period 1970–90, both passenger and freight movements had continued to grow throughout the EU, while at the same time investment in transport systems in most member states continued to decline in relative terms. Since the growth in traffic was mainly concentrated in the road transport sector, this evolution led to increasing problems for both users and non-users in the form of congestion, air pollution, noise and accidents. In view of these developments, the 1992 White Paper *The Future Development of the Common Transport Policy: A Global Approach to the Construction of a Community Framework for Sustainable Mobility* represented a major reappraisal of the EU's role in transport policy. It represented a belated first step in defining the goals of common transport policies, and in establishing a work programme to achieve it. The emphasis was on *sustainable mobility* for the EU as a whole. Underlying the document is the importance of transport to the successful working of the single market, both as an industry in itself and as a necessary input for other industries. Therefore, the paper stresses the importance of minimising red tape and quantitative restrictions, while at the same time maintaining regulations necessary to ensure fair competition.

Despite its relatively general provisions the White Paper sets out a statement of policy which gives a clear preference towards the use of price-based measures, reflecting the full social costs of transport. It identifies the failure to charge for high external costs and for the full infrastructure costs associated with the network as the major problems following the growth of road traffic. As the potential for expanding the road network in much of the EU is seen as very limited, other pricing and regulatory measures are suggested. Moreover, the use of fiscal instruments is argued to have some clear advantages over regulatory measures. Pricing policies have the advantage of giving operators a choice while ensuring better utilisation in time and space of the existing capacity of different transport modes. It is realised that if external costs were internalised through appropriate pricing, road use becomes much less attractive as compared to other modes. The paper also points out the advantages of price differentiation to tackle specific externalities (for example, congestion charges, vehicle taxes in function of pollution characteristics, and so on) and emphasises that user charges can easily and quickly be changed in response to new circumstances. Finally, externality pricing would generate additional funds that could be used to improve alternative, more sustainable, transport systems that cause less damage to both users and the wider community.

The White Paper recognises that improved pricing of the transport sector might be damaging the sector itself because of the increase in (especially) road transport prices. It therefore suggests stimulating the use of intermodal systems, especially for freight transport, throughout the EU. Moreover, in order to prevent distortions of international competitiveness, the paper argues that policies should be decided upon and implemented at the EU level. If they were to be implemented at national or local level, the internal market could be unbalanced by member states that use the transport pricing mechanism to gain an unfair advantage. Another reason for supranational policymaking is to ensure compatibility amongst the emerging technologies that may be used in the future to implement pricing policies (for example, electronic road pricing).

3.2.2 Green Paper *Towards Fair and Efficient Pricing in Transport*

The 1996 Green Paper *Towards Fair and Efficient Pricing in Transport: Policy Options for Internalising the External Costs of Transport in the European Union* reinforces the view that more emphasis on pricing instruments is highly desirable, and it offers specific suggestions for making pricing systems fairer and more efficient. The central theme is that the price paid by the end user should be more closely aligned to the full social cost of the journey; since costs often vary across time, space and modes, this implies the need for prices to be differentiated in these dimensions.[2]

In the long run, it is argued that telematics could become sufficiently sophisticated to provide a system meeting all requirements (in terms of spatial and temporal differentiation) while still maintaining the privacy of individuals. Such a system would significantly reduce transport problems, since it would allow each individual road user to pay costs which are related to the type of vehicle, route chosen, distance driven, time of travel, and so on. In the short and medium term, possible actions which are consistent with the pricing principles advocated in the paper include:

- Adjusting existing Community legislation on road charges for heavy goods vehicles;
- Kilometre charges for heavy road vehicles based on infrastructure damage and possibly other parameters (for example a charge on heavy goods vehicles related to the number of axles);
- Road tolls in congested or congestion-sensitive areas;
- Differentiated fuel taxes reflecting differences in fuel quality and environmental characteristics;
- Differentiated vehicle taxes in accordance with the vehicle's environmental and noise characteristics, possibly to be linked with electronic kilometre charges;
- The provision of information on safety performance of vehicles and modes.

The Green Paper sends a clear and urgent signal that adjusting the tax and pricing system is likely to generate significant benefits. Although the problems of estimating exact marginal external costs are acknowledged, it is suggested that often enough is known about the direction and magnitude of the required charges to allow a gradual phasing in of policy instruments, using more information as it becomes available. At the administrative level, it is stressed that transparency of costs and prices is important. To increase social acceptance of externality charges, end users must be able to see the relation between the price they pay for a given journey in relation to the social costs generated. Users must be convinced that the pricing system is not designed in the first place as a source of government revenue.

3.2.3 Green Paper *The Citizens' Network*

The early focus on the improvement of the EU's basic high-level transport infrastructure, and the more recent policy emphasis on internalising external costs through adjustment of the tax and price structure, have generated another concern. It is explicitly recognised that better pricing policies may improve efficiency but that, unless some accompanying measures are taken, this may come at the expense of increasing inequality in access to the transport system. It is argued, therefore, that developing acceptable alternatives for private road transport is crucial. This is, in a nutshell, the significance of the Green Paper *The Citizens' Network: Fulfilling the Potential of Public Passenger Transport in Europe*. The paper argues in favour of public transport systems that are integrated and interconnected at all levels. Long-distance services should connect easily with local services, and networks of public transport systems (for example, rail and bus in major urban areas) should fit together, so that passengers can change easily between the various modes of public transport. Moreover, transfer between public transport and other modes, such as bicycle and car, should be facilitated.

The paper further suggests that the European Commission, in partnership with the member states, should contribute towards the funding of improved public transport systems. Different regulatory and financing options for public transport are identified, with varying degrees of public and private input. The paper proposes a strong emphasis on co-financing projects that promote further integration and encourage greater use of inter-modal systems. It argues that a fully deregulated approach to the provision of public transport services (such as that adopted in the UK) often implies a reduced scope for the achievement of predefined transport policy objectives, such as the integration within and between modes.

3.3 THE POLICY PACKAGES STUDIED IN THIS BOOK

In this section, we turn to the definition of appropriate packages of policy instruments that are broadly in line with the suggestions of recent EU policy documents, and that can be analysed with the models constructed for application in this book. Intuitively, one expects considerable scope for welfare gains from well-designed policy packages, especially those that include pricing measures that move us closer to social cost pricing. The reason is simply that current taxation of the transport sector in Europe is only marginally inspired by external cost considerations. At the risk of oversimplifying, in many European countries annual vehicle taxes, fuel taxes, parking fees, public transport subsidies and (in some cases) road tolls are used as the main pricing instruments. As discussed before, many of these instruments are not efficient. For example, a fixed tax on vehicle purchase and/or a yearly tax does not relate well to the externality generating characteristics of the vehicles. Fuel taxes may differ according to fuel type (gasoline, diesel or LPG) and to other characteristics (leaded or unleaded), but they are totally unrelated to spatial and temporal congestion differences. Parking tariffs can of course be differentiated by location and according to the time of the day, but in many cities they are mainly designed for revenue collection. They typically are related to length of stay rather than time of arrival or departure. Public transport prices are not inspired by efficiency considerations in many countries, and they poorly approximate the sort of second-best correction of relative prices discussed in Chapter 1. Finally, in cases where road tolls are used, they are typically not applied with external cost considerations as the main objective.

Of course, not all suggestions for better pricing are equally realistic in the short run, as implementation may require the introduction of currently unavailable pricing instruments. In what follows, we therefore present a number of different policy packages. They all fit within the changing emphasis in EU policy identified in the previous section of this chapter. They range from fairly modest adjustments in policy, that is, combinations of measures that can be implemented with existing instruments, to quite drastic changes that are only feasible if new price instruments become available (that is, some form of electronic road pricing) that allow price differentiation in time and over space.

3.3.1 The TRENEN Policy Packages

The implementation of identical policy proposals in different countries guarantees comparability of results; moreover, differences in implications can be identified and traced back to variations in cities' or regions' characteristics. The following major packages will be studied, where it should be noted that for some of them several variations are possible depending on specific additional assumptions.

a. The reference scenario

To analyse the welfare effects of the various policies, we systematically compare the results with those of a *reference scenario*. This reference situation is chosen to be the transport market equilibrium that would result in 2005 on the assumption that current policy remains in effect, and assuming no major changes in the capacity of the transport system. In other words, it reflects the transport taxes, prices and volumes that one expects for 2005 on the assumption of unchanged transport policy and in the absence of large infrastructure adjustments. Determining all relevant information for the reference case involves the calculation, for each transport service and vehicle type considered, of all resource costs, prices, transport demand, external costs, and so on, implied by the current policy regime. The reference situation implies, among others, that not all external costs are charged to users, that parking is typically not charged at its full cost, that public transport is heavily subsidised, and so on.

b. Optimal pricing

Apart from the reference situation, the optimal pricing scenario serves as a second benchmark. The idea is to determine the welfare-optimal prices for all types of transport services considered, that is, to determine that set of prices that maximises the net benefits to the economy. In determining optimal prices, the obvious assumption is that all currently existing prices and taxes are abolished and replaced by the optimal ones. The authorities are assumed to have perfect pricing instruments available that allow price differentiation reflecting external cost differences according to mode, vehicle type, period of the day, and so on. Although such a scenario might be difficult to implement in the short run, since it implies highly differentiated charging for different drivers, it provides a valuable long-run benchmark with respect to the maximal welfare improvement that pricing measures can achieve. Moreover, the other policy packages can be compared to this second benchmark so as to evaluate their effectiveness in terms of contributions to overall welfare.

c. Congestion pricing

Clearly, optimal pricing may be an objective that is too ambitious for the near future. A more modest alternative is the policy package 'congestion pricing'. Its main purpose is to allow for some price differentiation in relation to differences in congestion so as to reduce external congestion costs. Of course, as the model we use does not allow continuous differentiation depending on traffic volumes and the corresponding average speed levels, this main idea is implemented in a fairly crude, but still quite informative, way. The model basically distinguishes between peak and off-peak periods and allows price differences between periods.

For obvious reasons, the practical implementation of congestion pricing in the model differs somewhat between the urban and the interregional applications of the models. In the urban version of the model, two variants are considered. In the first variant a city cordon is defined, and the distinction is made between those residing inside and outside the cordon. It is then assumed that, for vehicles entering the cordon, different prices can be charged in the peak and the off-peak periods. Public transport prices are equal to their resource costs, eliminating all variable subsidies. A second variant of the 'congestion pricing' scenario introduces parking charges, at resource cost, as an additional policy instrument.

In the interregional models, congestion pricing involves imposing a time-differentiated highway toll that can be levied per passenger- and per tonne-kilometre. Time differentiation is again limited to peak versus off-peak period. The use of other roads is priced at the reference levels. Again, public transport is priced at resource cost, eliminating all variable subsidies.

d. Uniform pricing

This policy package aims at increasing the cost of private road transport (both for freight and passenger transport) using only currently available pricing instruments, such as fuel prices and a Eurovignette on highways. This scenario can be interpreted as an across the board increase in the costs of road transport that leaves public transport prices at their reference level (including the existing level of subsidy where applicable).

Again, there are some slight differences in implementation between the urban and interregional versions of the model. In both model versions, the levels of fuel prices are assumed to correspond to the minimum target levels proposed by the EU for 2002. These are fixed at 0.5 Euro/litre for gasoline and 0.393 Euro/litre for diesel. Country-specific VAT rates are then applied to the sum of resource costs and the excise levels in order to arrive at the relevant fuel price. In the interregional setting, the fuel price increases are combined with an annual licence for the use of highways (equal to 1000 Euros per year for trucks and 100 Euros per year for passenger cars) as an additional instrument. For the urban model applications, as in the congestion scenario, two variants were applied: one variant changes only the fuel prices, with other prices left at their reference levels, the second charges in addition the resource cost of parking to all users.

e. Emission technology regulation

Finally, note that in both the urban and interregional models all scenarios can be implemented with and without the possibility of imposing improved emission technology for cars. Basically, it is assumed that in addition to the standard policy scenarios described above it is possible to subsidise improved vehicle emission technologies, if the external pollution cost reductions exceed the cost of the subsidies. The improved emission technologies imply, among others, to add to the standard technologies a three-way catalytic converter for gasoline cars and a particulate filter for diesel cars.

3.3.2 A Schematic Overview of the Selected Policy Packages

A summary of the common policy packages analysed is provided in Table 3.1. The table clearly indicates the set of currently used taxes and subsidies that are abolished in the different scenarios, and it lists the policy instruments that are proposed. Interestingly, the 'optimal pricing' and 'congestion pricing' packages require to numerically optimise the values of the different policy instruments, whereas 'uniform pricing' is merely a simulation exercise in which the values of the relevant instruments are introduced in the model to analyse the corresponding welfare effects. This illustrates the different ways in which the model can be employed. Finally, note that the 'emission regulation' scenario can be combined with each of the other packages listed. For example, it is perfectly possible to analyse the combined effect of congestion pricing and emission regulation.

3.4 CONCLUSION

This chapter first briefly reviewed recent changes in EU transport policy. Taking into account the observed change of emphasis in policymaking, we then proceeded to present a number of specific policy packages that will be carefully analysed using a large-scale optimisation model. All policy packages place more weight on pricing instruments in an effort to internalise external costs. Apart from a reference scenario that reflects the transport market equilibrium at unchanged policies, we suggested analysing an optimal pricing scenario, a congestion-pricing package and a uniform pricing package.

The optimal pricing scenario is considered a benchmark that indicates the maximal welfare gain that can be achieved if perfect pricing instruments are available. As it has to be recognised that implementation may be difficult in the short run because of technical, political and administrative problems, some alternative interim policies may be necessary. We have therefore identified two basic alternatives: congestion pricing aims at price differentiation between peak and off-peak periods, uniform pricing allows taking into account some of the external costs of transport by using only existing price instruments. Several variations of the different scenarios were suggested by allowing parking charges and emission regulation as additional policy instruments.

Table 3.1 Description of common scenarios

Scenario	Existing taxes and subsidies that are abolished	Policy instruments used
Optimal pricing (benchmark)	All abolished	Taxes and subsidies can be differentiated by vehicle km or pass km according to mode, type of vehicle, time of the day
Congestion pricing	All subsidies to public transport except for fixed cost	– URBAN: define one cordon; prices are optimally differentiated between peak and off-peak – INTERURBAN: highway toll that optimally differentiates between peak and off-peak – Public transport prices are equal to marginal resource cost
Uniform pricing	Fuel taxes	– URBAN: fuel taxes are increased to a common EU level (0.5 Euro/l per gasoline and 0.393 Euro/l of diesel). This implies small increases – INTERURBAN: same fuel taxes as for urban, but annual highway licence as extra instrument
Congestion pricing + parking charges (urban model only)	All subsidies to public transport except for fixed cost Subsidies to parking	– One cordon, optimal price differentiation between peak and off-peak – Parking charges at resource cost – public transport prices are equal to marginal resource cost
Uniform pricing + parking charges (urban model only)	Fuel taxes Subsidies to parking	– Fuel taxes are increased to a common EU level (0.5 Euro/l for diesel), this implies small increases Parking charges equal to resource costs
Emission technology regulation for cars	Existing technology regulation for cars	More expensive but cleaner emission technologies reduction of emissions (except CO_2) of some 50%

NOTES

1. It should also be recognised that, in addition, important transport issues have been addressed, either explicitly or implicitly, in both general economic strategy documents, such as the White Paper on *Growth, Competitiveness and Employment*, or those on spatial development such as the *Europe 2000* studies.
2. The Paper estimates the aggregate cost to the EU for the four main external costs. The results are: 0.2 per cent of GDP for noise, 0.4 per cent of GDP for air pollution, 2 per cent of GDP for congestion, and 1.5 per cent of GDP for accidents.

PART II

Modelling

4. Methodology and structure of the urban model[1]

Stef Proost and Kurt Van Dender

4.1 INTRODUCTION

The graphical presentation of Chapter 1 introduces the microeconomic framework of analysis used throughout this book. It shows that the current transport situation may be inefficient because of the presence of non-internalised externalities and because of the presence of unjustified subsidies. The suggested approach to improve the efficiency of the transport system is to bring prices in line with social costs. This requires the internalisation of external costs, through taxation and/or regulation as well as an abolishment of unjustified subsidies.

It is our objective to apply this framework in case study work for European regions and cities. The policy reform packages discussed in Chapter 3 need to be assessed in terms of their impact on the efficient operation of transport systems. Policy assessment requires a careful analysis of the quantitative importance of the different mechanisms. Because of the complexity of transport systems, in particular because of the large number of interacting transport markets and because of constraints on policy instruments, graphical analysis will not suffice for such a task. A solution is to translate economic theory into a mathematical model, suitable for implementation as computational software.

The economic literature provides several theoretical and graphical analyses of the optimal structure of transport prices, but only few actual computations of optimal prices. Our model extends a previous urban transport model (De Borger et al., 1997), which focussed on optimal pricing policies only, did not use an explicit welfare criterion and relied on a strongly simplified demand and supply structure. The principal contribution of the present model is the explicit computation of optimal taxes and regulations that internalise different types of externalities in a second best framework. Previous contributions to the optimal transport pricing problem in a second best framework include the seminal papers by Glaister and Lewis

(1978) and Small (1983). These papers focussed on congestion externalities only and were limited to two modes.

This chapter presents the structure and properties of the URBAN model. The next chapter does the same for the INTERREGIONAL model. The next section of this chapter introduces the basic idea of the model. Section 4.3 elaborates on the representation of demand, Section 4.4 covers supply. Section 4.5 deals with the treatment of tax revenues. Section 4.6 presents the equilibrium and optimality principles, and Section 4.7 discusses the use of the model and the different model versions. The appendix contains a brief mathematical description.

4.2 THE BASIC IDEA

From Chapter 1 we know that the transport sector is an important cause of external costs specific to transportation like congestion and accidents, but also of other external costs like air pollution and noise. In addition, transport prices may fail to reflect the resource costs (exclusive of external costs), for example when mass transit is subsidised or free parking is provided. Several types of pricing and regulation instruments can be used to tackle these problems. The basic idea of the urban model is to look for the optimal combination of price and regulatory policies in the transport and environment domain. This is achieved by the constrained optimisation of a welfare function. The approach is further explained by using a model flowchart (Section 4.2.1) and by explaining the structure of the welfare function (Section 4.2.2).

4.2.1 Model Flowchart

Figure 4.1 shows the models' main components: a demand module, a supply module and an equilibrium price module. These modules are treated in detail in Sections 4.3, 4.4 and 4.5 respectively. The simultaneous interaction of the three modules allows to compute transport prices, taking account of restrictions on the flexibility of prices when relevant, such that the value of the welfare function is maximised. Figure 4.1 is reminiscent of the graphs in Chapter 1, which show a demand curve, a supply curve and an equilibrium price. Only now the modules represent a large number of markets (graphs) simultaneously, taking account of their interdependence. The interdependencies between transport markets exist through two mechanisms. First, a (generalised) price change in one market will have demand effects in other markets. Since transport modes are, to a certain extent, substitutes, an increase in the price in a market will lead to lower demand in that market and higher demand in other markets. Second, given that most modes use the same road transport network, the time cost component of the generalised price in one market will depend on the intensity of use of that same road network by other modes of transport. For example, the time required for a bus trip strongly depends on the number of passenger cars present on the network. So we have an interdependency between markets via demand substitution and via the time costs.

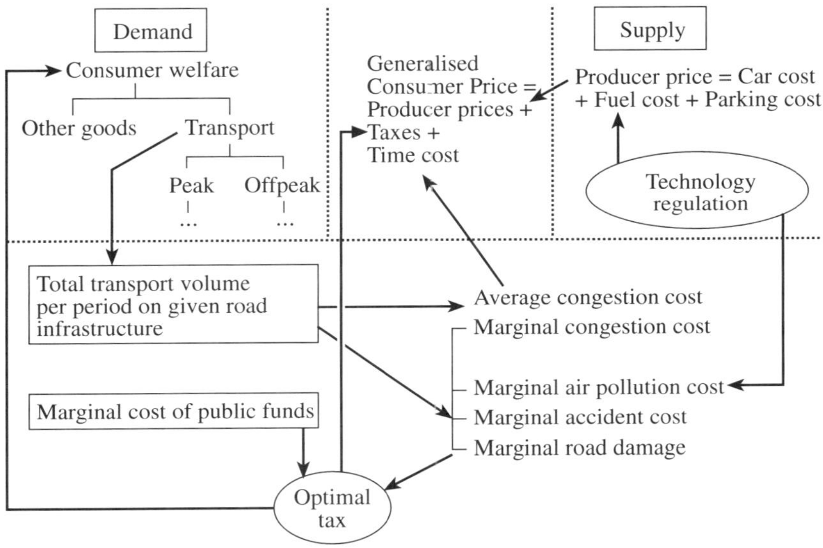

Figure 4.1 Model flowchart

In Figure 4.1, the two policy instruments are shown as ellipses. The optimal regulation of technology will affect the producer price of cars (a cleaner car will be more expensive) and will affect the emission characteristics and therefore the marginal air pollution cost. The second policy instrument is the taxes (or subsidies) that can be levied on the different markets. A market is defined in terms of the number of passenger kilometres with a given transport mode at a given time. These taxes will represent the different marginal external costs and will also be influenced by the marginal cost of public funds. For given values of the two policy variables, the supply part (the right hand upper part of Figure 4.1) determines the generalised cost functions. These are indeed functions because, even with constant marginal resource costs for car and bus kilometres, the average congestion (or time) cost component still depends on the volume of transport on that mode and on other modes. The equilibrium on the transport market can only be determined by allowing full interaction between the supply (or cost) functions and the demand functions. The demand part represents a set of interdependent demand functions. The demand for each mode (for example total passenger kilometre in peak with a given type of car) is a function of the generalised price of that mode, the generalised price of all other modes and of the level of income. We represent also the demand for non-transport goods to account for the possibility of substitution between other goods and transport: the total demand for trips is therefore not fixed. The standard way to derive a consistent set of interdependent demand functions is to maximise a utility function. This utility function serves to represent the consumers' welfare, this is an important component of the total welfare level of a given transport equilibrium. The model is mostly used not to compute one equilibrium but to select the best equilibrium by choosing optimal values for the policy parameters.

4.2.2 Structure of the Welfare Function

The structure of the welfare function is important because it drives the selection of optimal policy parameters. The welfare function represents in a mathematical form the different model components shown in the flowchart. The approach is rather general, because we want to trade off inefficiencies on the different transport markets. Nevertheless, the model relies on a partial equilibrium structure, because we do not deal explicitly with the labour market and do not model the feedback from freight transport prices into the prices of non-transport commodities. The latter assumption is acceptable because urban freight transport prices are a relatively small fraction of consumer prices. The interregional model (Chapter 5) drops this simplification.

Table 4.1 details the structure of the welfare function. The control variables used by the government in maximising this function are the taxes and subsidies in the transport sector, as well as the environmental standards on cars or other vehicles. Two types of constraints are used: (1) demand for a particular transport mode must equal supply and (2) some tax instruments can not be used.

The first element in the welfare function can be seen as a generalised consumer surplus (area under the demand curve minus the consumers' expenses, see Chapter 1). There are three specific elements in this utility function formulation. First, it is expressed in terms of generalised costs rather than money prices. This allows to take into account time losses due to congestion and the reaction of consumers on variations in speed, waiting and walking time, and so on. Second, the utility formulation allows to treat the different transport modes simultaneously. This is difficult with a traditional consumer surplus approach defined on each market when transport modes are substitutes, because the consumer surplus is not uniquely defined anymore in that case: it depends on the path of integration. Third, the income term takes into account the effect of changes in tax revenue. In other words it is assumed that the change in tax income is ultimately redistributed to the consumers. The income term also takes into account the profits or losses of the suppliers of transport ('producer surplus'). Assume a transport provider decreases his price below the marginal cost. This benefits the consumer directly but the loss must be paid for by society, which implies ultimately an income decrease for the consumer.

Table 4.1 The structure of the welfare function

Welfare is the sum of:	
Utility of households from private goods	Utility is a function of three elements: • Prices of non-transport goods, which are taken as given; • Generalised costs of all alternative passenger transport options; the generalised price includes the resource costs and the time costs (incl. on board, waiting, walking time for mass transit); • Exogenous income + profits of the suppliers of transport + recycled tax revenue.
+ Utility of freight transport users	Represented by minus the total cost function of the production sector that is a function of three elements: • The level of production, specified exogenously; • The generalised cost of all freight transport options; these equal the money costs plus the time costs; • The prices of other production factors, which are taken as given.
− Environmental and accident costs	Represents the product of environmental damage and the monetary valuation of the damage + the external accidents costs.
+ Tax revenue use correction	This correction is necessary to take into account the efficiency effects on the labour markets of the particular way in which tax revenues are assumed to be used.

The second term in Table 4.1 represents the cost level of firms. We assume that firms choose that mix of freight transport services that minimises their overall production costs for given production levels. The benefit of any change in generalised freight transport prices equals the change in total production costs for the economy. This can be seen as a consumer surplus term for the users of freight transport. The level of production is taken as fixed here, because (a) there is only a small feedback effect from urban freight costs on production levels, and (b) the expected variation in the demand for non-transport consumption that can result from changes in urban transport prices will be small. The overall level of production is no longer kept fixed in the INTERREGIONAL model (see Chapter 5).

The third term takes into account the environmental and accident externalities that have been expressed in monetary terms. They could be integrated into the utility function of the consumers but this would complicate the formulation. The congestion externalities are integrated in the utility function via the average time costs in the generalised prices.

The fourth term in the welfare function is a correction term to take into account the secondary effects of changes in tax revenues. When there are no other distortions in the economy and when additional tax revenue is redistributed to the consumers in a lump sum form, this term drops out: the tax increase and the redistribution of the receipts are taken into account in the utility function. Other forms of revenue use lead to positive or possibly negative correction terms. This is a difficult issue and the interested reader can find a detailed explanation of this element of the welfare function in Section 4.6.2.

The objective function is maximised using the prices of transport and the environmental regulation of cars as control variables. It can be shown that in the absence of constraints on the instruments, the optimum can be reached via prices equal to marginal social costs corrected for a tax revenue term. When there are constraints on the policy instruments, the marginal social cost pricing result no longer holds and complicated second-best pricing rules need to be computed. The Appendix to this chapter contains an abbreviated version of the mathematical formulation of the model.

4.3 DEMAND

4.3.1 Principle

The *demand part* shows the consumption choices that a representative household has. The choice possibilities are represented in detail for transport consumption, but not for other consumption. In particular, a household can

- increase or decrease the overall level of consumption;
- vary overall demand for transport, that is it can choose between transport and other goods;

- choose the time of day for its travel (peak or off-peak);
- choose between motorised and non-motorised transport;
- choose between two modes in order to fulfil its transportation needs: private or public mode;
- more specifically, it can choose between metro or tram and bus, for the private side there is a choice between: solo driving or shared driving (car pool);
- if the car mode is chosen, different sizes of vehicles are available;
- finally there is a choice between several types of fuel, namely diesel and petrol.

Carpooling is considered as a separate mode. By doing so the overall occupancy rate for cars becomes endogenous. The non-motorised modes are aggregated into one mode because we emphasise congestion and air pollution problems, which are related to motorised transport.

In the demand part, consumers choose between alternative types of transportation on the basis of their subjective preferences and on the basis of the relative prices of the different transport alternatives supplied to them. The transport goods consumed have the dimension passenger kilometre in a specific type of vehicle in a given period.

Demand functions are defined as a function of the generalised price of transport: the cost of transport consists of a money cost (the public transport fare or the expenditures for the use of a car) and a time cost (the time necessary for the trip, times the value of time). The time requirement may depend on the mode of transport (passenger or freight, car or public transport) and on the discomfort of the users (a minute lost when driving to work in the morning peak probably has a higher subjective value than a minute lost during a shopping trip in the afternoon). Trip distances are fixed by assuming fixed locations for all activities. The use of generalised prices is a shortcut for a more elaborate model with endogenous values of time. The shortcut is justified as long as values of time do not change between two equilibria. The generalised price plays an important role in the model: travel times are endogenous, as they depend on the level of congestion of the transport mode used.

4.3.2 Implementation

The transport choice possibilities are represented using a nested constant elasticity of subsitution (CES) utility function (Keller, 1976). Figure 4.2 is a graphical representation of the type of nests that are used. Only the peak branch is shown completely. The off-peak branch has a similar structure. The advantage of this functional form is that only information about the ease of substitution at each division of the tree in branches is needed (transport versus transport goods, peak versus off-peak and so on) together with the quantities and prices of the 23 final goods (the lowest level in the tree) in a reference equilibrium. This information is sufficient to construct the 23×23 matrix of price and cross-price elasticities. Of course imposing structure on the choices of individuals also implies some limitations. The main limitations are the unitary income elasticities and the separable structure. Unitary income elasticities imply that expenditure shares for goods are independent of income levels, which makes the model unsuited for long-term forecasting. Separability means that goods on a branch of the tree will react identically to price changes for all goods on other branches.

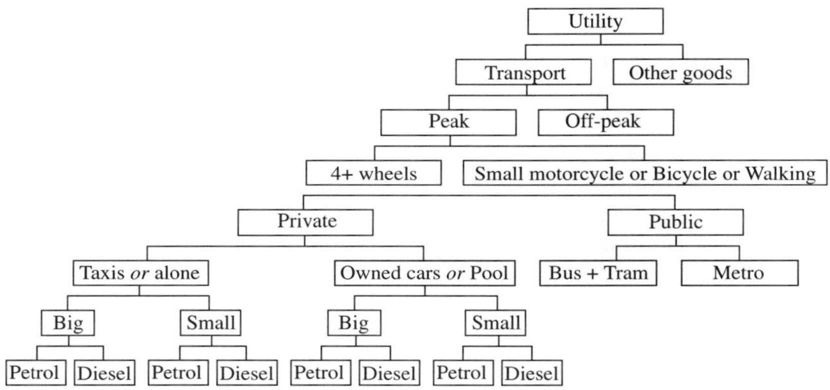

Figure 4.2 CES utility structure of URBAN model

4.4 SUPPLY

The supply part of the model (right hand side of Figure 4.1) represents the activities and choices made by the producers of cars and the suppliers of other inputs such as fuels, car maintenance and so on. Choices in the supply part of the model are made on the basis of profit maximisation, subject to government regulation of vehicle technology and equipment. Assuming perfect competition among the suppliers, supply will deliver at marginal resource costs plus producer taxes. In the absence of producer taxes, producer prices will equal the least cost combination of marginal resource costs. This implies, for example, that if there is no pollution regulation or taxation, suppliers will typically supply vehicle kilometres with dirty cars, as these are cheaper to produce. The combined assumptions of perfect competition and constant returns to scale in production ensure that producers will sell the demanded quantities at marginal resource cost.

The supply module is simple. Its main function is to represent the resource costs of alternative transport modes. In the present version, for most parts of the supply process there will be no real choice possibility included in the model, except for the vehicle emission technology. The producer can be forced by regulation to offer a particular emission technology.

Two types of modes are distinguished: public and private transport modes. We consider each in turn.

4.4.1 Private Transport Modes

For the private passenger transport modes, a distinction is made between large and small cars (where size relates to engine capacity), between diesel and petrol cars and between cars with one or more occupants ('non-pooled' and 'pooled' cars). Resource costs are taken as constant per vehicle-kilometre for each of these categories. The costs of ownership and of cars use are not explictly distinguished. This is acceptable for a static implementation of a model that represents a long-run adjustment of the stock of cars.

Two technological options are distinguished for petrol cars: standard technology includes a normal 3-way catalytic converter whereas improved technology contains a pre-heated 3-way catalytic converter. The latter is more efficient in reducing harmful emissions in urban areas (where trips are shorter on average). For diesel cars there are also two possibilities. The improved technology adds a particulate filter to the standard technology.

Six different inputs are combined to produce a car-km. There is no substitution possible between these inputs; their proportions are fixed. To obtain one km in period X by individual of type Y with cartype Z, a fixed amount of fuel and parking time is assumed to be required. The other costs are vehicle depreciation costs, insurance costs, maintenance costs and (possibly) road toll costs. The relevant costs are the marginal costs per vehicle-km.

Fuel costs are determined by the resource cost per litre of fuel and the fuel consumption in litre per km. The first part is the cost (exclusive of taxes) of a litre of petrol or a litre of diesel. The second part is not only different between fuel types, but will also depend on the size of the car and the occupancy rate (car pooling is slightly more fuel consuming per vehicle kilometre than cars driven solo). Fuel consumption also depends on traffic speed. As regards *vehicle costs*, since we do not distinguish fixed and variable cost components, we express the cost of the vehicle as a cost per vehicle-km (assuming a certain amount of km driven during the lifetime of an average vehicle). A constant cost for each vehicle type (size and fuel type) is used. The *parking cost* consists of two components: the resource cost per hour of parking and the average parking time per trip. The cost of an hour of parking can differ according to time of day and vehicle size. Parking time may depend on time of day as well, and it can differ between residents and non-residents of the city. In the applications discussed in this book, parking costs will be constant – on a per trip basis – over all these categories, however. The remaining resource costs (of oil, tyres, maintenance and insurance) are grouped in one cost component. Their level depends on vehicle and fuel type.

4.4.2 Public Transport Modes

It is assumed that public transport is completely controlled by the government. There are two types of public transport: buses and trams, and metro. Buses and trams are considered as one mode because they are perceived by the user as transport modes with the same quality. Buses and trams are assumed to use the same network, and both contribute to the overall road congestion

Both public transport modes are represented by a linear cost function that contains a fixed cost and a proportional variable cost which differs by period: capacity costs are fully allocated to the peak period as extra vehicles are only needed in this period.

We have introduced walking times to the public transport stops and waiting times at stops as part of the generalised cost of public transport, where we allow waiting times to vary in respect to public transport volumes. The relation between waiting times, bus frequencies and public transport volumes is based on the optimality rule derived by Mohring (1972). We assume that frequency can be changed (increased or decreased) at constant marginal costs. It is assumed that the average occupancy rate in the peak is constant. For example for Brussels it amounts to 40 persons/vehicle in the peak and in the off-peak: 9 persons/vehicle.

4.5 EQUILIBRIUM AND OPTIMAL TAX RULES

In the *equilibrium price module* (middle and lower part of Figure 4.1) generalised prices are computed for the different types of transportation modes. The generalised price is the sum of three elements:

- a producer price for different types of vehicle-km – this price is determined by the supply module;
- a transportation time cost that is a function of the total (peak or off-

peak) volume of traffic in equilibrium; this transportation time contains the average congestion cost;
- a tax (or subsidy) that has two functions: first, to raise tax revenue or to subsidise[2] certain modes of transportation and, second, to correct for marginal external costs like air pollution, marginal congestion costs and so on. This tax is differentiated for the different types of transport goods, that is the tax is differentiated across markets. The magnitude of the taxes is codetermined by the marginal cost of public funds (the benefit of raising tax revenue in the transport sector equals the cost of public funds raised in other sectors, see Section 4.6) and by the level of the marginal external costs.

Besides taxes, the policymaker can also impose certain *environmental regulations* under the form of ad hoc constraints on the supply part of the model: minimum energy efficiency, banning certain types of fuels and so on. This will increase the producer price but will decrease the external effects associated to vehicle use.

In the transport market equilibrium:

- government regulates the supply technologies to be used,
- producers maximise profits, taking prices as given,
- consumers select their preferred consumption bundle given the consumer prices, and
- government combines regulations and consumer taxes to maximise overall welfare (in as far as the government optimizes welfare).

The transport market equilibrium is computed as an optimal tax equilibrium under constraints on tax and regulatory instruments (see Appendix 1). The limiting case is where constraints on tax instruments simply implement the present values so that there is no scope for policy changes. Table 4.2 describes the optimal tax rules (or transport pricing rules) for some simplified cases when there are no constraints on the tax instruments. The table is restricted to passenger transport. A detailed discussion of the marginal cost of public funds parameter is postponed until Section 4.6.3.

We consider several cases. First, when there are no constraints on instruments and there is no interaction with other tax distortions (lump-sum taxes are available so that the marginal cost of public funds equals one), the optimal price of transport goods equals the marginal resource cost plus the VAT rate on other consumption goods. The VAT rate on non-transport goods is taken as given in the model set up. The optimal allocation in the economy is reached when the relative price of transport and non-transport goods is not altered via taxes, so that the same VAT taxes should apply.[3] The same VAT rate on all consumption goods together with a subsidy on

Table 4.2 Optimal tax rules

Constraints on transport tax instruments?	External costs present?	Marginal cost of public funds?	Optimal pricing rule
No	No	1	Price passenger transport = marginal resource cost + tax rate on non-transport goods (VAT).
No	No	>1	Price passenger transport = marginal resource cost + tax rate on non-transport goods + Ramsey mark up.
No	Yes	1	Price passenger transport = marginal resource cost + marginal external cost + tax rate on non-transport goods.
Yes One mode is subsidised	No	1	Price passenger transport = marginal resource cost + tax rate on non-transport goods – subsidy if this mode is substitute.

labour does indeed not distort choices of consumers. Take the case of metro, where there are increasing returns to scale. The implication of the tax rule is that subsidies are required so that the metro prices equal the marginal resource cost. The operating deficit of the public transport company is covered via lump sum taxes that do not cause distortions.

Second, when there is a premium on government revenue (marginal cost of public funds larger than one), it becomes interesting to raise revenue whenever the loss of consumer surplus due to tax distortions is lower than the premium on government revenue. The tax will be raised more on those transport goods that are relatively price inelastic. This is the Ramsey rule: revenue-raising taxes should be inversely proportional to the price elasticity, as losses in consumer surplus due to taxation are smaller for goods with lower price elasticities. In fact, with many interacting markets the rule is more complex, because the net effect on all other markets has to be taken into account. The marginal cost of public funds also has its implications for the subsidies to public transport operations that are characterised by increasing returns to scale. The premium on government revenue will tend to reduce the optimal subsidy level because subsidies are more costly.

The third case is the typical textbook case, with external costs in transport markets and the marginal cost of public funds equal to one. Now the price should equal the marginal social cost plus the VAT rate so that the marginal rate of substitution between consumer goods equals the ratio of marginal social costs.

In the fourth case we restrict ourselves to only two modes and assume that one mode is underpriced. This could be car transport when free parking is provided or when marginal external costs are not charged for. In this case the optimal price for the substitute mode (say metro) is lower than the marginal resource cost.

In the case studies that we will discuss in the next chapters, we will have to deal mostly with mixed cases: external costs, tax constraints and a premium on government revenue will have to be combined. The tax rules lose their transparency and numerical optimisation becomes necessary.

4.6 ADDITIONAL ISSUES

4.6.1 Economies of Density in Public Transport

In the basic formulation of the model the marginal resource cost of supplying public transport was taken to be constant, as was the quality of public transport (reflected in the appropriate value of time). Mohring (1972) and Viton (1983) have shown that this assumption is not realistic. When demand for public transport in a given hour increases, one can increase the load factor of buses and/or increase the frequency of the bus service. Keeping the load factor constant, an increase in demand for public transport allows an increase in frequency without any increase in marginal costs. The increase in frequency reduces average waiting times at bus stops, implying a decrease of the generalised trip cost. Keeping the service frequency constant, an increase in public transport demand allows an increase in the load factor and a decrease in the marginal cost per passenger.

In the URBAN model we have included a simplified version of the Mohring effect. This is done by using fixed occupancy rates and assuming that a variation of demand increases the frequency of service. The implication is that increased demand reduces the waiting time for the public transport users. This can be considered a positive externality, in the sense that one extra user of public transport reduces the waiting time of the existing users. The positive externality rule leads to an optimal price that is, *ceteris paribus*, below the marginal resource cost.

4.6.2 The Marginal Cost of Public Funds

In the welfare function, changes in tax revenue (including public transport deficits) are valued at the marginal cost of public funds minus 1, and tax revenue is returned in a lump sum way to the individual. This is a reduced form formulation for a partial equilibrium framework, as we will now explain in more detail.

Our model is a partial equilibrium model, in which only the allocation of the income of consumers over transport goods and one non-transport good is studied. The level of income is fixed and the labour market is not explicitly modelled.

To understand the role of the marginal cost of public funds, it is useful to examine the effects of an increase in transport taxes in a broader context than that of our model. The increase will have a straightforward first effect on the transport market, but other markets are affected as well. There are direct effects on other markets (for example the labour market) when the other good is a complement or substitute, and indirect effects when the revenue of the transport tax is used to lower taxes on that market. When there are important distortions on this second market, these indirect effects have potentially important welfare effects. In the urban model, we capture the direct and indirect effects on other markets through a 'marginal cost of public funds' parameter. Obviously, a general equilibrium approach where the labour market is explicitly represented would be better. In the current model versions the implicit assumption is that all changes in tax revenue from the transport sector are compensated by changes in the labour tax. If this assumption holds, all direct and indirect effects can be captured by a correction factor for the changes in public funds. The labour tax was selected because it is the most important tax, so that lowering it may have important beneficial welfare effects.

Let us now examine in more detail the effects of an increase in the level of taxes on transport and check how they are accounted for in the model. On the market of consumption goods a tax increase on transport will generate a shift to non-transport consumption goods. This will probably also increase the total tax revenue raised on consumption goods. The two effects are included in the model: utility is defined over transport and the other consumption good. Assume that the net increase in tax revenue is used to reduce the tax rate on labour. As long as the labour supply is fixed we can represent this as a lump sum increase in the level of exogenous income. If the labour supply is indeed fixed, the marginal cost of public funds on labour equals 1, as there is no extra inefficiency created by raising revenue from labour taxes. This is the simplest case.

When labour supply is no longer fixed, we have to take into account different types of secondary effects on the labour market. Following Bovenberg and De Mooij (1994) and Goulder et al. (1999), we distinguish between four effects (none of which is explicitly represented in our model).

- Complementarity effect: When transport is directly related to work trips (leisure), making transport more expensive has a direct negative (positive) effect on labour supply. One should be aware that the majority of trips are not work related so that the net complementarity effect (aggregated over all trips) is indeterminate.
- Tax interaction effect: Higher transport taxes reduce the purchasing power of the net wage, and this reduces the supply of labour.
- Tax recycling effect: When the extra transport tax revenue is used to reduce existing labour taxes, this tends to increase the supply of labour.
- Tax shifting effect: When not all individuals supply labour, but all consume transport goods, an increase in the transport tax recycled via a decrease in labour taxes means shifting taxes from labour income to non-labour income. This has a positive labour supply effect.

It is the combination of these four effects that will determine the value we attribute to changes in tax revenue from transport goods and consumption goods. We discuss several cases in Table 4.3.

In the model we use the third case of Table 4.3 as a benchmark. More precisely, we assume that the complementarity effect, the tax interaction effect and the tax recycling effect balance each other (which is an approximation) so that the tax shifting effect becomes important. In practice, all changes in tax revenue from transport and consumption taxes are added to the exogenous income term so that only the difference ($MCPF-1$) needs to be used to account for the value of changes in tax revenue. The changes in tax revenue $dREV$ are added as a separate term in the objective function with as coefficient λ:

$$\lambda = (MCPF - 1)^{*}\kappa^{*}\, dREV$$

where κ is the share of non labour income and $MCPF$ is the marginal cost of raising public funds via labour taxes. This formulation takes into account the tax shifting effect: taxes on labour are reduced by using the transport tax revenue raised on non-labour earners to reduce the labour taxes. For $MCPF$ a value of 1.20 is used, in the Brussels case study. This value was computed by applying the formulas of Snow and Warren (1996) to Belgian data. For κ, a value of 0.3 is used. This gives a λ value of 0.066.

4.6.3 Non-Identical Individuals

The model is formulated for multiple types of individuals. Individuals can differ in the transport opportunities they have, in the income and prices they face, and in their preferences. The applications in this book distinguish

Table 4.3 Assumptions on the marginal cost of public funds

Who supplies labour	Net complementarity between transport and labour supply	Different effects present	Value attributed to increase in transport tax and consumption tax revenue (marginal cost of public funds)
All individuals	No	Tax interaction Tax recycling	<1 because tax interaction is always larger than tax recycling
All individuals	Yes – complement to labour	Tax interaction Tax recycling complementarity	$\ll 1$ because additional negative effect of complementarity on labour supply
Not all individuals	Yes – complement to leisure	Tax interaction and complementarity balanced by Tax recycling and Tax shifting	>1 because increased tax on transport paid by non labour income is used to reduce tax on labour
All individuals	No	Tax interaction Tax recycling via lump sum transfer	$\ll 1$ because positive tax recycling effect is missing
All individuals	No	Tax interaction Tax revenue is wasted in bad projects	Negative because all revenue raised is wasted

four types of individuals: inhabitants of and commuters to the urban area, and within these groups a distinction is made between drivers who do and those who do not pay for parking at the trip destination. Aggregate welfare is an unweighted sum of the welfare of these individuals.

In order to take account of distributional issues, the welfare function can be adapted by using social welfare weights, which are taken as constant in the optimisation of transport prices. These weights are defined as the relative social marginal utility of income. All the elements of the objective function (distribution of tax revenue, distribution of changes in real profits, distribution of efficiency gains on the labour market and the distribution of the damage of external effects) have to be allocated to the different types of individuals for this system to work.

4.6.4 Constraints on Policy Instruments

Constraints on the use of policy instruments exist. In fact, only certain inputs to the use of transport means can be taxed (fuel, vehicle, tolls, and so on), rather than the actual use of the modes itself. This heavily restricts the pricing possibilities. The model can handle these constraints. When more constraints are introduced on the pricing instruments, the first order conditions become analytically more and more intractable so that only numerical simulations can bring definite answers (see Appendix).

4.7 THE USE OF THE MODEL

4.7.1 The Use of the Model for Comparative Statics

The model is calibrated by plugging in observed or expected taxes and prices, quantities and regulations. This generates a reference market equilibrium. The combination of elasticities of substitution and data on prices on quantities produces price elasticities for the reference equilibrium. The elasticities of substitution are chosen such that the generated elasticities conform to estimates which are available from the literature.

The problems with the method described are (a) that there are no estimates available for all trade-offs present in the model, and (b) that it is difficult to check whether the available estimates are constructed from a context which is relevant to the model. For problem (a), there is no real solution, except common sense. For (b), it is helpful to consider as wide a range of estimates as possible. The mathematical relation between elasticities of substitution and price elasticities is presented in Keller (1976), and is reproduced in the software.

Table 4.4 Price elasticities literature

	Car peak	Car off-peak	Pub peak	Pub off-peak
Car peak	−0.3	0.049	0.708	0
Car off-peak	0.05	−0.6	0	0.578
Pub peak	0.03	0	−0.35	0.036
Pub off-peak	0	0.02	0.03	−0.87

Source: Ochelen and Proost (1996)

Table 4.4 presents money price elasticities taken from a literature survey. Table 4.5 gives the corresponding elasticities for the URBAN model, averaged over all consumer groups. The approximations are reasonable. The largest deviation from the literature is found for the elasticities of public transport: they are below the values reported in the literature. The reason is the inclusion of walking and waiting time costs in the generalised price of public transport, leading to a low share of money costs in the generalised price. Manipulation of the substitution elasticities so as to arrive at higher money price elasticities in the model, leads to unlikely demand reactions. Hence we opted for consistency in the pattern of generalised price elasticities.

Table 4.5 Corresponding price elasticities

	Car peak	Car off-peak	Pub peak	Pub off-peak
Car peak	−0.36	0.025	0.12	0.0002
Car off-peak	0.025	−0.54	0.001	0.65
Pub peak	0.025	0.0007	−0.19	0.0051
Pub off-peak	0.003	0.05	0.0054	−0.35

The values used in the urban model are in line with the results of the TREMOVE model (DRI-KULeuven, 1999) and the EUCARS model (Denis and Koopman, 1998). Alternative market equilibria can be generated by changing the taxes or regulations. This is done by solving again the optimisation problem to which constraints on the values of tax parameters and the type of technologies are added. An infinity of market equilibria can be generated by the model in this simulation mode. Of particular interest are the best equilibria obtainable with a given set of tax and regulation instruments. These can be found by using the model in an optimisation mode, where the value of the tax parameters is the solution to the welfare maximum problem with restrictions on the type (not the value) of policy instruments.

4.7.2 Software Implementation

TRENEN II is programmed in GAMS v2.25. The core of the model is formed by two files, T2CAL.GMS and T2OPT.GMS, the calibration and optimisation programmes. Once a calibration has been constructed and an idea of the initial values for counterfactual equilibria has been formed, a complete model run takes approximately three minutes (on a Pentium 133 Mhz for TRENEN II URBAN). Since the solver performs a non-linear optimisation, the construction of the calibration and of the first counterfactual equilibria can be quite time-intensive, because not much is known about initial values.

The global programme structure is as follows:

- CALIBRATION
  - Declaration of sets, variables, equations
  - Specification of data for calibration (incl. declaration of scalars and parameters)
    - Elasticities of substitution
    - Prices and quantities in reference situation
      - non-transport data
      - transport data
  - Specification of equations
  - Specification of starting values and bounds
  - Solve statement for non-linear optimisation
  - Fixing of reference values
  - Computation of implicit price elasticities
- OPTIMISATION
  - Declaration of additional sets, variables, equations
  - Specification of equations
  - Specification of starting values and bounds
  - Solve statement for non-linear optimisation
  - Output management

The calibration determines the demand functions and welfare function, starting from data on elasticities of substitution, the income level, duration of periods, values of time, and on the prices and quantities for the reference equilibrium. Intermediate calculations are performed for traffic flows and speeds, generalised prices at all levels and expenditures.

The optimisation starts from the calibrated equilibrium and optimises a welfare function (including external costs and the valuation of public funds). The welfare function is optimised by selecting optimal values for a given set of policy instruments (including different types of taxes and regulations).

Our model simulates and/or optimises the impact of pricing and technology instruments on external effects in transport markets and on social welfare. In a simulation, the effect of a predefined value of an instrument is calculated. In an optimisation the optimal value of an instrument is computed. Simulation and optimisation elements can be combined in one scenario (for example optimal private transport prices with fixed values of public transport prices). Constraints on instruments can be added in an optimisation exercise (for example private transport taxes cannot be different for petrol and diesel cars but look for their optimal level).

In the case of simulation, a scenario is defined by specifying the values for policy variables. In the case of optimisation a scenario is defined by the constraints on optimal values. This is done in three blocks of equations, one for the use of technology, one for all pricing instruments not related to parking, and one for parking-related instruments.

4.7.3 Model Versions

Several types of TRENEN models have been developed. They all use the same principles but are adapted to the question one wants to answer:

Table 4.6 Different model versions

TRENEN-URBAN:	<u>focus</u> on representation of passenger transport in urban areas, distinction between commuters and inhabitants and between those who have and do not have access to free parking Versions: 0. Basic 1. Model with two government levels 2. Model with explicit transport network
TRENEN-INTERREGIONAL:	<u>focus</u> on interregional passenger transport and freight transport, tolled and untolled roads, freight transit transport Versions: 0. Basic with one country model 1. Two-country model where two country governments may behave strategically

Note that for the urban model, only the basic version is operational. The other versions of the urban model are to be considered as research tools.

APPENDIX 4A.1 THE MATHEMATICAL FORMULATION OF THE TRENEN-URBAN MODEL

This appendix briefly describes the formal structure of the TRENEN-URBAN model. In order to keep things simple, only one consumer type is taken into account and economies of density are abstracted from. We consecutively discuss the basic model set-up, the structure of the welfare function, market equilibrium conditions, and welfare maximisation conditions.

4A.1.1 Model Components

Assume N identical individuals and $i=1,...,I$ different passenger transport demand categories. Each mode can be produced by $j=1,...,J$ car technologies (for example for $i=$ *small car* we could have a small car without or with catalytic converter ($j=1$ *or* 2)). Similarly there are $f=1,...,F$ different freight transport demand categories, satisfied by J different supply categories. Individual passenger transport demand for transport services of type i equals x_i and is satisfied by a total supply of J different car technologies z_{ij}. Freight demand using mode f is denoted x_f and can be satisfied by j technologies (z_{fj}).[4]

We use a partial equilibrium approach in the sense that the feedback on non-transport markets are neglected. More specifically, prices on other markets, including the price of inputs for transport, are fixed. The supply side representation is simple. The producer price per vehicle-km with mode i is p_i. The marginal resource costs of supplying vehicle-km with mode i and technology type j are taken constant and equal rc_{ij}.

The demand functions are defined as a function of the generalised price of transport: the cost of transport consists of a money cost (the public transport fare or the expenditures for the use of a car, q_i) and a time cost (the time necessary for the trip, t_i, times the value of time of that mode, ρ_i). The generalised price for a passenger-km with modus i is thus defined as:

$$generalised\ price_i = q_i + \rho_i t_i \tag{4A.1}$$

The use of generalised prices is a shortcut for a more elaborate model with endogenous values of time. The shortcut is justified as long as values of time do not change between two equilibria. The generalised price plays an important role in the model: travel times are endogenous, as they depend on the level of congestion of the transport mode used. More specifically, it is assumed that some transport modes share a common infrastructure of fixed capacity. The unit time t_i for a passenger-km using mode i depends on the total traffic volume sharing the road network. Let S denote the set of (passenger and freight transport) modes that use the same infrastructure (for example cars, trucks and public buses in the peak period), and let m_i be the contribution of mode i to the overall congestion (for example a bus with 40 people adds per person less to congestion than a car with 1 person), then the general form of the congestion function is:

$$t_i = T_i\left(\sum_{l \neq f \varepsilon S} m_l N x_l + \sum_{f \varepsilon S} m_f x_f\right) \tag{4A.2}$$

4A.1.2 The Structure of the Social Welfare Function

Social welfare is the unweighted sum of four basic components: monetised utility of the consumers, the costs of freight transport supply, weighted tax revenues from passenger transport (the weight is the marginal cost of public funds, *MCPF*, symbol λ in the equations, of which the value depends on assumptions on revenue use), and external costs from accidents, air pollution and noise. We briefly discuss each of these components.

The indirect utility function

Preferences are captured in the utility function $U = U(x_o, x_i \ (i = 1, \ldots, I))$, where o stands for a composite other commodity and i for the transport commodities. Utility is maximised subject to a generalised budget constraint, stipulating that $TY = q_o x_o + \sum_i (q_i + \rho_i t_i)\, x_i$, where TY is total generalised income. Note that abstraction is made of the time component in non-transport consumption. Each consumer's total generalised income consists of an exogenous component (Y), an equal share of the producer surplus of transport supply (PS), and an equal share in transport tax revenue from all transport modes ($TAXREV$).

We use the indirect utility function $V(q_o, q_i + \rho_i t_i, (i = 1, \ldots, I), Y + PS + TAXREV)$, which is a function of generalised prices and income. After division by the marginal utility of income in the reference equilibrium (μ_r) the value of the indirect utility function is a monetary welfare measure for transport consumers.

The cost function for freight transport

Assuming competitive conditions in the freight transport sector and a constant level of production, it is possible to represent the consumer surplus of the demand for freight transport services by an aggregated cost function for the whole production sector where only generalised freight prices are varied (C).

The tax revenue weight

The tax revenue weight (λ) captures the efficiency effects of using tax revenue raised on the transport market to reduce labour taxes. The weight in this case is positive. It is applied only to tax revenue collected from private consumption. Tax revenue based on freight demand does not receive an extra weight because, in general, production efficiency is desirable so that prices should equal marginal social costs (see Diamond and Mirrlees, 1971a,b; Mayeres and Proost, 1997).

The non-congestion external costs

Marginal external costs ec_{ij} other than congestion can in principle be a function of any of the variables of the model. For simplicity they are taken as constant per vehicle km. These external costs depend on technology used (for example the polluting emissions of a car depend on the pollution abatement equipment j). As is clear from equation (4A.2), external congestion costs are implicitly accounted for in the time costs of transport.

Taking these components together, we arrive at the welfare function in (4A.3)

$$\frac{N}{\mu_r} V \left[\begin{array}{l} q_o, q_i + \rho_i t_i; (i=1,\ldots,I), \\ Y + \frac{1}{N} \sum_{l,i} (p_l - rc_{li}) z_{li} + \frac{1}{N} \sum_{f} (q_f - p_f) x_f + \sum_{i} (q_i - p_i) x_i \end{array} \right]$$

$$- C(q_f + \rho_f t_f; f=1,\ldots,F) + \lambda \sum_{i} (q_i - p_i) N x_I - \sum_{l,i} (ec_{li} z_{li}) \quad (4A.3)$$

4A.1.3 COMPUTATION OF THE MARKET EQUILIBRIUM

A market equilibrium is computed by maximisation of the welfare function with respect to p_i, q_i and z_{ij}, subject to the following constraints:

$$\sum_{j} z_{ij} \geq N x_i \; \forall i = 1,\ldots,I \quad (4A.4)$$

$$\sum_{j} z_{fj} \geq x_f \; \forall f = 1,\ldots,F \quad (4A.5)$$

$$p_l \geq rc_{lj} \; \forall l = 1,\ldots,I \text{ and } 1,\ldots,F; \forall j = 1,\ldots,J \quad (4A.6)$$

In addition we require that all variables take positive values. The constraints (4A.4) and (4A.5) state that demand has to be satisfied by the sum of the car and other transport technologies supplied. The supply of transport has to be corrected for the occupancy rate in order to match the demand for passenger-kilometres (this is left out of the equations for reasons of clarity). The third constraint states that producer prices are larger than the marginal resource costs, which is justified by incentive compatibility constraints for producers. The use of the indirect utility function and the production cost function in the objective function guarantee that the first-order conditions for a maximum contain demand functions so that all solutions are a consumer equilibrium for households and firms. A competitive supply behaviour is introduced because producer prices will, in an optimum of (4A.3) and in the absence of pricing restrictions on parking, always be equal to marginal costs. Subsidies to private or public transport are represented by a producer price larger than the consumer price.

It is assumed that the objective function is well behaved and that the maximum problem has a solution. A unique solution is not guaranteed.[5] We use Lagrange multipliers α_i, α_f for the first set of constraints and γ_{ij} for the second set of constraints, and look for an optimum with respect to the control variables q_i, q_f and $z_{i,j}$, $z_{f,j}$. This implies that the demand levels x are controlled indirectly via the consumer prices q so that all optima of the model are by construction consumer optima (passenger transport) or cost optima (freight transport). Taxes on consumer goods are implicitly determined by the difference between q and p. The optimum will satisfy the complementary slackness conditions associated to (4A.4), (4A.5) and (4A.6) as well as the following first order Kuhn–Tucker conditions for an interior optimum (x_{kq_i} represents the derivative of x_k with respect to the consumer price of good i and μ stands for the marginal utility of income in the new equilibrium):

$$\begin{aligned}
&-\mu\frac{N}{\mu_r}x_i - N\frac{\mu}{\mu_r}\sum_{l\neq f\varepsilon S}\rho_l x_l t_{lq_i} - \sum_{f\varepsilon S}\rho_f x_f t_{fq_i} \\
&+\frac{\mu}{\mu_r}Nx_i + N\frac{\mu}{\mu_r}\sum_k (q_k - p_k)x_{kq_i} \\
&+\lambda N x_i + \lambda\sum_k (q_k - p_k)Nx_{kq_i} + \sum_k \alpha_k N x_{kq_i} = 0
\end{aligned} \tag{4A.7}$$

$$\begin{aligned}
&-N\frac{\mu}{\mu_r}\sum_{l\neq f\varepsilon S}\rho_l x_l t_{lq_f} - \sum_{f\varepsilon S}\rho_f x_f t_{fq_f} + \frac{\mu}{\mu_r}\sum_g (q_g - p_g)x_{gf} \\
&+\frac{\mu}{\mu_r}x_f - x_f + \sum_g \alpha_g x_{gf} = 0
\end{aligned} \tag{4A.8}$$

$$\frac{\mu}{\mu_r}\left(\sum_j z_{ij} - N\,x_i\right) - \lambda N\,x_i - \gamma_{if} = 0 \tag{4A.9}$$

$$\frac{\mu}{\mu_r}\left(\sum_j z_{fj} - x_f\right) - \gamma_{fj} = 0 \tag{4A.10}$$

$$\frac{\mu}{\mu_r}(p_l - rc_{lj}) - ec_{lj} - \alpha_l = 0 \tag{4A.11}$$

4A.1.4 The Maximum as a Policy Optimised Market Equilibrium

It can be shown that the solution to the maximisation problem of the previous section corresponds to a market equilibrium where:

- government regulates the supply technologies to be used,
- producers maximise profits, taking prices as given,
- consumers select their preferred consumption bundle given the consumer prices, and
- government combines regulations and consumer taxes to maximise overall welfare.

Given the construction of the objective function, all solutions are optimum budget allocations or minimum cost allocations for given generalised prices. Assume provisionally that there is no excess supply at the optimum, because this would constitute a pure loss at least equal to the resource cost. This implies via the complementary slackness condition associated to (4A.4) that $\alpha_i > 0$. For each final transport good k at least one technology g is used such that $z_{kh} > 0$. This implies through (4A.11) that for whatever technologies g and h used in the optimum to satisfy demand k, we must have:

$$rc_{kl} + ec_{kl} = rc_{kn} + ec_{kn} \tag{4A.12}$$

Consequently in each welfare optimum the sum of resource costs and external costs determines which technologies should be used. Hence, choice of technology does not depend on any other parameter (not on λ, in particular).

Because the producer price p_i is identical for g and h and because the producer only has to pay for resource costs, a cost minimising producer would not necessarily select the socially optimal technology. Therefore, we need to introduce the regulation of the type of technology to be used, as a policy instrument.[6] In the optimum and for normal values of $\lambda > 0$, producer prices will, for all technologies used, always be equal to the resource costs. To see why, assume that prices are higher than the resource costs. Then the government can increase its tax revenue at the expense of the lower valued producer surplus by keeping constant q but lowering p until it reaches the resource costs. We conclude that, in the selected optimum, producer prices equal the lowest marginal resource costs of the set of technologies allowed by the policymaker. This corresponds to the outcome of a perfectly competitive market with regulations on the type of transport technologies that can be used.

For the interpretation of the optimal tax rules it helps to restrict the analysis first to the case where demand for each transport good only depends on its own price. Using (4A.7) and (4A.11) we obtain for the optimal tax on passenger transport:

$$\left[t_k - \frac{tmcong_k + ec_k}{(1+\lambda\mu_r/\mu)}\right]\frac{E_{kk}}{q_k} = -\frac{\lambda\mu_r/\mu}{1+\lambda\mu_r/\mu} \tag{4A.13}$$

Here $tmcong_k$ is the total marginal congestion cost of increasing the use of passenger transport mode k (T_{ii} and T_{ff} represent their derivative of unit transport time of respectively passenger and freight transport with respect to the total volume of transport and m_k the contribution of mode k to congestion):

$$tmcong_k = m_k\left[N\sum_{i\varepsilon S}\rho_i x_i T_{ii} + \frac{\mu}{\mu_r}\sum_{f\varepsilon S}\rho_f x_f T_{ff}\right] \tag{4A.14}$$

When there are no external effects, (4A.13) becomes the familiar Ramsey expression where taxes are inversely proportional to their own price elasticity. The general level of taxes on consumer goods will increase when the shadow cost of public funds λ increases. The term μ_r/μ is an approximation term with a value close to 1.

Consider now the case with external costs. The external congestion cost of an increase of passenger transport of type k is defined in (4A.14) and consists of the value of the time losses for all transport users (passengers and freight). In (4A.13), taxes become Pigouvian taxes when $\lambda = 0$.

When λ increases, the externality part of the optimal tax decreases below the pure Pigouvian component and the Ramsey component increases. Intuitively a higher λ means that the second role of the tax (to raise revenue) becomes more important and that therefore the policymaker can afford less tax differentiation aimed at environmental protection as this counteracts the revenue raising objective of the tax system.

When we consider the cross-price effects between passenger transport goods, existing price distortions for complements and substitutes have to be taken into account. Cross-price effects become very important when there are restrictions on the taxation of certain modes (for example car use in the peak period). In this case there are large distortions between the social cost and the price of that mode and this can require important deviations from social cost pricing for substitute modes (for example subsidies for public transport).

Restricting ourselves to the case without cross-price effects for optimal taxes on freight transport, (4A.8) and (4A.11) imply:

$$[t_f - tmcong_f - \mu_r/\mu . ec_{fj}]\frac{E_{ff}}{q_f} = (\mu_r/\mu - 1) \quad (4A.15)$$

When the μ_r/μ approximation is perfect, we have pure Pigouvian taxes that preserve production efficiency. The difference between (4A.15) and (4A.13) lies in the λ parameter: public revenue considerations are absent when setting indirect taxes to firms. Optimality conditions (4A.12), (4A.13) and (4A.15) drive all model results. When there are restrictions on tax instruments, these conditions become quite complex.

NOTES

1. Different case studies may use slightly different demand and supply representations. These will not alter the interpretation of the model and its results. The discussion in this chapter refers to the Brussels case study.
2. Given the model assumptions, subsidies are only justifiable on the basis of characteristics of the cost function (increasing returns to scale, positive externalities), or because of imperfect pricing for substitute modes. Redistributional issues are not taken into account.
3. Note that the assumed existence of acceptable lump sum instruments implies that optimal VAT rates should be zero – in the applications, we focus on the pricing of transport and take the existing VAT rates on other goods as fixed.
4. The notation of indices is as follows: i and k are used to denote the different passenger transport modes, f and g denote the different freight transport modes and l denotes both passenger and freight transport modes. The type of technology is indexed with j.
5. Optimal tax problems can have local maxima (Diamond and Mirrlees, 1971a,b). In the model applications we experienced no problems as we always start from a feasible reference situation.
6. In an alternative model set-up, not discussed here, the policymaker could replace the technology regulations by a tax on producers or on consumers in function of the type of technologies that are used. The choice between regulation, taxing externalities at the stage of producers or at the stage of consumers is not important in this model where the policymaker is perfectly informed and disposes of perfect policy instruments.

REFERENCES

Bovenberg, A.L. and De Mooij, R.A. (1994), 'Do environmental taxes yield a double dividend', *American Economic Review*, **4**, 1085–9.

De Borger, B., Ochelen, S., Proost, S. and Swysen, D. (1997), 'Alternative transport and regulation policies: a welfare theoretic analysis for Belgium in 2005', *Transportation Research-D*, **2**(1), 177–98.

Denis, C. and Koopman, G.J. (1998), 'EUCARS: A partial equilibrium model for European CAR emissions (version 3.0),' *Economic Papers*, 130, CE.

Diamond, P.A. and Mirrlees, J.A. (1971a), 'Optimal taxation and public production I: production efficiency', *American Economic Review*, 8–27.
Diamond, P.A. and Mirrlees, J.A. (1971b), 'Optimal taxation and public production II: tax rules', *American Economic Review*, 261–78.
DRI, Kuleuven (1999), 'OIL II cost-effectiveness study; Part II: the TREMOVE model 1.3', European Commission (DGII), Standard & Poor's DRI and CES-KULeuven.
Glaister, S. and Lewis, D. (1978), 'An integrated fares policy for transport in London', *Journal of Public Economics*, **9**, 341–55.
Goulder, L.H., Parry, I.W.H., Williams III, R.C. and Burtraw, D. (1999), 'The cost-effectiveness of alternative instruments for environmental protection in a second best setting', *Journal of Public Economics*, **72**, 32–60.
Keller, W.J. (1976), 'A nested CES-type utility function and its demand and price-index functions', *European Economic Review*, **7**, 175–86.
Mayeres, I. and Proost, S. (1997), 'Optimal tax and investment rules for congestion type of externalities', *Scandinavian Journal of Economics*, **99** (2), 261–79.
Mohring, H. (1972), 'Optimization and scale economies in urban bus transportation', *American Economic Review*, 591–604.
Small, K.A. (1983), 'The incidence of congestion tolls on urban highways', *Journal of Urban Economics*, **13**, 90–111.
Snow, A. and Warren, R.S. (1996), 'The marginal welfare cost of public funds: theory and estimates', *Journal of Public Economics*, **61**, 289–305.
Viton, P.A. (1983), 'Pareto-Optimal Urban Transportation Equilibria', in T.E. Keeler, *Research in Transportation Economics*, Connecticut: JAI Press, 75–101.

5. Methodology and structure of the interregional model

Bruno De Borger

5.1 INTRODUCTION

The purpose of the interregional version of the model is to analyse optimal pricing and regulatory policies for interregional transport. Although the overall structure of the model is quite similar to that of the urban version described in Chapter 4, there are a number of important differences. Some are induced by the specific characteristics of interurban transport (for example, the more detailed treatment of freight transport in an interurban environment, taking account of the effects of freight transport prices on production costs and consumer prices, the relatively minor role of parking costs, and so on), others are related to the specific complications that arise because of the incorporation of international traffic flows. This seems desirable when modelling (freight) transport flows in small open economies characterised by very intense trade flows with other countries.

Indeed, the international component of transport flows creates a number of complications that were captured in the design of the interregional model. For example, since in some countries a non-negligible share of all (especially freight) flows consists of international transport and pure transit, a substantial fraction of external congestion, accident and pollution costs in such countries is generated by foreign transport firms. Moreover, it is well known that some transport externalities generate international spillovers; emissions of particular pollutants spill over to other regions (acid rain, global warming, and so on) and therefore generate external costs abroad. In addition, the prevalence of international transport flows and pure transit implies the possibility for countries to shift the burden of transport taxes to foreigners. Generally speaking, individual countries are likely to ignore or underestimate the implications of their policies on the welfare of foreigners, so that an international setting introduces the potential for tax exporting and tax competition between countries.

In the interregional version of the model the different complications were incorporated to various degrees, depending on the perceived importance of international transport flows. First, a one-country version of the model was developed in which the international dimension of transport pricing was captured in a very rudimentary way. This may well be acceptable for the analysis of pricing policies in fairly closed economies, or in countries in which the share of transit flows is very small. This particular version of the model was used to analyse pricing issues in Ireland (see Chapter 16). Second, a two-region model was developed that allows a detailed analysis of strategic transport pricing behaviour by individual countries. The model allows studying the implications of external cost spillovers and of tax exporting and tax competition between countries within the simplest possible setting. The theoretical underpinnings are discussed in De Borger, Courcelle and Swysen (1999).[1] The two-region version of the model was used to study optimal pricing in Belgium, a small open economy characterised by a large share of international traffic (see Chapter 15).

The models are designed to determine welfare-optimal prices and environmental policies, taking into account all relevant external effects associated with interregional transport. In other words, we take the view of a benevolent higher authority (say government) that is interested in finding the set of policy instruments that maximises social welfare. The objective function to be optimised captures the impact of pricing and regulatory policies on the welfare of consumers and producers (both directly and indirectly via their effect on externality levels) and on the tax revenues for the government (including possible public transport deficits to be covered). The model assumes perfect information on the part of the policymaker: he knows all demand functions, he is aware of the marginal private and external costs of the different supply options, and he knows the implications of introducing new vehicle technologies for private and external costs. The policymaker then determines optimal user prices for the various transport services and he may encourage the supply of new technologies if this is deemed to be welfare improving. The model allows the introduction of various constraints on the pricing and regulatory instruments available, and it takes account of the heterogeneity of transport services.

The model has at least three important limitations. First, although it is quite general in its treatment of the transport market, it remains very rudimentary in its treatment of the rest of the economy. Moreover, it only considers transport taxes among the set of taxes to be optimised. Second, it models transport flows in a spatially aggregated way. Third, at this stage of model development, distributive considerations have not yet been incorporated.

The structure of this chapter is as follows. In Section 5.2 we provide an intuitive general overview of the structure of the model. Section 5.3 considers the various model components in more detail. We pay attention to the structure of the demand side of the transport market and to the heterogeneity of transport services, we review the modelling of the supply of transport, and we discuss the introduction of externalities in the model. Moreover, we clearly point out the main differences between the one and two-country versions of the model. Finally, we briefly summarise the optimal tax rules that can be theoretically derived for the type of models constructed. In Section 5.4, the operation of the empirical model both for simulation and optimisation purposes is carefully explained. Section 5.5 concludes.

5.2 GENERAL DESCRIPTION OF THE INTERREGIONAL MODEL

5.2.1 A Summary Overview of the Model

In this section we review the structure of the interregional model. Of course, in developing models of this type one faces a trade-off between the level of detail in the sector one is most interested in and the level of detail in the rest of the economy. As previously suggested, we have opted for a detailed treatment of the transport sector at the cost of a very aggregate treatment of other relevant components of the economy. The model does not distinguish different types of consumer goods, it does not contain an explicit labour market, it only focuses on transport taxes (that is, no other tax instruments are considered), and it ignores distributive considerations. The model does incorporate a link between (freight) transport and production activities, and there is a direct impact of freight transport prices on the price of consumer goods in the economy.

To simplify the exposition, in this section we focus on the one-country version of the model. The extensions required for the two-region model are considered in the more detailed model description in the next section. The overall structure of the one-region version is given in Figure 5.1. It consists of a demand module, a supply module, and an equilibrium price module. The demand for passenger transport services is assumed to directly result from the optimising behaviour by consumers, who trade off transport versus other consumer goods. The demand for freight transport is modelled as a derived demand for input in the production process of these consumer goods, which are assumed to be produced according to a constant-returns-to-scale technology in a perfectly competitive setting. International flows (that is, flows in the country by foreign trucks) are modelled as a function of domestic pricing and regulatory policies.

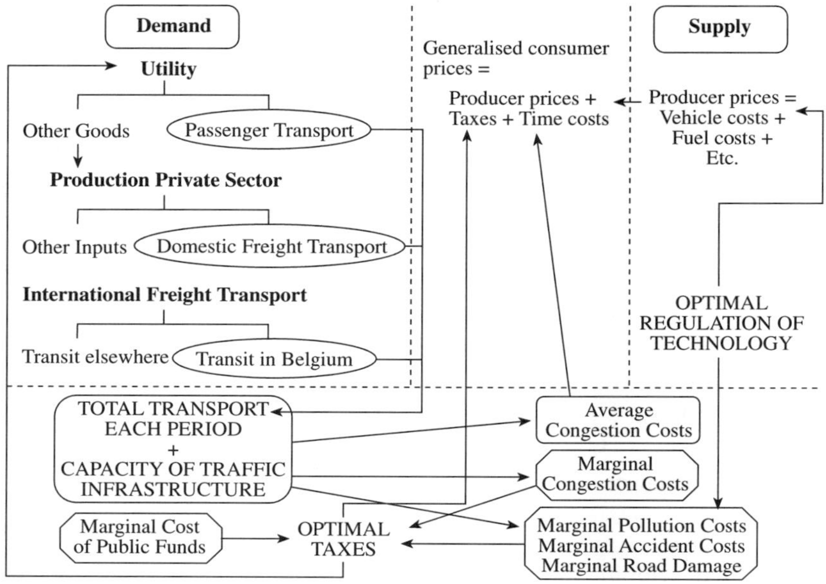

Figure 5.1 Structure of the one-region interregional model

The supply part of the model (see the right-hand side of Figure 5.1) captures the resource costs of the various modes and services. It is assumed that public transport is completely controlled by the government. For private car use the supply module reflects, among others, the choices made by the producers of cars and the suppliers of other inputs like fuels, car maintenance services, and so on. It is assumed that these choices are based on profit-maximising behaviour, subject to government regulation of vehicle technology and equipment. Assuming perfect competition among suppliers, transport services will be delivered at marginal resource costs plus producer taxes. Within the framework of our model this has an important implication: in the absence of producer taxes car kilometres will not be produced with clean technologies, unless explicit incentives (subsidies, regulation) are introduced. The intuition is obvious: introducing cleaner technologies raises production costs, and unless explicitly motivated to do so (for example, government subsidies for clean technologies) producers have no direct advantage in supplying vehicles with improved technologies. It raises costs at no direct benefit for the producer.

In the equilibrium price module (see the middle and lower part of Figure 5.1) generalised prices are computed for the different types of transportation modes. For each transport service the generalised price per vehicle-kilometre is the sum of three elements:

1. the producer price (determined in the supply module);
2. the time cost, which is a function of the total traffic volume. The time cost is the average congestion cost;
3. the tax (or subsidy) per unit. Taxes (subsidies) serve a double function: they allow the government to raise tax revenue (or to subsidise certain modes of transportation) and they may be required to correct for marginal external costs associated with air pollution, congestion, and so on. The tax is differentiated according to the different types of transport services. The overall tax levels are partially determined by the marginal cost of public funds and by the level of external costs.

It is assumed that both passenger and freight transport generate environmental externalities. In addition, the overall demand for road transport is responsible for congestion. The policy instruments the government has available to correct externalities include indirect taxes (subsidies), the possibility to impose certain environmental regulations (for example, minimum energy efficiency requirements, banning certain types of fuels), and the possibility to provide explicit incentives for the introduction of improved vehicle technologies. The optimal set of prices and regulatory instruments depends on marginal external costs and on the marginal cost of public funds.

5.2.2 Structure of the Welfare Function

The model determines optimal taxes and regulation by maximising a welfare function subject to an appropriate set of constraints. More specifically, the policy variables under control by the government are the taxes and subsidies in the transport sector, as well as the environmental standards on cars or other vehicles. The constraints reflect first, that on each transport market demand must equal supply and second, that in some cases there may be restrictions on the tax instruments. For example, if fuel taxes are used as the main instruments it is not feasible to impose different taxes in peak and off-peak periods.

Table 5.1 details the structure of the welfare function to be maximised in the one-country version of the model. It consists of three broad terms: consumer welfare, capturing the effects of price changes of both passenger and freight transport prices, external costs other than congestion, and a correction term related to the efficiency effects associated with the use of the tax revenues generated in the transport sector.[2] We discuss each term in turn.

Table 5.1 The structure of the welfare function

Utility of households from private goods	(Indirect) utility is a function of • Prices of non-transport goods. These prices depend on freight transport prices: freight prices affect production costs and therefore output prices; • Generalised prices of all alternative passenger transport options; the generalised prices include resource costs, time costs and taxes (+) or subsidies (−); • Generalised income: includes exogenous consumer income, redistributed profits of the suppliers of transport, and recycled transport tax revenues.
− Environmental and accident costs	Represents the product of environmental damage and the monetary valuation of the damage plus the external accidents costs.
+ Correction term for tax revenue use	The value of the correction term depends on the particular way in which tax revenues are assumed to be used (see Chapter 4 for details).

1. Consumer welfare is represented by an indirect utility function. It depends on generalised prices of passenger transport services, on the price of an aggregate private non-transport consumption good, and on generalised income. To start with the latter, generalised income consists of three components: exogenous consumer income, profits of the suppliers of transport services, and recycled indirect tax revenues from freight and passenger transport. In other words, it is assumed that the revenues from taxing externalities in the transport sector are lump-sum reimbursed to the consumer. The generalised prices include the value of the time spent in traffic, so that the welfare effect of congestion is directly captured in the consumer's utility function and the associated demand functions. The time cost of transport may depend on the transport mode and on the discomfort of the users (for example, the subjective value of time will probably be higher for the journey to work in the peak than for a leisure trip on a Sunday afternoon). Note that the generalised prices imply endogenous travel times as they depend on the level of congestion of the transport mode used.[3] Finally, consumer utility depends on the price of non-transport goods. The latter is a function of the generalised freight transport prices of the different modes. Indeed, the model assumes that the generalised prices of freight transport affect marginal production costs and therefore prices in the private sector. Also note that the model implicitly assumes perfect competition in the private sector, so that

producer profits in the private production sector of non-transport goods are zero.
2. The value of tax revenues evaluated at the shadow cost of public funds. When there are no other distortions in the economy and when additional tax revenue is redistributed to the consumers in a lump sum form, this term drops out: in that case tax increases and the lump-sum redistribution of the receipts are taken into account in the utility function. Other forms of revenue use lead to positive or possibly negative correction terms. This is a difficult issue that was explained in more detail in Section 4.6.2 of Chapter 4.
3. The external costs other than congestion. This term takes into account the environmental and accident externalities, expressed in monetary terms.

Maximising the welfare function with respect to the policy variables, taking into account the market equilibrium constraints and possible restrictions on instruments, yields a set of optimal taxes (subsidies) and optimal values for the regulatory control variables. This allows us to study optimal policies under a large number of policy scenarios that impose various types of constraints on the pricing instruments.

5.3 DETAILED MODEL STRUCTURE

In this section we provide more details on the structure of the demand side and the supply side, on the construction of the generalised prices, and on the introduction of the externalities. A mathematical formulation of a simplified version of the models is provided in Appendix.

5.3.1 Structure of the Demand Side of the Transport Market

5.3.1.1 The demand for passenger transport

To capture the heterogeneity of passenger transport services the transport sector is disaggregated according to the mode of transport and the time of day at which travel occurs. Consumer preferences in a given country have been modelled using nested CES-type utility functions (see Keller, 1976). The nested utility structure used for the optimisation exercises is represented in Figure 5.2. At the highest level (level zero) utility is specified as a function of two aggregate goods, passenger transport and an aggregate consumption good. Passenger transport is then systematically disaggregated. First, the transport subutility component contains transport demands in two periods of the day (peak and off-peak) as arguments. At a second level, both peak and off-peak passenger transport are disaggregated in private and public transport demand. The public transport subaggregate further captures both the demands for bus and train services. For private car transport the distinction is made between highways and other major roads, and between carpooling and driving alone.[4] Towards the bottom of the utility tree two car sizes are being considered, large and small. Finally, there are two possible fuels, gasoline and diesel, and two possible types of technology for each fuel type, cc and nc, the precise meaning of which will become clear below.

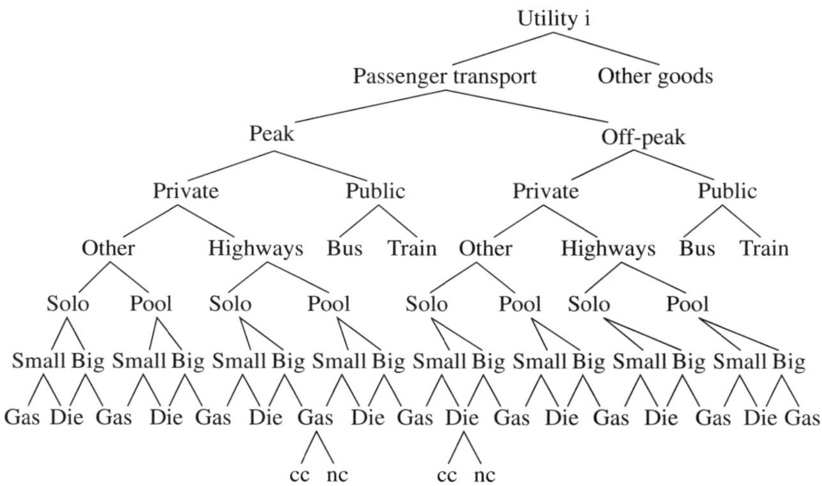

Figure 5.2 The nested CES utility function for passenger transport

The nature of the CES implies that, at each level, quantity and price indices can be constructed as a weighted sum of lower-level quantities and prices, respectively. Moreover, each quantity index has a subutility interpretation. Formally, the aggregate quantity index of transport service k (for example, kilometres by a small car in the peak period) belonging to a given level n is given by:

$$x_{n,k} = \left(\sum_{l \in k} \alpha_{n-1,l}^{1-\rho_{n,k}} \, x_{n-1,l}^{\rho_{n,k}} \right)^{\frac{1}{\rho_{n,k}}},$$

$$\text{where } \rho_{n,k} = \frac{\sigma_{n,k} - 1}{\sigma_{n,k}}$$

for all $n = 1,\ldots,N$ and all k. The parameter $\sigma_{n,k}$ is the (constant) elasticity of substitution within aggregate k at level n. The notation $l \in k$ means that all components of the level $n-1$ associated with $x_{n,l}$ are considered (for example, kilometres by small and large diesel cars in the peak period). The $\alpha_{n-1,l}$ are distribution parameters ($0 \leq \alpha_{n-1,l} \leq 1$). The corresponding aggregate price index related to $x_{n,k}$ is given by

$$q_{n,k} = \left(\sum_{l \in k} \alpha_{n-1} q_{n-1,l}^{\rho'_{n,k}} \right)^{\frac{1}{\rho_{n,k}}}$$

where

$$\rho'_{n,k} = \frac{\sigma'_{n,k} - 1}{\sigma'_{n,k}} \text{ and } \sigma'_{n,k} = \sigma_{n,k}^{-1}$$

With the above-described structure, it is easy to show that the utility maximising demand functions for commodity $x_{n,k}$ (for example, demand for kilometres by car in the peak period) can be written as (see Keller, 1976)

$$x_{n,k} = \frac{y}{q_{n,k}} \prod_{n=1}^{N} \alpha_{n-1,k} \left(\frac{q_{n,k}}{q_{n-1,k}} \right)^{\sigma_{n,k}}$$

where y is the consumer's income. Note that the demand for an arbitrary good is a function of all prices via the aggregate price indices at the various levels.

The use of nested CES utility functions has a number of advantages. It is easy to calibrate and requires a minimum of behavioural information, namely prices and quantities in a reference equilibrium together with substitution elasticities at each level. Of course, the flexibility offered by the CES has to be traded off against a serious drawback. The homotheticity of the CES implies that at each level subutility is separable in the different goods, with obvious restrictions on substitution possibilities. All goods that are located on the same branch of a tree will react identically to a price change of a good that is situated on another branch of the tree. Moreover, the CES implies unitary income elasticities, which makes it unsuited for long-term forecasting. Nested logit functions would, at least in theory, be a superior way to represent transport demand. However, they are more data-intensive and cannot easily be used for the computation of optimal taxes.

5.3.1.2 The demand for freight transport

As indicated before, the importance of international freight flows (including pure transit) in some countries and the possibility of strategic behaviour related to this international dimension, induced us to develop both a one-country and a two-country model version. Both versions assume that in a given country the aggregate consumption good that enters the utility of the representative consumer is produced by an aggregate private sector.

Cost-minimising behaviour by producers then generates a derived demand for freight transport. Again, to model a large number of freight transport alternatives we use a tree structure based on a CES specification, this time for the production and cost functions of the producers of the aggregate consumption good.

The differences between the two model versions lie in the approach towards international freight transport flows. In the one-region version we took a very ad hoc approach. The demand for freight flows on the country's territory by foreign firms was simply specified as an ad hoc function of domestic pricing and regulatory policies (see Figure 5.1 above). Given the opportunities for international and especially pure transit traffic to consider alternative routes, demand is specified to be quite elastic with respect to domestic prices.

To capture some of the implied complications associated with the international dimension (spillover effects of externalities, tax exporting, and tax competition), the two-country model uses the simplest possible structure that allows us to illustrate some of the most relevant issues. Specifically, as the focus of the models is on transport pricing, we wanted to avoid having to incorporate a formal international trade model, where trade generates international transport flows. Instead, it is simply assumed that in each country domestic production activities generate a demand for both domestic and international freight transport. The assumption is that domestic production activities not only require domestic freight transport as an input but also some international freight transport abroad (for example, for the delivery of foreign intermediate inputs to domestic firms). Pure transit can be modelled as an extreme case.

The above hypothesis results in the type of interaction between the two countries presented in Figure 5.3. In each country, utility maximisation generates a demand for passenger transport and a demand for the aggregate consumer good. From the former the further disaggregation towards modes, periods and car types starts off, as presented earlier in Figure 5.2. The demand for the aggregate consumer good on the other hand generates demands for freight transport and for an aggregate other input, treated as numeraire. Freight flows associated with production in region i are disaggregated in domestic flows (that is, in region i) and international transport in the other region j (see Figure 5.3). This modelling procedure implies that there is some (possibly very small) substitution possibility between domestic and international flows. Perfect complementarity can be modelled as an extreme case.

In each region three relevant freight modes (road, rail, inland waterways) are distinguished. Further down in the tree structure for freight within a given region road transport is divided in flows on highways and on other

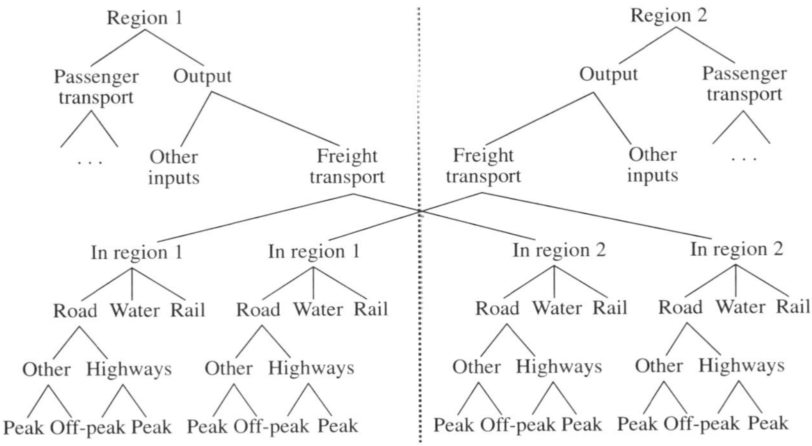

Figure 5.3 The nested CES production function for freight transport

major roads, and the distinction is made between peak and off-peak demand. These latter distinctions seem only relevant for road transport. Moreover, note that no distinction has been made according to the type of fuel. The reason is simply that almost all trucks use diesel.

Importantly, note that the model distinguishes domestic and international (transit) freight flows, but that the demand for passenger transport is assumed to be entirely domestic. Although this is not entirely realistic, international passenger transport was excluded because of data limitations and because of its much smaller share in total flows, at least compared to international freight flows.

5.3.2 The Structure of the Supply Side of the Market for Transport Services

The supply of the various transport modes is introduced in both versions of the model via cost functions for the different modes and alternatives. We assume that in the absence of taxes the various services will be supplied at marginal resource cost. For freight transport and public passenger transport, resource costs include expenditures on labour, energy, materials, rolling stock and so on. For private passenger transport (that is, for the car mode) resource costs consist of expenditures on ownership, fuel, maintenance, parking and so on.

As indicated before, the model also considers optimal choices of new emission technologies. The costs of different emission technologies are also captured as part of the supply component. Remember that if there is no pollution regulation and there are no taxes or subsidies, then within our model structure there are no incentives for suppliers of transport services to implement cleaner technologies. Indeed, the required investment expenditures (for example, to install particulate filters in diesel cars) increase the private resource costs of transport services, whereas the benefits consist of reductions in external, not private, costs. Without government intervention, suppliers will therefore have no incentive to select cleaner technologies. As a consequence, we chose to analyse the potential desirability of the introduction of new emission technologies by assuming that the government is willing to subsidise the installation of cleaner technologies if the latter are welfare improving. In other words, the choice of emission technology is the result of the overall welfare optimisation in which the government trades off the reductions in external costs and the required investment expenditures.

In view of the above we distinguish two technological options with respect to gasoline operated cars. It is assumed that by 2005 the standard technology will include a normal 3-way catalytic converter. However, the government also has the option to subsidise an improved technology that contains a pre-heated 3-way catalytic converter. The latter is more efficient in reducing harmful emissions. For diesel cars there are also two possibilities available. The standard technology for 2005 includes an oxidation catalyst and electronic engine control. The improved technology consists in adding a particulates filter to the standard technology.

5.3.3 Generalised Prices of Transport Services

The generalised prices of the various transport services are the sum of three components: the marginal resource cost, the imposed tax and the time cost. The taxes have a double function, namely to generate government revenues and to correct for external costs. The time costs were included into the generalised prices so as to capture the value of the time losses associated with travel, and to allow a straightforward calculation of the marginal external congestion cost (see Section 5.3.4 below). The time component of the generalised price is simply equal to the average congestion cost and, for road transport, obviously depends on total traffic flows.

Although resource costs and taxes typically include both fixed (for example, annual vehicle taxes) and variable (for example, fuel taxes) components, the model does not explicitly consider two-part tariffs. The various price components are translated so as to be expressed per passenger- or ton-kilometre. This is clearly somewhat less than desirable, since transport economists have long pointed out the different implications of, for example, taxing car ownership versus car use. However, since the focus of this chapter is on issues of tax exporting and pricing of transport externalities, it is assumed that the planner determines welfare-optimal prices per passenger- or ton-kilometre.[5]

5.3.4 Externalities Taken into Account

The model incorporates congestion, air pollution, noise, accident costs and road depreciation. The externalities were introduced in the model in different ways. More details on the valuation of the externalities can be found in Chapter 7 of this volume.

First consider congestion. The impact of congestion was captured in the time cost component of the generalised prices of transport services (see above). A congestion increase directly affects consumers' indirect utility functions (and the demand for passenger transport and other goods) and producers' cost functions (and the derived demand for freight transport). The marginal external congestion cost represents the extra time loss of all other road users when one extra vehicle is added to the traffic flow. It is the product of three elements: the average time loss due to the speed reduction caused by the extra vehicle, the number of vehicles on the road, and the monetary value of the time loss. The time needed to travel one kilometre was based on an endogenously determined non-linear speed-flow relationship. This gives the traffic's speed as a function of the number of passenger car units (PCU) per hour for each period considered. It is assumed that large and small cars have the same impact on congestion and are equal to one PCU while buses and trucks equal two PCUs. One speed-flow relation for each type of road (highways, 'other' major roads) was constructed by calibrating the functional form given in Kirwan, O'Mahony and O'Sullivan (1995) on the basis of observed traffic data. Both the functional form and estimation of the speed-flow relationship is discussed in more detail in Chapter 10 of this volume. The monetary value of travel time per kilometre is simply the value of time per hour times the inverse of travel speed.

In view of the international dimensions of traffic flows taken into account in the two-country model version, it seemed instructive to incorporate the distinction between local and global external costs in the model. This is especially relevant in order to analyse the role of external cost spillovers in the optimal pricing rules. To make the distinction for congestion, consider a marginal increase in traffic flow in Belgium. The local marginal external congestion cost captures the monetary value of the time losses imposed on passengers and Belgian truckers (or, more precisely within the terminology of the model, on freight transport related to Belgian production activities). The global marginal external cost of congestion incorporates in addition the time losses imposed on foreign truckers (on transport in Belgium that is related to foreign production activities).

All externalities other than congestion were assumed to have a constant cost per kilometre. We considered six air pollutants: SO_2, NO_x, HC, CO, CO_2 and PM. The level of pollution in each region is a function of the level of depositions of each pollutant in the region. Deposition of each pollutant in region *j* is related to the level of emissions in region *i* by an 'emission-deposition' matrix. This allows us again to make the distinction between local and global marginal external pollution costs. In each region, the former only capture the pollution costs which affect utility of the region's own representative consumer. Global marginal pollution costs also include the spillover effect on the welfare of consumers in the other region due to transboundary pollution.

The marginal external accident costs consist of that part of the extra accident costs caused by an additional vehicle that are not taken into account by the driver either directly or via his insurance premium. Valuation takes into account both material losses (output loss, ambulance costs, and so on) and the willingness to pay of the victim and his close friends and relatives to avoid accidents. Moreover, account is taken of the impact of additional traffic on the risk of accidents. Finally, consistent with Newbery (1988), road depreciation was fully attributed to trucks.

5.3.5 Optimal Tax Rules: an Intuitive Summary

Although the numerical optimisation models described in this chapter are too complex for theoretical analysis, the nature of the optimal tax rules they imply can be appreciated by considering simplified versions. In this subsection we provide a very brief intuitive summary of optimal tax rules. A full discussion is provided in De Borger, Courcelle and Swysen (1999); the Appendix to this chapter has a brief technical summary.

Assuming zero cross-price elasticities, the optimal tax rules that follow from the one-country version can be interpreted as externality-corrected Ramsey rules (see, for example, Oum and Thretheway, 1988). They relate the optimal taxes plus a fraction of the marginal external cost to the inverse of the price elasticity of demand. Moreover, the tax increases when the shadow cost of funds increases because in that case the revenue raising function of the tax becomes more important. The tax rules imply marginal social cost pricing if no extra value is assigned to tax revenues.

When we consider the cross-price effects between passenger transport goods, existing price distortions for complements and substitutes have to be taken into account. Cross-price effects become very important when there are restrictions on the taxation of certain modes (for example car use in the peak period). In this case there may be large deviations of the price from the marginal social cost.

As far as the two-country version of the model is concerned, the optimal tax rules obviously strongly depend on the assumptions made with respect to the behaviour of individual countries and with respect to the pricing instruments used. If countries cooperate and determine all policy variables so as to maximise their joint welfare then, assuming zero cross-price elasticities and a marginal cost of funds equal to zero, all transport taxes in each country equal the 'global' marginal external cost. This global external cost captures not only the external costs experienced by country's residents, but it also includes all spillovers to the other country. It includes the marginal external cost associated with spillovers of pollution to the other region and the value of the time losses imposed on foreign truckers. If cross-elasticities are non-zero, more complicated rules result that take account of substitution possibilities between services.

If countries do not cooperate but instead behave strategically, there are two important changes in the optimal tax results. First, individual countries will tend to ignore the spillovers of externalities to other countries. Tax rules will be based on local marginal external costs only, that is, external costs imposed on foreigners will be ignored. Second, the tax rules will reflect the impact of tax exporting behaviour. The degree of tax exporting behaviour depends on the pricing instruments used. For example, if countries cannot price discriminate between domestic and foreign trucks on the domestic road system, then the tax rate on road freight transport will positively depend on the importance of foreign freight flows. More international freight flows will induce an individual country to raise the tax on freight because taxes can be exported abroad to a larger extent. Finally, again note that more complicated rules are obtained if the shadow cost of funds is non-zero and cross-elasticities are relevant.

5.4 OPERATION OF THE MODEL

5.4.1 Calibration of the Model

The first step in the operation of the model is to produce a reference equilibrium that can be used as a starting point for the optimisation procedures. At the same time, this reference situation serves as a benchmark with which to compare the results of the different welfare optimisation exercises. Using observed or predicted information on the transport market and estimates of the price elasticities at the different levels of the CES trees, we calibrate the remaining parameters of the model (utility and cost function parameters, and so on). Basically, the parameters are chosen so as to make them consistent with the observed prices, flows, and relevant demand and cost information. This reference situation in other words corresponds to a market equilibrium that reflects an initial transport situation.

The reference situation differs from a welfare optimum in the presence of externalities because current policies that are reflected in the reference equilibrium are not aimed at internalisation of external costs. Importantly, note that for the same reasons the reference situation in the two-country version of the model cannot be considered a Nash equilibrium (see below for details).

5.4.2 Using the Model

The model can be used for both simulation and optimisation purposes. Moreover, the two-country version allows modelling a variety of strategic interaction patterns between countries.

5.4.2.1 Simulation versus optimisation

Starting from the calibrated reference case we can use the model for optimisation or for simulation purposes. Both techniques will be used in this book. When using the model for simulation purposes we simply compute the impact of imposing specific values for the policy instruments. For example, one could be interested in evaluating the effect of a 20 per cent increase in fuel taxes, study the impact of changing current subsidies to public transport modes, or investigate the implications of new regulatory measures. Optimisation on the other hand searches for the best possible value of the instruments, possibly subject to constraints.

5.4.2.2 Optimal policies in a federal framework

Importantly, for the two-country model the objective function can be the welfare of a given country or the welfare of the 'federation' of the two countries. This depends on the specific assumptions made with respect to the countries' behaviour. Various optimal taxation exercises can be implemented. We consider three such possibilities, each of which can be executed with various constraints imposed on the instruments. Table 5.2 summarises the various alternatives.

Local optimum for a given country The model determines the optimal policy from the viewpoint of an individual country. In other words, we maximise the welfare of a given country i with respect to all policy variables (prices, choice of technology) the country directly controls, assuming that all instruments in the other region j ($\neq i$) are kept at the reference level. If

Table 5.2 Overview of possible exercises

Objective function		Instruments used: Perfect instruments	Constrained instruments	Instruments at their reference levels
Welfare of region *i*	–Unilateral	Local full optimum	Local second best optimum	Reference situation for both regions
	–Competition	Nash equilibrium	Constrained Nash equilibrium	Reference situation for both regions
Welfare of federation		Full federal optimum	Federal second best optimum	Reference situation for both regions

policy instruments for country *i* are unconstrained then the output of this exercise yields a local full optimum for country *i*. If instruments are constrained a variety of second-best local optima can be considered. For example, it may or may not be feasible to differentiate peak and off-peak taxes on road transport, it may or may not be possible for country *i* to price differentiate between domestic freight transport and foreign freight flows on its territory, and so on.

Nash equilibrium between countries or regions In the previous type of exercise, we implicitly assumed that the other country does not adjust its policies in reaction to the unilateral decisions made by country *i*. However, in practice it is probably more realistic to assume that the two regions are involved in a non-cooperative game. It seems plausible that *both* countries are interested in maximising their welfare. Therefore, they may behave strategically using as instruments ('strategies') the prices and technologies they can unilaterally decide upon. The payoffs of a country's strategies are measured in terms of the value of its welfare function. A Nash equilibrium is then an equilibrium outcome for this non-cooperative game in which the instruments chosen by *each* region are locally optimal, given the optimal choice of instruments made by the other region. In other words, it consists of a set of jointly determined local optima for both countries.

A Nash equilibrium can be easily illustrated graphically (see Figure 5.4) for the case where each region has only one instrument. Suppose for example that p_1 is the price of a transport service in region 1 and p_2 is the price of the same transport service in region 2. The curve AB gives the optimal price for region 1 for each choice of price by region 2. It is the reaction curve of region 1. Similarly, CD relates the optimal price for region 2 to the choice of price by region 1. Now suppose that the pair of prices in the reference situation is given by point E on Figure 5.4. An iterative process can then be imagined that ultimately leads the two regions to the Nash equilibrium point H (where the two reaction curves intersect). The pair of prices which corresponds to this point (p_1^*, p_2^*) are the Nash equilibrium prices. The Nash outcome implies that *each* country maximises its own welfare, conditional on the policies selected by the other country. Again, the analysis can be performed with and without constraints on instruments.

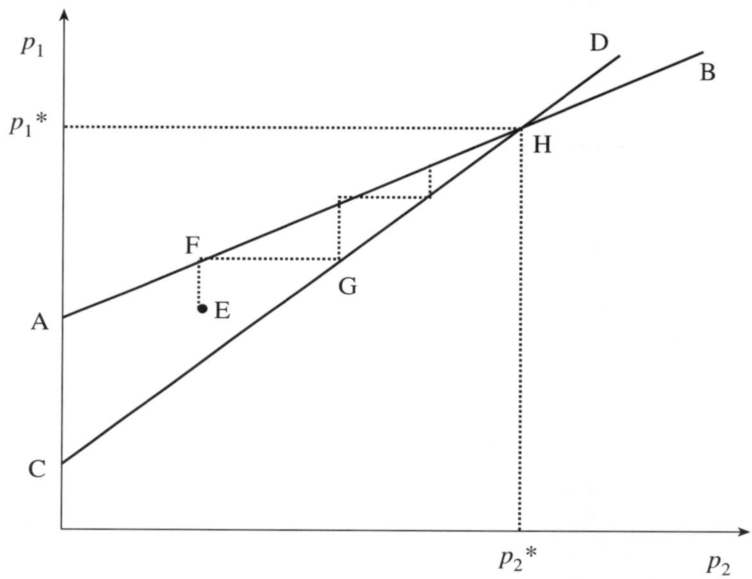

Figure 5.4 Illustration of a Nash equilibrium

The Nash equilibrium is obtained in our framework by an iterative process in which both regions maximise their welfare using perfect or constrained instruments. Starting from the reference situation, we compute a local optimum for one region. Relative to the optimal choice of instruments made by the first region, we then run the model to obtain a local optimum for the other region. We repeat for each region this second stage of the process until we reach convergence.

A 'federal optimum' In a third type of exercise we consider the optimal values of all policy instruments in the hypothetical two-country federation by maximising the welfare of the federation. We obtain then a cooperative equilibrium, a 'federal optimum'. This type of exercise is especially relevant if policymaking can be implemented at the federal level (for example at the EU level) so as to avoid tax competition and tax exporting behaviour.

5.5 SUMMARY AND CONCLUSIONS

The purpose of this chapter was to explain in a non-technical way the construction and the operation of the interregional model designed for the analysis of interurban traffic in a country or a system of countries (federation). The focus was on the one-country version of the model, although the required extensions for the federal version were clearly indicated as well.

The chapter started out with an overall model structure. It then provided a more detailed description of the structure of the demand and supply sides of the model, it considered the incorporation of external costs and it explained the objective function to be used in the optimisation exercises. Finally, the use of the model was discussed.

APPENDIX: SUMMARY OF MODEL FORMULATION AND OPTIMAL TAX RESULTS

In this appendix a brief overview of the formal structure of the interregional model is given. We keep as much as possible the same notation as in the description of the urban model (see the appendix to Chapter 4). Moreover, we consider a simplified version that illustrates the differences with the urban version, especially with respect to the important role of freight transport. Only one consumer type is taken into account. Moreover, technology choice is ignored (in this appendix; not in the applications reported later in the book) because modelling, derivations and results on this issue are the same as in the urban model. Indeed, one easily shows that the welfare-optimal technology is the one with the lowest marginal social cost per kilometre. In what follows, we therefore assume that only one technology is available.

We first focus on the one-country version. Next we discuss the extension to a federal setting where countries or regions may behave strategically. The importance of international freight flows then leads to problems of tax exporting. Moreover, spillovers of externalities to other regions deserve special attention.

The One-Country Version

Assume there are N identical individuals and $i=1,...,I$ different passenger transport demand services. Similarly, let there be $f=1,...,F$ different freight transport demand services. Individual demand for passenger transport service i is denoted by x_i. Freight demand for service f is denoted x_f. This freight demand is the sum of domestic and international freight flows. Domestic flows reflect the demand for freight transport by cost minimising producers; that is, they are treated as input demands related to production activities in the country. The demand for international flows on the country's territory (for example, foreign trucks on the domestic road network) is modelled as a simple ad hoc function of (generalised, see below) freight transport prices in the country. Producer prices per vehicle km are given by p_i and p_f for passenger service i and freight service f, respectively. Corresponding marginal resource costs are assumed constant and equal to rc_i and rc_f.

The demand functions for passenger transport services are defined as a function of the generalised prices of transport. The generalised price for service i per kilometre consists of a monetary cost q_i (including taxes) and a time cost. The latter is calculated as the time it takes to travel one kilometre using transport service i, t_i, times the appropriate value of time of that service or mode, ρ_i. The generalised price for a passenger-km with mode i, $\tilde{q}_i$, is therefore defined as:

$$\tilde{q}_i = q_i + \rho_i t_i$$

Similarly, generalised prices for freight transport can be defined as

$$\tilde{q}_f = q_f + \rho_f t_f$$

where q_f is the monetary user price for freight transport service f, ρ_f is the value of time for service f, and t_f is time needed for one kilometre.

It is assumed that some transport modes share a common infrastructure of fixed capacity. The unit time t_i for a passenger-km using mode i depends on the total traffic volume sharing the road network. Let S denote the set of (passenger and freight transport) modes that use the same infrastructure and let m_i be the contribution of mode i to overall congestion, then the general form of the congestion functions for passenger and freight services is given by

$$t_i = T_i\left(\sum_{l \neq f \varepsilon S} m_l N x_l + \sum_{f \varepsilon S} m_f x_f\right)$$

$$t_f = T_f\left(\sum_{l \neq f \varepsilon S} m_l N x_l + \sum_{f \varepsilon S} m_f x_f\right),$$

respectively.

Producers of the aggregate consumption good use domestic freight transport services as inputs in production. Assuming perfect competition and constant returns to scale production, the output price q_0 of the non-transport consumer good reflects the marginal production cost, which depends on input prices. In other words,

$$q_0 = \mathrm{q}_0(\tilde{q}_f; f = 1,\ldots,F)$$

Social welfare is the unweighted sum of three basic components. First, consumer welfare is captured by an indirect utility function that depends on the price of non-transport goods, the generalised prices of passenger transport commodities, and generalised income. The latter consists of exogenous consumer income Y, tax revenues out of the transport sector (assumed to be recycled in a lump-sum way towards consumers), and producer surplus of the suppliers of transport commodities. After division by the marginal utility of income in the reference equilibrium (μ_r) the value of the indirect utility function is a monetary welfare measure for transport consumers. Second, an extra weight is assigned to tax revenues that can be considered a crude way of capturing the efficiency effects of the use of the tax revenues in a partial equilibrium setting. Its meaning was explained more fully in Chapter 4. Tax revenue on passenger transport flows is assigned an extra weight λ_P. A weight λ_F, possibly zero, is assigned to tax revenues on freight flows. As explained in Chapter 4, in a general equilibrium setting optimal taxation requires production efficiency. In principle then input prices, including freight transport prices, should equal marginal social costs (see Diamond and Mirrlees, 1971). In that case no extra weight should be assigned to freight tax revenues. Finally, the third component of the welfare function reflects the monetary value of the external costs of transport other than congestion. Marginal external costs other than congestion (ec_i and ec_f) for passenger transport service i and freight service f, respectively, are taken as constant per vehicle-km. Note that congestion costs have already been captured through the generalised prices in the indirect utility function.

For simplicity, we normalise $N=1$ without loss in generality. Taking all the above components together, we arrive at the following welfare function

$$W = \frac{1}{\mu_r} V\left[q_0, \tilde{q}_1, \tilde{q}_2, \ldots, \tilde{q}_I, Y + \sum_i (p_i - rc_i)x_i + \sum_f (q_f - p_f)x_f + \sum_i (q_i - p_i)x_i \right]$$
$$+ \lambda_P \sum_i (q_i - p_i)x_i + \lambda_F \sum_f (q_f - p_f)x_f - \sum_i (ec_i\, x_i) - \sum_f (ec_f x_f)$$

where $q_0 = q_0(\tilde{q}_f; f = 1,...,F)$, and the generalised prices and congestion functions have been defined above.

Maximising the objective function subject to the restriction that producer prices should exceed resource costs yields optimal tax rules that are very similar to those obtained for the urban model. If cross-price elasticities are zero and assuming that the approximation to the marginal utility of income is perfect, we find the following rules for passenger and freight services, respectively

$$\left[q_i - p_i - \frac{MEC_i}{(1+\lambda_P)}\right]\frac{E_{ii}}{q_i} = -\frac{\lambda_P}{1+\lambda_P}$$

$$\left[q_f - p_f - \frac{MEC_f}{(1+\lambda_F)}\right]\frac{E_{ff}}{q_f} = -\frac{\lambda_F}{1+\lambda_F},$$

where the E_{kk} are the own price elasticities of demand for transport service k and

$$MEC_i = tmcong_i + ec_i$$

$$MEC_f = tmcong_f + ec_f$$

are the marginal external costs of services i and f, respectively. Note that the E_{ff} are the price elasticities of the unconditional factor demand functions for freight transport; that is, they take account of the impact of generalised freight prices on the price of the aggregate consumption good. Marginal external costs consist of marginal external congestion costs and other marginal external costs (pollution, noise, road damage). Marginal external congestion costs are given by

$$tmcong_k = m_k\left[N\sum_{i\varepsilon S}\rho_i x_i T_{ii} + \sum_{f\varepsilon S}\rho_f x_f T_{ff}\right],$$

where T_{ii} and T_{ff} represent the derivative of unit transport time of respectively passenger and freight transport with respect to the total transport volume.

The pricing rules can be interpreted as externality-corrected Ramsey rules (see, for example, Oum and Thretheway, 1988) that relate the optimal taxes plus a fraction of the marginal external cost to the inverse of the price elasticity of demand. The tax increases when the shadow cost of funds (the tax revenue weights) increase. In that case the externality component of the optimal tax decreases and the pure Ramsey component increases because the revenue-raising function of the tax becomes more important. The tax rules imply marginal social cost pricing for freight transport services if one assumes a zero shadow cost of freight tax revenues. More generally, all taxes equal marginal external costs if the shadow cost of funds is zero.

When we consider the cross-price effects between passenger transport goods, existing price distortions for complements and substitutes have to be taken into account. Cross-price effects become very important when there are restrictions on the taxation of certain modes (for example car use in the peak period). In this case there may be large deviations of the price from the marginal social cost. Of course, cross-price effects are taken into account in the numerical optimisation exercises reported later in the book.

Extensions for the Two-Country Version

Consider two countries. Call them arbitrarily 1 and 2. Welfare in a given country is defined as before, but output requires both domestic and foreign freight. Let q_f^{cd} denote the money price charged for freight service f in country c (c=1,2) by firms from country d (d=1,2). For example, consider production of the private aggregate consumption good in country 1. This generates a demand for domestic freight transport (denoted x_f^{11}) as well as a demand for freight transport abroad (denoted x_f^{21}). The corresponding unit prices are q_f^{11} and q_f^{21}. Note that if countries charge the same freight prices to domestic transport and to foreign transport on their territory then $q_f^{11} = q_f^{12}$ and $q_f^{22} = q_f^{21}$. If countries price discriminate then these equalities may not hold. Whether price discrimination can and will be applied depends on the legal setting and on the type of price instruments used. For example, price discrimination does not seem technically feasible when fuel taxes are used, but they may be feasible if highway tolls are used.

Generalised prices for passenger services and freight services are indexed by country. We have

$$\tilde{q}_i^c = q_i^c + \rho_i^c t_i^c$$

$$\tilde{q}_f^{cd} = q_i^{cd} + \rho_f^{cd} t_f^c$$

for passenger service i in country c and for freight transport service f by country d in country c, respectively. The congestion functions used to define external congestion costs take into account that congestion in a given country is not only due to flows by domestic firms but also by foreign firms. For example, the time a one-kilometre passenger and freight trip takes in country c (c=1,2) is given by

$$t_i^c = T_i^c\left(\sum_{l \neq f \varepsilon S} m_l^c N^c x_l^c + \sum_{f \varepsilon S} m_f^c x_f^c\right)$$

$$t_f^c = T_f^c\left(\sum_{l \neq f \varepsilon S} m_l^c N^c x_l^c + \sum_{f \varepsilon S} m_f^c x_f^c\right)$$

respectively, where $x_f^1 = x_f^{11} + x_f^{12}$ and $x_f^2 = x_f^{22} + x_f^{21}$. Similarly, external costs other than congestion (ec_k^{cd}) are country-specific and they depend on both domestic and international flows.

Given the above description, the price of the aggregate consumption good in country c ($c=1,2$) depends on both domestic generalised freight prices and on generalised freight prices abroad:

$$q_0^1 = q_0^1(\tilde{q}_f^{11}, \tilde{q}_f^{21}; f=1,\ldots,F)$$
$$q_0^2 = q_0^2(\tilde{q}_f^{12}, \tilde{q}_f^{22}; f=1,\ldots,F)$$

The welfare function for a given country takes account of the welfare of its inhabitants, of all tax revenues collected on its territory and of all external costs experienced by its inhabitants. For example, welfare in country 1 is given by (again normalising the number of consumers at one)

$$W^1 = \frac{1}{\mu_r} V^1\left[q_0^1, \tilde{q}_1^1, \tilde{q}_2^1, \ldots, \tilde{q}_I^1, Y^1 + \sum_i (p_i^1 - rc_i^1)x_i^1 + \sum_f (q_f^{11} - p_f^{11})\, x_f^{11}\right.$$
$$\left. + \sum_f (q_f^{12} - p_f^{12})x_f^{12} + \sum_i (q_i^1 - p_i^1)x_i^1)\right] + \lambda_P^1 \sum_i (q_i^1 - p_i^1)x_i^1$$
$$+ \lambda_F^1\left[\sum_f (q_f^{11} - p_f^{11})x_f^{11} + \sum_f (q_f^{12} - p_f^{12})x_f^{12}\right] - \sum_i (ec_i^1 x_i^1)$$
$$- \sum_f (ec_f^{11} x_f^{11}) - \sum_f (ec_f^{12} x_f^{12})$$

Welfare for the second country is defined analogously.

The optimal tax rules derived from this model strongly depend on the assumptions made with respect to the behaviour of individual countries and with respect to the pricing instruments used. First, consider a federal optimum in which it is assumed that the two countries determine all policy variables so as to maximise the joint welfare of the federation as a whole. In other words, in this case the objective function is simply the sum of the objective functions for the two regions, $W^1 + W^2$. Moreover, as previously suggested we redistribute the net tax revenues of the government to the representative consumer in the appropriate region. If we again focus on the case of zero cross-elasticities the optimal taxes for country 1 are described by (analogous rules hold for country 2):

$$\left[q_i^1 - p_i^1 - \frac{GMEC_i^1}{(1+\lambda_P^1)}\right]\frac{E_{ii}^1}{q_i^1} = -\frac{\lambda_P^1}{1+\lambda_P^1}$$

$$\left[q_f^{11} - p_f^{11} - \frac{GMEC_f^{11}}{(1+\lambda_F^1)}\right]\frac{E_{ff}^{11}}{q_f^1} = -\frac{\lambda_F^1}{1+\lambda_F^1}$$

$$\left[q_f^{12} - p_f^{12} - \frac{GMEC_f^{12}}{(1+\lambda_F^1)}\right]\frac{E_{ff}^{12}}{q_f^1} = -\frac{\lambda_F^1}{1+\lambda_F^1}$$

where the *GMEC* are the 'global' marginal external costs, and definition of all other parameters is as before. External costs are 'global' in the sense that they capture not only the external costs generated in country 1 imposed on country 1's residents, but they also include spillovers to the other country. For example, they include the cost associated with spillovers of pollution to region 2 due to traffic in region 1, and the time losses imposed on country 2's truckers because of congestion in region 1. Note that the optimal tax rules imply identical taxes in the two countries only if marginal external costs, price elasticities and shadow costs of funds are the same in both countries (the latter automatically holds if an overall shadow cost of funds applies for the federation as a whole).

If countries behave strategically, then tax rules will reflect the impact of tax exporting behaviour and the fact that countries will ignore the spillovers of externalities abroad in their welfare optimisation. For example, suppose each country maximises its own welfare function with respect to the policy variables it controls, subject to given values for transport prices abroad. To illustrate the potential for tax exporting consider the extreme case where countries can actually price discriminate between domestic and foreign freight flows on their territory. We obtain the following tax rules for country 1 (similar rules apply to country 2):

$$\left[q_i^1 - p_i^1 - \frac{LMEC_i^1}{(1+\lambda_P^1)}\right]\frac{E_{ii}^1}{q_i^1} = -\frac{\lambda_P^1}{1+\lambda_P^1}$$

$$\left[q_f^{11} - p_f^{11} - \frac{LMEC_f^{11}}{(1+\lambda_F^1)}\right]\frac{E_{ff}^{11}}{q_f^{11}} = -\frac{\lambda_F^1}{1+\lambda_F^1}$$

$$\left[q_f^{12} - p_f^{12} - \frac{LMEC_f^{12}}{(1+\lambda_F^1)}\right]\frac{E_{ff}^{12}}{q_f^{12}} = -1$$

where the *LMEC* are local marginal external costs.

There are two important differences with the federal optimum. First, the marginal external cost taken into account for tax setting is the local cost which excludes all spillovers to other countries. Second, although apart from this qualification the structure of the tax rules for passenger transport and domestic freight flows are the same as before, tax exporting behaviour implies that international flows will be taxed as in the case of monopoly pricing. Indeed, if there were no externalities the tax rule for international flows in region 1 suggests a tax $(q_f^{12}-p_f^{12})$ as a fraction of the price which equals the inverse of the absolute value of the price elasticity of demand. This is precisely the monopoly pricing rule: it amounts to maximising the tax revenue on international freight flows. If externalities do prevail, the tax can be interpreted as maximising the difference between tax revenues and social costs as seen from the perspective of the country, not the federation.

Finally, consider the more likely case where price discrimination between domestic and foreign freight flows is not feasible so that $q_f^{11}=q_f^{12}=q_f^1$. This does not affect the tax rule for passenger transport, but optimal taxes for freight transport services in country 1 (similar rules apply for the other country) are described by

$$\left[q_f^1-p_f^1-\frac{LMEC_f^1}{(1+\lambda_F^1)}\right]\frac{1}{q_f^1}=-\left[\frac{\dfrac{\lambda_F^1}{1+\lambda_F^1}+\dfrac{x_f^{12}}{x_f^{11}}}{E_{ff}^{11}+E_{ff}^{12}\dfrac{x_f^{12}}{x_f^{11}}}\right]$$

where we have assumed for simplicity that resource and external costs are the same for domestic and international freight flows. Note that tax-exporting behaviour now yields tax rates that positively depend on the importance of foreign freight flows in the country (x_f^{12}). The reason is that more international freight flows induce an individual country to raise the tax on freight simply because taxes can be shifted to a larger extent to foreigners.

NOTES

1. Tax exporting is studied in, for example, Arnott and Grieson (1981), Wildasin (1987) and Krelove (1992). Detailed analyses of tax competition between regions are provided by Gordon (1983), Mintz and Tulkens (1986) and Wildasin (1988). Optimal policies in the presence of externalities with international spillovers are studied in, for example, Markusen (1975), Merrifield (1988), Krutilla (1991) and Markusen, Morey and Olewiler (1995).
2. Note the slight difference in the structure of the welfare function in this chapter with that of the urban model in Chapter 4. The difference is due to a different treatment of freight transport. In the urban model an increase in freight transport prices affect the exogenously specified production costs in the private production sector, but production and output prices are unaffected. In the interregional model freight prices affect production costs, output prices, and therefore consumer welfare.

3. The described approach is a simplification of a more general approach with endogenous values of time; it is justified as long as values of time do not change between two equilibria.
4. Carpooling is considered as a particular mode in order to allow different prices (per car km) according to the car's occupancy rate.
5. Importantly, note that the use of prices per unit of service does not prevent the model from being able to approximate the implications of implementing different price instruments (for example, fuel taxes, road tolls and public transport prices). The reason is that, although all pricing instruments ultimately translate into variations in prices per passenger- and ton-kilometre, they have very different implications for specific transport services. For example, fuel taxes do not differentiate between peak and off-peak transport but do differentiate between fuel types. A road toll on the other hand can differentiate between cars and trucks and between peak and off-peak but does not distinguish fuel types. In other words, depending on which prices are affected different pricing policies can be introduced in the model (for more detail see De Borger et al., 1997 and De Borger and Swysen, 1998).

REFERENCES

Arnott, R. and Grieson, R.E. (1981), 'Optimal fiscal policy for a state or local government', *Journal of Urban Economics*, **9**, 23–48.

De Borger, B. and Swysen, D. (1998), 'Optimal Pricing and Regulation of Transport Externalities: A Welfare Comparison of Some Policy Alternatives', in R. Roson and K.A. Small (eds), *Environment and Transport in Economic Modelling*, Dordrecht: Kluwer Academic Publishers, pp. 10–38.

De Borger, B., Ochelen, S., Proost, S. and Swysen, D. (1997), 'Alternative transport pricing and regulation policies: a welfare analysis for Belgium', *Transportation Research D*, 177–98.

De Borger, B., Courcelle, C. and Swysen, D. (1999), 'Optimal transport pricing in a federation', Department of Economics Working Paper 99-004, University of Antwerp (UFSIA).

Diamond, P. and Mirrlees, J. (1971), 'Optimal taxation and public production: production efficiency', *American Economic Review*, **61**, 8–27.

Gordon, R. (1983), 'An optimal taxation approach to fiscal federalism', *Quarterly Journal of Economics*, **98**, pp. 567–86.

Keller, W.J. (1976), 'A nested CES-type utility function and its demand and price-index functions', *European Economic Review*, **7**, 175–86.

Kirwan, K.J., O'Mahony, M.M. and D. O'Sullivan (1995), 'Speed-flow relationships for use in an urban transport policy assessment model', working paper, Trinity College, Dublin.

Krelove, R. (1992), 'Competitive tax theory in open economies', *Journal of Public Economics*, **49**, 361–75.

Krutilla, R. (1991), 'Environmental regulation in an open economy', *Journal of Environmental Economics and Management*, **20**(2), 127–42.

Markusen, J. (1975), 'International externalities and optimal tax structures', *Journal of International Economics*, **5**, 15–30.

Markusen, J., Morey, E. and Olewiler, N. (1995), 'Competition in regional environmental policies when plant locations are endogenous', *Journal of Public Economics*, **56**, 55–72.

Merrifield, P. (1988), 'The impact of selected abatement strategies on transnational

pollution, the terms of trade and factor rewards: a general equilibrium approach', *Journal of Environmental Economics and Management*, **15**(3), 259–84.
Mintz, J. and Tulkens, H. (1986), 'Commodity taxation between member states of a federation: equilibrium and efficiency', *Journal of Public Economics*, **29**, 173–97.
Newbery, D. (1988), 'Road user charges in Britain', *Economic Journal*, **98**, 161–76.
Oum, T.H. and Thretheway, M. (1988), 'Ramsey pricing in the presence of externality costs', *Journal of Transport Economics and Policy*, **22**, p. 307–17.
Wildasin, D. (1987), 'The demand for public goods in the presence of tax exporting', *National Tax Journal*, **40**, 591–601.
Wildasin, D. (1988), 'Nash equilibria in models of fiscal competition', *Journal of Public Economics*, **35**, 229–40.

6. Introducing spatial disaggregation and zoning in the Amsterdam model

Erik T. Verhoef, Frans Bal and Jeroen C.J.M. van den Bergh

6.1 INTRODUCTION

Transport is an inherently spatial phenomenon: if there were no space, there would be no demand for transport as most transport demand serves to satisfy spatial mismatches between the demand for and supply of goods and factors (for instance, peak passenger travel often serves to overcome the spatial mismatch between the supply of labour, in residential areas, and the demand for labour, in centres of economic activity). Transport policies therefore often have spatially differentiated impacts, both in terms of efficiency and in terms of equity. A closely related feature of transport is that it takes place in a network environment.

Nevertheless, the TRENEN model, so far, has been largely non-spatial in nature, and has been lacking a spatial transport network representation. The present chapter reports on recent efforts to develop a spatial version of the TRENEN model for Greater Amsterdam. Section 6.2 discusses the technicalities of introducing these elements in TRENEN, and will propose a mathematical formulation. Section 6.3 reports on a linearized application to a basic network for Greater Amsterdam. Section 6.4 concludes.

6.2 A NETWORK IN TRENEN: THEORETICAL CONSIDERATIONS

In this section, we will give a discussion of the first attempt we made to introduce zones and networks in the TRENEN model. A number of important choices had to be made in terms of modelling characteristics (see Verhoef and Van den Bergh, 1996). Before turning to a mathematical formulation, it is important to mention two of these briefly.

First, a decision had to be made on the modelling of the consumers' spatial behaviour, giving rise to the choice of origins and destinations of trips. In line with earlier exercises with the Brussels model, it was decided to introduce a representative consumer for each origin–destination pair considered. For the Amsterdam model, with four zones, this would imply the introduction of a maximum of 16 representative consumers, including intra-zonal traffic and taking account of two possible directions between each pair of zones. In the application in Section 6.3, intra-zonal traffic in the peripheral zones is ignored, so that 13 representative consumers remain.

A second choice that had to be made concerned the modelling of route choice (within a mode). Rather than including a layer in the utility structure relating to the choice of routes, we proposed to model route choice on basis of Wardropian principles (Wardrop, 1952).[1] The reason is that the first possibility would, under the assumption of fully rational consumers, imply an elasticity of substitution between routes of ∞, yielding no additional information over the Wardropian principle, in which case it is also only (generalised) cost differences between routes that govern route choice. Wardrop's principle can be introduced by adding some appropriate complementary slackness conditions on route usage.

Turning to the mathematical formulation, in comparison with the standard TRENEN model described in Chapter 4 of this volume, various representative consumers are considered, which will be distinguished by subscript g ('group'). For the ease of representation, we will consider only passenger transport below. Denoting the set of possible routes for mode i and group g as $R_{i,g}$, the representative consumer's demand for transport by mode i can be given as the sum of the demand over all possible routes:

$$x_{i,g} = \sum_{r \in R_{i,g}} x_{i,g,r} \tag{6.1}$$

In other words, in the current representation, only uni-modal trips are considered yet. The modelling of multi-modal trips is, at least for the time being, complicated due to the structure of the utility function. Hopefully, this problem can be solved.

Whereas demand can be subdivided according to routes, congestion should be considered on a link basis. This is exactly where interdependencies between various consumer groups may occur. Denoting each link (within a mode) with subscript a, the following link-specific congestion functions apply, defining travel times $t_{i,a}$ per link:

$$t_{i,a} = T_{i,a}\left[\sum_{g}\sum_{l \in S_i}\sum_{r \in R_{i,g}} \delta_{a,r} \cdot m_l \cdot N_g \cdot x_{l,g,r}\right] \tag{6.2}$$

where $\delta_{a,r}$ takes on the value of 1 when link a belongs to route r, and is equal to zero otherwise. N_g gives the size of group g; m_1 enables us to consider various congestion factors for a given mode i (for example buses and passenger cars use the same infrastructure S_i). The generalised price on a link is thus given by the sum of the money cost $q_{i,a}$ and the value of time ρ_i times the travel time $t_{i,a}$, so that the following generalised price gp applies for a certain route:

$$gp_{i,r} = \sum_a \delta_{a,r} \cdot (q_{i,a} + \rho_i \cdot t_{i,a}) \tag{6.3}$$

In comparison with the basic version of TRENEN, also the producer price p, the resource costs rc and the external cost ec now have to be made link-specific. It is assumed that each of these vary between links according to the length of the link l_a, that is:

$$p_{i,a} = l_a \cdot p_i \tag{6.4}$$

$$rc_{i,j,a} = l_a \cdot rc_{i,j} \tag{6.5}$$

$$ec_{i,j,a} = l_a \cdot ec_{i,j} \tag{6.6}$$

Completely in accordance with the basic version of TRENEN, the following objective function can then be written down (where [0] denotes skipped terms due to the present neglect of freight transport):

$$\begin{aligned} MAX \sum_g w_g \cdot \frac{N_g}{\mu(0)_g} \cdot V_g \Bigg[& q_o, gp_{i,g}^{\min}(i = 1,\ldots,I), Y \\ & + \frac{1}{N_g} \sum_{i,j} \sum_{r \in R_g} \sum_a \delta_{a,r} \cdot (p_{i,a} - rc_{i,a}) \cdot z_{i,j,g,r} + [0] \\ & + \sum_i \sum_{r \in R_g} \sum_a \delta_{a,r} \cdot (q_{i,a} - p_{i,a}) \cdot x_{i,g,r} + [0] \Bigg] \\ & + \lambda \cdot \sum_i \sum_g \sum_{r \in R_g} \sum_a \delta_{a,r} \cdot (q_{i,a} - p_{i,a}) \cdot x_{i,g,r} \cdot N_g \\ & - \sum_{i,j} \sum_g \sum_{r \in R_g} \sum_a \delta_{a,r} (ec_{i,j,a} \cdot z_{i,j,g,r}) \end{aligned} \tag{6.7}$$

where $gp_{i,g}^{\min}$ denotes the minimum generalised price that a traveller in group g faces for mode i (see also equation (6.10) below). In the present formulation, it is assumed that tax revenues are transferred to the group from which they are obtained; of course, it can also be assumed that all tax revenues are first pooled and then transferred to all actors involved. Also the supply of transport is assumed to be group-specific (see $z_{i,j,g,r}$). Furthermore, it can be noted that the terms w_g are added so as to enable us to attach different weights to different groups. Again, as in the basic version, the objective function can be maximised with respect to $p_{i,a}$, $q_{i,a}$ and $z_{i,j,g,r}$, subject to the following constraints:

$$\sum_j z_{i,j,g,r} \geq N_g \cdot x_{i,g,r} \qquad \forall i\, \forall g\, \forall r \tag{6.8}$$

$$\sum_a \delta_{a,r} \cdot p_{i,a} \geq \sum_a \delta_{a,r} \cdot rc_{i,j,a} \qquad \forall r\, \forall i,j \tag{6.9}$$

In addition, the following constraints guarantee Wardrop's principle to hold:

$$x_{i,g,r} \geq 0; \quad gp_{i,r} - gp^{\min}_{i,g} \geq 0; \quad x_{i,g,r} \cdot (gp_{i,r} - gp^{\min}_{i,g}) = 0 \qquad \forall i\, \forall g\, \forall r \tag{6.10}$$

In principle, the GAMS software is able to deal with such complementary slackness conditions. This means that equations (6.1)–(6.10) give the network version of TRENEN in a general representation.

6.3 THE AMSTERDAM ROAD NETWORK

The spatial and network representation of Amsterdam in the TRENEN model that is being developed, including the multimodal infrastructural network, can be found in Verhoef and Van den Bergh (1996). In this section, we will present some results with the road network only. The purpose of this exercise lies primarily in the development of a GAMS procedure for solving a model as given in equations (6.1)–(6.10) above.

A specific complication in solving the type of network models considered here is caused by the general non-uniqueness of equilibria in terms of *route choice per OD pair*; albeit that equilibria will be unique in terms of *modal split* (or: total road usage) for each OD pair, and also unique in terms of *link usage*. It may seem odd at first sight that the latter two types of uniqueness would not imply uniqueness of route choice per OD pair. However, a simple example may clarify this.

Consider a network where in equilibrium, users from two different OD pairs (say group A and B) use two parallel routes (say R_1 and R_2). Because it is an equilibrium, we know that user costs should be equal on R_1 and R_2 (Wardrop's principle), and that marginal benefits for both groups should be equal to these user costs. Suppose that in this equilibrium, 50 users of group A and 50 of group B use route R_1, and also 50 users of group A and 50 of group B use route R_2. It is then a simple thought experiment to take out one driver of group A from R_1 and put him on R_2, while doing the opposite to a driver from group B on R_2. Clearly, the resulting configuration with 49 (51) A-drivers (B-drivers) on R_1 and 51 (49) *A*-drivers (*B*-drivers) on R_2 is again an equilibrium, equivalent to the one considered before when evaluated in terms of user costs on both routes. We can thus find 101 different equilibria when defined on the level of route choice per OD pair. This intuitive example will illustrate the basic point that equilibria will be unique only in terms of link usage, and total usage per OD pair, but not in terms of route choice per OD pair as soon as two OD pairs both use the same parallel routes.

A second complication that may arise, comparable to the one mentioned above, is that an optimum need not be unique in terms of *tolls per link*. Again a simple thought experiment may clarify this. Consider a simple two-link serial network. Suppose that in the optimum, marginal external costs and hence the tolls are 2 Euros on the first link and 3 Euros on the second one. Now if there is only one group of users, all of which want to use both links, then any combination of tolls t_i for which $t_1 + t_2 = 5$ Euros would produce the optimum. Evidently, a redefinition of the network to one link would in this case solve the problem. The important point in the present context, however, is that the implied interdependencies between tolls may complicate the convergence process in the numerical solving process.

We now turn to a discussion of some preliminary experiments with a network model for TRENEN-Amsterdam. Figure 6.1 shows the *road* network configuration used for the TRENEN model of the Amsterdam region. In the model, four zones are distinguished: the city centre inside the ring road (I), and three surrounding zones (II–IV). The road network consists of main roads (m) and secondary roads (s).

Ignoring intrazonal traffic for the regions II–IV, a total of 13 groups (OD combinations) can be distinguished, implying that the model will have to use 13 representative consumers (see Table 6.1 for an overview of the dimensions of the model). Given the revealed limited capabilities of GAMS to deal with more complex versions of TRENEN than those developed for the Brussels region, it is not unlikely that either some of these OD pairs, or, alternatively, some 'utility layers' will have to be given up in order to keep the model with the TRENEN demand specification solvable for GAMS.

This is, however, not our concern here, because the experiments we are reporting on now were performed with a simulation model in GAMS containing the road network given in Figure 6.1, but which is much simpler on the demand-side of the model than TRENEN: the inverse demand relations for each OD pair are assumed to be given, and linear. Also the

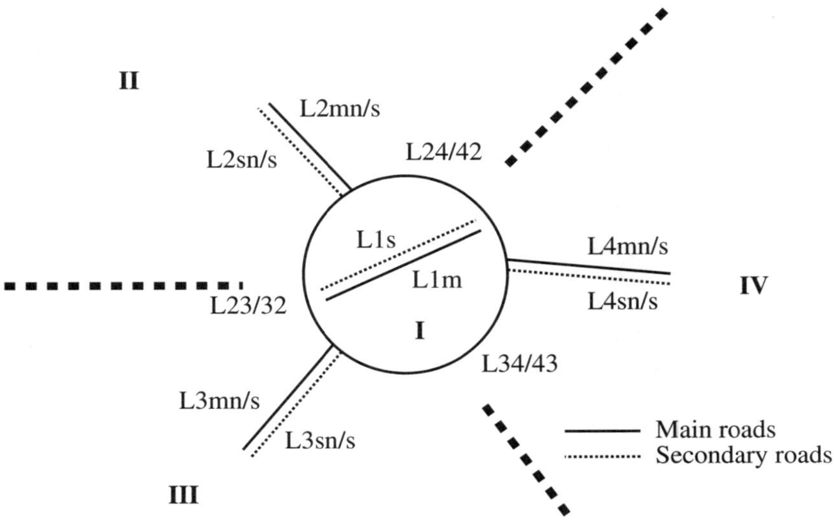

Figure 6.1 The spatial configuration and road network for the Amsterdam version of the TRENEN model

link-congestion functions are assumed to be linear: the private generalised costs of using the link rise linearly with usage.

This means that we can fully concentrate on the programming of the network structure, the route choice decisions and the modal split decisions in GAMS. Since TRENEN is solved numerically, there should be no fundamental differences between the programming of this linearised model and the model that uses the TRENEN structure with non-linear demand and congestion cost formulations.

Table 6.1 shows the dimensions of the spatial version of the TRENEN-Amsterdam model. As mentioned, four zones and 13 groups (or OD pairs) are considered. Since all roads, apart from the two links representing the city centre, have two directions, and since for all connections, apart from the ring, a distinction is made between main roads and secondary roads, the network has 20 links in total. In Figure 6.1, these links are shown. The link codes have the following logic: the code LZyn/s stands for the **L**ink in **Z**one Z (links belonging to the ring have two digits, showing the 'origin' and 'destination' zones of the link) of type y (y = **m**ain or **s**econdary), running **n**orthbound or **s**outhbound.

Perhaps surprisingly, this rather simple network leads to a total of (actually more than) 98 routes. This total is reached after strictly inferior routes are cancelled out (for instance those involving 'an extra round' on the ring),

Table 6.1 Dimensions of the spatial version of the TRENEN-Amsterdam model

Zones	Groups or OD pairs	Routes	Links
4	13[1]	98[2]	20

Notes
1. With four zones, a maximum of 4·4 = 16 OD combinations could in principle be distinguished. In the present model *intra*zonal traffic in zones II, III and IV is ignored.
2. Theoretically speaking, there is an infinite number of possible routes. It is generally assumed that strictly inferior routes (for example, including a number of extra rounds on the ring) are not used. In addition, it is assumed that no user will use two-thirds of the ring when one-third will do.

and also after cancelling those that use two-thirds of the ring. This latter type of route becomes relevant when congestion is stochastic and accidents can block a certain part of the ring, but in the present deterministic setting, such routes are unlikely to be used on a structural basis. Clearly, there is nothing that prevents us from including these routes in the model, they are simply ignored in this version. Table 6.2 gives some more details of the groups, OD pairs and number of routes per group. These details can be verified by inspection of Figure 6.1. In the network model, a route-link matrix filled with 0s and 1s (if a link belongs to a certain route) was used to determine prices on a route level.

Table 6.2 Details of groups, OD pairs and numbers of routes per group

Group	A	B	C	D	E	F	G	H	I	J	K	M	N
Origin	I	I	I	I	II	II	II	III	III	III	IV	IV	IV
Destination	I	II	III	IV	I	III	IV	I	II	IV	I	III	II
# routes	2	4	4	4	4	12	12	4	12	12	4	12	12

It would take too much space to include the entire model, as written in GAMS, in the present chapter. However, the general structure can be outlined as follows:

1. Define the sets L and R, containing all links and all possible routes in the model; and the sets $A(R) - N(R)$, defining per OD pair the possible routes. Next, define all parameters, the link-route table CHOICE, the variables, equations, constraints and objective.
2. Some relevant variables are, on the *group* level: the marginal benefit ($DEMx$), total benefits ($BENx$), total usage ($TOTQx$) which is the

sum of usage of all relevant routes $Q(R)$, the equilibrium cost level for every possible route ($RC(R)$) and the minimum costs for each group ($RCminx$); and, on the *link* level: link usage ($X(L)$), tolls ($TOLL(L)$) and the 'price' $P(L)$, which is equal to the average costs *plus* the toll.

3. The objective of social welfare can then be defined as the sum *over all groups* of total benefits, minus the sum *over all links* of total costs.
4. For the linearised version of the model, some typical equations from the GAMS model are given in Table 6.3.

Table 6.3 Characteristic equations from the network model for Amsterdam

PRICE(L):	$P(L) = \kappa(L) + \beta(L)*X(L) + TOLL(L);$
EQRCa(A):	$RCa(A) = \{SUM[L, CHOICE(A,L)*P(L)]\};$
LOWRCa:	$RCmina = min(RCa(\text{'}R11a\text{'}), RCa(\text{'}R11b\text{'}));$
EQX(L):	$X(L) = \{SUM[R, CHOICE(R,L)*Q(R)]\};$
EQTOTQa:	$TOTQa = \{SUM[A, Q(A)]\};$
DEMANDa:	$DEMa = \delta a - \alpha a*(TOTQa);$
BENEFITa:	$BENa = \delta a*TOTQa - 0.5*\alpha a*(TOTQa)^2;$
TOTBEN:	$TTBEN = BENa + BENb + BENc + BENd + BENe + BENf +$ $BENg + BENh + BENi + BENj + BENk + BENn + BENm;$
TOTCOSTS:	$TTCOS = \langle SUM\ \{L, \kappa(L)*X(L) + \beta(L)*[X(L)]^2\}\rangle;$
WELFARE:	$WEL = TTBEN - TTCOS;$
EQCOND4a(A):	$COND4a(A) = Q(A)*[RCa(A) - RCmina];$
CONSTR1a(L):	$X(L) \geq 0;$
CONSTR1b(R):	$Q(R) \geq 0;$
CONSTR2a:	$DEMa = RCmina;$
CONSTR4a(A):	$COND4a(A) = 0$

It may be clear from the equations in Table 6.3 that the fixed term in the average cost (marginal benefit) relation is $\kappa(\delta)$, and the parameter in the variable term $\beta(\alpha)$.

In order to produce an 'easy-to-check' simulation, the respective parameters in the model were chosen so as to produce a highly symmetric configuration. On the demand side, three types of groups were distinguished: those who come from but stay in the centre (Type 1); those who travel to or from the centre (Type 2) and those who travel between two peripheral zones (Type 3). Also on the cost side, three types of links are considered: parts of the ring (Type 1), all other main roads (Type 2), and all secondary roads (Type 3). Table 6.4 gives the parameter values.

The implied model was solved successfully for the first-best optimum using the GAMS 2.25 software. Given the assumed symmetry, the results

Table 6.4 Some parameter values for the simulation presented

Demand side			Cost side		
Type 1 Group A	*Type 2* Groups BCDEHK	*Type 3* Groups FGIJMN	*Type 1* Parts of ring	*Type 2* Main roads	*Type 3* Secondary roads
$\delta=750$ $\alpha=0.1$	$\delta=1000$ $\alpha=0.1$	$\delta=500$ $\alpha=0.1$	$\kappa=20$ $\beta=0.02$	$\kappa=20$ $\beta=0.01$	$\kappa=20$ $\beta=0.05$

Table 6.5 Some simulation results of the linearised TRENEN-Amsterdam model

Groups (OD pairs)			Links		
Type 1 Group A	*Type 2* Groups BCDEHK	*Type 3* Groups FGIJMN	*Type 1* Parts of ring	*Type 2* Main roads	*Type 3* Secondary roads
$Q=2843$	$Q=3983$	$Q=1487$	$X=1487$	$X=5797$ $X_{1M}=22286$	$X=1159$ $X_{1S}=4457$
$DEM=RCmin=466$	$DEM=RCmin=602$	$DEM=RCmin=351$	$P=79$	$P=136$ $P_{1M}=466^*$	$P=136$ $P_{1S}=466^*$
			$TOLL=30$	$TOLL=58$ $TOLL_{1M}=223^*$	$TOLL=58$ $TOLL_{1S}=223^*$

Note: Refers to the two links in the central zone

obtained are also highly symmetric. Only the main and secondary link in the centre have different equilibrium usage, costs and tolls than the other main and secondary links, since more groups start and/or end their trips in the centre.

Table 6.5 summarises the results. Note that in the optimum, the marginal social costs (which are equal to 'Price' P) are equalised on parallel main and secondary roads, which is a feature of optimal route split. Furthermore, note that for each group, DEM – which gives the marginal benefits – is equal to the sum of the marginal social costs over the links used. Putting on the left-hand side of the equation the marginal benefit DEM, and on the right-hand side the marginal private cost including tolls ('Price' P) over all links used, we can check Table 6.5 by observing:

* For group type 1: **466** = **466** (link type 2_1 = link type 3_1)
* For group type 2: **602** = **466** (link type 2_1 = link type 3_1) + **136** (link type $2_{\neq 1}$ = link type $3_{\neq 1}$)
* For group type 3: **351** = **79** (link type 1) + **136** (link type $2_{\neq 1}$ = link type $3_{\neq 1}$) + **136** (link type $2_{\neq 1}$ = link type $3_{\neq 1}$)

These conditions are in line with optimal overall equilibrium usage of the network.

The feature of the present model that tolls on parallel main and secondary roads are exactly equal in the optimum is a direct consequence of the linear cost curves assumed, *in combination with* the identical fixed component in these cost curves (to reflect equal length of the links), and the optimality condition that marginal social costs should be equal on parallel routes.

Because of the linear average cost curves, it is easy to derive that the marginal external congestion costs in the optimum on a link L are $\beta_L \cdot X(L)$. It is therefore easy to check that the results presented in Table 6.5 must be correct: the tolls on all routes satisfy the intuitive optimality condition that they should be equal to the marginal external congestion costs in the optimum.

Hence, the model works in principle. It is, however, fair to acknowledge that the GAMS programme does not always find an equilibrium. Convergence problems were experienced in cases where second-best problems were studied. These still have to be analysed further. Two possible causes for these difficulties were touched upon in the beginning of this section: first, equilibria in terms of *route choice per OD pair* are not unique; albeit that equilibria will be unique in terms of *modal split* (or: total road usage) for each OD pair, and also unique in terms of *link usage*; and second, an optimum need not be unique in terms of *tolls per link*. The GAMS solver may experience difficulties with finding an outcome for such models.

6.4 CONCLUSION

This chapter reported on the development of a network version for TRENEN-Amsterdam. The results with a linearised version of this model are encouraging. Nevertheless, the GAMS solver may experience difficulties with finding an outcome for such models. It is questionable whether the more elaborate demand specification in TRENEN, in combination with these network complications, still yield models that the GAMS software can handle. Otherwise, it is advisable to use derived demand curves (from the TRENEN model) directly in the network model. It may well be that analytically specified Marshallian demand functions for road usage at the group level, consistent with the utility functions used, are less computationally demanding than the utility functions used in the full model. The disadvantage would be that the full model can be solved only by iterating between the network model and the full TRENEN model.

NOTE

1. In short, Wardrop's first principle states that between a certain origin and destination, all routes that are used in equilibrium should have equal generalised costs, and the routes that are not used should have higher generalised costs. Hence, no individual can obtain a higher utility by switching route.

REFERENCES

Verhoef, E.T. and van den Bergh, J.C.J.M. (1996), 'Spatial disaggregation and zoning in the TRENEN model', TRENEN report, Free University, Amsterdam.

Wardrop, J. (1952), 'Some theoretical aspects of road traffic research', *Proceedings of the Institute of Civil Engineers*, **1**(2), 325–78.

PART III

External and Internal Costs

7. The external costs of transport

Inge Mayeres and Kurt Van Dender

7.1 INTRODUCTION

The aim of this chapter is to describe the methodology used in this book to determine the marginal external costs of transport. As different concepts of external costs are used in the literature, it is useful to restate the definition and the use of external cost information in economics. Our main interest here is in the measurement of the marginal external costs of transport by road, rail and inland navigation. According to the definition by Baumol and Oates (1988) an 'externality is present whenever some individual's (say *A*'s) utility or production relationships include real (that is, nonmonetary) variables, whose values are chosen by others . . . without particular attention to the effects on *A*'s welfare'. The marginal external costs of transport use correspond therefore to the costs caused by an additional transport user that are not borne by the user himself but by others. They may consist not only of costs in the monetary sense, but also of, for example, time losses, pollution, noise and so on. We focus on marginal rather than total external costs because the former are the necessary ingredient for computing the marginal social cost. This is the sum of the marginal private resource costs paid by the user and the marginal external costs. Prices fulfil their allocative function best when they are based on the marginal social cost rather than on the average social cost.

Recently, a number of studies have tried to determine the marginal external costs of (mainly road) transport use. They include, *inter alia*, the studies by Newbery (1988), Jones-Lee (1990), Mayeres (1993, 1994), Boniver and Thiry (1994), Jansson (1994), Peirson, Skinner and Vickerman (1994), Small and Kazimi (1995), Maddison et al. (1996), Mayeres, Ochelen and Proost (1996) and Bickel et al. (1997).

Before starting the analysis, we want to stress the following points. First, the marginal external costs are always computed for a given economic equilibrium. This implies that the size of the external costs will depend on transport pricing and regulation policies that affect equilibrium transport volumes. Specifically, currently observed external costs may be reduced substantially by the introduction of social cost pricing. Thus, what is needed is a marginal external cost function rather than a point estimate of the external cost in a given equilibrium.

Second, as explained in Chapter 1, simply charging consumers the 'equilibrium' social cost of transport use per km is not necessarily the best pricing principle. There are two reasons for this. First, other objectives (equity, tax revenue), imperfections of the instruments (for example, the impossibility to discriminate between peak and off-peak traffic) or pricing imperfections in related markets (for example, disequilibrium on the labour market) may require optimal deviations from marginal social cost pricing. In addition, the present equipment of cars and trucks can be inefficient in the sense that additional pollution abatement investments can reduce the external costs per vehicle km drastically. This calls for external cost information expressed in function of the externality problems themselves (for example, per gram of a pollutant) rather than per vehicle-km.

Table 7.1 gives an overview of the different categories of marginal social costs of transport use. They are subdivided in costs which are internalised in the decision process of the additional transport user, and costs that are external. The main marginal external cost categories are the marginal external congestion, air pollution (including global warming), noise, accident and road damage costs. In this chapter, the functions are constructed for both urban and interregional transport. Throughout the main text, their use is illustrated for the case studies for Brussels and for interregional transport in Belgium. All values are expressed in prices of 1990. The results for the other case studies are summarised in the appendices. The calculations are made for the transport situation of 2005 assuming that there is no policy change. A detailed description of the prevailing transport situations is offered in the case study chapters in Part IV. The marginal external costs are determined for different transport modes: cars, buses, trams, metro, trucks, (passenger and freight) rail and inland navigation. To a large extent the methodology is similar to Mayeres, Ochelen and Proost (1996). However, we have chosen to integrate as much as possible recent information provided by the ExternE-Transport project (Bickel et al., 1997).

The next sections discuss the different types of marginal external costs.

7.2 THE MARGINAL EXTERNAL CONGESTION COSTS

The marginal external congestion costs are present whenever an additional vehicle in the transport network reduces the speed of the other transport users. The marginal external congestion costs of road transport are determined endogenously in our models. Due to data problems, they are not calculated in the case of rail transport and inland navigation.

A lower speed has several effects. First of all, it affects the time and operating costs of the other road users. Second, it may also have an impact on environmental costs and accident risks. In the models it is assumed that the average fuel consumption per km and the other average resource costs remain constant in each of the periods considered. It is also assumed that the accident risks do not change as an additional vehicle joins the traffic flow (see Table 7.1). The analysis therefore focuses on the time losses of the other road users.

Table 7.1 The marginal social costs of motorised road transport

Description	Internal	External
Private resource costs	Average resource costs	Change in resource costs of other vehicles due to the decrease in speed caused by the additional vehicle
Time costs	Average time costs	The time losses of all other road users due to the decrease in speed caused by the additional vehicle
Accidents	Costs associated with average risk (except direct economic costs)	Cost of the increased accident risk + direct economic costs associated with average accident risk
Air pollution (including global warming)	–	Damage to the rest of society and to future generations
Noise	Damage to the vehicle users	Damage to the neigbourhood
Road damage		Increased repair cost of the road borne by the government

7.2.1 The Time–flow Relationship

In principle, congestion is different for each part of the road network. An additional vehicle on a four-lane road has different congestion effects than an additional vehicle on a two-lane road. Our models compute the marginal external congestion costs in a more aggregate way. The basic premise is that the area under consideration has homogeneous traffic conditions and can be represented as if it were a one-link system. Adding one vehicle to the traffic flow then slows down all other vehicles using the same network at that moment.

The time–flow relationship is of crucial importance in the calculation of the marginal congestion costs. It describes how the traffic flow influences the time needed to drive one km. Traffic flow is measured in millions of passenger car unit (PCU) km per hour. PCU is used, instead of the number of vehicles, to reflect the difference in congestive effect of the vehicle types considered. Generally, a bus, a tram or a truck is assumed to correspond with 2 PCU. The aggregate time–flow relationship is derived from simulations with a network model. Its construction is explained in Chapter 10 of this volume. A network model is necessary to compute the impact of a proportional increase in all trips on the average speed. In Chapter 10 it is concluded that an exponential type of time–flow relationship is the most satisfying. The following general form is proposed:[1]

$$t_{i,j}=\frac{60}{s_{i,j}}=A_{1,j}[A_2+A_3\exp(A_4\cdot q_i)] \qquad (7.1)$$

It expresses $t_{i,j}$, the time needed to drive one km (in minutes) by mode j (j = car, bus, tram, truck) in period i (i = peak, off-peak period), as a function of the number of PCU km per hour in that period (q_i). $s_{i,j}$ is the speed of vehicle type j in period i in km per hour. A_2, A_3 and A_4 are parameters of the time–flow relationship. The speed of the bus and tram mode is assumed to be proportional to that of cars and trucks. This is expressed by the parameter $A_{1,j}$. In the case studies it is assumed to equal one for the car and truck mode and 1.30 for bus and tram, which reflects the fact that in the benchmark equilibrium the speed of public transport is approximately 77 per cent of that of the car mode (UK, Department of Transport, 1982). The average speed of non-motorised transport is assumed to be independent of the volume of other traffic. In addition, non-motorised transport is assumed not to affect the speed of the other modes. The time–flow relationship is calibrated on the basis of three observation points.[2]

The time–flow relationship allows us to compute the time loss suffered by the other road users if an additional PCU joins the traffic flow. This has to be combined with information on the value of a marginal time saving in order to calculate the marginal external congestion cost (*MECC*) of an additional PCU km. This is given by:

$$MECC_{qi}=\sum_{j=car,bus,tram,truck}\frac{\partial t_{i,j}}{\partial q_i}x_{i,j}\,VOT_{i,j} \qquad (7.2)$$

$X_{i,j}$ being the number of pkm travelled in period i by mode j in the case of passenger transport, and the number of tkm in the case of freight transport. $VOT_{i,j}$ is the value of a marginal time saving per passenger or per tonne per hour. In order to get the *MECC* of a truck, tram or bus vkm the *MECC* of an additional PCU km needs to be multiplied by 2.

7.2.2 The Value of Marginal Time Savings

In order to assign a value to the time losses suffered by other road users, we use recent value-of-time studies. Such studies exist both for passenger and freight transport. For passenger transport, all case studies, except the one for Dublin, use the results of a willingness-to-pay (WTP) study carried out for the Netherlands by the Hague Consulting Group (HCG, 1990). This study provides empirical evidence about monetary valuations of travel time savings or losses for different modes (private cars and public transport) and for different trip purposes. The methodology and the results are discussed extensively by the HCG (1990).[3] In order to derive the values for Belgium, Amsterdam and London, the HCG findings are combined with the relative importance of the different trip purposes.[4] This gives the results of Table 7.2, which presents the value of marginal time savings for the year 2005. The values for 2005 are derived from those for 1990 using the relationship between the VOT and income. MVA Consultancy et al. (1987) and HCG (1990) have found that the VOT increases with income, but less than proportionally. From the results of the stated preference analysis by HCG (1990), we estimate a linear relationship between VOT and income. According to this relationship the elasticity of the VOT with respect to income equals 0.368. It is assumed that on average income increases annually by 2 per cent. The values for Ireland are based on Steer Davis Gleave (1995).

The value of marginal time savings in freight transport is taken from De Jong, Gommers and Klooster (1993), in which the value for 1990 is estimated by means of a contextual stated preference method. The value for 2005 is obtained by assuming that the labour cost, which is one of the main components of freight transport, increases by 2 per cent annually between 1990 and 2005.

7.2.3 Results

Table 7.3 presents the resulting MECC per vkm for the reference situation in Brussels and Belgium in 2005.[5] The MECC are very high, especially in the peak period. The high costs for peak transport in Brussels reflect the fact that one expects to be close to the saturation of the Brussels' network by 2005. As a consequence one arrives in a very steep part of the speed–flow relationship. The expected increase in traffic between 1991 and 2005 makes the average peak period speed in Brussels drop from 38 km/h

Table 7.2 The value of marginal time savings in passenger and freight transport in 2005

	Peak	Off-peak
Passenger transport: private		
(Euro/passenger/hour)		
Urban		
Amsterdam, Brussels, London	7.7	7.3
Dublin	4.2	5.1
Interregional		
Belgium	7.5	7.5
Ireland	4.2	5.1
Passenger transport: public		
(Euro/passenger/hour)		
Urban		
Amsterdam, Brussels, London	5.4	5.7
Dublin	1.6	5.1
Interregional		
Belgium	5.5	5.5
Ireland	1.6	5.1
Freight transport: truck		
(Euro/tonne/hour)	2.2	2.2

Source: Own calculations based on HCG (1990), De Jong, Gommers and Kloosters (1993), Stratec (1992), MVA Consultancy et al. (1987) and Steer Davis Gleave (1995)

Table 7.3 The marginal external congestion costs for Brussels and Belgium in 2005 (Euro/vkm)

	Peak			Off-peak		
	Car	Bus[a]	Truck	Car	Bus[a]	Truck
Brussels	1.796	3.592		0.003	0.006	
Belgium interregional						
Highways	0.928		1.856	0.009		0.018
Other roads	0.086	0.172	0.172	0.004	0.009	0.009
Average	0.381		1.081	0.006		0.014

Note: [a] Includes tram for Brussels

to 23.7 km/h. For urban public transport the MECC equal twice the cost of passenger cars. For interregional transport in the peak period the MECC are lower than those for urban transport. Note that when averaged over transport on highways and other roads, the MECC of heavy vehicles (trucks and buses) does not equal twice the MECC of passenger cars because the share of vkm driven by these vehicle types on highways and other roads is different.

7.3 THE MARGINAL EXTERNAL AIR POLLUTION COSTS

This section determines the social costs of a marginal increase in the emission of air pollutants by road and rail transport and by inland navigation. This generally requires four steps. The first step consists of the calculation of the emissions caused by an additional vehicle-km. The second step establishes the relationship between the change in emissions and the resulting ambient concentrations of the primary and secondary air pollutants. This requires atmospheric dispersion models predicting the spread of the pollutants from their origin, and chemical transformation models describing how different air pollutants react together to form so-called secondary air pollutants. The third step consists of relating the change in the ambient concentration to its effects on health, vegetation, materials, visibility, ecosystems and so on. This requires the use of so-called exposure–response relationships. The final step assigns a monetary value to the different effects of air pollution.

First, we describe the approach which is used in the case studies to calculate the marginal external air pollution costs. This approach is used for all transport modes except for public transport in the urban case studies. Next, we turn to the marginal external air pollution costs of urban public transport.

7.3.1 The Marginal External Air Pollution Costs of all Transport Modes Except Urban Public Transport

For all transport modes except urban public transport the case studies use the findings of the ExternE-Transport project for the last three steps in the calculation of the air pollution costs. The ExternE-Transport project provides data on the damage cost per g of pollutant emitted, which are combined with the emission factors of the different vehicle types. An overview of the main ExternE-Transport results and a brief discussion of the methodology is presented in Bickel et al. (1997). Table 7.4 summarises the

Table 7.4 The impacts of air pollutants considered by ExternE-Transport (Bickel et al., 1997)

		Impacts								
Precursor emissions by road transport	Ambient concentration	Health	Materials soiling	Materials	Visibility	Crops	Forests	Eco-systems	Fisheries	Climate change
CO	CO	XX								
PM	PM	XX	XX		X					
NO_x	NO_2	XX								
	O_3	XX		XX		XX				
	nitrates	XX	X		X					
	acidity			XX		XX	X	X	X	
Pb	Pb	X								
SO_2	SO_2	XX				XX				
	sulphates	XX	X		X					
	acidity			XX		XX	X	X	X	
VOC	O_3	XX		XX		XX				
CO_2	global warming									XX
N_2O	global warming									XX
benzene	benzene	XX								
1,3-butadiene	1,3-butadiene	XX								
formaldehyde	formaldehyde	XX								
ethene	ethene	XX								
PAH	PAH	XX								
CH_4	global warming									XX

impacts of air pollution considered by ExternE-Transport. The impacts marked by 'XX' are valued in monetary terms by the project, while the ones marked by 'X' are not. In the case studies the health effects of carcinogens and lead are not taken into account, nor is the contribution of the N_2O and CH_4 emissions to global warming.

The results of ExternE-Transport for the damage cost per g of each pollutant are used. From Bickel et al. (1997) we derive the damage costs per g of pollutant as reported in Table 7.5.[6] Table 7.6 summarises the way in which the findings of ExternE-Transport are used in the case studies. For CO_2, the maximum of the ExternE-Transport range is used (that is, 25.2 Euro/tonne CO_2).

Table 7.5 Damage cost per g of pollutant (10^{-3} Euro/g) (Bickel et al., 1997)

	PM	NO_x	SO_2	CO	HC	CO_2
Urban						
Paris	2620	21	38	0.020	0.78	0.0008–0.0252
Stuttgart	348	10	10	0.003	0.78	0.0008–0.0252
Amsterdam	304	5	8	0.002	0.78	0.0008–0.0252
Barnsley	389	6	16	0.004	0.78	0.0008–0.0252
Average Amsterdam, Stuttgart and Barnsley	347	7	11	0.003	0.78	0.0008–0.0252
Interregional						
Stuttgart-Mannheim	185	14	8	0.002	0.78	0.0008–0.0252
Tiel drive	155	5	10	0.002	0.78	0.0008–0.0252
Average Stuttgart-Mannheim and Tiel	170	9	9	0.002	0.78	0.0008–0.0252

Table 7.6 The use of the ExternE-Transport results in the case studies

Case study	Values of ExternE-Transport used in the case study
Urban	
London	Paris
Amsterdam	Amsterdam
Brussels, Dublin	Average of Stuttgart, Amsterdam and Barnsley
Interregional	
Belgium, Ireland	Average of the route Stuttgart-Mannheim and the Tiel drive

In order to calculate the marginal external air pollution costs these findings are combined with constant emission factors (per vkm, pkm or tkm) for different vehicle types (vehicle size, fuel type, emission technology, fuel efficiency) in the different transport markets (time of day, occupation rate). An overview of the emission factors is given in Appendix 7A.4. The appendix also describes the main assumptions underlying these emission factors. For cars the emissions are given for standard and for improved emission technology, and for standard and increased fuel efficiency. In the reference situation all cars are assumed to use standard technology with a standard fuel efficiency. Improved technology or increased fuel efficiency can be imposed by regulation or by emission taxes.

Table 7.7 The marginal external air pollution costs of passenger cars in Brussels in the reference equilibrium (10^{-3} Euro/vkm)

	Brussels						
	NO_x	CO_2	VOC	CO	PM	SO_2	Total
Gasoline car							
Peak small	0.788	5.015	0.133	0.005	2.706	0.305	8.952
Peak large	1.110	6.754	0.187	0.008	2.706	0.305	11.069
Off-peak small	0.702	4.259	0.108	0.003	2.706	0.305	8.083
Off-peak large	0.972	5.242	0.152	0.005	2.706	0.305	9.382
Diesel car							
Peak small	2.270	4.511	0.091	0.001	28.064	1.572	36.509
Peak large	3.638	5.569	0.194	0.002	45.930	1.958	57.291
Off-peak small	1.774	3.301	0.055	0.001	17.449	1.148	23.728
Off-peak large	2.575	4.183	0.097	0.002	26.781	1.462	35.100

Table 7.7 presents the marginal external air pollution costs of standard passenger cars in Brussels in 2005. Even among private cars the variation in air pollution costs between the different car types and uses is quite important (compare, for example, the marginal external air pollution costs of a large diesel car in the peak period and those of a small gasoline car in the same period). For gasoline vehicles, CO_2 is the dominant cause of air pollution costs, followed by PM. For diesel cars, PM have the dominant share. Table 7.8 presents the results for interregional transport in Belgium.

7.3.2 The Marginal External Air Pollution Costs of Urban Public Transport

The marginal external air pollution costs of urban public transport are taken from the ExternE-Transport project. Table 7.9 presents the findings

Table 7.8 The marginal external air pollution costs of interregional transport in Belgium in the reference equilibrium

	Highways	Other roads	Average Belgium interregional
Gasoline car (10^{-3} Euro/vkm)			
Peak small	3.15	3.05	3.09
Peak large	3.58	3.78	3.71
Off-peak small	3.67	3.00	3.23
Off-peak large	4.01	3.50	3.68
Diesel car (10^{-3} Euro/vkm)			
Peak small	11.12	13.17	12.45
Peak large	14.15	20.12	18.03
Off-peak small	15.92	10.36	12.31
Off-peak large	19.14	13.97	15.78
Public transport[a] (10^{-3} Euro/pkm)			
Peak bus			10.50
Off-peak bus			16.81
Truck[b] (10^{-3} Euro/tkm)			
Peak	8.46	8.46	8.46
Off-peak	6.38	6.38	6.38

Notes:

[a] The following occupancy rates are assumed for bus: peak bus: 36.95 passengers/vehicle; off-peak bus: 22.66 passengers/vehicle

[b] A truck is assumed to have an average load factor of 11.30 tonnes/vehicle

Table 7.9 The marginal external air pollution costs of urban public transport

Vehicle type	Marginal external air pollution costs (10^{-3} Euro/pkm)
Diesel bus	31.0
Electric bus	3.8
Tram	3.2
Light rail	4.2
Train (urban)	5.0

Source: Bickel et al. (1997)

of this project. The values are best estimates for a typical medium-sized urban area. They are used in the case studies for Brussels. For diesel buses in London, a marginal external air pollution cost of 224 10^{-3} Euro/pkm[7] is assumed. Note that no differentiation is made between peak and off-peak transport. The values are for average occupancy rates and average emission factors. In the peak period the emission factors and the occupancy rates can be expected to be higher than the average, in the off-peak period, the reverse is true.

7.4 THE MARGINAL EXTERNAL ACCIDENT COSTS

From the economic literature we know that the accident cost relevant for pricing is the difference between the marginal social and the average private accident cost. This difference is the marginal external accident cost. Following Jansson (1994), the total accident cost (TAC) of a given equilibrium can be written as:

$$TAC = \sum_{j=1}^{6} \sum_{n=1}^{4} (c_A^n + c_B^n + c_C^n) \sum_{v=1}^{7} ar_{jv}^n V_j \tag{7.3}$$

The indices j and v represent the transport modes. In the case of road transport these include: car, bus, tram, metro, truck and non-motorised transport. In addition, index v includes external objects (such as a wall or a tree) as a category (indexed by $v=7$). Index n indicates the severity of the accident. A distinction is made between fatal accidents, accidents with serious injuries, accidents with light injuries and accidents with only material damage. c_A^n stands for the victim's own WTP to avoid an accident of type n. c_B^n is the WTP of the relatives and friends of the victim to avoid an accident of type n. c_A^n and c_B^n are the so-called 'warm-blooded' costs as opposed to the 'cold-blooded' cost category c_C^n which consists of the pure economic costs (net output loss, ambulance costs, police and medical costs) which are borne by the rest of society. V_j is the number of vehicle-km travelled by transport mode j. Finally, ar_{jv}^n is the probability that an accident of severity n occurs between transport modes j and v and in which j is the victim. It is defined as

$$ar_{jv}^n = ACC_{jv}^n / V_j$$

$$ACC_{jv}^n = ACC_{jv}^n (V_j, V_v) \; \forall j,v \tag{7.4}$$

ACC_{jv}^n giving the number of accidents between modes j and v in which j is the victim. It is assumed not to depend on the number of vehicle-kilometres driven by transport modes other than j and v.

The marginal social accident cost (*MSAC*) of a car is the derivative of the *TAC* with respect to the number of car km:

$$
\begin{aligned}
MSAC_{car} &= \sum_{n=1}^{4} (c_A^n + c_B^n + c_C^n) \sum_{v=1}^{7} ar^n_{car,v} \\
&+ \sum_{n=1}^{4} (c_A^n + c_B^n + c_C^n) \sum_{v=1}^{7} \frac{\partial ar^n_{car,v}}{\partial V_{car}} V_{car} \qquad (7.5)\\
&+ \sum_{j \neq car} \sum_{n=1}^{4} (c_A^n + c_B^n + c_C^n) \frac{\partial ar^n_{j,car}}{\partial V_{car}} V_j \\
&= MSAC^1_{car} - MSAC^2_{car} + MSAC^3_{car}
\end{aligned}
$$

This derivative consists of three terms. The first term gives the social costs of the risk that the car occupants themselves are involved in an accident. The second and the third term give the social cost of the increased accident risk for other cars and road users due to the additional car-km. A similar formula can be obtained for the marginal social accident cost of buses, trucks and so on. However, to keep the explanation as simple as possible, we limit ourselves to cars.

Part of the marginal social cost is internalised in the transport users' decision process. From the literature on accident costs we know that road users take into account the average private accident costs. These include the insurance premium and two cost categories associated with their own accident risk, namely their own utility loss due to the accident risk (c_A) and possibly also the utility loss of their relatives and friends (c_B).[8] Thus in the first term of equation (7.5), only the c_C cost category would be external. However, this depends on the type of insurance that is in place. If an insurance covering costs of type c_C is compulsory, then the cold-blooded costs associated with the own accident risk are internalised through the insurance premium. In Belgium, this is the case for car passengers but not for car drivers. Therefore, the cold-blooded costs are external for car drivers only. For public transport, these costs are assumed to be external for both the driver and the passengers.[9]

The second term of equation (7.5) can be written as:

$$MSAC^2_{car} = \sum_{n=1}^{4} (c_A^n + c_B^n + c_C^n) \sum_{v=1}^{7} el^n_{(car,v)car}\, ar^n_{car,v} \qquad (7.6)$$

in which $el^n_{(car,v)car}$ is the elasticity with respect to the number of car-km of the probability of an accident of type n between the car mode and mode v ($ar^n_{car,v}$) in which car users are the victims. If an additional car-km does not increase the risk of accidents of cars with other road users, the elasticities $el^n_{(car,v)car}$ equal zero so that expression (7.6) reduces to zero. However, if for some transport modes $el^n_{(car,v)car}$ is positive, the marginal external costs associated with increased accident risks for cars are non-zero. The value of $el^n_{(car,v)car}$ depends on the relationship between the number of accidents and the traffic flow. In the literature, different views are taken of this relationship. For the accidents between two motorised road users an accepted convention[10] is to assume that the number of accidents is proportional to the traffic volume, so that the elasticities $el^n_{(car,v)car}$ are zero. This assumption is supported by recent empirical work for London. This is discussed by Dickerson, Peirson and Vickerman in Chapter 8 of this volume.

The third term in expression (7.5) can be rewritten as:

$$MSAC^3_{car} = \sum_{j \neq car} \sum_{n=1}^{4} (c^n_A + c^n_B + c^n_C)\, el_{(j,car)car}\, ar^n_{j,car} \frac{V_j}{V_{car}} \tag{7.7}$$

$el^n_{(j,car)car}$ is the elasticity with respect to the number of car-kms of the risk of accidents between mode j and the car mode in which the users of mode j are the victim (with $j \neq$car). If the number of these accidents is proportional to the number of car km, these elasticities are equal to one.[11] We have assumed this to be the case for all modes (see also Chapter 8 in this volume). In addition, we have assumed that the car driver is confronted with the average accident costs he causes to these transport modes, because of the insurance premiums he pays.[12] The combination of these two assumptions entails that there are no marginal external accident costs with respect to the non-car transport modes.

Under the assumptions specified above, the total external accident costs ($TEAC$) can be defined as

$$TEAC = \sum_n c^n_C \sum_{j=1}^{6} \sum_{v=1}^{7} ar^n_{j,v}\, V_j \tag{7.8}$$

and the marginal external accident costs of a vkm driven by mode j ($MEAC_j$) are given by

$$MEAC_j = \sum_n c^n_C \sum_{j=1}^{6} \sum_{v=1}^{7} ar^n_{j,v} \tag{7.9}$$

This is simply the accident risk multiplied with that part of the social cost which is external, namely the direct economic costs c^n_C.

By way of illustration we apply this methodology to the city of Brussels and the interregional transport in Belgium. From our discussion it follows that we need information on the accident risks of all transport modes and on the 'cold-blooded costs' of the different accident types. The accident risk

Table 7.10 The accident risks in the benchmark equilibrium

	Accident risk		
	Fatality or fatal injury	Serious injury	Light injury
Brussels			
Car driver or occupant	$1.68\ 10^{-8}$	$9.56\ 10^{-8}$	$170.70\ 10^{-8}$
Bus driver or occupant	$0.00\ 10^{-8}$	$6.93\ 10^{-8}$	$311.98\ 10^{-8}$
Tram driver or occupant	$0.00\ 10^{-8}$	$8.03\ 10^{-8}$	$128.49\ 10^{-8}$
Metro driver or occupant	$0.00\ 10^{-8}$	$0.84\ 10^{-8}$	$3.52\ 10^{-8}$
Truck driver or occupant	$4.14\ 10^{-8}$	$28.97\ 10^{-8}$	$329.05\ 10^{-8}$
Belgium interregional			
Car driver or occupant	$1.80\ 10^{-8}$	$14.02\ 10^{-8}$	$59.34\ 10^{-8}$
Bus driver or occupant	$0.63\ 10^{-8}$	$19.53\ 10^{-8}$	$274.11\ 10^{-8}$
Truck driver or occupant	$1.73\ 10^{-8}$	$14.67\ 10^{-8}$	$63.42\ 10^{-8}$

Source: Own calculations on the basis of NIS (1990)

Table 7.11 The pure economic costs of the different accident categories (Euro)

	Fatality or fatal injury	Serious injury	Light injury	Material damage
Pure economic costs	126882	306631	709	0
= output loss	298172	298172		
+ police and medical costs	8459	8459		
− discounted consumption	179749	0		

Source: Jones-Lee (1990) and Newbery (1987) and own assumptions

figures for Belgium are summarised in Table 7.10. For each transport mode the table gives the probability per vkm that it is involved in an accident of a certain type (fatality, serious injury, light injury) and that it is the victim of that accident. The figures are based on NIS (1990). No reliable data exist on the risk of accidents with material damage only. Therefore, they are not included in our calculations.

We need information on the so-called 'cold-blooded' costs c_C^n of the different accident types. Table 7.11 presents the values used for the pure economic costs of the different accident types. In the case of fatal accidents these costs consist of the sum of the net output loss and the police, medical and ambulance costs. The net output loss equals the gross output loss minus the discounted present value of the victim's future consumption. The values correspond with those used to calculate the health costs resulting from air pollution. In the case of a serious injury, the discounted present value of the victim's reduction in future consumption is assumed to be zero. The monetary value of a light injury is based on Newbery (1987).

The resulting marginal external accident costs for the initial equilibrium are summarised in Table 7.12 for the Brussels and Belgium case study. The main share of these costs is accounted for by the accidents causing serious injuries. The accidents causing light injuries are only of relatively minor importance, despite their relatively high probability.

Table 7.12 The marginal external accident costs of transport in Brussels and Belgium in the initial equilibrium (10^{-3} Euro/vkm)

	Brussels			
	Car	Bus	Tram	Metro
MEAC associated with the accident risk of the transport users	32.65	23.47	25.53	2.62
– fatality or fatal injury	2.13	0.00	0.00	0.00
– serious injury	29.32	21.26	24.62	2.59
– light injury	1.20	2.21	0.91	0.03
	Belgium interregional			
	Car	Bus	Truck	
MEAC associated with the accident risk of the transport users	45.70	62.64	54.00	
– fatality or fatal injury	2.28	0.80	2.48	
– serious injury	43.00	59.90	51.01	
– light injury	0.42	1.94	0.51	

7.5 THE MARGINAL EXTERNAL NOISE COSTS

The marginal external noise costs are calculated only for the urban case studies. Due to data problems the noise costs are not computed for interregional transport. However, previous studies (see, for example, Mayeres, 1993) show that this entails only a slight underestimation of the marginal external costs of interregional transport. Here we describe how the values for Brussels are derived.

7.5.1 Noise Function

In order to calculate the marginal external noise costs, one needs to determine the effect on the noise level of an additional vehicle-km. The index used for noise is the energy mean sound level, $L_{eq}(\mathrm{dB}(A))$, representing the average sound level over a given period. The Institut Bruxellois pour la Gestion de l'Environnement (1995) presents a number of functions that relate the noise level in a street to, *inter alia*, the traffic flow. We assume that the average street in Brussels has houses on both sides of the street. In that case the function is:

$$L_{eq}(A) = 53.9 + 10\log(V_{light} + E\,V_{heavy}) - 10\log l + K \qquad (7.10)$$

$L_{eq}(A)$ being the equivalent noise level at two metres of the façade. V_{light} stands for the flow of light vehicles ($<3.5\ t$) in vehicles per hour. V_{heavy} is the flow of heavy vehicles ($>3.5\ t$) in veh/h. E is an equivalence factor. For slopes smaller than 2 per cent one heavy vehicle is assumed to be equivalent to 10 light vehicles. The width between the façades (in m) is given by l. K is a correction factor for speed which means that one decibel is added for each 10 km/h above a speed of 60 km/h.

The practical problem we face is that this function is established to compute the noise in a particular street, and not the average city-wide noise level. We have to make several assumptions to deduct an average noise function from this information. More specifically, we have to convert the PCU city-wide to the PCU of an average street. We know that the road network is approximately 2000 km long, taking all types of roads into account. However, the study of the Institut Bruxellois (1995) takes into account only the roads with relatively heavy traffic. This amounts to 500 km. We will assume that 75 per cent of all traffic is concentrated on this 500 km network, and that this is the only area where noise externalities occur.[13] This means that expression (7.10) becomes:

$$L_{eq}(A) = 53.9 + 10\log\left\{\frac{0.75[V_{car} + 10(V_{bus} + V_{tram} + V_{truck})]}{500}\right\} - 10\log l + K \qquad (7.11)$$

7.5.2 Monetary Valuation

For the monetary valuation we use the hedonic housing market method, which is the most widely used method for the valuation of the social costs of noise. The basic idea underlying this technique is that the value of a house depends not only on its intrinsic characteristics, but is also a function of a number of environmental attributes, such as accessibility, proximity to schools, shops and parks and pollution. If the value of a house is, amongst other factors, a function of noise, this means that when individuals buy or rent a house, within their price range they have the possibility of buying a property in a quiet location rather than a similar property in a noisy location. It is reasonable to expect that, *ceteris paribus*, houses located in noisy areas are of less value than those located in quiet areas. Therefore, the housing market constitutes a surrogate market for noise (Pearce and Markandya, 1989). For a detailed description of the method and its strengths and weaknesses we refer to Pearce and Markandya (1989).

Nelson (1982) summarises the results of North American hedonic price studies on traffic noise. The majority of the findings correspond with a house value depreciation in the range of 0.2 per cent to 0.6 per cent per dB(A), giving a mean of 0.4 per cent. The results refer to a standardised house value. This way one tries to eliminate the possibility that higher priced properties may have a greater depreciation than lower priced ones. Traffic noise is expressed in L_{eq} units. According to Alexandre and Barde (1987), as a rule of thumb a 0.5 per cent house value depreciation per dB(A) constitutes a reasonable guide and is based upon a substantial number of studies. However, they point to the fact that it is probable that this depreciation rate is valid only above a certain noise threshold, say 50 dB(A) L_{eq}, since most surveys show a very low level of annoyance below this level. Furthermore, they mention the possibility that the unit percentage of depreciation increases both with the noise level and with the value of the house.

From the literature we use the average house depreciation rule of 0.5 per cent. We assume a standardised value of 70 600 Euros per house. Thus for an increase of 1 dB which would continue during 50 years, the value of one exposed house decreases with 355 Euros. However, we need to know the value of a brief increase of the noise level. We assume an expected house life time of 50 years and a discount factor of 5 per cent. This gives a value of 0.003 Euro(90) per dB(A) during one hour for one house. Assuming an average of 200 exposed houses per km, we obtain 0.6 Euro per dB per street of 1 km.

We assume that real housing prices remain constant between 1991 and 2005 and the valuation of 1 dB is also supposed to remain the same in the future reference situation.

7.5.3 Results

The total external noise cost for Brussels is the monetary value per dB, multiplied by the noise level above the threshold of 50 dB(A), multiplied by the number of road km where a noise externality is generated (we assumed 500 km above).[14]

To compute the resulting marginal external noise cost (*MENC*) in the reference equilibrium, we derive the total external noise cost function with respect to the number of vehicle km. Using the noise formula (7.11) given above we find that the *MENC* of a car km is given by:[15]

$$MENC_{car} = 0.6\left[\frac{10}{\ln 10}\frac{1}{V_{car} + 10\,(V_{bus} + V_{tram} + V_{truck})}\right]500 \quad (7.12)$$

The resulting marginal external noise cost for the 2005 reference situation is given in Table 7.13. As expected, the marginal external noise cost generated by a vehicle is much higher in the off-peak period than in the peak period hours of the day. Indeed, an extra vehicle on a quiet moment causes more disturbing noise than an extra vehicle under congested conditions. By definition, the MENC of heavy vehicles is ten times higher than that of passenger cars.

Table 7.13 Marginal external noise cost in Brussels in 2005 (10^{-3} Euro/vkm)

	car	bus, tram
Peak	1.9	19
Off-peak	7.3	73

7.6 THE MARGINAL EXTERNAL ROAD DAMAGE COSTS

The external road damage costs are discussed extensively in Newbery (1988). They arise when the passage of trucks causes damage to the road surface. Two types can be distinguished: the increased repair cost of the road, borne by the government and the increased vehicle operating costs for the other road users. Under a number of conditions, Newbery shows that the second type of road damage costs are negligible in all reasonable cases and that, if road damage is not only caused by vehicle passage but also by weather conditions, the cost to be charged is a fraction of the average repair cost allocated over the total number of equivalent standard axles (ESA).[16] In his 1990 study for the UK he estimates them to be 3.5 pence per ESAkm, which corresponds to approximately 0.049 Euro per ESAkm. For a 5-axles-truck with an average load capacity of 25.3 tons and an average load factor of 44.66 per cent (see De Borger and Swysen, 1995), the average road damage externality then amounts to 1.411 10^{-3} Euro per vkm.[17]

Table 7.14 General overview of the marginal external costs in the initial equilibrium in Brussels and Belgium (Euro/vkm)

	Brussels					
	Congestion	Air pollution	Noise	Accidents		Total
Passenger car[a]						
PK.GS.SM	1.796	0.009	0.002	0.033		1.840
PK.DI.SM	1.796	0.037	0.002	0.033		1.868
OF.GS.SM	0.003	0.008	0.002	0.033		0.046
Bus						
PK	3.592	0.496	0.019	0.023		4.130
OF	0.006	0.496	0.073	0.023		0.598
Subway	0	0.080	0	0.003		0.083
	Belgium interregional					
	Congestion	Air pollution	Noise	Accidents	Road damage	Total
Passenger car[a]						
PK.GS.SM	0.381	0.003		0.046		0.430
PK.DI.SM	0.381	0.012		0.046		0.439
OF.GS.SM	0.006	0.003		0.046		0.055
Bus						
PK	0.172	0.388		0.063		0.623
OF	0.009	0.381		0.063		0.453
Truck						
PK	1.842	0.096		0.054	0.001	1.993
OF	0.004	0.072		0.054	0.001	0.141

Notes:
[a] The occupancy rate of the car is assumed to be 1
PK Peak OF Off-peak
GS Gasoline DI Diesel
SM Small

7.7 SUMMARY AND CONCLUSIONS

Table 7.14 presents the marginal external costs of transport in Brussels and in Belgium in 2005 for the different transport modes.[18] The marginal external costs vary widely in respect to the network considered, the volume of traffic and the vehicle type. Since only results for standardised cars are presented, the variation in external costs (noise, air pollution) is underestimated in these tables. Cars without a properly functioning catalytic converter or without noise abatement technology have marginal external costs that are much higher. It is important to note that public transport vehicles entail external costs as well. For meaningful comparisons between modes, the occupancy rates must be taken into account. These were presented in note 5.

It is very important to note that the marginal external cost calculations are only valid for the particular transport situations considered here. A different equilibrium will imply a different level of external costs,[19] hence the importance of external cost functions rather than point estimates.

The marginal external cost calculations are subject to many uncertainties which depend primarily on the quality of the valuation techniques. In the domain of air pollution, for example, the uncertainty is mainly situated in the emission-concentration and the exposure-response relationships. In the case of accidents, the relationship between the number of accidents of different types and the traffic flow is hard to establish.

NOTES

1. Appendix 7A.1 provides a list of symbols.
2. Table 7A.1 of Appendix 7A.2 summarises the information used for the calibration of the time–flow relationships for each of the case studies, together with the resulting values of the parameters of that relationship.
3. For cars the time-weighted average VOT in 1990 is 5.1 Euro/h for commuting, 16.9 Euro/h for business trips and 4.1 Euro/h for other trips. For bus users the values are 4.3 Euro/h, 16.9 Euro/h and 2.5 Euro/h respectively.
4. The share of the trip purposes in Brussels and Belgium in 1990 is as follows (figures in percent):

	commuting	business	other
Brussels			
peak car	51	18	31
peak public transport	47	10	43
off-peak car	27	17	56
off-peak public transport	23	15	62
Belgium interregional			
car	38	17	45
bus	34	13	53

The values are taken from Stratec (1992). The shares for Amsterdam and London are assumed to be the same as those for Brussels.

5. In order to compute the costs per passenger-km and per tonne-km, we use the following occupancy rates and load factors:

	Passengers/Vehicle		Tonnes/Vehicle	
	Car solo	Car pooling	Bus	Truck
Brussels				
peak	1	2.5	40	
off-peak	1	2.5	9	
Belgium interregional				
peak	1	2.5	36.95	11.30
off-peak	1	2.5	22.66	11.30

6. The data underlying these results are presented in Appendix 7A.3.
7. This value is obtained by multiplying the value for medium sized areas in ExternE by the ratio between the marginal external air pollution costs of diesel cars in London and those in medium-sized urban areas.
8. See the articles of Newbery (1988), Jones-Lee (1990) and Jansson (1994).
9. This point calls for investigation on the insurance systems used by the public transport firms.
10. We refer to Vitaliano and Held (1991), Jones-Lee (1990), UK, Department of Transport (1987) and US Federal Highway Administration (1982).
11. Indeed, using the definition of $ar^n_{j,car}$ one can easily show that

$$el^n_{(j,car)car} = \frac{\partial ar^n_{j,car}}{\partial V_{car}} \frac{V_{car}}{ar^n_{j,car}} = \frac{\partial ACC^n_{j,car}}{\partial V_{car}} \frac{V_{car}}{ACC^n_{j,car}}$$

which equals one if the number of accidents is proportional to the number of car km.
12. This is a strong assumption. First of all, it can be argued that insurance mainly covers the so-called 'cold-blooded' accident costs and only to a minor extent the other cost categories. If this is the case, the costs associated with the WTP of the victims and their relatives and friends are partially external. Second, it can be argued that the insurance premiums are perceived as fixed rather than as variable costs by the car users, so that they are not taken into account in their decision whether or not to travel. This implies that the marginal social accident costs associated with the risk to non-car and non-motorised road users are completely external. Both aspects need further analysis.
13. In the 2005 reference peak period we have a volume of 0.922 million car units per hour (bus, tram and truck being equivalent to 10 cars). Assuming that the noise externality is generated by 75 per cent of this total volume on the busiest 500 km of the road network, we have 1383 car units per hour per road km. Assuming an average width between façades of 12 m, we obtain a noise level of 74.5 dB using the noise formula for U-shaped roads. Applying the same assumptions in the off-peak period, we have an average flow of 337.5 car units per hour per km, generating a noise level of 68.3 dB.
14. For the reference peak period 2005 this gives (74.5dB–50dB)* 0.6 Euro * 500km, or a total external noise cost of 7350 Euros per peak period hour in Brussels.
15. In the reference peak period 2005 the marginal external noise cost of a car amounts to 0.6 Euro * 0.0000047 * 500 = 0.00141 Euro per car km. For a truck or bus this is 10 times higher. The marginal external cost in the off peak period is 0.0058 Euro per car km.
16. One ESA is defined as $(W/8.2)^4$, W being the load on a dual tyre single axle in tonnes.
17. 1.411 = 5*0.0489*1000*((25.3*0.4466/5)/8.2)^4.
18. The results for the other case studies are presented in Appendix 7A.5.
19. In the case studies only the marginal external congestion costs are assumed to depend on the traffic flow. The other marginal external cost categories are assumed to be constant.

REFERENCES

Alexandre, A. and Barde, J.-Ph. (1987), 'The Valuation of Noise', in P.M. Nelson (ed.), *Transportation Noise Reference Book*, London: Butterworths, pp. 23/1–23/10.

Baumol, W.J. and Oates, W.E. (1988), *The Theory of Environmental Policy*, Cambridge: Cambridge University Press.

Bickel, P., Schmid, S., Krewitt, W. and Friedrich, R. (eds) (1997), *External Costs of Transport in ExternE, Final Report*, Stuttgart: IER.

Boniver, V. and Thiry, B. (1994), 'Les coûts marginaux externes du transport public de personnes en milieu urbain, Estimations chiffrées pour la Belgique', *Cahiers Economiques de Bruxelles*, 203–40.

De Borger, B. and Swysen, D. (1995), *TRENEN-Interregional, Model Documentation*, Antwerp: SESO.

De Jong, G.C, Gommers, M.A. and Klooster, J.P.G.N. (1993), 'De reistijdwaardering in het goederenvervoer', *Tijdschrift vervoerswetenschap*, **29**, 77–85.

Dickerson, A., Peirson, J. and Vickerman, R. (1999), 'The relationship between road accidents and traffic flows', Chapter 8 in this volume.

EC (1995), *A Welfare Cost Assessment of Various Measures to Reduce Pollutant Emissions from Passenger Road Vehicles for the Year 2010*, EC DOCII/576/95–EN, Brussels: EC.

Hague Consulting Group (1990), *The Netherlands' 'Value of Time' Study: Final Report*, The Hague: Hague Consulting Group.

Harrington, W. (1997), 'Fuel economy and motor vehicle emissions', *Journal of Environmental Economics and Management*, **33**, 240–52.

Institut Bruxellois pour la Gestion de l'Environnement (1995), *Bruit du trafic routier, Region bruxelloise*, Bruxelles: I.B.G.E.

Jansson, J.O. (1994), 'Accident externality charges', *Journal of Transport Economics and Policy*, 31–43.

Jones-Lee, M.W. (1990), 'The value of transport safety', *Oxford Review of Economic Policy*, **6**, 39–60.

Khazzoom, J.D. (1995), 'An econometric model of the regulated emissions for fuel-efficient new vehicles', *Journal of Environmental Economics and Management*, **28**(2).

Maddison, D., Pearce, D., Johansson, O., Calthrop, E., Litman, T. and Verhoef, E. (1996), *The True Costs of Road Transport, Blueprint 5*, London: CSERGE, Earthscan.

Mayeres, I. (1993), 'The marginal external cost of car use: with an application to Belgium', *Tijdschrift voor Economie en Management*, **38**, 225–58.

Mayeres, I. (1994), 'The marginal external costs of trucks – an empirical exercise for Belgium', *Tijdschrift Vervoerswetenschap*, **30**, 121–38.

Mayeres, I., Ochelen, S. and Proost, S. (1996), 'The marginal external costs of urban transport', *Transportation Research D*, **1**(2), 111–30.

MVA Consultancy, Institute of Transport Studies University of Leeds, Transport Studies Unit University of Oxford (1987), *The Value of Travel Time Savings*, Policy Journals.

Nelson, J.P. (1982), 'Highway noise and property values', *Journal of Transport Economics and Policy*, **16**, 117–32.

Newbery, D.M. (1987), 'Road user charges in Great Britain', CEPR Discussion Paper no. 174, London: Centre for Economic Policy Research.

Newbery, D.M.G. (1988), 'Road user charges in Britain', *The Economic Journal*, **98**, 161–76.
NIS (1990), *Verkeersongevallen op de openbare weg met doden en gewonden, Jaar 1990*, Brussel: NIS.
O'Mahony, M. (1999), 'Speed-flow relationships and the feasibility of road pricing', Chapter 10 in this volume.
Pearce, D.W. and Markandya, A. (1989), *Environmental Policy Benefits: Monetary Valuation*, Paris: OECD.
Peirson, J., Skinner, I. and Vickerman, R. (1994), 'Estimating the External Costs of U.K. Passenger Transport: The First Step Towards an Efficient Transport Market', Discussion paper 94/2, Canterbury: CERTE.
Small, K. and Kazimi, C. (1995), 'On the costs of air pollution from motor vehicles', *Journal of Transport Economics and Policy*, **29**, 7–32.
Steer Davis Gleave (1995), *Transport Modelling in DTI Phase 2 – Final Report*, Dublin: Department of the Environment.
Stratec (1992), *Plan régional des déplacements, Analyse de l'enquête 'Ménages'*, Bruxelles: Région de Bruxelles-Capitale.
UK, Department of Transport (1982), *Urban Public Transport Subsidies: An Economic Assessment of Value for Money. Summary Report*, London: Department of Transport.
UK, Department of Transport (1987), *COBA 9*, London: Department of Transport, Assessments Policy and Methods Division.
US Federal Highway Administration (1982), *Final Report on the Federal Highway Cost Allocation Study*, Washington: USGPO.
VIA (Verkehrswissenshafliches Institut der Ruth-Aachen), final report of the Trenen Project, 12 Dec., 1995.
Vitaliano, D.F. and Held, J. (1991), 'Road Accident External Effects: An Empirical Assessment', *Applied Economics*, **23**, 373–8.

APPENDIX 7A.1 A LIST OF SYMBOLS AND ABBREVIATIONS

CO	Carbon monoxide
CO_2	Carbon dioxide
ESA	Equivalent standard axles
HC	Hydrocarbons
$L_{eq}(dB(A))$	Equivalent noise level
MEAC	Marginal external accident costs
MECC	Marginal external congestion costs
MENC	Marginal external noise costs
MSAC	Marginal social accident costs
NO_x	Nitrogen oxides
PCU	Passenger car units
pkm	Passenger km
PM	Particulate matter

SO_2	Sulphur dioxide
TAC	Total accident costs
TEAC	Total external accident costs
tkm	Tonne km
vkm	Vehicle km
VOC	Volatile organic compounds
VOT	Value of a marginal time saving
$A_{1,j}$, A_2, A_3, A_4	Parameters of the time–flow relationship
ar_{jv}^n	The probability of an accident of type n between transport modes j and v in which j is the victim
ACC_{jv}^n	The number of accidents of type n between modes j and v in which j is the victim
c_A^n	The willingness-to-pay to avoid an accident of type n
c_B^n	The willingness-to-pay of the relatives and friends of the victim to avoid an accident of type n
c_C^n	The pure economic costs of an accident of type n
$el_{(j,v)j}^n$	The elasticity with respect to the number of km driven by mode v of the risk of accidents of type n between mode j and v in which mode j is the victim
K	Correction factor for speed in the noise function
l	The width between façades (in m)
q_i	The traffic flow in million PCU per hour
$s_{i,j}$	The speed of mode j in period i in km/h
$t_{i,j}$	The minutes needed to drive one km by mode j in period i
V_j	The number of vehicle km travelled by mode j
$VOT_{i,j}$	The value of a marginal time saving
$X_{i,j}$	The number of pkm travelled in period i by mode j

APPENDIX 7A.2

Table 7A.1 The time–flow relationship

	Peak period in 2005		Off-peak period in 2005						Elasticity of $t_{i,j}$ w.r.t. 10^6 PCU km	
	10^6 PCU/h	km/h	10^6 PCU/h	km/h	Free-flow km/h	A_2	A_3	A_4	Peak	Off-peak
Urban										
Amsterdam	1.26	14	0.24	36	40	0.940	0.560	1.454	1.46	0.14
Brussels	0.64	23	0.15	49	50	1.198	0.002	9.910	2.50	0.00
Dublin	2.60	21	1.08	36	40	1.418	0.075	1.183	1.70	0.22
London	6.32	28	2.88	33	34	1.739	0.026	0.442	0.58	0.09
Non-urban										
Belgium										
other roads	5.74	57	1.97	72	75	1.183	0.017	0.893	1.38	0.21
highways	10.34	36	3.31	110	115	0.585	0.003	0.339	0.24	0.02
Ireland	3.34	55	1.62	83	96	0.582	0.043	0.744	1.17	0.24

APPENDIX 7A.3

Table 7A.2 Damage estimates (vehicle use only) for a gasoline passenger car in different locations (best estimate) in 10^{-3} Euro(1995)/vkm

	Agglomerations		Urban areas		Extra-urban areas	
	Paris	Stuttgart	Amsterdam	Barnsley	Stuttgart-Mannheim	Tiel drive
Primary PM	53.41	3.73	1.96	4.17	1.1	0.74
SO_2	1.05	0.12	0.10	0.33	0.06	0.07
CO	0.06	0.02	0.02	0.03	0.00	0.00
Cancers	0.33	0.18	0.06	0.76	0.03	0.06
Sulphates	0.66	0.09	0.21	0.26	0.07	0.22
Nitrates	16.14	4.58	1.60	2.76	5.89	2.59
O_3	1.24	0.54	0.51	1.42	0.64	0.83
Global warming	3.58	2.98	3.20	3.48	2.38	2.49
Total	76.47	12.24	7.66	13.21	10.17	7.00

Source: Bickel et al. (1997), p. 101

Table 7A.3 Average emission factors of a gasoline car in g/vkm (including cold start emissions)

	Agglomerations		Urban areas		Extra-urban areas	
	Paris	Stuttgart	Amsterdam	Barnsley	Stuttgart-Mannheim	Tiel drive
Primary PM	0.017	0.009	0.005	0.009	0.005	0.004
NO_x	0.672	0.420	0.336	0.462	0.399	0.559
SO_2	0.038	0.018	0.032	0.031	0.013	0.023
CO	2.580	6.450	9.030	5.805	1.549	0.465
VOC	0.237	0.593	0.890	0.771	0.107	0.086
CO_2	268.24	191.60	210.76	249.08	153.40	168.74

Source: Bickel et al. (1997), p. 71 and p. 102

APPENDIX 7A.4 THE EMISSION FACTORS

1. Passenger Cars

The models distinguish between two types of passenger car technology. In some exercises a distinction is made between cars with standard and improved emission technology. In other exercises cars with normal and increased fuel efficiency are considered. This fuel efficiency is for cars with standard emission technology. We do not distinguish according to emission technology and fuel efficiency simultaneously.

The emissions for passenger cars with standard emission technology and improved emission technology are calculated as follows:

Table 7A.4 ExternE emissions for urban and interregional passenger car traffic (g/vkm)

		NO_x	CO_2	VOC	CO	PM	SO_2
Interregional	Petrol	0.24	153.4	0.044	0.609	0.005	0.013
	Diesel	0.478	120.3	0.049	0.293	0.055	0.117
Urban	Petrol	0.22	191.6	0.252	2.65	0.009	0.018
	Diesel	0.587	137.8	0.138	0.83	0.084	0.15

Source: Bickel et al. (1997), p. 71

From Bickel et al. (1997) we take emissions per vehicle kilometre for the newer cars in the 1996 car stock. For petrol cars, EURO2 cars are used, for diesel cars, the 90s diesel is taken. Table 7A.4 gives the ExternE values. Interregional values are for the Stuttgart-Mannheim drive, urban values for Stuttgart conditions.

Conversion to 2005 emissions is achieved by applying Auto-Oil I scenarios on emission reductions to the ExternE values for 1996. The same methodology is used for urban and interregional transport. The models distinguish standard and improved technology for 2005. Standard technology is assumed to coincide with Auto-Oil I Scenario II, improved technology with Scenario III. Table 7A.5 presents the emission reductions. The average urban and interregional emission factors are adapted to the different case studies by using ExternE ratios (Bickel et al., 1997, p. 102) for different cities and regions.

The resulting emissions still need to be adapted to the model structure. The disaggregation to large and small cars, to occupancy rate and to peak and off-peak traffic is based on the VIA ratios for these criteria (VIA, 1995).

The models make a distinction between vehicles with a standard fuel efficiency and those with an improved fuel efficiency. The standard fuel

Table 7A.5 Auto-Oil I emission reductions for 1996–2010 (in %)

		NO_x	CO_2	VOC	CO	PM	SO_2
Scenario II	Petrol	40	–	40	30	0	–
	Diesel	35	–	20	40	35	–
Scenario III	Petrol	65	–	65	45	0	–
	Diesel	30	–	30	50	50	–

Source: EC (1995), p. 8

Table 7A.6 Fuel consumption with standard and improved fuel efficiency (l/100km, for Brussels 2005)

	Standard fuel efficiency		Improved fuel efficiency	
	Gasoline	Diesel	Gasoline	Diesel
PK.AL.SM	7.118	5.167	4.583	4.480
PK.AL.BG	9.602	6.421	6.182	5.567
PK.PO.SM	7.692	5.472	4.952	4.745
PK.PO.BG	10.040	6.774	6.464	5.874
OF.AL.SM	6.052	3.766	3.896	3.265
OF.AL.BG	7.438	4.818	4.789	4.178
OF.PO.SM	6.394	3.987	4.117	3.457
OF.PO.BG	7.793	5.114	5.017	4.434
Average	7.766	5.190	5.000	4.500

Notes:

PK	Peak	OF	Off-peak
AL	Occupancy rate = 1	PO	Occupancy rate = 2.5
SM	Small car	BG	Large car

efficiency in 2005 is the result of technological progress. There have been proposals by the European Commission to impose minimum fuel efficiency of 5l/100km for gasoline cars and 4.5l/100km for diesel cars by 2005. In the case studies this case is called the improved fuel efficiency case. The computation of emissions from passenger cars with increased fuel efficiency starts from emission factors for cars with standard emission technology, and assumes a direct proportional link between fuel consumption and emissions. This has been investigated in the literature (see Khazzoom, 1995; and Harrington, 1997). The proportionality assumption is justifiable in a static model which compares two cars of average age and with proper maintenance. The disaggregation to car types and other conditions (time of day, occupancy rate) builds on VIA (1995). Table 7A.6 shows the fuel consumption for both fuel efficiency levels.

Given these assumptions, one obtains emission factors for passenger cars in 2005 for different emission technologies and levels of fuel efficiency. Table 7A.7 and Table 7A.8 summarise the emission factors for gasoline and diesel cars used in the urban case studies.

Table 7A.7 The emission factors for gasoline cars – urban case studies (g/vkm; CO_2: kg/vkm)

	NO_x	CO_2	VOC	CO	PM	SO_2
PK.AL.GS.SM.ST	0.108	0.199	0.170	2.003	0.008	0.027
PK.AL.GS.BG.ST	0.152	0.268	0.240	2.917	0.008	0.027
OF.AL.GS.SM.ST	0.096	0.169	0.139	1.239	0.008	0.027
OF.AL.GS.BG.ST	0.133	0.208	0.195	1.808	0.008	0.027
PK.PO.GS.SM.ST	0.119	0.214	0.182	2.105	0.008	0.027
PK.PO.GS.BG.ST	0.166	0.281	0.254	3.039	0.008	0.027
OF.PO.GS.SM.ST	0.104	0.179	0.147	1.301	0.008	0.027
OF.PO.GS.BG.ST	0.142	0.218	0.206	1.911	0.008	0.027
PK.AL.GS.SM.IM	0.063	0.199	0.099	1.576	0.008	0.027
PK.AL.GS.BG.IM	0.089	0.268	0.140	2.299	0.008	0.027
OF.AL.GS.SM.IM	0.056	0.169	0.081	0.974	0.008	0.027
OF.AL.GS.BG.IM	0.078	0.208	0.114	1.423	0.008	0.027
PK.PO.GS.SM.IM	0.070	0.214	0.106	1.652	0.008	0.027
PK.PO.GS.BG.IM	0.097	0.281	0.148	2.388	0.008	0.027
OF.PO.GS.SM.IM	0.061	0.179	0.086	1.022	0.008	0.027
OF.PO.GS.BG.IM	0.083	0.218	0.120	1.499	0.008	0.027
PK.AL.GS.SM.IF	0.070	0.128	0.110	1.290	0.005	0.017
PK.AL.GS.BG.IF	0.098	0.173	0.154	1.879	0.005	0.017
OF.AL.GS.SM.IF	0.062	0.109	0.089	0.798	0.005	0.017
OF.AL.GS.BG.IF	0.086	0.134	0.126	1.165	0.005	0.017
PK.PO.GS.SM.IF	0.077	0.138	0.117	1.355	0.005	0.017
PK.PO.GS.BG.IF	0.107	0.181	0.164	1.957	0.005	0.017
OF.PO.GS.SM.IF	0.067	0.115	0.095	0.838	0.005	0.017
OF.PO.GS.BG.IF	0.092	0.140	0.133	1.231	0.005	0.017

Notes:
PK Peak — OF Off-peak
AL Occupancy rate = 1 — PO Occupancy rate = 2.5
GS Gasoline car
SM Small car — BG Large car
ST Standard 2005 technology, standard fuel efficiency
IM Improved emission technology, standard fuel efficiency
IF Standard 2005 technology, improved fuel efficiency

Table 7A.8 The emission factors for diesel cars – urban case studies (g/vkm; CO_2: kg/vkm)

	NO_x	CO_2	VOC	CO	PM	SO_2
PK.AL.DI.SM.ST	0.311	0.179	0.117	0.431	0.081	0.139
PK.AL.DI.BG.ST	0.498	0.221	0.249	0.875	0.132	0.173
OF.AL.DI.SM.ST	0.243	0.131	0.070	0.340	0.050	0.102
OF.AL.DI.BG.ST	0.353	0.166	0.124	0.732	0.077	0.129
PK.PO.DI.SM.ST	0.319	0.189	0.117	0.444	0.083	0.148
PK.PO.DI.BG.ST	0.512	0.234	0.249	0.875	0.136	0.183
OF.PO.DI.SM.ST	0.249	0.138	0.070	0.366	0.058	0.108
OF.PO.DI.BG.ST	0.364	0.176	0.124	0.718	0.081	0.138
PK.AL.DI.SM.IM	0.239	0.179	0.102	0.498	0.063	0.139
PK.AL.DI.BG.IM	0.383	0.221	0.218	0.498	0.102	0.173
OF.AL.DI.SM.IM	0.187	0.131	0.061	0.498	0.039	0.102
OF.AL.DI.BG.IM	0.271	0.166	0.109	0.498	0.060	0.129
PK.PO.DI.SM.IM	0.245	0.189	0.102	0.498	0.063	0.148
PK.PO.DI.BG.IM	0.394	0.234	0.218	0.498	0.104	0.183
OF.PO.DI.SM.IM	0.192	0.138	0.061	0.498	0.045	0.108
OF.PO.DI.BG.IM	0.280	0.176	0.109	0.498	0.063	0.138
PK.AL.DI.SM.IF	0.270	0.155	0.101	0.374	0.070	0.121
PK.AL.DI.BG.IF	0.432	0.192	0.216	0.759	0.115	0.150
OF.AL.DI.SM.IF	0.211	0.114	0.061	0.294	0.044	0.088
OF.AL.DI.BG.IF	0.306	0.144	0.108	0.634	0.067	0.112
PK.PO.DI.SM.IF	0.276	0.164	0.101	0.385	0.072	0.128
PK.PO.DI.BG.IF	0.444	0.203	0.216	0.759	0.118	0.159
OF.PO.DI.SM.IF	0.216	0.120	0.061	0.317	0.050	0.094
OF.PO.DI.BG.IF	0.315	0.153	0.108	0.623	0.070	0.120

Notes:

PK Peak OF Off-peak
AL Occupancy rate = 1 PO Occupancy rate = 2.5
DI Diesel car
SM Small car BG Large car
ST Standard 2005 technology, standard fuel efficiency
IM Improved emission technology, standard fuel efficiency
IF Standard 2005 technology, improved fuel efficiency

2. Interregional Public Passenger Transport

The emission factors for rail transport are based on VIA (1995), in which emission factors for 1990 are presented. They are assumed not to have changed by 2005. For bus transport the emission factors are calculated on the basis of VIA (1995) and Bickel et al. (1997). For each pollutant the emission factor for a standard diesel car (obtained from Bickel et al., 1997) is multiplied by the ratio of emissions of a bus and a diesel car found in VIA (1995).

Table 7A.9 The emission factors for interregional public passenger transport (g/pkm; kg/pkm for CO_2)

	NO_x	CO_2	VOC	CO	PM	SO_2
Peak bus	0.951	0.021	0.173	0.104	0.008	0.023
Off-peak bus	1.586	0.033	0.281	0.137	0.010	0.035
Peak rail	0.031	0.012	0.001	0.000	0.003	0.048
Off-peak rail	0.061	0.024	0.001	0.000	0.006	0.095

3. Interregional Freight Transport

The basic emission factors for trucks are those of a EURO-II diesel truck (>17t) (Bickel et al., 1997, p. 96). For freight rail and inland navigation they are taken from VIA (1995). For these three transport modes it is assumed that the standard technology in 2005 reduces the emissions per vehicle-km by 35 per cent for NO_x, by 20 per cent for VOC, by 40 per cent for CO and by 35 per cent for PM (cf. Auto-Oil I Scenario II for diesel cars). This results in the following emission factors:

Table 7A.10 The emission factors for interregional freight transport (g/tkm; kg/tkm for CO_2)

	NO_x	CO_2	VOC	CO	PM	SO_2
Peak truck	0.596	0.078	0.033	0.079	0.013	0.035
Off-peak truck	0.479	0.058	0.025	0.046	0.008	0.027
Rail	0.116	0.034	0.006	0.046	0.010	0.032
Inland navigation	0.151	0.044	0.008	0.059	0.013	0.042

APPENDIX 7A.5

Table 7A.11 The marginal external costs in the initial equilibrium – Amsterdam (Euro/vkm)

	Congestion	Air pollution	Noise	Accidents	Total
Passengercar					
PK.GS.SM	1.362	0.024	0.001	0.100	1.486
PK.DI.SM	1.362	0.022	0.001	0.100	1.484
OF.GS.SM	0.045	0.021	0.001	0.161	0.232
Bus					
PK	2.724	0.558	0.010	0.788	4.079
OF	0.090	0.499	0.054	0.738	1.381
Subway	0	0.685	0	0.001	0.693

Notes:
PK Peak OF Off-peak
GS Gasoline DI Diesel
SM Small

Table 7A.12 The marginal external costs in the initial equilibrium – Dublin (Euro/vkm)

	Congestion	Air pollution	Noise	Accidents	Total
Passenger car					
PK.GS.SM	0.454	0.009	0.001	0.033	0.497
PK.DI.SM	0.454	0.037	0.001	0.033	0.525
OF.GS.SM	0.045	0.008	0.001	0.033	0.087
Bus					
PK	0.909	0.025	0.005	0.024	0.963
OF	0.090	0.025	0.011	0.024	0.150
Subway		0.005		0.003	0.008

Notes:
PK Peak OF Off-peak
GS Gasoline DI Diesel
SM Small

Table 7A.13 The marginal external costs in the initial equilibrium – London (Euro/vkm)

	Congestion	Air pollution	Noise	Accidents	Total
Passenger car					
PK.GS.SM	0.204	0.056	0.000	0.033	0.293
PK.DI.SM	0.204	0.201	0.000	0.033	0.438
OF.GS.SM	0.021	0.055	0.000	0.033	0.109
Bus					
PK	0.410	0.027	0.002	0.024	0.463
OF	0.042	0.027	0.004	0.024	0.097
Subway	0	0.007		0.003	0.010

Notes:
PK Peak
GS Gasoline
SM Small
OF Off-peak
DI Diesel

Table 7A.14 The marginal external costs in the initial equilibrium – Ireland (Euro/vkm)

	Congestion	Air pollution	Noise	Accidents	Road damage	Total
Passenger car						
PK.GS.SM	0.252	0.007		0.053		0.312
PK.DI.SM	0.252	0.011		0.053		0.316
OF.GS.SM	0.033	0.008		0.053		0.094
Truck						
PK	0.504	0.157		0.064	0.016	0.741
OF	0.067	0.121		0.064	0.016	0.268

Notes:
PK Peak
GS Gasoline
SM Small
OF Off-peak
DI Diesel

8. External accident costs and the relationship between road accidents and traffic flows

Andrew Dickerson, John Peirson and Roger Vickerman*

8.1 INTRODUCTION

The previous chapter considers the estimation of the marginal external costs of different modes of transport. This short chapter examines one unresolved aspect of the estimation of the external costs of road accidents. The attention devoted to just one aspect of the estimation of the external costs of transport may be justified by the suggested substantial size of road accident external costs[1] and, as will be shown shortly, there being a major problem with previous attempts to estimate these costs.

The process of preparing estimates of the external costs of road accidents is usually divided up into three parts (see, for example, Maddison et al. 1996; Mayeres, Ochelen and Proost, 1996, and Peirson, Skinner and Vickerman, 1998). First, the relationship between road accidents and traffic flows is examined. Second, those parts of accident costs that are external are considered. Finally, values are placed on these externalities. This chapter only examines the first stage in the estimation of road accident externalities, that of identifying the functional relationship between accidents and vehicular flows.

The accident–flow relationship is investigated by matching the UK's Department of Transport's London traffic flow data for the mid-1990s with

* We would like to thank, without implication, the Department of Transport for giving us access to the automatic count data used in this study. Particular thanks are due to Daniel Aromire for his assistance in the provision and explanation of these data. The accident data were supplied by the ESRC Data Archive at the University of Essex. Neither the original collectors of the accident data nor the Archive bear any responsibility for the analyses or interpretations presented here. This research was funded in part by the TRENEN project of the European Commission's Fourth Framework RTD Programme, DG VII (Project ST-96-SC-116).

police data on all road traffic accidents in the corresponding areas during the same period.

8.2 PREVIOUS STUDIES OF ROAD ACCIDENTS AND TRAFFIC FLOWS

It is generally accepted that an additional vehicle imposes an increased risk of an accident on other road users. The increased risk gives rise to important externalities, but the relationship between road accidents and traffic flows is complex and has been the subject of few empirical studies. Maddison et al. (1996, p. 122) noted that 'given the policy relevance of . . . the degree of market failure in road transport, it is unfortunate that not more is known regarding traffic flows and accident rates'. Vitaliano and Held (1991, p. 373) commented that 'there is a significant gap in our understanding of this important facet of highway economics'. The difference between the marginal and average accident rates is usually considered to be the most important determinant of road accident externalities (see Jones-Lee, 1990). Intuitively, this follows from the idea that an additional vehicle imposes an increased risk of an accident on all other vehicles, but the occupants of the additional vehicle only face the average risk of an accident. This intuition is developed into a model of road accidents and traffic flows which is then related to past empirical studies.

It is assumed that all road users are identical, the road network is homogenous and all vehicles are driven in an identical manner whatever the level of traffic flow.[2] An accident is assumed to be caused by two vehicles colliding.[3] Then the probability of any particular vehicle having an accident is proportional to the number of other vehicles on the road, as represented by the traffic flow F. If we denote the constant of proportionality by λ, then consider all possible accidents between two vehicles, the expected total number of accidents, A, is given by (the half occurs because an accident is defined to involve two vehicles):

$$A = \tfrac{1}{2}\lambda F^2$$

An additional vehicle gives rise to λF more expected accidents, that is the marginal risk, but the occupants of the additional vehicle only face the risk to one vehicle, that is, the average risk which is given by $\tfrac{1}{2}\lambda F$. The form of the above function is important since it determines the difference between the marginal accident rate and average accident rate. The divergence between the marginal and average risks represents the extent of the accident externality. The expected value of the externality is given by this difference multiplied by the accident costs for one vehicle in a two-vehicle accident. This derivation of the marginal external accident cost makes the simplifying assumption that the occupants of the additional vehicle fully internalise the risk and all the risk imposed on other road users is not internalised. However, one might expect higher levels of traffic flow to reduce average speeds and make driving behaviour safer (see Bailey, 1970 and Peirson, Skinner and Vickerman, 1998 for a more detailed explanation) and, thus, λ will be a function of traffic flow.

Only a few studies have modelled the relation between road accidents and traffic flow in the context of estimating the consequent road accident externalities. Using simple arithmetical calculations on Californian freeway driving in the early 1960s, Vickrey (1968) suggested that the marginal accident rate was 1.5 times the average rate.

Vitaliano and Held (1991) is one of the few studies that produces econometric estimates of the relationship between road accidents and traffic flows. They used data on annual road accident and traffic flows on segments of urban and rural roads in New York State in 1985. Control variables included the number of lanes, annual snowfall, speed limit, length of road segment studied, and so on, although the slope of the accident–flow relationship was assumed to be constant across all types of roads. They conclude that the relationship between accidents and flows is nearly proportional and thus the external accident effect is close to zero, although when the 19 highest flow observations with more than 50000 vehicles per day were separately analysed, there is some evidence of a small negative external effect. However, it is not possible from their results to determine whether the difference is significantly different from the estimated external effect for the remaining 380 observations.

The empirical studies discussed above can be criticised on two important grounds. First, differences in the accident–flow relation between different types of roads are not distinguished. While some of the differences are random (see Fridstrøm et al., 1995), some are likely to be systematic. Roads have particular characteristics which determine their ability to carry different levels of traffic safely and the relationship between accidents and flows is unlikely to be the same for all road types. Aggregation of data on accidents and flows on different types of roads may seriously bias estimates of the underlying accident–flow relationship. Observations from roads which can only take low flows will typically be associated with a small number of accidents (and thus will be close to the origin), whilst observations from roads designed to take high flows will typically have more accidents. Thus, simple aggregate regression techniques which do not distinguish between road types are likely to produce near-proportional relationships between accidents and traffic flows which will give near equality between the marginal and average accident risk rates.

The second point to be noted is that the previous empirical studies do not yield sufficiently flexible specifications for accident–flow relationships to allow for the possibility that the ratio of the marginal to the average accident rates might vary with traffic flows.

8.3 ESTIMATION OF THE ACCIDENT–FLOW RELATION

8.3.1 Data Description

This study amalgamates two data sets on accidents and vehicular flow for London over the period July 1993 to December 1995. The data on hourly vehicular flows have been generously provided by the Department of Transport from their automatic data recorders at 54 representative sites spread throughout the London boroughs. These flow data consist of more than 2 million hourly observations.

The data on accidents are taken from the Road Accident Data deposited at the ESRC Data Archive by the Department of Transport Road Accident Statistics Branch. These data record every accident and its circumstances occurring on the public highway where at least one road vehicle and one casualty are involved. From these data, we select the 96 440 accidents that occurred within the area and during the period covered by the automatic count data.

These two sources of data have different units of observation, and can be amalgamated in a number of ways. We choose to use year–month–hour as our basic time dimension on which to merge the two datasets – so that each observation in the combined dataset comprises the total number of accidents, A_{hmy}, that occurred in a particular hour, h, in a given month, m, and year, y, together with the average vehicular flow, F_{hmy}, in that year–month–hour from the automatic count data.[4] We also investigate the sensitivity of our results to this particular choice of unit of observation.

8.3.2 Econometric Analysis of the Accident–Flow Relationship

The previous section argues that the formulation of the accident–flow relationship should be capable of allowing for differences between road types and for variations in the ratio of the marginal to average risk rates. Some preliminary evidence on the necessity of the former can be obtained from Figure 8.1 which plots the total number of accidents against the average vehicular flow, where both total accidents A_{hmy} and average flows F_{hmy} are calculated separately for four different road classifications (A-roads, B-roads, C-roads and Unclassified roads[5]) and are also classified by area into Inner London and Outer London.[6] Figure 8.1 reveals that there are groups of observations and these can be seen to correspond to different road–area categories as shown in Figure 8.2. Graphically, the marginal accident–flow relation corresponds to the local slope of the relationship between accidents and vehicle flows while the average accident rate corresponds to the slope of the line that connects the origin to the data. Figure 8.2 clearly reveals important differences in the marginal and average accident rates according to different road types and area.

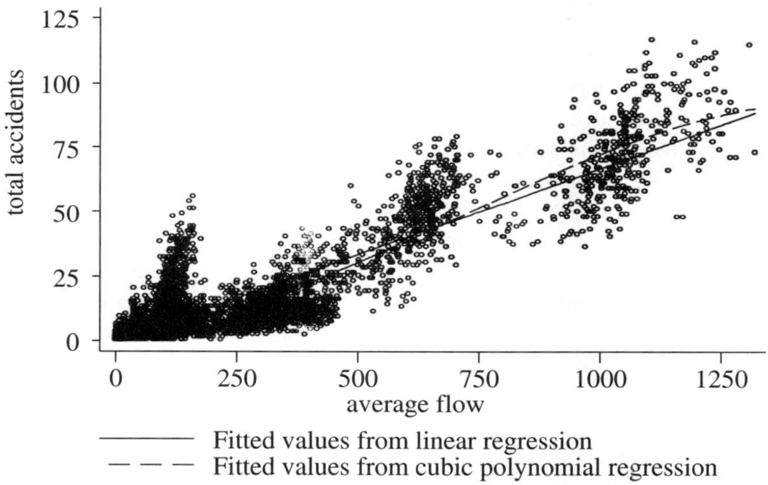

Figure 8.1 Accidents vs flows: aggregated

If the evidence is examined at an aggregate level, differences in the road-area accident–flow relationship may well result in an erroneous conclusion. Figures 8.1 and 8.2 together suggest that while the aggregate relationship is near proportional, the disaggregated relationships appear different from one another and are non-linear. Superimposed on Figure 8.1 are the fitted values from linear and cubic polynomial regressions.[7] These regressions indicate that the average and marginal accident rates are very similar and fairly constant, confirming the results of previous studies and from which one might easily conclude that the accident externality is negligible. Dickerson, Peirson and Vickerman (1998) show more formally that the accident–flow relationships are statistically different between the various road and area classifications depicted in Figure 8.2.

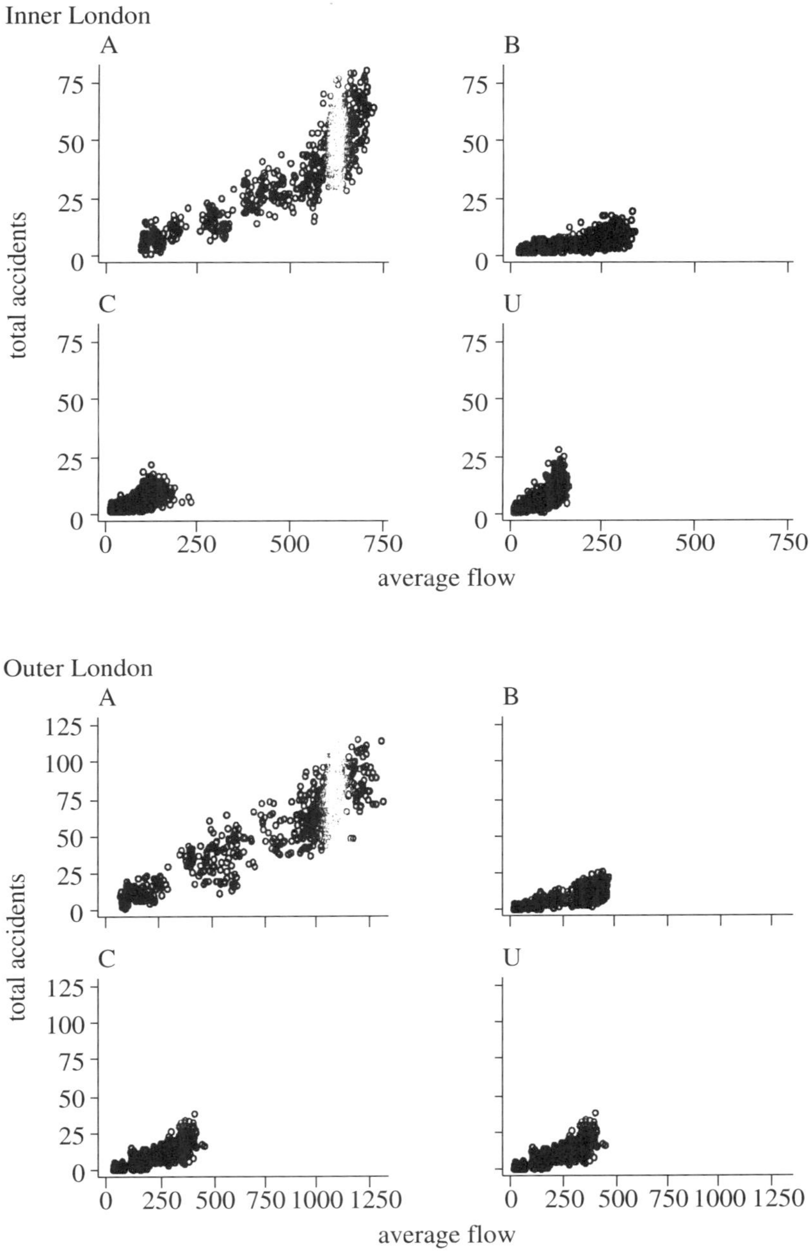

Figure 8.2 *Accidents vs flows: disaggregated*

In the disaggregated econometric analysis of the accident–flow relationship, we utilise a semi-parametric specification – namely piecewise linear splines – to estimate the different area and road class accident–flow relationships. This approach has the advantage that it gives continuity in the accident–flow relationship without imposing a functional form, whilst also allowing the average and marginal rates to be directly calculated. The specification is superior to a simple polynomial representation of the accident–flow relationships on two counts. First, polynomial specifications are very sensitive to observations at the ends of the data range (see, for example, Royston and Altman, 1994a). Even fractional polynomial estimation is not immune to such end-effect and/or outliers (Royston and Altman, 1994b). Second, a polynomial specification does not allow the mathematical relationship between marginal and average accident rates to vary in an unrestricted manner with traffic flow.

Following the above preliminary analysis, we estimate separate spline functions for each road–area combination. Visual inspection of the data, together with some pre-testing, indicates that three spline segments (that is two nodes) are sufficient. The results from estimating the spline functions are illustrated in Figure 8.3 – full details of the regressions for the eight road–area types can be found in Dickerson, Peirson and Vickerman (1998). All eight estimated regressions pass a standard RESET test for misspecification, and thus can be regarded as econometrically satisfactory. As can be seen, the third segment in each road–area classification typically has a slope greater than that of the first two segments, and thus at high flows, the marginal rate is greater than the average rate.[8] In order to show the difference between the marginal and average accident rates at different flows, Table 8.1 tabulates the marginal accident rate, M (the slope of each spline segment), the average accident rate, A (evaluated at the mid-point of each spline segment), and the ratio of the marginal to average accident rate, M/A, for each road–area combination.

The results confirm what is apparent in Figure 8.3. For low-to-moderate traffic flows on each road–area classification, the marginal and average accident rates are approximately equal, and hence the ratio of the marginal to average rate is close to unity. This indicates that there is a negligible accident externality at low-to-moderate traffic flows. However, at high flows, the M/A ratio is considerably greater than unity for almost all road–area classifications, indicating that there are substantial accident externalities at high traffic flow rates. It is only by allowing the M/A ratio to differ by traffic flow that this relationship becomes apparent. Moreover, a three-segment piecewise linear spline function applied to the aggregated data depicted in Figure 8.1 actually indicates a *falling* M/A ratio at high flows. This confirms the danger in using aggregated accident–flow relationships to estimate the degree of accident externality.

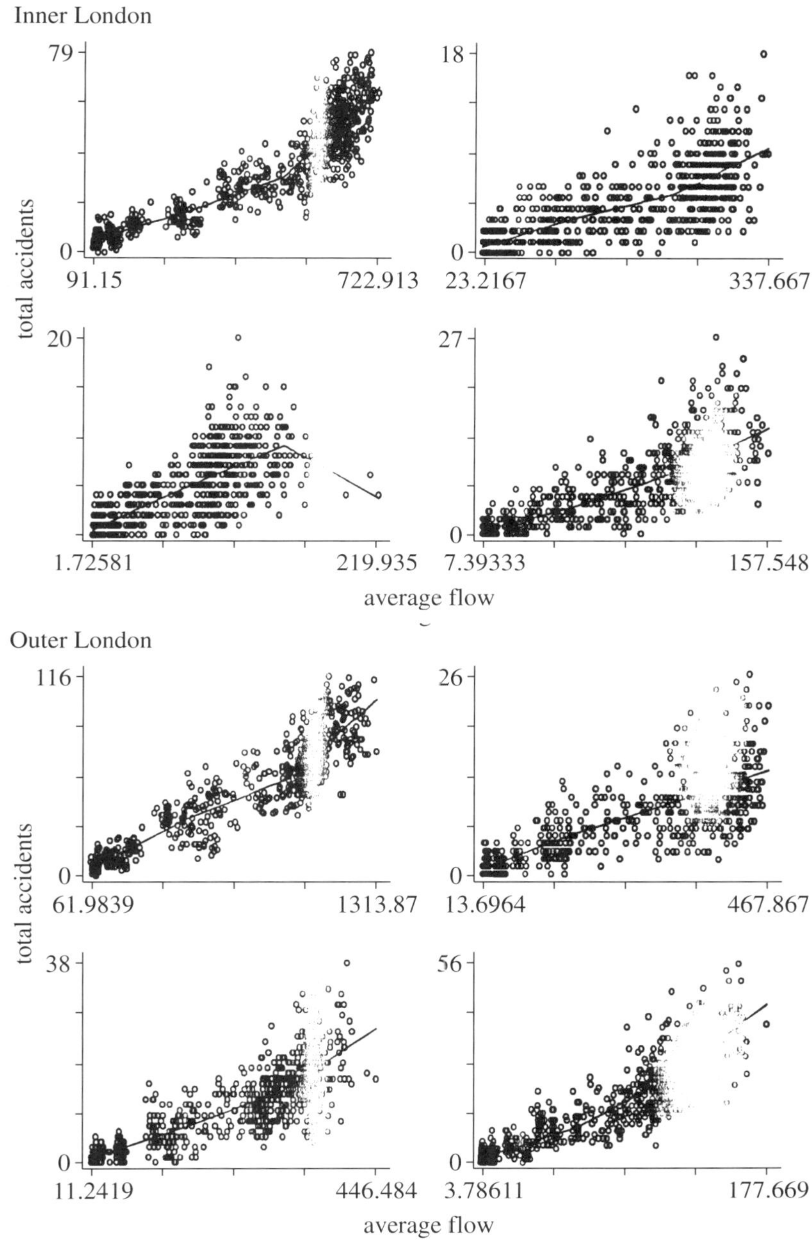

Figure 8.3 Accidents vs flows: piecewise linear splines

Table 8.1 Estimates of the marginal and average accident risk

			Spline Segment		
Road	area		(1) low flow	(2) moderate	(3) high flow
A	inner	M	0.0540	0.0648	0.1674
		A	0.0549	0.0572	0.0773
		M/A	0.9845	1.1325	2.1654
A	outer	M	0.0686	0.0521	0.1134
		A	0.0721	0.0650	0.0717
		M/A	0.9521	0.8023	1.5820
B	inner	M	0.0253	0.0198	0.0400
		A	0.0252	0.0237	0.0260
		M/A	1.0051	0.8374	1.5405
B	outer	M	0.0315	0.0257	0.0280
		A	0.0343	0.0307	0.0292
		M/A	0.9178	0.8378	0.9585
C	inner	M	0.0595	0.0572	−0.0741
		A	0.0717	0.0629	0.0347
		M/A	0.8309	0.9089	−2.1378
C	outer	M	0.0417	0.0463	0.0823
		A	0.0470	0.0451	0.0525
		M/A	0.8868	1.0268	1.5670
U	inner	M	0.0663	0.0896	0.1267
		A	0.0652	0.0730	0.0863
		M/A	1.0169	1.2284	1.4686
U	outer	M	0.1445	0.2462	0.3555
		A	0.1731	0.1873	0.2316
		M/A	0.8346	1.3144	1.5353

Notes: M denotes marginal risk; A denotes average risk; M/A is the ratio of the marginal to average risk

Finally, the robustness of our results to the chosen aggregation methodology was examined. Clearly there are differences in traffic flows by time of day, and one might suspect there to be differences in accident rates according to the season of the year (due to driving conditions and daylight hours). If these differences systematically impinge upon accidents and traffic flows, then they represent omitted factors from our analysis, while if they are completely stochastic influences, they will only affect the error variances. In order to assess the importance of time of day and seasonal effects, we re-estimate the spline functions using a fixed-effects panel estimator. Our fixed effects are all twenty combinations of five time-of-day periods (am-peak, inter-peak, pm-peak, evening and night) and four seasons (spring, summer, autumn and winter). The results are qualitatively similar to those in Table 8.1. In particular, the marginal to average risk ratio is increasing in traffic flows, and at high flows there is a clear accident externality with the M/A ratio in excess of unity.[9]

8.4 CONCLUSIONS

The relationship between accidents and traffic flows is not well understood and past studies have suggested that there is a negligible road accident externality. The present study finds that there are important differences in the accident–flow relationships between different types of roads and geographical areas. Our results indicated that while there is a near-proportional relationship at low-to-moderate traffic flows, the marginal accident rate rises above the average rate at higher traffic flows. This implies that there is a substantial road accident externality at high traffic flows.

These results have important implications for transport policy. Such policy should take account of the fact that the magnitude of road accident externalities varies between road classifications, geographical areas and traffic flows. In particular, policies which attempt to internalise accident externalities, for example through road pricing, need to be carefully devised (see CEC, 1996). Our results parallel the findings on congestion externalities in that only at high traffic flows is there a large external accident cost (see Maddison et al. 1996; Newbery, 1988).

It should be noted that our analysis does not distinguish between the severity of road accidents. As traffic flows increase, the distribution of accidents types between slight, severe and fatal accidents may shift towards less serious accidents. Thus, though the marginal accident rate may be increasing at high flows, the marginal accident *cost* may be constant or even decreasing. We intend to investigate this possibility in future work.

NOTES

1. For the United Kingdom, the annual total costs have been estimated at between £5 billion and £26 billion (see Maddison et al., 1996; Pearce, 1993; Fowkes, Nash and Tweddle, 1990; Hopkins and O'Reilly, 1993; Hansson and Marckham, 1992 and Newbery, 1988).
2. This model is in the spirit of Newbery (1987, 1988), Jansson (1994) and Peirson, Skinner and Vickerman (1998).
3. Approximately two-thirds of all road accidents involve two vehicles (calculation from Department of Transport *Road Accident Data 1992–1995*).
4. Note that we cannot match the two data sources by location since accidents are only located on a road *class* within a borough rather than at an exact location in order to retain the confidentiality of the victims. Moreover, even if the geographical location of each accident was known, each would only ever be in the vicinity of any one of the limited

number of automatic count sites. However, our methodology is able to accommodate any spatial mismatch between accidents and flow as we discuss below.

5. A, B, C and Unclassified roads correspond loosely to major trunk roads and through routes, secondary through roads, minor roads and residential streets respectively, although, for practical reasons, the distinction between the latter two categories is not always clear.
6. We choose to disaggregate on these two dimensions of the data since accident rates and traffic flows differ substantially across both road classification and area.
7. The econometric methodology should really take account of the fact that the number of accidents is bounded below by zero. However, only 7 per cent of our observations have zero accidents and hence we restrict ourselves to ordinary least squares estimation.
8. The exception is C-roads in Inner London where the third segment is actually downward sloping. This is purely a site-specific problem in that we only have one representative site for this particular road–area combination and thus the results for this road–area classification should perhaps be treated with some caution. The distribution of the 54 sites between road types and area is as follows:

	Road classification			
area	A-roads	B-roads	C-roads	U-roads
inner	13	2	1	7
outer	21	2	2	6

Hence, the results for A-roads and Unclassified-roads are based on traffic flows averaged across rather more sites than those for B-roads and C-roads and thus can perhaps be regarded with greater confidence, although the Department of Transport chooses the sites for its automatic recorders to be representative of traffic flows throughout London.

9. The key difference is that the estimated M/A ratios are typically significantly less than unity at low traffic flow rates. This would appear to be due to the fact that low flows are almost exclusively associated with the night period, and thus the lower accident rates at low flows are more properly due to a fixed night effect rather than associated with low traffic flows.

REFERENCES

Bailey, M. (1970), 'Comment on Vickrey's Paper', in J. Margolis (ed.), *Analysis of Public Output*, New York: NBER, pp. 336–8.

CEC (1996), *Towards Fair and Efficient Pricing in Transport: Policy Options for Internalising the External Costs of Transport in the European Union*, COM (95) 691 Final Report, Brussels.

Department of Transport Road Accident Statistics Branch, *Road Accident Data 1992–1995* (computer file) Colchester, Data Archive.

Dickerson, A., Peirson, J. and Vickerman, R. (1998), 'Road Accidents and Traffic Flows: An Econometric Investigation', Department of Economics Discussion Paper 98/9, University of Kent, England.

Fowkes, A.S., Nash, C.A. and Tweddle, G. (1990), 'The Track and External Costs of Road Transport', ITS Working Paper 312, University of Leeds.

Fridstrøm, L., Ifver, J., Ingebrigtsen, S., Kulmala, R. and Thomsen, L.K. (1995), 'Measuring the contribution of randomness, exposure, weather, and daylight to the variation in road accident counts', *Accident Analysis and Prevention*, **27**, 1–20.

Hansson, L. and Marckham, J. (1992), *Internalisation of External Effects in Transportation*, Paris: UIC.
Hopkins, M. and O'Reilly, D. (1993), 'Revaluation of the Cost of Road Accident Casualties: 1992 revision', Crowthorne: TRL RR378, Transport Research Laboratory.
Jansson, J.O. (1994), 'Accident externality charges', *Journal of Transport Economics and Policy*, **28**, 31–43.
Jones-Lee, M.W. (1990), 'The value of transport safety', *Oxford Review of Economic Policy*, **6**, 39–60.
Maddison, D., Pearce, D., Johansson, O., Calthrop, E., Litman, T. and Verhoef, E. (1996), *Blueprint 5: The True Costs of Road Transport*, London: Earthscan.
Mayeres I., Ochelen, S. and Proost, S. (1996), 'The marginal external costs of urban transport', *Transportation Research, Part D – Transport and Environment*, **1**, 111–30.
Newbury, D. (1987), 'Road User Charges in Britain', Centre for Economic Policy Research, Discussion Paper 174, April 1987.
Newbery, D. (1988), 'Road User Charges in Britain', *Economic Journal*, **98**, 161–76.
Pearce, D.W. (1993), *Blueprint 3: Measuring Sustainable Development*, London: Earthscan.
Peirson, J., Skinner, I. and Vickerman, R. (1998), 'The microeconomic analysis of the external costs of road accidents', *Economica*, **65**, 429–40.
Royston, P. and Altman, D.G. (1994a), 'Regression using fractional polynomials of continuous: parsimonious parametric modelling', *Applied Statistics*, **43**, 429–67.
Royston, P. and Altman, D.G. (1994b), 'Using fractional polynomials to model curved regression relationships', *Stata Technical Bulletin*, **21**, 11–23.
Vickrey, W. (1968), 'Automobile accidents, tort law, externalities and insurance: an economist's critique', *Journal of Contemporary Law and Problems*, 464–84.
Vitaliano, D.F. and Held, J. (1991), 'Road Accident External Effects: An Empirical Assessment', *Applied Economics*, **23**, 373–8.

9. Computation of the internal costs of transport in the model

John Peirson and Roger Vickerman

9.1 INTRODUCTION

The major purpose of the models used in this book is to investigate the welfare effects of policies that improve the pricing of passenger and freight transport. The investigation of these welfare effects requires data on the demand, supply and internal and external costs of transport with which to calibrate the transport models and investigate the effects of different transport policies. This chapter considers the estimation of the internal costs that are required as input for the models. We start with some conceptual issues in Section 9.2. Then an overview is given of different methods for estimating the various internal cost components (Section 9.3). In a fourth section we review the methods used for the purpose of this book. Finally, a conclusion follows.

9.2 INTERNAL COST INPUTS: SOME CONCEPTUAL ISSUES

The models require estimates of the marginal resource cost of the supply of the different transport modes. Unless otherwise noted all models assume linear cost functions for all transport modes. In other words, costs are described by a fixed cost and a constant marginal resource cost. For convenience, we take the term 'resource cost' as referring to the 'marginal resource cost' from hereafter.

The models take the infrastructure of each transport mode as given. Thus, infrastructure costs are a sunk fixed cost and should not appear in the estimates of resource cost. For both private and public transport, additional demand for transport requires a proportionate increase in the provision of vehicles/trains/buses/trams and so on. It is assumed that the existing average occupancy rates and load rates for freight are maintained. As discussed in Chapter 4, increased/decreased service frequencies increases/ decreases demand as waiting times are reduced/increased. These effects are explicitly allowed for.

Conceptually, the resource cost of a unit of transport can be defined in two ways:

(i) Resource Cost = Consumer Price − Tax + Subsidy − Abnormal Profit
(ii) Resource Cost = Sum of Individual Components of Resource Cost (fuel, capital, labour, . . .)

The approaches leading from the two definitions may be characterised as top down and bottom up, respectively. In the former approach, the overall price for the input is taken and adjusted to give the resource cost. In the latter approach, each component of the resource cost is identified and estimated. The resource cost is the sum of the different individual components.

The two definitions are in theory equivalent but in practice require different approaches. The first definition requires information on consumer prices, tax, subsidies and abnormal profit. The first three types of data are straightforward and may be easily available. It is correct to include normal profit in the measure of resource costs as this reflects the opportunity cost of capital. However, profits above the normal rate of return inflates the price measure of the resource cost. Deduction of abnormal profits is necessary to get the correct measure. However, in reality this is difficult to achieve; therefore, we make the typical but strong assumption that the supply of transport services is in the long-run perfectly competitive equilibrium. In these circumstances, there are no abnormal profits.

In practice, the top-down approach may not be feasible as the consumer price does not directly relate to the resource cost. Thus, in the case of private car travel there is no identifiable price of passenger transport and the price has to be constructed from the individual components of car travel. In the case of public transport, the consumer price of peak travel does not usually directly relate to the capital cost of trains/buses/trams and again the resource cost has to be constructed using the bottom-up approach. For these reasons, the bottom-up approach is the preferred method for estimating the internal costs. Of course, this requires information on all the different elements of costs in the resource cost. This information is not always publicly available and specific research has to be carried out to identify the costs (for an example, see Department of Transport, 1996).

With both approaches it is necessary to remove all taxes and subsidies from resource cost estimates. However, it is very difficult to remove income and social security taxes. The resource cost inputs that are used in the empirical models in this book take labour supply as fixed and the full burden of income and social security taxes are borne by labour. As the supply of labour is fixed, its resource cost is the opportunity cost of labour in terms of foregone production. In perfect competition, this foregone production is measured by the gross wage paid by producers to labour. Therefore, given the assumption of a fixed supply of labour, income and social security taxes are not removed from prices in the estimation of resource costs. The assumption of not adjusting for income and social security taxes, but removing indirect taxes and subsidies, means that inputs used in the model can be regarded as producer prices.

Finally, note that the models consider the resource cost of transport in terms of cost (measured in EURs) per passenger kilometre for passenger travel and cost per tonne kilometre for freight (measured in EURs).

9.3 DIFFERENT APPROACHES TO ESTIMATING THE COST OF TRANSPORT

Waters (1997) has identified and examined three different approaches to the estimation of the costs of transport, namely accounting, engineering and statistical approaches.

The accounting approach uses existing accounting cost data on the output of transport services to estimate resource costs. This approach is simple and cheap to use. However, three problems are identified with the approach. First, the reported cost of assets may be a historical cost or a book value that does not reflect the true opportunity cost. Second, the accounting process may not distinguish between costs that vary with output and those that do not. Thus, it is not possible to estimate accurately true marginal resource costs and fixed costs. Third, the costs may be so aggregated that it is not possible to identify the costs of a particular output, for example the cost of peak transport. These issues suggest that methods relying on accounting cost data should not be followed.

The second approach consists of relating inputs to outputs (consider, for example, the relation between vehicle speed and fuel consumption) following a theoretical engineering approach; alternatively, it can be based on empirical observation. The inputs are then valued to determine the cost of the output. The potential problem with this approach is one of time and cost. It is probably the preferred method to determine the internal costs of transport.

The final approach is that of statistically estimating the relation between output and cost. The latter is typically accounting information, though it may be sufficiently disaggregated to ensure that it confirms with economic definitions of appropriate cost variables. However, there are problems with the availability of suitable data, differences between short- and long-run costs and definitions of variables. Quinet (1993, p. 38) concluded that 'econometrics provides only approximate indicators . . . of the probable structure of the [costs] under consideration'. Thus, to the extent possible the use of statistical studies to estimate the internal cost inputs for the models was avoided in this book.

9.4 ESTIMATION OF RESOURCE COSTS

9.4.1 Estimation of Resource Costs of Private Transport

The urban and interregional models separate out different types of private transport (small or large cars; gasoline or diesel fuel; cars driven alone or with passengers; and standard or improved technology). The different components of resource costs are estimated for each of the different types of private transport.

The definition of large and small cars varies slightly between countries depending on the most useful categorisation that made groups of appropriate sizes. For gasoline cars, the standard technology is a three-way catalytic converter and the improved technology contains a pre-heated three-way catalytic converter. The improved technology reduces the emissions for urban car use. For diesel cars, the standard technology is direct fuel injection, a turbo supercharger, exhaust gas recirculation and charge cooling. The improved diesel technology adds a particulates filter to the standard technology. When appropriate, the following discussion does not always distinguish between the different types.

In general, the private resource costs for a given transport service are defined as:

Private Transport Resource Costs = occupants' time + fuel + implicit capital cost of car + depreciation + parking + other costs (maintenance, oil, tyres and so on)

Transport costs consist clearly of material resource costs and time costs. The determination of average and marginal time costs was dealt with in Chapters 4 and 5. In this section the focus is on the other cost elements.

The fuel resource cost is estimated by considering the resource cost of a litre of fuel and the fuel used in travelling one vehicle-kilometre. The fuel use per kilometre varies by type of vehicle and by speed. It is desirable, but complicated, to incorporate how fuel resource costs vary with speed (for example see Rouwendal, 1996). In the empirical models we distinguish between the fuel consumption rates for the peak and off-peak periods, but within these periods fuel use is assumed to be fixed for each type of private transport.

The specification of capital costs associated with the use of a car is complex. We treat infrastructure costs as a sunk fixed cost that should, therefore, not appear in the estimates of resource cost. It is assumed that the average use of private vehicles remains constant. Thus, additional demand for private transport requires a proportionate increase in the ownership of vehicles. It is further assumed that the existing average occupancy and kilometres per vehicle rates are maintained.

Car capital costs have to be allocated to off-peak and peak use. Unlike public transport, where non-use-related capital costs should be charged to the peak period, the situation is more complicated in the case of car capital costs. A car provides the joint products of off-peak and peak travel. As we use aggregate models, the natural assumption is made that in both off-peak and peak periods capital costs of cars are allocated proportionately with the number of vehicle-kilometres to these periods. This gives a fixed capital cost per vehicle-kilometre, whether travel is in the peak or off-peak period.

The implied annual cost of the capital value of a private vehicle is the discount rate multiplied by the present capital value. The estimated capital value of a private vehicle must allow for indirect taxes on the initial purchase of the vehicle, for example value added tax, and the depreciation in the value of the car across time. The capital value of each type of vehicle is estimated for each year of the life of the vehicle and the average capital value calculated. For a particular type of vehicle, examples of particular makes of car are used to estimate the initial resource value and the value in succeeding years. The product of this average value and the discount rate gives the implied average annual capital cost. The average annual depreciation is calculated similarly. The sum of these two values gives the total annual capital cost. Division of this estimate by the estimated annual number of vehicle-kilometres gives the capital cost per vehicle-kilometre. It is important to avoid the double counting of depreciation in the calculation of the capital and operating costs of cars.

For urban private transport, the price and resource cost of parking can be large parts of the overall price or cost of a trip. Additionally, many car-users park free and thus receive a substantial subsidy. Parking resource costs per passenger-kilometre vary greatly between insiders and outsiders as the latter usually travel significantly greater distances. Information on parking prices and costs is limited, in spite of its importance in price and resource cost of urban private transport (see Calthrop, Proost and Van Dender, 2000). Estimation of prices and cost is complicated by the availability of very different types of parking, for example on street, multi-storey, employer provision, and so on.

The other resource costs of private vehicles include the cost of oil, tyres, maintenance and insurance. These costs depend on the type of vehicle and are estimated net of indirect taxes. They may be either reported net of indirect taxes (for example see Department of Transport, 1996), or the adjustment may have to be estimated.

Finally, note that road maintenance and capital costs were ignored in the definition of the private marginal resource cost of vehicle use. These costs are clearly important for investment analyses, and they are known to strongly vary between countries (for example, see Newbery, 1989; Hansson and Markham (1992) and Skarstad, Thune-Larsen and Lea, 1992). For the purpose of optimal pricing of transport services, as studied in this book, they are not very relevant. First, road capital costs are not marginal costs. Second, road maintenance costs do not affect private transport decisions by individual travellers. These costs should be allocated to vehicles on the basis of use-related damage, and they are typically considered an external cost. In general, since heavy vehicles cause most of such damage, these costs are therefore ignored for private cars; for heavy vehicles, they are treated as an external cost.

9.4.2 Estimation of the Resource Cost of Public Transport

The resource costs of public transport are different from those of private transport for two important reasons. First, there are large economies of scale in the provision of public transport. Second, the provision of public transport is a multi-output product with peak and off-peak travel. For these reasons, the total resource costs were approximated as:

Total Resource Costs of Public Transport = Fixed Cost + Resource Cost in Peak · Peak Volume + Resource Cost in Off-peak · Off-Peak Volume

The specification of the fixed cost approximates the economies of scale in the provision of public transport. London Transport (1992) estimated large economies of scale in providing underground public transport. Their estimates suggest that marginal operating costs per passenger-kilometre are about 20 per cent of the average cost. McGeehan (1993) estimated that, for the railway system in Eire, the ratio of the marginal to average variable cost is about one half. The fixed costs for bus and coach travel are usually considered to be relatively less. As with private transport, the infrastructure costs are taken as given and, thus, the resource costs do not include any part of these sunk fixed costs.

The vehicle resource cost of peak public transport is:

Peak Vehicle Resource Costs of Public Transport = Capital Cost + Depreciation Unrelated to Use + Use Related Depreciation + Driver Time + Cost of Fuel + Other Costs

The models assume constant occupancy rates that are different for the peak and off-peak periods. Changes in the peak demand for each of the public transport modes are met by proportionately equal changes in the service frequencies, so maintaining the occupancy rates. The estimates of peak resource costs of additional peak use of public transport include these additional capital costs. Typically, these capital costs are taken from the vehicle and carriage asset values of the companies providing rolling stock. Using the assumption that the existing vehicles and carriages are optimally adjusted to the level of peak demand, then multiplication of the capital value of these assets by the discount rate gives the annual capital cost of the vehicles and carriages.

The depreciation unrelated to use of the vehicles and carriages is added to the above annual capital cost. Deprecation related to use is apportioned between the peak and off-peak according to number of vehicle-kilometres.

The total capital and depreciation costs are normalised by division through by the number of vehicle peak kilometres. Cost per passenger-kilometre are estimated by simple division by the peak occupancy rate.

Turning to the other resource costs, the cost for the peak period is estimated on the basis of vehicle-kilometres. The driving time taken for a bus/train and so on to travel one kilometre is estimated and multiplied by the appropriate wage rate (for example normal or overtime rate) to give the value of driving time per vehicle-kilometre. The fuel cost per vehicle-kilometre is also estimated.

The vehicle resource cost of off-peak public transport is:

Off-peak Vehicle Resource Costs of Public Transport = Use Related Depreciation + Driver Time + Cost of Fuel + Other Costs

A major issue in the estimation of internal costs and the frequency of service is the optimal adjustment of service provision. In the case of buses, coaches, railways, and so on, the price and frequency of service both determine demand (for example, see Wardman, 1995, and TRRL, 1980, for estimates of service elasticities). The models in this book adjust demand to service frequencies through allowing service frequencies to determine waiting times and, thus, the generalised price.

The fixed costs of public transport are computed through taking the difference of total costs and the total marginal costs (including both peak and off-peak costs).

9.4.3 Freight Internal Costs

The internal costs of freight transport can be considered in a very similar manner to the internal costs for bus and rail passenger travel. The equations for and explanations of the resource costs, fixed costs and non-infrastructure costs are identical. The costs are defined in terms of EURs per tonne kilometre.

It should be noted that in the urban models only road freight is considered. Road freight is transported by small or large trucks. In the case of the interregional model road, rail and inland waterways are considered. By comparison with the cost definition of bus and rail passenger travel, occupancy rates are replaced by average freight carried rates.

9.5 CONCLUSION

The use of the numerical optimisation models requires that the marginal resource and capital costs of transport be clearly separated out and appropriately allocated. This apparently simple process is complicated and difficult in practice. Accurate data is not always available and simplifications or approximations are sometimes necessary. Where possible, the internal cost inputs for the models were taken from good engineering studies of the resource and capital costs which were related to the output of transport services.

REFERENCES

Calthrop, E., Proost, S. and Van Dender, K. (2000), 'Parking policies and road pricing', *Urban Studies*, **37**(1), 63–76.

Department of Transport (1996 and revisions), *COBA 10*, London: Department of Transport.

Goodwin, P. (1996), 'The real effects of "environmental friendly" transport policies', ESRC Conference on the Transport and the Environment, March 1996, London.

Hansson, L. and Markham, J. (1992), *The Internalisation of the External Effects in Transportation*, Stockholm and Paris: UIC-C6, Strategic Planning Committee.

London Transport (1992), *Estimating LUL's Marginal Costs*, October 1992.

McGeehan, H. (1993), 'Railway costs and productivity growth', *Journal of Transport Economics and Policy*, **27**, 19–32.

Newbery, D.M. (1989), 'Cost recovery from optimally designed roads', *Economica*, **56**, 165–85.

Quinet, E. (1993), 'Transport between Monopoly and Competition: Supply Side and Markets', in J. Polak and A. Heerte (eds), *European Transport Economics*, Oxford: Blackwell.

Rouwendal, J. (1996), 'An economic analysis of fuel use per kilometre by private cars', *Journal of Transport Economics and Policy*, **30**, 3–14.

Skarstad, O., Thune-Larsen, H. and Lea, R. (1992), *NSBs Road Use Costs*, Oslo: TOI Report 140/1992.

Transport and Road Research Laboratory (1980), *The Demand for Public Transport*, TRRL.

Wardman, M. (1995), 'Forecasting the impact of service quality changes on the demand for inter-urban rail travel', *Journal of Transport Economics and Policy*, **28**, 287–306.

Waters, W.G. III (1997), 'Statistical Costing in Transportation', in T.H. Oum et al. (eds), *Transport Economics: Selected Readings*, Netherlands: Harwood Press.

10. Speed–flow relationship and feasibility of road-pricing technology

Margaret O'Mahony and K.J. Kirwan

10.1 INTRODUCTION

This chapter is divided into two parts. In the first, the research into selecting the most appropriate speed–flow relationship for use in the development of the TRENEN models is described. The selected function type was used in all of the applications. In the second part of the chapter the current state-of-the-art in road-use pricing is summarised including indications of likely future developments and uses of technology. The final part of the chapter describes a road-use pricing trial underway in Dublin which is using the TRENEN evaluations of external costs as the road-use charging levels.

10.2 SPEED–FLOW RELATIONSHIP RESEARCH OBJECTIVES

The first objective was to quantify the external costs of congestion for which it was necessary to obtain a function describing the relationship between average speed on an urban network and the overall level of demand for car travel. The second objective was to examine the possibility of estimating the function from network parameters, such as, for example, junction capacities and number of junctions per unit length of network.

10.2.1 Link-based Speed–flow Relationships

Link-based speed–flow relationships have been used mainly in engineering studies and for economic cost–benefit analysis. The relationships describe speeds and associated time costs at each level of traffic flow and are usually defined for road sections of homogeneous properties with few junctions. The Highway Capacity Manual (TRB, 1992) outlines the standard approach for deriving this type of speed–flow relationship. Dewees (1979) found that such a relationship for non-homogeneous roads with a significant number of junctions per unit length can be difficult to determine.

In addition to speed and flow, another variable often used to describe flow characteristics is density. Density is normally defined as the average number of vehicles occupying a unit length of a roadway at any given instant. A typical speed–density function is presented in Figure 10.1.

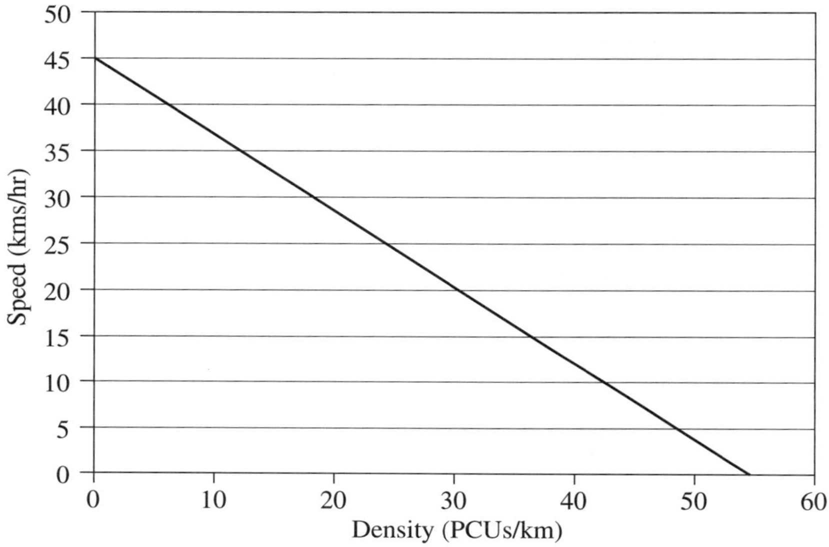

Figure 10.1 Speed–density relationship for a single link (O'Flaherty, 1979)

Traffic flow is generally defined as the number of vehicles that pass over a given section of roadway for some specified period. It can be calculated by multiplying the speed by the density. From Figure 10.1 the speed–flow relationship presented in Figure 10.2 can be produced. The relationship is quadratic by nature where the highest speed is achieved at free-flow and low flow levels. As flow increases, speed decreases up to a point of maximum flow (F_{max}). The relationship then displays backward bending indicating a region of instability in highly congested conditions. The interpretation of this part of the curve continues to be a subject of debate (Evans, 1992 and Hills, 1993).

Travel cost is usually calculated from travel times and in that context an inverse of the speed–flow relationship is more useful for use in our models. Such a function is presented in Figure 10.3. The time taken to travel one kilometre will be referred to as unit-time and will be measured in minutes per kilometre.

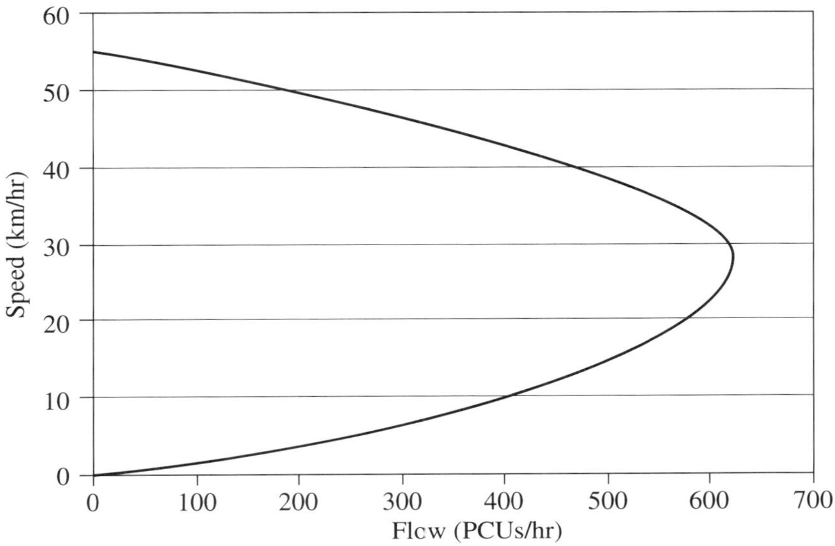

Figure 10.2 Speed–flow relationship for a single link (O'Flaherty, 1979)

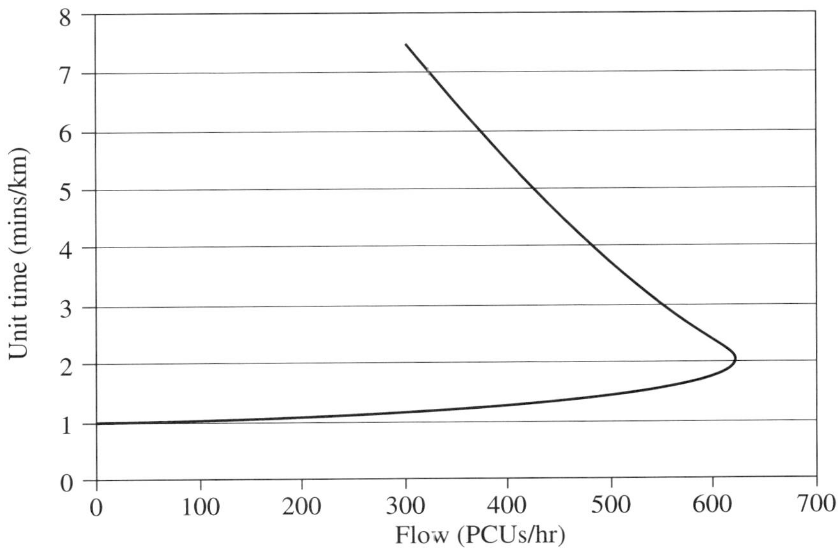

Figure 10.3 Unit time–flow relationship for a single link

10.2.2 Network Speed–flow Relationships

The flow-delay characteristics on a link-by-link basis are not particularly useful for the TRENEN model as direct inputs because it requires an aggregate congestion function representing the delay characteristics of a city, similar to that shown in Figure 10.4. The method developed to determine this type of function is described below but in summary it involved extracting selected results from a series of different demand outputs from a network model.

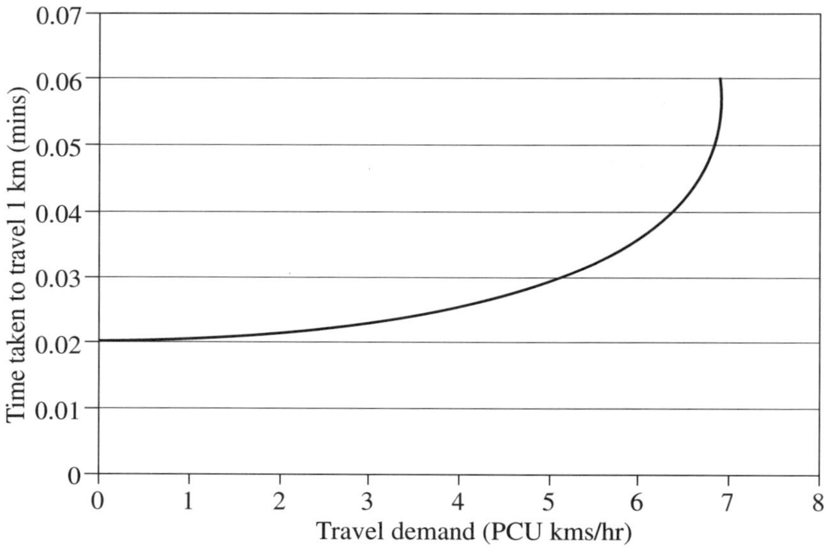

Figure 10.4 Network congestion function (De Borger et al., 1996)

The unit of flow over a given section of road is no longer a suitable indicator when examining speed–flow relationships at a network level. A more suitable measurement is the total equivalent passenger car unit (PCU) kilometres travelled on the network although in the strictest terms this cannot be described as 'flow', the units of which are vehicles/unit time. A more correct representation would be 'travel demand'. The function should be monotonically increasing, as defined by De Borger et al. (1996) to support uniqueness and convergence properties of the model, that is average travel times increase as network usage increases. The impact of an additional vehicle on the network can be easily assessed by such a function. Using additional information on the values of time and the total vehicle-kilometres travelled the marginal congestion costs can be evaluated. Henceforth, this type of function will be referred to as a congestion function.

10.2.3 Network Speed–flow Relationships for Dublin

To derive an aggregate congestion function for Dublin, the SATURN network model was used to calculate average traffic delays at a series of travel demand levels. A method is suggested whereby a relationship, not only for Dublin but for other cities as well, can be developed using a series of model runs. A variety of functions to describe the relationship are investigated and the most appropriate is selected. Congestion functions for sub-areas of the network, in this case an outer and inner region of Dublin city, are also described. To test transferability of the method it was applied to another city. The network model of Dubai was available to the authors at the time that this work was underway and a similar procedure to that used in Dublin was used to determine a delay–demand relationship for Dubai also.

10.2.4 Simulation of Demand Variation

In the preliminary part of the research, the 1991 peak and off-peak hour matrices for Dublin were used (DTI, 1994). To represent changes in demand levels, manipulation of the base year matrices was required. This was done by factoring the base year matrices by factors ranging from 0.5 to 1.5 in steps of 0.1. The matrix at a factor of unity represents traffic demand and conditions in Dublin in the 1991 reference year. Multiplying the matrix by 50 per cent reduces the number of trips by 50 per cent. This is quite a simplistic approach to reducing demand on the network as the level of reduction is applied at a uniform rate across the network. However, there was no other means of representing various demand levels at that time. The peak and off-peak trip matrices were factored in the same manner. Average speeds will be a function of the number of trips made and also the distribution of those trips across the network. Typically distribution in the off-peak period is different from that in the peak period but the exercise of looking at both allows an enriching view of how the changes in trip distribution impacts on the aggregate congestion function to be developed. The model was run for each new factored matrix and the unit travel time was calculated as follows (Kirwan, 1995):

$$\textit{Unit travel time} = T = \frac{\textit{Total travel time (PCU}\cdot\textit{min s)}}{\textit{Total travel distance (PCU}\cdot\textit{kms)}} = \frac{\sum_i V_i t_i + \sum_j V_j t_j}{\sum_i V_i d_i}$$

where V_i = actual volume of traffic per hour on link i
t_i = time taken for traffic to traverse link i
V_j = actual volume of traffic per hour making turn j
t_j = average delay to traffic making turn j
d_i = length of link i

Figure 10.5 shows the data points obtained from the model runs for each level of demand using the peak period matrix. The type of function mapped out by the points is indeed monotonically increasing and at low levels of demand the slope of the curve is equal to zero, that is when flow is equal to zero the inverse of unit-time represents the average free-flow speed.

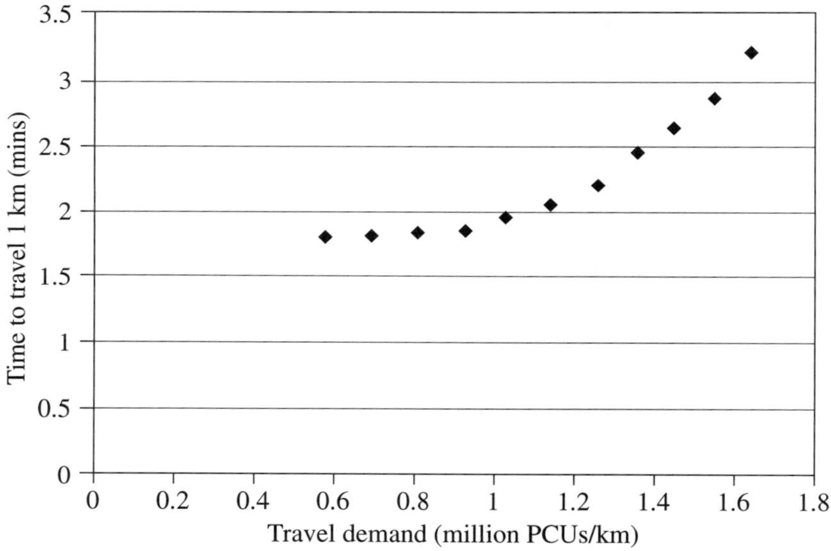

Figure 10.5 Data points for travel demand–unit time relationship from 1991, Dublin peak-hour matrix

10.2.5 Speed–flow Congestion Function Formats

The TRENEN models requires a single function to describe the demand–delay relationship. It was therefore necessary to fit a curve to the data points shown in Figure 10.5. The first step in this process was to determine what type of function most adequately describes the relationship. In the first instance, a quadratic function similar in format to that of Figure 10.4

(De Borger et al., 1996) was tried. For units of demand in million pcu.kms (X) and speed in km/min (S) the quadratic function for Dublin was derived as follows:

$$X = 0.62 + 0.115S - 0.0033S^2$$

Solving for S and taking the inverse gives the relationship for unit time against demand

$$T = \frac{2(0.0033)(60)}{0.1146 + \sqrt{0.1146^2 + 4(0.0033)(0.62 - X)}}$$

One of the difficulties with this function type is that it has a positive finite slope when demand is zero. The slope of a valid relationship should be equal to zero for free-flow conditions (O'Flaherty, 1979). A second difficulty with the quadratic function type is that it is discontinuous when the numerator goes to zero (in this case at approx. 1.6 million PCU kms) and this implies that the flow reaches a set capacity and does not go beyond this capacity. The simulation runs indicate that this does not truly represent what is happening for the demand level simulated. In order to find a more suitable function to describe the relationship the function types summarised in Table 10.1 were tested using a non-linear curve fitting routine. Summary parameters and statistics related to the suitability of each function for the Dublin data are given in Table 10.2. It is apparent from Table 10.2 that the power and exponential functions requiring three parameters to describe the relationship give the best-fit curves with R^2 coefficients of 99.78 and 99.92 respectively. On the basis of this statistic it was decided to use the exponential form to describe the congestion function relationship for our case studies.

Table 10.1 Functional forms tested in selection of unit time–flow relationship for TRENEN

Function Type	Equation
Power function type 1	$T = A + X^C$
Power function type 2	$T = A + BX^C$
Exponential function type 1	$T = A + e^{CX}$
Exponential function type 2	$T = A + Be^{CX}$

Source: Kirwan (1995)

Table 10.2 Summary statistics derived from non-linear curve-fitting routine

Function	Parameter	Value	t Statistic	R^2 Statistic
$T = A + X^C$	A	0.998	23.41	88.94
	B	–	–	
	C	1.345	12.73	
$T = A + BX^C$	A	1.741	64.1	99.78
	B	0.198	5.41	
	C	3.99	23.28	
$T = A + e^{CX}$	A	0.084	1.09	92.38
	B	–	–	
	C	0.646	22.54	
$T = A + Be^{CX}$	A	1.633	181.93	99.92
	B	0.263	22.52	
	C	2.49	47.2	

Source: Kirwan (1995)

10.2.6 Congestion Functions for the Whole Dublin Study Area

Figure 10.6 shows the data points from the simulations using matrices based on peak and off-peak hour demands and an exponential function fitted through each of the two sets of points. The functions for the data shown in Figure 10.6 are as follows:

$$\text{Peak:} \quad T = 1.633 + 0.0263e^{2.486X}$$

$$\text{Off-peak:} \quad T = 1.523 + 0.0574e^{1.833X}$$

The relationships appear similar at low levels of demand. Free-flow unit times derived from the off-peak matrix are 5 per cent lower than those derived from the peak hour matrix. The difference between the curves appears negligible up to demand levels of 1.2 million PCU kms but becomes more pronounced after this level. This difference may be attributed to the variation in demand distributions between matrices. Demand in the peak hour includes a large proportion of commuting trips and is concentrated on inbound radial routes and on low-capacity city-centre streets. Off-peak hour car travel generally consists of business and shopping trips and as a result the demand is more widely distributed.

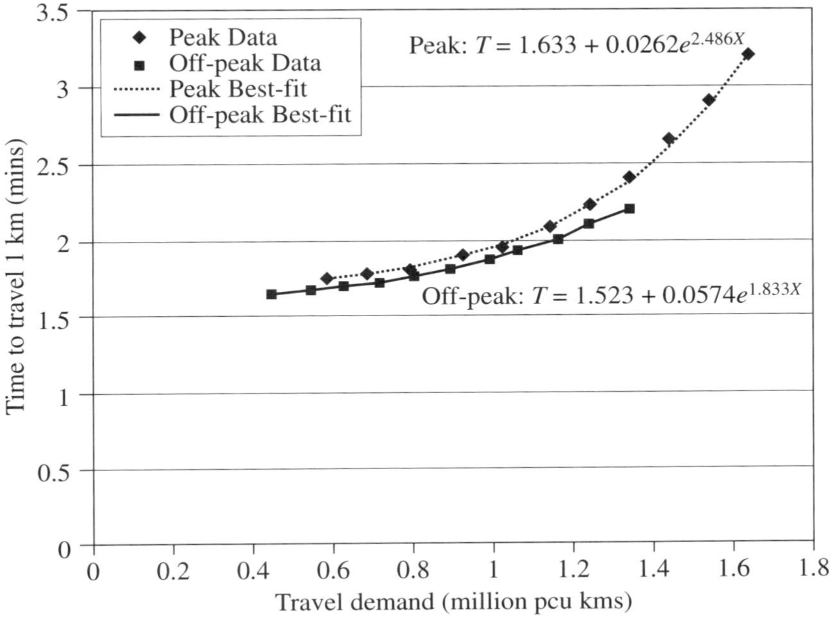

Figure 10.6 Peak and off-peak Dublin congestion functions

10.2.7 Congestion Functions for Inner and Outer Regions of the Dublin Study Area

The Dublin area can be divided easily, both geographically and with respect to land use, into two distinct areas; the city centre and an outer area consisting primarily of residential and industrial zones. The database analysis facilities of SATURN can be used to extract link flows and delays for specified portions of the network (Van Vliet and Hall, 1993). To further investigate the relationship between average speeds and demand, congestion functions were derived for the city centre and outer study areas.

Congestion functions for inner city centre are similar in shape to that of the whole study area but as expected the average free-flow speeds are considerably lower. The functions are as follows:

$$\text{Peak:} \quad T = 2.372 + 0.023e^{30.51X}$$
$$\text{Off-peak:} \quad T = 2.329 + 0.0382e^{22.6X}$$

For the outer area the following functions were obtained:

$$\text{Peak:} \quad T = 1.539 + 0.0288e^{2.661X}$$
$$\text{Off-peak:} \quad T = 1.361 + 0.112e^{1.516X}$$

As one might expect, the average speed in the outer area is considerably higher than in the city centre given that the quality of the road network is higher in the outer areas. Generally the scatter between the data points is lower for the outer area than for the inner city area. This is because the buffer links which make up much of the outer area are described by simple flow delay functions whereas the simulation of traffic interactions within the simulation (city centre) area gives relationships between demand and delay that are non-linear by nature.

The total level of travel (in vehicle-kms) for any given demand level, in the outer area, is considerably higher than for the city centre. For example, in the case of the peak hour matrix factored by one, flow in the outer study area is of the order of 0.8 million equivalent PCU kms which is approximately 80 per cent of the total flow in the full study area (approximately 1.0 million equivalent PCU kms).

Free-flow speeds range from 25.05 km/hr for the city centre for the peak matrix compared with 40.73 km/hr for the off-peak matrix applied to the outer area. The peak period matrix applied to the total study area gives a speed of 36.2 km/hr compared with a speed of 37.8 km/hr for the off-peak period.

10.2.8 Testing the Application of Derivation of Congestion Function in Another City: Dubai

Dubai is the capital city of the United Arab Emirates and is an old city which has undergone a period of considerable expansion as a result of the oil boom of the 1960s and 1970s. As a result the city consists of an older network of relatively narrow streets surrounded by a high quality network of overpasses, signalised junctions and signalised roundabouts. The peak hour is between 1.00 pm – 2.00 pm. A comparison is made in Table 10.3 between the characteristics of Dublin and Dubai. The Dublin network is considerably larger in length than the Dubai network. The number of lanes per km in Dubai is higher than in Dublin, with an average of approximately three lanes compared with just under two for Dublin. Hence traffic on the Dublin network encounters more junctions per unit network length and as a result delays at junctions are more likely to account for a greater proportion of total travel time. Both network quality indicators can be combined as a single indicator; that is the number of simulation nodes per lane km (modelling junctions). This network indicator is 72 per cent higher for

Table 10.3 Network parameters for Dublin and Dubai

Network Parameter	Dublin	Dubai
Simulation network		
Total link length (km)	837.2	266.5
Total length (lane/km)	1534.8	766.5
Average no. of lanes (lanes/km)	1.83	2.88
No. of simulation nodes	814	237
No. of simulation turns	6035	2253
Average link length (kms)	1.03	1.12
No. of simulation nodes (/ lane km)	0.53	0.309
Buffer network		
Total length (kms)	13685	3058
No. of buffer nodes	381	166
Average link length (kms)	36	18
Simulations nodes consist of		
Priority junctions	443	106
Traffic signals	320	85
Roundabouts	13	19
Additional information		
No. of zones	367	164
No. of bus routes	186	0

Dublin than for Dubai, indicating that the Dubai network should be more efficient than the Dublin network in catering for increases in demand. The congestion function for Dubai is as follows:

$$T = 1.165 + 0.0031e^{15.7X}$$

The function fits the data well with an R^2 value of 98.9 per cent. The exponential functional form is an acceptable representation of the aggregate congestion function for an urban area.

10.3 TECHNOLOGY FEASIBILITY OF ROAD-USE PRICING

Road-use pricing is defined as charging for the use of road space. In effect this means internalising some of the external costs imposed by car travel. The technology options for road-use pricing are described in detail in Blythe (1995). A summary of those options is presented below.

Road-use charges can be fixed or can be made to vary based upon the following:

- Time of day
- Class of vehicle
- Level of congestion
- Environmental factors
- Purpose of journey
- Vehicle occupancy
- Other access rights.

Payments may be in terms of a transaction at a point of charging, purchasing a prepaid permit, vignette or licence or the control of access based on a set of parameters. A variety of methods are available from manual to a combination of manual and automatic to fully automatic systems. Each method is summarised below.

10.3.1 Manual Systems

For the manual stop and pay method, the driver is required to stop the car and use cash or a card for the transaction. Specialised road infrastructure is required in the form of toll plazas to support this method of road-use pricing. Typically three toll booths are required to serve one lane of traffic. The requirement for land area to do this is a problem in most cities and the time required for each driver to conduct the transaction results in long queues. Manual stop and pay methods therefore are not popular or conducive to reducing delay in peak periods and in particular in urban areas. The typical method of enforcement used is a barrier at the point of charge but in some cases vehicle counters are also used.

Manual payment methods include manned toll booths, automatic coin receptors, card readers and paper stickers (area licences and vignettes). The first of these needs little explanation. In this case, the toll booths are manned by an individual who collects the money, tokens or paper tickets from the drivers and also gives change if required. In the case of the automatic coin receptors, manning of all toll booths is not required as the coin validation unit performs the task of deciding whether the vehicle should proceed or not based on the coins put in the basket/hopper.

Journey tickets or prepaid cards are another variation where the car driver inserts the card into a card reader and then collects the returned card before continuing. Each transaction takes approximately 15 seconds. The last type in the category of manned systems is the paper sticker or 'vignette'. The sticker is placed on the windscreen of the car and can be observed by manual observers or cameras. This system has been used in Bergen (Norway) and Singapore although in the latter case an upgrade to an automatic system took place in 1998.

10.3.2 Automatic Road-use Charging Systems

Automatic systems rely on in-vehicle units, roadside units, a computer system and an enforcement system. The technology supporting the systems includes Dedicated Short Range Communication (DSRC), wide area or video.

10.3.2.1 Short-range systems

Short-range systems can use read-only tags, read and write tags or automatic vehicle transponders. A read-only tag contains a fixed identification code which when passing the roadside reader will be passed to the roadside system to the user's account. Read–write tags allow information not only to be translated from the vehicle to the roadside but also from roadside to vehicle.

The automatic debiting transponder requires more sophisticated on-board vehicle equipment to allow for the additional features such as holding the user's credit balance. There is one example of this system in Europe in Austria and other examples exist in USA and in Singapore.

10.3.2.2 Area-wide Systems

An area-wide system makes use of a Global Positioning System (GPS) allowing the location of suitably equipped vehicles to be calculated. To achieve suitable accuracy for road pricing differential GPS is used. GSM (cellular radio) is also required to allow two-way communications over a wide area. The difficulty is the lack of proven and effective enforcement. This system has been tested in trials in Germany but as yet has not been implemented anywhere at a full-scale level.

10.3.2.3 Video-based systems

Automatic vehicle registration plate recognition relies on the vehicle's numberplate as an identifier for the vehicle. Cameras photograph the plate number and the system identifies the number without human intervention. No full implementation of this technology for road-use pricing exists although it has been used for enforcement of paper licence systems.

10.3.3 Examples of Road-use Pricing

Road-use pricing in the Norwegian cities of Oslo, Trondheim and Bergen was introduced as revenue generation measures. The pricing levels were deliberately set at low levels to ensure that demand was maintained and that revenue would be guaranteed. The funds raised from the toll rings were used for the construction of new road infrastructure.

This approach is in distinct contrast to those cities currently examining the potential of road-use pricing as a traffic demand measure where the aim is to reduce car travel demand. Singapore is the only city in the world that has introduced such a system. Recently, Singapore upgraded to an electronic system from an area-based licensing system. In the first few weeks after implementation a 24 per cent decrease in volume was noticed on the priced routes with an increase of 50 per cent on the alternative unpriced routes. Some delays were evident in the first few days of the system where drivers slowed down when passing the gantries to check that the correct amount was debited from their account. Since then the system has settled down and is working quite well.

There have been several trials of road-use pricing including those in Cambridge, London, Netherlands, Leicester, Lisbon, Goteborg, Newcastle and Dublin. These trials attempt to replicate real life conditions if road-use pricing were to be introduced on a full scale. Many of the trials show little impact at low pricing levels but more significant impacts at higher levels, such as decreases in car demand. However, the pricing levels at which impacts were realised are likely to pose acceptability problems at political and public levels. Trials suffer to some degree from the fact that all benefits to the road-use payers cannot be easily realised, such as shorter travel times, assuming that if road-use pricing was applied at a full-scale level there would be an overall decrease in car travel demand. Given that there has only been one example of road-use pricing implemented for traffic demand management purposes in the world and no example in Europe, the next stage in researching its potential is for a city to take on full-scale implementation.

Road-use pricing was recently endorsed in the UK White Paper on Transport (DETR, 1998) with the prospect of associated trials in the near future. Recent indications would suggest that the trials will take place in Bristol, Leeds and Edinburgh.

Increasingly issues other than technology have become important in developing road-use pricing as a successful traffic demand measure. These include public and political acceptance, system administration, hypothecation of the revenue, the ability of the authority to enforce and ensure compliance and handling of occasional users to an adequate degree.

10.3.4 Infrastructural Tolling

Infrastructural tolling offers useful experience for urban road use pricing, particularly in reference to the technological aspects. One example of toll roads using automatic debiting systems exists in Austria on the Breneer

Autobahn AG. It uses automatic licence-plate number recognition to establish whether a vehicle user is a subscriber or not. A camera reads the licence-plate number automatically. If the number corresponds to a stored record of a subscription then the barrier is raised to allow the vehicle through.

Motorway tolling in Italy is not new. The main operator is Autostrada Italiano, which owns a large proportion of the motorway network. The payment system has two variants; one acting as a credit card related to a central account and the other as a value card with a prepaid value assigned to it before use.

In Illinois, one million vehicles travel on the Illinois Tollway every day making it one of the most heavily trafficked toll roads in the USA. In 1993 an electronic system moved from trial stage to a full-scale project involving 196 lanes in strategic and selected locations on the 270 plus mile tollway. The transponder on each vehicle has a two-way communication facility. It is an active read–write unit with a large memory and integrated microprocessor. At the toll plaza the Toll Transaction Management System receives messages from a passing transponder via a radio signal and automatically deducts the toll. The transponder displays the amount paid by the driver and the account balance.

In California, the SR 91 Express Lanes, a privately funded and operated 10-mile toll facility built in the median of State Route 91 in Orange County opened to traffic in 1995. It is located on one of California's most congested highway corridors and offers a faster alternative to motorists who are willing to pay a toll which is varied by time of day. High occupancy vehicles go free but in the future there is likely to be a charge for these vehicles although it will be below that of single occupancy vehicles.

In 1993 the provincial government in Ontario decided to accelerate the construction of the 407 ETR, an urban highway that runs 69 kilometres across Ontario's busiest corridor. It was developed as a 'user pay' facility because of the likely delay in implementation if traditional approaches were used. When the facility was complete no tolls were applied for an initial period. During that time there were 250 000 to 270 000 trips per day using the facility, well in excess of the 100 000 trips per day predicted for use on the tolled infrastructure. When tolling was introduced, traffic immediately dropped to approximately 100 000 vehicles per day but it has been rising steadily since.

The system works as a closed system matching entries and exits to form a 'trip' and then applies the appropriate time, distance and vehicle classification charge rates to translate the trip to a revenue transaction. The toll equipment at the entry/exit locations consists of: tag readers, vehicle classifiers and cameras to deal with licence plate capture, tracking antennae and local field processors to provide interfacing to the communications system.

10.4 CONCLUSIONS

The aims of this chapter were twofold; first to explain how the demand–delay relationship was developed using network models for input to our model, and second to present a summary of the technical aspects of implementation of road-use pricing.

The first part of the chapter described in detail the research conducted to arrive at a reasonable, technically feasible function to describe congestion. The marginal costs of congestion are a considerable part of the externalities and this function is used to calculate these costs in the model. The function, by nature of the model requirement, is aggregate by nature and represents the traffic conditions of the city. A network model is recommended to establish the relationship to be used for any city to be analysed by TRENEN. A system of factoring the demand matrix in the model is used to establish a series of demand levels and the model output runs for each of these levels of demand are used to establish the data points for development of the speed–flow relationship. The functional form found to best represent the data is an exponential relationship and this type of function was used for all the case studies.

The second part of the chapter summarises the technical aspects of the alternative technologies available for road-use pricing. There has only been one full-scale implementation of road-use pricing for traffic demand management purposes, in Singapore. Given the controls on car ownership in Singapore it is doubtful that its experience is useful for applications in Europe where such car ownership constraints would be considered highly unacceptable. Many trials across Europe advocate further investigation of it as a traffic demand management measure but no government, as yet, has endorsed it fully and promised introduction. The UK government has prepared the groundwork necessary for introduction of road-use pricing and it is likely that trials will take place shortly. The chapter ends with a description of some examples of infrastructural tolling, the technology and experience of which may be useful for road-use pricing applications in urban situations.

REFERENCES

Blythe, P. (1995), 'The use of smart cards in road pricing and tolling systems', Proceedings IEE Colloquium on Electronics Techniques for Road Pricing and Tolling, London, March.

De Borger, B., Mayeres, I., Proost, S. and Wouters, S. (1996), 'Social cost pricing of urban passenger transport – with an illustration for Belgium', *Journal of Transport Economics and Policy*, January, 31–54.

Dewees, D.N. (1979), 'Estimating the time costs of highway congestion', *Econometrica*, **47**(6) Nov., 1499–512.

DETR (1998), *A New Deal for Transport*, The Government's White Paper on the Future of Transport, July 1998, Department of Environment, Transport and the Regions.

DTI (Dublin Transportation Initiative) 1999, final report, Department of the Environment, Dublin, Ireland.

Evans, A.W. (1992), 'Road congestion pricing: When is it a good idea?', *Journal of Transport Economics and Policy*, **26**, 213–43.

Hills, P.J. (1993), 'Road congestion pricing: When it is a good policy? A comment', *Journal of Transport Economics and Policy*, **27**(1), 91–105.

Kirwan, K.J. (1995), 'Optimal transport pricing for Dublin', MSc Thesis, University of Dublin, Trinity College, Dublin, Ireland.

O'Flaherty, C.A. (1979), *Highways and Traffic – Volume 1*, Edward Arnold.

Oscar Faber, Goodbody, TSRG & TORG (1999), *Technology Options. Dublin Road Pricing Study*, Dublin, Ireland: Department of the Environment.

Steer Davies Gleave (1994), *Dublin Transportation Initiative*, Dublin, Ireland: Department of the Environment.

TRB (1992), *Highway Capacity Manual*, Washington DC: Transportation Research Board.

Van Vliet, D. and Hall, M.D. (1993), *Saturn User Manual – Version 8.4*, Epsom, UK: WSAtkins.

PART IV

Case Studies

11. Testing alternative transport pricing policies for Brussels

Kurt Van Dender

11.1 INTRODUCTION

This chapter presents the case study on urban transport pricing and technology regulation policies for Brussels in 2005. Section 11.2 presents a general overview of the expected transport situation in Brussels in 2005, in case there are no policy innovations with respect to 1995. Section 11.3 gives a detailed description of this reference situation. We focus on the prevailing price structure, and on subsequent inefficiencies in transport markets. Next, Section 11.4 deals with the results of an optimal pricing and regulation policy. The main results of other counterfactual equilibria, more specifically cordon pricing and fuel taxes, are given in Section 11.5. Section 11.6 presents a conclusion.

11.2 BACKGROUND TO THE CASE STUDY[1]

11.2.1 Transport Markets and Traffic Flows

The geographical area for this case study is the zone within the outer ring-road of Brussels. This area was chosen for two reasons: (a) an analysis of available data on transport flows shows that magnitude of flows and average speed clearly differ within and outside the ring; (b) the area within the ring is serviced by one urban public transport operator. The geographical scope also closely relates to the administrative boundaries of the Brussels Capital Region.

Data on traffic flows are derived from the projection for 2005, from IRIS (1993). These flows are measured for a representative day. A day is the most relevant time scale for an analysis of urban transport problems. All prices, costs and taxes are for 2005, on the assumption that there is no change in policy with respect to 1995. The case study is for 2005, hence the effect of alternative policies is measured on a realistic time span, assuming that alternative policies are implemented around the year 2000. Compared to 1991, traffic volume increases by 22 per cent in 2005, the share of private transport increases, and speeds decline with 34 per cent on average. Only passenger transport flows have been modelled. Adding freight transport to the analysis did not generate important new insights in urban transport policy, because it represents only a minor share of traffic volume. This is the major difference with the interregional model applications.

Transport flows inside the Brussels ring are generated by inhabitants of the region and by commuters. There are 936 200 inhabitants and 649 274 commuters who make trips in the considered area. Each of these travellers makes 1.24 trips per day, on average. The average length of car trips by inhabitants is 4 km. For commuters, the average distance of a car trip is 13.07 km, of which 5.5 km are within the Brussels ring. Since the case study only considers the external costs of traffic within the ring, the relevant trip distance for commuters is, in the analysis of policy instruments, 5.5 km. Some costs of car trips, notably parking charges and costs, are related to journey distance. A journey is defined as the complete round trip. As such, parking costs in the city centre incurred by a commuter are linked to a distance driven of 26.14 km. The average length of a public transport trip, again within the ring, is 4.4 km for inhabitants and 6 km for commuters. Non-motorised transport, in Brussels almost exclusively walking, has average distances of approximately 0.5 km and 1.5 km in peak hours and off-peak hours, respectively.

Daily traffic flows in Brussels are spread unequally over time, as Figure 11.1 shows. For analytical and computational reasons, only two time intervals are considered in the model. The off-peak period stretches over 17 hours (02.00 am–07.00 am, 09.00 am–04.00 pm, 19.00 pm–00.00 pm), the peak period contains the morning and the afternoon peak (07.00 am–09.00 am, 16.00 pm–19.00 pm). The period from 00.00 pm to 02.00 am is not taken up in the analysis. Inhabitants make 52 per cent of all trips during peak hours. This share is higher for commuters, who mainly make peak hour work-related trips: 72 per cent of all commuter trips are peak hour trips.

The distinction between peak (5 hours long) and off-peak (17 hours long) is essential, since travel times differ strongly between both periods: more than half of all trips are done in less than a quarter of the 'transport day' (22 hours long). The relation between traffic flows and travel times, or travel speeds, is summarised in the congestion function (Figure 11.2). The congestion function is constructed by calibrating a given functional form with observations on traffic flows and speeds for Brussels. The functional form is taken from extensive experiments with a network model, reported in Chapter 10 of this volume. With a fixed road capacity, higher traffic

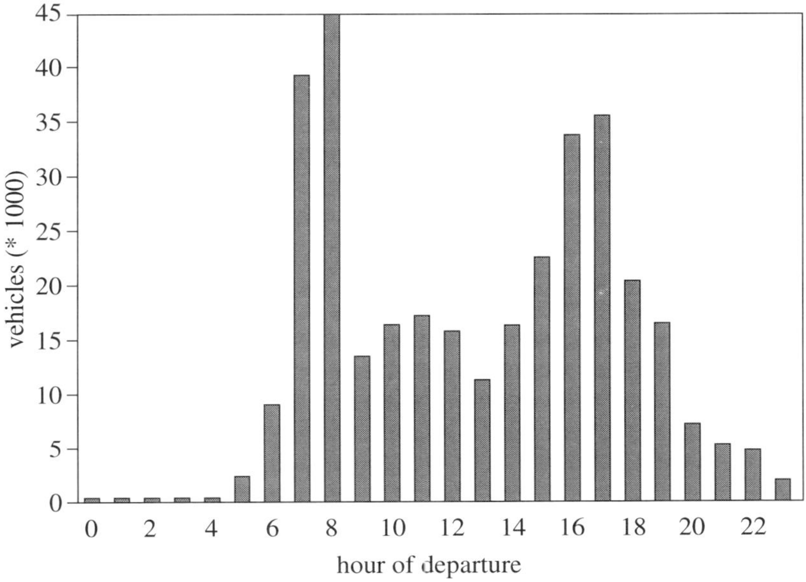

Source: IRIS (1993)

Figure 11.1 Load curve of traffic for a representative day in Brussels

volumes imply lower average speeds. Moreover, the decline in speed caused by an increase of traffic volume is larger as the initial traffic level is higher. Hence the congestion function is strongly non-linear. The marginal external congestion cost is the time loss caused by an additional kilometre driven on the network, affecting all transport already present on the network. These marginal external congestion costs will be proven to be essential variables in an improved urban transport policy.

Apart from the time distribution of traffic flows, the analysis of urban transport externalities requires information on environmental characteristics of vehicles, on modal choice and on cost structures of the different modes. Based on these criteria, the urban transport situation is split into a number of interrelated 'transport markets'. For Brussels 2005, the following criteria have been used to distinguish motorised[2] transport markets.

- Private and public (or collective) transport, private transport being passenger car transport and public transport consisting of transport by bus, tram and metro. The distinction between private and public

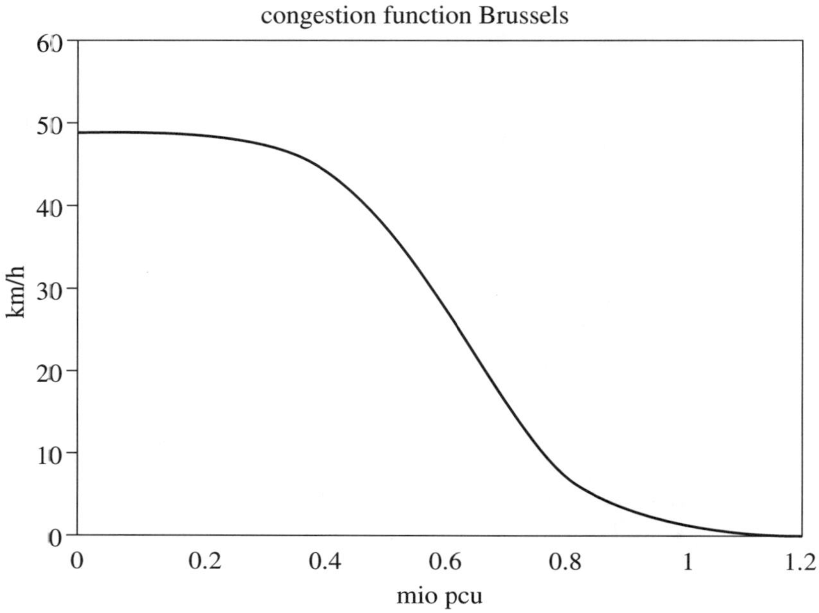

Source: based on IRIS (1993) and O'Mahony and Kirwan (2000)

Figure 11.2 Speed–flow function for Brussels, 2005

transport is essential, because of differing cost structures, different external costs and differences with respect to availability of policy instruments vis-à-vis both modes.

- For passenger cars, separate markets are defined according to occupancy rates (solo driving, or pooled driving), to the size of the car (small or large cars) and according to fuel type (petrol or diesel). The occupancy rate of cars has important consequences on costs per passenger-kilometre. The size of the car is related to fuel consumption and air pollution, but also to consumers' preferences. Fuel types are closely related to air pollution characteristics of cars.

Detailed information on modal split, on costs, taxes and external costs on the different transport markets is given in Section 11.3.

A last important characteristic of the urban transport situation concerns parking. As by far the largest share of urban trips is motivated by working, shopping or entertainment objectives, it is safe to assume that approximately all passenger car trips lead to a demand for parking space at the trip destination (in, or close to, the city centre). However, not all travellers have to pay for this parking space, either because the employer or the shop or the entertainment centre provides free parking, or because free (legal or illegal) on-street parking is available. For Europe, it is estimated that 70 per cent of all city centre-bound trips end in free parking. Since the resource cost of a parking space is clearly not zero, provision of free parking implies a distortion of the urban transport market. The distortion is taken up in the model, by dividing the inhabitants and the commuters into travellers who do and who do not have access to free parking at the trip destination. Applying the share of 70 per cent of 'non-payers', the sizes of the four consumer groups which are distinguished are the following:

- inhabitants, non-payers: 655 340 individuals,
- inhabitants, payers: 280 860 individuals,
- commuters, non-payers: 454 492 individuals,
- commuters, payers: 194 782 individuals.

Since a price difference exists between payers and non-payers, and price differences have an impact on demand through the price elasticity of demand, the impact of the parking charges system on the level and the modal split of transport demand by the four consumer groups are taken into account. Travellers having to pay for parking will consume less transport services, and the share of public transport in their total transport demand will be higher, when compared to non-payers for parking.

It should be noted that parking demand at the trip origin, mostly residential on-street or off-street parking, is not taken up in the model.

11.2.2 Recent Trends in Urban Transport Policy in Brussels

This case study results in a number of recommendations concerning the improvement of urban transport policies in Brussels. It is therefore useful to summarise the characteristics of the present lines of policy in Brussels. The results of the IRIS traffic study suggest that an integrated policy to control traffic demand and to optimise modal split and modal complementarity is required. The objectives of this policy are to decrease congestion and discomfort or damages caused by traffic to users and inhabitants. The set of measures put forward in the IRIS study includes:

Spatial organisation of the city:

- local employment and housing to be concentrated along public transport lines
- parking near to railway stations on city borders

Public transport

- integration of products and fares
- better exploitation of existing infrastructure
- extension of underground network
- increased bus and tram frequency (especially during off-peak), increased number of routes
- separate lanes for buses and trams
- fast train services from 30km outside the city to the city centre ('regional express net')

Passenger car

- investments in alleviation of bottlenecks in infrastructure
- 'avoid saturation of the network'
- more parking space for residents, introduction of residential parking permit
- stimulate intermodality by parking on city borders
- less on-road parking space, more off-road space
- progressive tariffs to decrease long duration parking

Freight transport

- zones for loading and unloading
- regulation of circulation, of noise and environmental characteristics of trucks

Institutional aspects

- better coordination of public transport, through an institution where bus, tram and train companies and the 19 municipalities of the Brussels region are present
- better parking policy regulated by an institution where the 19 municipalities of the Brussels region are present
- systems for financing the national and international service functions of the region

It is interesting to note that the IRIS study contains almost no pricing measures.

The general description of the transport situation in Brussels in 2005 being completed, we can now move on to descriptions and interpretations of our results. First, a detailed account is given of the reference situation which we have described in general terms here. This description points out the major inefficiencies which are related to the current pricing system of urban transport. Knowledge of the size and type of the inefficiencies suggests which policies are suitable to tackle the urban transport problems. The model computes the effects of policies in so-called 'counterfactual equilibria' (the reference situation may be called the 'factual equilibrium'). These are computed by implementing tax changes and changes in the environmental regulation on vehicle technology. In some counterfactual equilibria, optimal tax changes are computed, subject to constraints on the policy instruments. Other counterfactual scenarios simulate the impact of predefined tax and regulation changes.

The following counterfactual equilibria will be presented:[3]

- *Full optimum*. This policy sets policy instruments almost perfectly in order to alleviate the existing inefficiencies in the transport markets. Private and public transport prices are optimised. Optimal taxes take account of all differences in external costs and of inefficiencies due to the parking pricing system of the reference situation. Implementation of this policy requires a highly sophisticated tolling system, linking taxes to congestion conditions in space and time, to polluting characteristics of vehicles, as well as to vehicle noise production and accident externalities. In addition, parking costs are charged to all drivers. While such a policy may be feasible in the long run, this counterfactual equilibrium should also be seen as a benchmark: it gives the maximal welfare gain to be expected from improvements in urban transport pricing.
- *Cordon pricing*. In this counterfactual equilibrium, commuter trips are taxed according to congestion conditions, while the reference tax levels stay put for inhabitants. This allows the analysis of the effect of installing a single toll ring around the city area. We focus on the results for the case where public transport prices are set at the reference level, but results for the case where public transport prices cover resource costs are also mentioned.
- *Uniform pricing*. Here, the effects of changing fuel costs of trips are analysed. More specifically, the effects of raising fuel taxes to the levels proposed by the EU for 2005 will be simulated.

The three counterfactual equilibria have all been computed with and without regulation on vehicle technology, and with and without improved parking charges. Regulation on vehicle technology implies that all passenger cars are to be equipped with less polluting engine technology, as compared to the reference situation (see Chapter 3). Improved parking charges imply that all travellers pay for the resource cost of parking directly, instead of having 70 per cent of non-payers as in the reference situation.

11.3 REFERENCE SITUATION 2005 (RF)

As explained in Section 11.2, the criteria for the distinction of motorised transport markets in our model are: time of day (peak, off-peak), mode (public, private), subdivisions of modes (large or small passenger car using petrol or diesel, tram, bus or metro) and occupancy rates (solo or pooled driving). This section presents the cost structures and traffic volumes on these markets, assuming an unchanged transport policy in 2005 with respect to 1995.

The total marginal cost to the consumer, or 'generalised price', of driving one kilometre by passenger car consists of resource costs (the cost of material inputs required to produce that particular kilometre with that particular mode), taxes and time costs. The sum of resource costs and taxes is called the 'money price'. The money price of public transport is equal to the per kilometre fare. The sum of the money price and the value of time spent driving the kilometre (time cost) is the generalised price. Apart from the generalised cost to the consumer, there are the marginal external costs related to each kilometre driven. The marginal external costs are the real costs to society which are not included in the generalised price. In our model, the following marginal external costs are distinguished (for an extensive description of the methodology, see Chapter 7 of this volume).

- *Marginal external congestion cost*. This is the value of the time loss that a traveller causes to all other travellers when he decides to drive an extra kilometre. Indeed, when a traveller drives an extra kilometre he will marginally slow down all other traffic on the network. In his decision to travel an extra kilometre, the traveller takes into account his own time loss but not the time loss caused to others. The decrease in speed is small, but it is multiplied by the total number of travellers. Hence, the marginal external congestion cost becomes significant during peak hours.
- *Marginal external air pollution cost*. This is the cost of health damage and mortality caused by harmful pollutants emitted by engines.
- *Marginal external accident cost*. Insurance premiums and drivers' decision behaviour are such that not all costs of accidents are taken into account when the decision to travel or not is taken.
- *Marginal external noise cost*. Traffic generates noise, which has negative effects on well-being and health effects.

The upper part of Table 11.1 presents the cost structure for a number of transport markets in Brussels in 2005. A selection of markets has been made so that the most important pricing inefficiencies become apparent. The first row shows the price per passenger-kilometre of a small petrol car driven alone, during peak hours, where the driver is an inhabitant and does not have to pay for parking at the trip destination. We note:

- The time cost (0.334 Euro/vkm), which is the difference between generalised price and money price, equals 54 per cent of the total trip cost. In the off-peak, for an otherwise identical trip, this share is only 35 per cent. Other price components only differ between peak and off-peak because of differences in speed between both periods, speed differences leading to differences in fuel consumption.
- The money price in row 1 is lower than the resource cost, which is explained by the fact that this inhabitant does not pay for parking. Since the parking cost per vehicle kilometre is 0.17 Euro, the money price minus the taxes (0.280 − 0.089 = 0.191) is 0.17 Euro below the resource cost (0.191 + 0.17 = 0.361). Commuters not paying for parking pay a money price of 0.280 Euro, while the resource cost is 0.261 Euro, so there is a small net tax. This difference does not exist for drivers having to pay for parking (compare row 3 for inhabitants and row 4 for commuters): the tax is added to the total resource cost.
- The resource cost per kilometre of an inhabitant is higher than for a commuter. This is because parking costs are converted from a per trip basis to a per kilometre basis, and average total trip distances are higher for commuters than for inhabitants (compare Section 11.2). As a consequence, the parking cost per kilometre is 0.17 Euro for inhabitants and 0.07 Euro for commuters.
- The difference in per kilometre costs between payers and non-payers for parking is large. For inhabitants, the money price of a kilometre is 28 per cent higher if they have to pay for parking. For commuters, the difference is 11 per cent. A different way to illustrate the importance of parking costs is their share in the resource cost: 47 per cent for inhabitants, and 27 per cent for commuters. The importance of parking costs is an essential difference between an urban and an interregional transport situation.
- The cost of a kilometre by diesel car is lower than the cost for a petrol car. This is due to lower taxes on diesel vehicles and the lower resource costs per kilometre of diesel vehicles (due to higher average mileage). The high share of diesel cars in the vehicle stock in Belgium is due to this tax regime. The share of diesel cars will probably diminish as old vehicles are replaced. Recently, the tax system has been

Table 11.1 Characterisation of the reference situation (Brussels, 2005)

Prices and costs (Euro/pkm)	Resource cost	Tax	Money price	Marginal external cost (per vkm)	Generalised price
Peak					
car, solo, small, petrol, free parking					
inhabitants	0.361	0.089	0.280	1.834	0.614
commuters	0.261	0.089	0.280	1.834	0.614
car, solo, small, petrol, paid parking					
inhabitants	0.361	0.089	0.450	1.834	0.784
commuters	0.261	0.089	0.350	1.834	0.684
car, solo, small, diesel, free parking					
inhabitants	0.326	0.083	0.271	1.863	0.547
bust/tram (inhabitants)	0.080	0.039	0.12	0.092	0.587
Off-peak					
car, solo, small, petrol, free parking					
inhabitants	0.359	0.083	0.271	0.047	0.419
bus/tram (inhabitants)	0.271	−0.151	0.12	0.014	0.521
Volume and composition of traffic	**mio pkm**	**Share (per cent)**	**Per cent carpool**	**Speed (km/h)**	
Peak, private	3.846	41.6	29.6	23.1	
Peak, public	1.839	19.9		20.6	
Off-peak, private	2.839	30.7	25.4	49.7	
Off-peak, public	0.727	7.9		44.2	
Tax revenue (mio Euro/day)					
Private	0.508				
Public	−0.010				
External costs other than congestion (mio Euro/day)	0.432				

reformed such as to increase the total tax on diesel cars (by increasing the tax on the fixed costs of diesel cars).

- Taxes are far below marginal external costs in the peak period, while the situation is reversed in the off-peak. This suggests that the present tax structure is badly suited for the internalisation of external costs. Marginal external costs are much higher in peak hours than in off-peak hours. The explanation for this difference is that the marginal external costs of congestion are very high during the peak (for a decomposition of marginal external costs into the different categories, see below).
- As for public transport, it is noted that the money price is equal in peak and off-peak. Resource costs differ strongly on a per passenger-kilometre basis, however, because of differences in occupancy rates. The same bus is used in peak and off-peak, but during peak hours there is an average of 40 persons on board, as opposed to circa 9 persons on average during the off-peak. As a consequence, peak period bus driving more than covers the marginal resource cost of the bus (including the capacity cost of the bus), whereas in the off-peak the net taxes are strongly negative (in other words, off-peak bus transport is heavily subsidised). For public transport, the share of time costs in the total travel costs is higher than for private transport (80 per cent in peak hours to be precise). The reason is that walking times to bus (or tram, or metro) stops, and waiting times at bus stops are included in the travel time.

In the lower part of Table 11.1, the level and the composition of traffic has been summarised. Peak period traffic accounts for 62 per cent of total traffic, expressed in passenger-kilometres. Public transport stands for 28 per cent of all passenger-kilometres. Within the peak period, 32 per cent of all passenger-kilometres is produced by public transport. In the off-peak period, this share is 22 per cent. The explanation is that commuting trips, which are concentrated in peak hours, make more frequent use of public transport modes. The share of carpooling in the total number of passenger-kilometres is also slightly higher during peak hours, because carpooling is more frequent in work trips than for trips with other motives. Given the expected traffic volumes, average speeds are expected to be about 23 km/h for passenger cars during peak hours, and about 50 km/h during the off-peak. Public transport travels slower than private transport. The share of passenger-kilometres by diesel car in the total demand for passenger km by passenger car is 38 per cent. This share is higher than in most European cities, because the tax structure on passenger cars used to be favourable to diesel cars.

Finally, Table 11.1 shows that aggregate tax revenues from private transport are positive, while those of public transport are slightly negative. The total value of the external costs of accidents, air pollution and noise (that is, *exclusive of congestion costs*) is 0.432 million Euro/day.

The following paragraphs translate the situation described in Table 11.1 to a per trip level, and point out the main inefficiencies related to the current pricing system.

Driving into the centre of Brussels during peak hours in 2005, from outside the larger ring of the city ('commuters'), will cost an estimated 3.4 Euros for the part of the trip inside Brussels. It is assumed that policy and infrastructure remain unchanged with respect to 1995. This is the price when the driver does not have to pay for parking space at his destination, for example when his employer provides free parking space. The price is a generalised price, which decomposes into a time cost of 1.55 Euros and a money cost of 1.85 Euros. A trip from inside the ring to another point in the city ('inhabitants'), under otherwise equal conditions, will cost 2.5 Euros, consisting of 1.4 Euros time costs and 1.1 Euros money costs. The length of the trips is 5.5 km and 4 km on average respectively. The cost of the same trips during off-peak hours is 2.3 Euros for commuters and 1.7 Euros for inhabitants.

The situation described here is inefficient, because of two reasons directly related to the transport sector.

1. For both trips, the resource cost of parking is not charged to the drivers. This resource cost is 0.07 Euro/km for commuters and 0.17 Euro/km for inhabitants, 27 per cent and 47 per cent of the total resource cost per kilometre respectively.[4] It is estimated that 70 per cent of all trips do not pay for parking. The resource cost of freely provided parking space is spread over society. This is an inefficient pricing system, since prices of trips do not reflect the resource costs for non-payers. Hence, their total transport demand, as well as the share of passenger car transport in their total transport demand, will be inefficiently high. This excess demand has negative effects on time costs of all travellers, and on the other external costs.
2. Prices are below social costs. Social costs are the total costs of a trip to society. Apart from resource costs, they include marginal external costs. These marginal external costs are related to (in Euro/km, for the reference situation):

   - congestion (1.796 Euro in peak period, 0.003 Euro in off-peak),
   - air pollution (0.004 Euro in peak period, 0.004 Euro in off-peak),
   - accidents (0.032 Euro in peak period, 0.032 Euro in off-peak),

- noise (0.002 Euro in peak period, 0.007 Euro in off-peak),
- total per km: 1.834 in peak period, 0.0465 in off-peak; this amounts to circa 7.3 Euros per inhabitant trip in the peak, 0.2 Euros per inhabitant trip in the off-peak, 10.4 Euros per commuter peak hour trip, and 0.26 Euro per off-peak trip of a commuter.

The discrepancy between prices and social costs leads to an inefficiently high demand for transport. Since the discrepancies differ according to transport modes and time periods, the modal distribution and the time distribution of transport demand will be suboptimal. However, the present size of marginal external costs is not a good guideline for policies, since price changes will induce demand reactions. This will lead to a new equilibrium with lower marginal external costs.

An additional reason why the current transport taxation system may be inefficient originates from the relation between transport taxation and the efficiency of the global tax system in the economy. Government raises tax revenue in order to pursue its objectives (provision of public goods and services, redistribution of income). Raising taxes distorts the economy, in as far as they create a wedge between marginal resource costs and consumer prices. Transport taxes are an instrument for the manipulation of the degree of distortion. This role of transport taxes is taken into account when counterfactual equilibria are computed. There are two aspects to this role.

- Transport tax revenue is used to shift taxes away from labour and this decreases the distortion on the labour market (see Chapter 4 of this volume).
- As transport expenditures are rather price inelastic compared to other consumption goods, one achieves an efficiency gain by shifting part of the tax burden on other goods to transport.

The model computes the effects of policies on the three types of inefficiencies mentioned above. There are two ways of doing this: (a) calculating optimal values for instruments, or, (b) simulating the effects of prespecified values of the instruments. The yardstick for policy evaluation is welfare, welfare then being the difference between benefits from consumption activities and their costs, including external costs. Note, however, that the implementation costs of the instruments are not taken into account in our analysis. The types of instruments that will be analysed are pricing tools and regulation of technology with respect to air pollution characteristics. We will analyse optimal pricing, cordon pricing and uniform pricing, every time with and without simultaneous technology regulation and improved parking charges.

11.4 OPTIMAL POLICY (FO)

11.4.1 Introduction

In the optimal policy, prices are set in such a way that they reflect marginal external costs as well as possible in all transport markets. Since resource costs are fixed per kilometre, taxes are used to achieve these optimal prices. In the optimal policy, there are (nearly) no restrictions on the flexibility of taxes: they may differ according to time of day, vehicle type, fuel type, between inhabitants and commuters (that is taxes are differentiated spatially). It is clear that implementation of such a pricing policy will require a highly sophisticated tolling mechanism. Only electronic road pricing systems are potentially suitable, but even then the question remains whether they will allow variable emission taxes. Note that taxes are optimised in public transport as well as in private transport, and that the optimal taxes are not only determined by marginal external costs, but also by the other inefficiencies mentioned in Section 11.3.

There is one restriction on the flexibility of taxes, since it was imposed that the toll should be equal for payers and non-payers for parking. The reason is that an electronic on-road tolling mechanism cannot observe whether drivers will or will not have to pay for parking at their destination. Of course, the distinction between payers and non-payers is no longer relevant when all drivers have to pay for parking at their destination. We will first look at the results of *optimal pricing* in this situation *with improved parking charges*. We will also assume that *no regulation of technology* has taken place, such that all vehicles will have the same emission characteristics as in the reference situation. When the results of this version of optimal pricing have been discussed, we return to the situation where parking charges have not been improved.

11.4.2 Welfare Changes and Volume Effects

Tables 11.2 and 11.3 summarise the results of the optimal pricing policy, when technology is not regulated and parking charges have been improved. The full optimum (FO) is compared with the reference scenario (RF). Table 11A.1 of the appendix provides more detailed information on the optimum pricing scenario.

Our principal standard for policy assessment is welfare; it is a quantitative measure (in our case, a monetary measure: generalised income) of the net benefits of a given economic equilibrium. It takes account of the benefits accruing to all consumers and producers, on the assumption that tax revenues are used by the government to improve consumer welfare. The

Table 11.2 Key results of optimal policy (Brussels, 2005)

	Welfare level	Per cent welfare gain	Per cent maximal welfare gain	Traffic level (mio/ pkm)	Per cent peak, private traffic	Per cent peak, public traffic	Per cent off-peak, private traffic	Per cent off-peak, public traffic	Other external costs (mio Euro/day)
RF	54.60	0	0	9.252	41.6	19.8	30.6	7.8	0.432
FO	55.31	1.30	97.3	8.410	35.3	28.2	29.1	7.4	0.374

Note: RF = reference equilibrium; FO = full optimum (optimised taxes and improved parking charges)

impact of negative externalities is accounted for by subtracting the monetary value of these impacts from welfare.

The simultaneous introduction of improved parking charges and optimal pricing with respect to external costs leads to a welfare gain of 1.30 per cent of generalised income, as compared to the reference situation. External costs of air pollution, noise and accidents ('other external costs', in the tables) decrease with 0.06 million Euro per day, a decrease with 13.4 per cent. The change in congestion conditions is reflected in the average travel speeds. Whereas peak hour driving in the reference situation was at an average speed of 23km/h, this increases to 40km/h. This increase will be reflected in a decrease of time costs of trips (see below). Off-peak speeds do not change significantly, because congestion is not problematic in the off-peak hours in the reference situation.

The increase in travel speeds is related to the change in traffic level, and in modal and time distribution of traffic. Overall daily traffic drops with 0.842 million passenger car units, i.e. a 9 per cent decrease. The share of peak traffic remains more or less constant (61.5 per cent in reference situation and 63.5 per cent in the optimum), but there is an important modal shift from private transport to public transport. Aggregated over peak and off-peak, the share of public transport rises from 27.6 per cent to 35.6 per cent. This effect decomposes into a small drop in the off-peak share of public transport, and a large peak share increase (+8.4 percentage point).

Thus, as a conclusion, the impact of optimal pricing on urban traffic in Brussels is that peak and off-peak traffic decrease, that the time distribution of total traffic remains more or less constant, and that the share of public transport in peak hours increases strongly. The combination of a decreased peak traffic level and a switch to collective modes leads to increased travel speeds.

Introducing optimal transport prices leads to a net welfare increase. The net effect is the sum of effects on different markets. First, there is a substitution of other consumption for transport consumption. All consumer groups consume more non-transport goods in the full optimum. The order of magnitude of the increase is 2.5 per cent. On the transport markets, the tax increase outweighs the decrease in time costs, resulting in a loss of consumer surplus on the transport markets. The total benefit of consumption (the consumer surplus) increases for all groups. For inhabitants who did not pay for parking in the reference situation, the increase is small. For this group, the per kilometre increase of private transport prices is so high that it largely offsets all other gains from the optimal policy.

11.4.3 Optimal Tax Levels

Table 11.3a gives information on the optimal tax levels and compares them to the reference taxes. Remember that the taxes are the instruments used to bring about the optimal changes in traffic demand, and that the new taxes substitute all existing taxes in transport (fuel, registration taxes, and so on). Note also that this scenario assumes that parking charges have been improved, so that all consumers now pay for the resource cost of parking. Hence, there is no need to use the tax instrument to correct inefficiencies in parking charges.

Taxes increase for all modes, but to a higher extent for peak passenger car traffic and for off-peak public transport, where a subsidy is transformed into a net tax. In the case of peak passenger car traffic, the main incentive for the tax increase is the high marginal external congestion cost. For off-peak public transport, the tax increase is motivated by the large discrepancy between resource costs per passenger-kilometre and prices per passenger-kilometre in the reference situation: when all modes are priced optimally, there is no reason why public transport should be subsidised beyond covering the difference between average and marginal resource cost.

Table 11.3a Taxes in reference situation and optimal pricing (Euro/passenger km, per cent change w.r.t. reference, Brussels, 2005)

	Euro/pkm			
	IN	IP	ON	OP
RF				
peak, car*	0.089	0.089	0.089	0.089
peak, bus	0.039	0.039	0.039	0.039
off-peak, car*	0.083	0.083	0.083	0.083
off-peak, bus	−0.151	−0.151	−0.151	−0.151
FO				
peak, car*	0.533	0.533	0.497	0.497
peak, bus	0.080	0.080	0.072	0.072
off-peak, car*	0.188	0.188	0.166	0.166
off-peak, bus	0.104	0.104	0.108	0.108

Notes:
* small petrol car driven alone
IN inhabitants non-payers for parking, IP inhabitants payers, ON commuters non-payers, OP commuters payers

Table 11.3b Generalised prices for reference and optimal pricing (Euro/passenger km, index w.r.t. reference, Brussels, 2005)

	ECU/pkm				per cent change			
	IN	IP	ON	OP	IN	IP	ON	OP
RF								
peak, car*	0.610	0.780	0.610	0.680	0	0	0	0
peak, bus	0.587	0.587	0.570	0.570	0	0	0	0
off-peak, car*	0.419	0.589	0.419	0.489	0	0	0	0
off-peak, bus	0.521	0.521	0.483	0.483	0	0	0	0
FO								
peak, car*	1.085	1.085	0.949	0.949	78	39	56	39
peak, bus	0.501	0.501	0.475	0.475	−15	−15	−17	−17
off-peak, car*	0.694	0.694	0.572	0.572	65	18	36	17
off-peak, bus	0.797	0.797	0.783	0.783	53	53	62	62

Notes:
* small petrol car driven alone
IN inhabitants non-payers for parking, IP inhabitants payers, ON commuters non-payers, OP commuters payers

Table 11.3c Generalised prices in reference and optimal pricing (small petrol car driven alone by an inhabitant not paying for parking in reference, Brussels, 2005, Euro/pkm)

	Peak		Off-peak	
	RF	FO	RF	FO
Generalised price	0.614	1.085	0.419	0.694
Time cost	0.334	0.191	0.148	0.148
Money price	0.280	0.894	0.271	0.546
Tax	0.089	0.533	0.083	0.188
Resource cost excl. parking	0.191	0.191	0.189	0.189
Resource cost of parking	0.170	0.170	0.170	0.170

Optimal taxes are much more differentiated between transport markets than in the reference situation. There is a differentiation between peak and off-peak taxes, as well as spatial differentiation: the per kilometre tax is higher for inhabitants than for commuters.[5]

As a reference order of magnitude, note that the optimal tax on a per trip level for driving in Brussels by passenger car during peak hours is between 2.1 and 2.7 Euros. During the off-peak, a charge of approximately 0.7 Euro to 0.9

Euro is optimal. These figures exclude parking resource costs, since these are charged directly to all drivers.

Taxes are the instruments of the optimal pricing policy. The more relevant variable for the consumer is the generalised price of transport. Table 11.3b compares generalised prices in the reference situation to those of the full optimum.

Generalised prices of transport increase, except in the case of peak public transport. Whereas the tax increase (Table 11.3a) is quite substantial, the increase in generalised prices is more moderate, even when parking charges are introduced for former non-payers. The reason is that tax increases, causing money price increases, are partly offset by gains in travel speeds, which lead to lower time costs. The net generalised price increase during peak hours for private transport is, due to internalisation of external costs, approximately 40 per cent. In the case of public transport, an additional cause of decreasing time costs is the Mohring effect: when public transport demand increases, the model assumes that the frequency of public transport services responds optimally. This leads to decreasing waiting times at public transport stops, when the demand increases. This effect is partly responsible for the decrease in the generalised price of peak public transport.

Table 11.3c supplies additional information on the changes in price structure between the reference situation and the optimal pricing scenario. The time cost component of the generalised price is found to decrease strongly in peak hours. This is the result of both the increase in the money price (tax increase) and the decrease in the time cost levels. For money prices, the opposite direction of effects holds. Tax rates increase, and are now higher in the peak than in the off-peak (while the relation was opposite in the reference situation). Taxes are more or less equal in peak and off-peak in the reference situation, but the peak tax is higher in peak hours under optimal pricing. Since external costs are internalised in the generalised price, the share of the resource costs in the generalised price becomes smaller.

In the optimal pricing policy taxes exceed marginal external costs. As explained before, this relates to the efficiency of the global taxation system. Marginal external costs for a small petrol car driven during peak hours are 0.407 Euro per kilometre (off-peak: 0.047 Euro/km). The optimal tax is between 0.497 and 0.596 Euro per kilometre (off-peak: between 0.17 and 0.19 Euro/km). The mark-up tax rate in terms of generalised prices (that is, the difference between tax and marginal external cost, divided by the generalised price) is 15 per cent in peak hours and 26 per cent in off-peak hours.

11.4.4 The Role of Parking Charges

In the discussion up to now, full optimal pricing has been discussed in the context where all drivers pay for parking charges at the trip destination. We now assume that optimal pricing is introduced, while the reference parking charges system remains unchanged (70 per cent non-payers), without environmental technology regulation. The welfare gain from this policy is almost identical to the gain from optimal pricing plus improved parking charges. The reason is that the optimal tax instrument is flexible enough to correct external costs and parking pricing inefficiencies simultaneously. However, compared to the optimal taxes in the presence of improved parking charges, the taxes required for this simultaneous treatment of both inefficiencies are much higher.

Since the same tax is levied on both payers and non-payers, the payers for parking will face a much higher price increase than the non-payers. So, while the global welfare effect of the policy is comparable to the case discussed above, the distributional consequences are more perverse.

Improving parking charges is an important element of urban transport policy, and should preferably (presumably, can only) be implemented separately from the introduction of road pricing schemes (see Calthrop, Proost and Van Dender, 2000 for a more detailed discussion). The importance of improving parking charges may be illustrated by a comparison of the welfare level of the reference situation to a situation where only parking charges are improved, while taxes and technology remain as they were. The results of this scenario, resource cost pricing of parking, are summarised in Table 11A.4 in the appendix. The welfare gain of this policy is circa 0.42 per cent with respect to the reference situation, which is approximately 32 per cent of the maximal welfare gain. In other words, *a third of the initial inefficiency on the urban transport markets is due to imperfect pricing of parking. Charging resource costs of parking to all drivers is essential in an efficient urban transport pricing system.*

11.5 ANALYSIS OF OTHER POLICIES

11.5.1 Cordon Pricing (CO)

In cordon pricing, as it is analysed here, the tax instrument for passenger cars has the same characteristics as the optimal tax instrument of Section 11.4, *but it is limited to commuters*. For this group, there is a tax differentiation according to time and to vehicle characteristics. For inhabitants, however, the taxes remain unchanged with respect to the reference situation, and public transport prices are the same as in the reference situation as well. This set-up of the model tries to compute the effect of installing a cordon around the city of Brussels. Drivers passing through this cordon are charged an optimal toll, while trips inside the city are not affected by the cordon at all.

The main effects of this policy can be explained intuitively. Levying an optimal tax on commuters will lead to increased generalised prices for this group. Their transport demand will decrease, and the composition of demand will be more in line with external costs. This is welfare improving. For inhabitants, however, money prices of transport do not change with respect to the reference situation. Additionally, time costs of transport will decrease because of the reduced demand from commuters. Hence, the generalised cost of transport decreases for inhabitants, so that their traffic demand increases, and part of the welfare gain from the improved pricing for commuters will be lost.

Note that, since taxes for commuters are optimised, these taxes will take into account the negative effect on the inhabitants' demand as well as possible. This implies that the optimal tax for commuters under cordon pricing will differ from the optimal commuter tax under full optimal pricing (it will be higher, since the policy objective is to maximise overall welfare, and there is no weighing of separate groups' welfare). Since the commuter tax is a very indirect instrument to control the inhabitants' demand, the performance of cordon pricing will be inferior to optimal pricing.

If cordon pricing is implemented without improved parking charges and without regulation of emission technology, welfare increases with 0.70 per cent with respect to the reference situation. This is 54 per cent of the welfare gain from full optimal pricing. Total external costs from air pollution, noise and accidents are 3.9 per cent lower than in the reference situation. Table 11A.2 (appendix) presents more detailed results for this scenario. The share of private transport in total transport demand is lower than in the reference situation, but higher than under full optimal pricing. The share of peak transport in total transport decreases slightly. Total transport demand decreases with 1.5 per cent (compared to a 9 per cent decrease under full optimal pricing). This last figure results from a demand decrease from commuters, which is partly offset by a demand increase from inhabitants. As a consequence, speeds are up to 33 km/h in peak hours (reference situation: 23 km/h; optimal pricing: 40 km/h).

The differential impact of cordon pricing on inhabitants and commuters is illustrated in Table 11.4, where changes in consumer surpluses[6] for the four consumer groups are compared, with respect to the reference situation, for optimal pricing and cordon pricing. In order to isolate the effect of restricting optimal pricing to commuters, it is assumed for both scenarios that parking charges and emission technology remain as they were in the reference situation.

Table 11.4 Changes in consumer surpluses for 2 scenarios (Brussels, 2005, per cent changes with respect to reference situation)

	IN	IP	ON	OP
Optimal pricing	0.35	1.90	0.96	1.84
Cordon pricing	2.24	2.11	−1.87	−1.60

In the optimal pricing scenario all consumers enjoy a welfare gain,[7] while in the case of cordon pricing inhabitants experience large gains and commuters face large losses. Urban transport policies may have different welfare impacts on different groups of transport users. In the case of cordon pricing, inhabitants will be in favour of the instrument. If pricing measures are within the competence of the urban authorities, and if these authorities only take the welfare of inhabitants into account, they may prefer cordon pricing above optimal pricing (assuming, not unrealistically, that cordon pricing is cheaper to install than a full optimal pricing system over the complete territory of the city). The question of competence of different layers of government with respect to urban transport policies is proven to be of considerable importance.

To conclude the discussion of cordon pricing, we indicate the impact of simultaneously introducing improved parking charges. The welfare gain of combined cordon pricing and improved parking charges is 0.97 per cent with respect to the reference situation, or 75 per cent of the maximum attainable gain. The comparable figures for pure cordon pricing are 0.70 per cent and 54 per cent. The importance of correct parking charges is illustrated clearly here. In contrast to the case of full optimal pricing, a cordon cannot be used to tackle inefficient parking pricing systems indirectly. The parking pricing problem must be dealt with separately, and it leads to substantial additional welfare gains.

11.5.2 Uniform Pricing (UP)

Uniform pricing involves setting the tax levels on fuel in line with the EU target levels for 2005. For Belgium, this implies a limited increase in the consumer price of fuels, since tax levels are relatively high in the reference situation already. More specifically, the price of petrol per litre increases by 11 per cent, that of diesel by 32 per cent. Detailed results are reported in Table 11A.3 of the appendix. Table 11.5 shows the change in the money price for a passenger car per kilometre caused by increased fuel prices, in case emission technology and parking charges do not change with respect to the reference situation. It will be observed that the relative price increase in Belgium is larger for diesel cars, which reflects the fact that taxes on diesel fuel are relatively low in the reference situation.[8] However, the overall increase of the price per kilometre is quite limited.

Table 11.5 Money price changes of a vehicle-kilometre caused by fuel price increases (Brussels, 2005)

	RF (Euro/vkm)	UP (Euro/vkm)	Per cent change
Peak, car, solo, petrol, free parking			
inhabitant	0.280	0.286	2.1
commuter	0.280	0.286	2.1
Peak, car, solo, petrol, paid parking			
inhabitant	0.450	0.456	1.3
commuter	0.350	0.356	1.7
Peak, car, solo, diesel, free parking			
inhabitant	0.214	0.223	4.2
Off-peak, car, solo, petrol, free parking			
inhabitant	0.271	0.276	1.8

The impacts of this policy on the urban transport equilibrium in Brussels will be limited. Besides the small size of the price increase there are three additional reasons that limit the effectiveness of the policy:

- Fuel costs take up a small share of the per kilometre transport cost in urban environments. Fuel costs are too narrow a tax base for setting urban transport prices correctly. The following orders of magnitude for the per kilometre cost in Brussels in 2005 (averaging over peak and off-peak, over vehicle types and over inhabitants and commuters) illustrate this point:
    - vehicle resource cost per kilometre: 0.21 Euro (60 per cent)
    - fuel resource cost per kilometre: 0.02 Euro (6 per cent)
    - parking resource cost per kilometre: 0.12 Euro (34 per cent)
    - total resource cost per kilometre: 0.35 Euro (100 per cent)

Setting fuel prices in order to correctly charge resource costs and external costs would lead to unacceptable tax rates on fuel.

The composition of per kilometre passenger car costs in Brussels once again illustrates the size of the inefficiency caused by providing free parking to 70 per cent of all drivers. The reduction of the total price is comparable to a price reduction caused by providing free fuel for the in-city trip to all drivers.

- Even if the tax rate on fuel could be set high enough to reach efficient pricing levels, this tax rate would be unsuited for efficient pricing in non-urban traffic. Since spatially differentiated fuel prices are not feasible, fuel taxes are not a good instrument if current pricing inefficiencies differ, for example, between cities and highways.
- Fuel prices cannot be time differentiated, so that the impact on congestion conditions will be small unless the taxes are sufficiently high to decrease the overall traffic level substantially.

Uniform pricing without regulation of technology and without improved parking charges leads to a welfare gain of 0.07 per cent with respect to the reference situation, which is 5.8 per cent of the maximal attainable welfare gain. The overall traffic level barely changes (−0.01 per cent), while there is a small increase in the share of public transport with circa 0.5 per cent. Travel speeds increase slightly.

Combining uniform pricing with improved parking charges results in a welfare gain of 0.46 per cent as compared to the reference equilibrium, which is 35 per cent of the maximal welfare gain. The inefficiency not tackled by any of the policy components (fuel prices or parking charges) is the excessive external congestion cost.

11.5.3 The Impact of Emission Technology Regulation

The impact of improving emission technology for passenger cars on emissions is given in Table 11.6. The resource cost of the improvement is between 225 Euros and 824 Euros per car, the precise figure depending on car size and fuel type (EC, 1995). This leads to a per kilometre increase of 0.0027 Euro on average in the capital cost of a car. We will now analyse the impact of a policy where government imposes the use of improved emission technology through regulation, in the assumption that consumers bear the capital cost increase caused by the regulation (see Table 11.7).

Table 11.7 summarises the main effects of the scenario and compares them with the reference situation. Imposing the improved technology by way of a regulation on all the vehicles does not yield net welfare gains. There is a small decrease in consumer surplus and in tax revenues from private transport. This loss is only partly offset by the decrease in air pollution costs.

Table 11.6 Emission reductions (in per cent)

		NO_x	CO_2	VOC	CO	PM	SO_2
Standard tech.	Petrol	40	–	40	30	0	–
	Diesel	35	–	20	40	35	–
Improved tech.	Petrol	65	–	65	45	0	–
	diesel	30	–	30	50	50	–

Source: EC doc II/576/95-EN, p. 8

Table 11.7 Main components of welfare (changes w.r.t. reference)

Levels	Improved Emission Technology Consumer pays
Welfare (mio Euro/day)	−0.003
Cons. surplus (average, mio Euro/day)	−0.005
Tax rev. priv. tr. (mio Euro/day)	−0.002
Ext. costs excl. congestion (mio Euro/day)	−0.005
Air pollution costs (mio Euro/day)	−0.006
per cent change w.r.t. reference	
Welfare	−0.01
Cons. surplus	−0.01
Tax rev. priv. tr.	−0.39
Ext. costs excl. congestion	−1.15
Air pollution costs	−4.76

This result should be interpreted with care. First, improved technology was imposed on all types of vehicles. It is probable that imposing enhanced technology for diesel cars exclusively would bring a small net benefit. Second, as the costs of improved technology are probably increasing with the degree of abatement, smaller improvements could be worthwhile. Finally, the air pollution damage estimates are only relevant for a medium-sized city like Brussels. In more densely populated areas, improved emission technologies could still be useful.

11.5.4 Comparison of Scenarios

Table 11.8 summarises the main results of the scenarios which have been explained in the previous sections. Apart from the reference situation, outcomes are given for optimal pricing, cordon pricing and uniform pricing, for the case with and without improved parking charges.

Table 11.8a Key results of counterfactual equilibria (case, 2005) reference parking charges, reference technology

	Per cent welfare gain	Per cent maximal welfare gain	Traffic level (mio/pkm)	Per cent peak, private traffic	Per cent peak, public traffic	Per cent off-peak, private traffic	Per cent off-peak, public traffic	External costs (mio Euro/day)
RF	0	0	9.252	41.6	19.9	30.7	7.9	0.432
CO	0.70	53.5	9.110	37.2	24.1	30.4	8.3	0.415
UP	0.07	5.7	9.251	41.6	20.0	30.4	8.0	0.431
FO	1.31	100	8.407	35.3	28.2	29.1	7.4	0.379

Table 11.8b Key results of counterfactual equilibria (case, 2005) improved parking charges, reference technology

	Per cent welfare gain	Per cent maximal welfare gain	Traffic level (mio/pkm)	Per cent peak, private traffic	Per cent peak, public traffic	Per cent off-peak, private traffic	Per cent off-peak, public traffic	External costs (mio Euro/day)
Parking charges	0.42	32.5	9.048	41.4	21.5	26.8	10.2	0.413
CO	0.97	73.8	8.890	36.6	25.5	27.3	10.6	0.396
UP	0.45	34.8	9.012	41.5	21.6	27.0	9.9	0.411
FO	1.30	99.0	8.410	35.3	28.2	29.1	7.4	0.374

The following comments repeat some of the conclusions of the previous sections.

- Pricing instruments that do not tackle the congestion externality are much less efficient than policies that do: the fuel price scenario (UP) performs substantially worse than cordon pricing (CO) and full optimum pricing (FO). In fact, the largest welfare gains are to be expected from internalisation of external congestion costs, as these are the dominant inefficiency in the present urban transport equilibrium.
- For the Brussels case, the reduction in external congestion costs is achieved by a reduction of peak period passenger car travel. There is no important shift of traffic to the off-peak period. The overall traffic level decreases, and the share of public transport in peak period demand increases.
- Among policies that address congestion externalities, the policies affecting a larger share of transport users perform better: full optimum pricing (FO) performs better than cordon pricing (CO). Gains from policies that affect part of the transport users will be offset by generalised price decreases for travellers not affected directly by the policy instrument. Additionally, policies that cover part of the transport users only may have adverse distributional effects.
- The use of less polluting technology imposed by government regulation, leads to a small net welfare loss.
- The improvement of the parking charges system, so that all passenger car users pay for the resource cost of parking at the trip destination, is crucial in any urban transport policy. Better parking charges as such lead to a welfare gain of about one-third of the maximal welfare gain of urban transport policy.

In the analysis of policy instruments, the implementation costs of the policy instruments have not been taken into account (except for the resource costs involved in the production of less polluting cars). It is likely that fuel price increases, technology regulation and improved parking charges do not require large investments in equipment. The situation is different for cordon pricing and optimal pricing, which require investments in high-tech metering and charging systems. Estimates of implementation costs suggest that these costs are outweighed by the benefits of the system.[9] The real difficulty in the decision on road pricing systems lies in the degree of spatial differentation of the system. In cordon pricing, one toll ring around the city centre is used. In optimal pricing, the external costs are measured on each road of the network. The optimal scheme is situated between those extremes. The determination of the optimal degree of spatial differentiation of a road pricing scheme can only be achieved in a network model in which the welfare benefits of road pricing can be measured and in which the costs of different degrees of spatial differentation of tolls are taken up.

The political and administrative feasibility and the public acceptance of the instruments are harder to judge. While improved parking charges may be relatively easy to implement, they are not beneficial to the majority of transport users at present. Road pricing is not popular either, although the analysis suggests that it may be beneficial to most transport users, depending on the way in which revenues are used. In order to 'sell' road pricing, it is necessary to emphasise the benefits of the system. These are not limited to the transport sector (decreasing pollution, noise and accidents costs, increasing travel speeds), as there are benefits from the reduction of non transport taxes.

11.6 CONCLUSIONS

The reference traffic equilibrium of Brussels in 2005 is characterised by a severe peak congestion problem. Policy instruments which differentiate taxes between peak and off-peak hours can therefore generate important welfare gains. A second important inefficiency in the reference situation is that the majority of drivers do not pay for the use of a parking spot in the city centre. Charging all drivers for the resource cost of parking is an important aspect of an improved urban transport policy package. Externalities related to air pollution, accidents and noise prove to be of relatively less importance in the Brussels case.

Optimal policies generate important welfare gains: a real income increase of 1.3 per cent is put forward as the maximum. These optimal taxes are, however, difficult to implement. The combination of charging commuters an optimal congestion toll and having all drivers pay for the resource cost of parking is probably a more realistic goal, and it yields approximately three-quarters of the maximal welfare gain. Relying on other studies for estimates of implementation costs, it is safe to conclude that the benefits of these policies by far exceed the costs. Note that it has been assumed in the welfare assessment of the policy options, that additional transport tax revenues are used to decrease labour taxes, which corresponds to optimal revenue use. Other types of revenue use may influence the result of the cost–benefit analysis.

As compared to other urban case studies, the road network of Brussels is characterised by a large sensitivity of travel times to changes in network flows at high traffic volumes. In other words, the congestion function is very steep at high traffic levels. In the reference situation of 2005, this characteristic is translated into high marginal external congestion costs during peak hours. Consequently, the optimal peak period congestion taxes are higher than in most other urban case studies (see Chapters 12, 13 and 14).

High subsidies for public transport in off-peak hours are also specific to the Brussels reference case. Other cities pay less subsidies for off-peak public transport, or even raise a net tax. The explanation can be found in the low occupancy rates of public transport vehicles during off-peak hours in Brussels. In the model, this inefficiency is mitigated by raising the off-peak public transport fares. A different approach might be to try to increase occupancy rates, or to adapt vehicle size. Our representation of public transport is not sufficiently detailed to model these policy options.

A comparison of the results for Brussels with the recently defined policy options for Brussels (see Section 11.2.2) shows a clear difference in emphasis. The model assessment of the reference situation identifies peak period congestion and the widespread lack of parking space charges as the main current sources of inefficiency. Substantial improvements of the transport situation can only be expected if these problems are tackled directly by using pricing policies. The Brussels policy proposals concentrate on initiatives to improve the attractiveness of public transport and to stimulate intermodality, so as to indirectly decrease demand for passenger car trips. The instruments are to improve the quality and density, in space and time, of public transport provision, and to provide parking spaces at city border public transport links so as to allow easy substitution between private and public.

The measures proposed may well be necessary if public transport and intermodality are to gain market share in the Brussels transport market, and our results do suggest that such an increase is required. However, these measures must be complemented by pricing measures. Improving public transport without pricing passenger car traffic according to time of day, will not result in decreased passenger car traffic, and thus will not result in decreased congestion during peak hours.

APPENDIX: OVERVIEW TABLES OF COMMON POLICY SCENARIO RESULTS

Table 11A.1 Characterisation of optimal pricing, improved parking charges (Brussels, 2005)

Prices and costs (Euro/pkm)	Resource cost	Tax	Money price	Marginal external cost (per vkm)	Generalised price
Peak					
car, solo, small, petrol, free parking					
inhabitants	0.361	0.533	0.894	0.407	1.085
commuters	0.261	0.497	0.758	0.407	0.949
car, solo, small, petrol, paid parking					
inhabitants	0.361	0.533	0.894	0.407	1.085
commuters	0.261	0.497	0.758	0.407	0.949
car, solo, small, diesel, free parking					
inhabitants	0.326	0.556	0.881	0.435	1.073
bus/tram (inhabitants)	0.080	0.08	0.160	0.020	0.501
Off-peak					
car, solo, small, petrol, free parking					
inhabitants	0.359	0.188	0.546	0.047	0.694
bus/tram (inhabitants)	0.271	0.104	0.375	0.016	0.797
Volume and composition of traffic	**mio pkm**	**Share (per cent)**	**Per cent carpool**	**Speed (km/h)**	
Peak, private	2.969	35.5	33	40	
Peak, public	2.372	28.2		36	
Off-peak, private	2.446	29.1	26	50	
Off-peak, public	0.623	7.4		44	
Tax revenue (mio Euro/day)					
Private	1.710				
Public	0.213				
External costs (mio Euro/day)	0.374				

Table 11.A.2 Characterisation of cordon pricing, reference parking charges (Brussels, 2005)

Prices and costs (Euro/pkm)	Resource cost	Tax	Money price	Marginal external cost (per vkm)	Generalised price
Peak					
car, solo, small, petrol, free parking					
inhabitants	0.361	0.089	0.280	0.865	0.514
commuters	0.261	0.760	0.951	0.865	1.185
car, solo, small, petrol, paid parking					
inhabitants	0.361	0.089	0.450	0.865	0.684
commuters	0.261	0.760	1.021	0.865	1.256
car, solo, small, diesel, free parking					
inhabitants	0.326	0.058	0.214	0.893	0.448
bus/tram (inhabitants)	0.080	0.0395	0.12	0.043	0.503
Off-peak					
car, solo, small, petrol, free parking					
inhabitants	0.359	0.083	0.271	0.047	0.419
bus/tram (inhabitants)	0.271	−0.151	0.12	0.014	0.521
Volume and composition of traffic	**mio pkm**	**Share (per cent)**	**Per cent carpool**	**Speed (km/h)**	
Peak, private	3.388	37.2	30.6	33	
Peak, public	2.192	24.1		29	
Off-peak, private	2.773	30.4	26.1	50	
Off-peak, public	0.757	8.3		44	
Tax revenue (mio Euro/day)					
Private	1.280				
Public	0.001				
External costs (mio Euro/day)	0.415				

Table 11.A.3 Characterisation of uniform pricing, reference parking charges (Brussels, 2005)

Prices and costs (Euro/pkm)	Resource cost	Tax	Money price	Marginal external cost (per vkm)	Generalised price
Peak					
car, solo, small, petrol, free parking					
inhabitants	0.361	0.095	0.286	1.855	0.612
commuters	0.261	0.095	0.286	1.855	0.612
car, solo, small, petrol, paid parking					
inhabitants	0.361	0.095	0.456	1.855	0.782
commuters	0.261	0.095	0.356	1.855	0.682
car, solo, small, diesel, free parking					
inhabitants	0.326	0.067	0.223	1.883	0.549
bus/tram (inhabitants)	0.080	0.039	0.12	0.093	0.581
Off-peak					
car, solo, small, petrol, free parking					
inhabitants	0.359	0.088	0.276	0.046	0.424
bus/tram (inhabitants)	0.271	−0.151	0.12	0.014	0.521
Volume and composition of traffic	**mio pkm**	**Share (per cent)**	**Per cent carpool**	**Speed (km/h)**	
Peak, private	3.853	41.7	29.7	24	
Peak, public	1.851	20.0		21	
Off-peak, private	2.810	30.4	25.5	50	
Off-peak, public	0.736	8.0		44	
Tax revenue (mio Euro/day)					
Private	0.548				
Public	−0.011				
External costs (mio Euro/day)	0.431				

Table 11.A.4 Characterisation of improved parking charges (Brussels, 2005)

Prices and costs (Euro/pkm)	Resource cost	Tax	Money price	Marginal external cost (per vkm)	Generalised price
Peak					
car, solo, small, petrol, free parking					
inhabitants	0.361	0.089	0.450	1.527	0.745
commuters	0.261	0.089	0.350	1.527	0.645
car, solo, small, petrol, paid parking					
inhabitants	0.361	0.089	0.450	1.527	0.745
commuters	0.261	0.089	0.350	1.527	0.645
car, solo, small, diesel, free parking					
inhabitants	0.326	0.058	0.384	1.555	0.679
bus/tram (inhabitants)	0.080	0.0395	0.12	0.076	0.552
Off-peak					
car, solo, small, pctrol, free parking					
Inhabitants	0.359	0.083	0.441	0.047	0.589
bus/tram (inhabitants)	0.271	−0.151	0.12	0.015	0.502
Volume and composition of traffic	**mio pkm**	**Share (per cent)**	**Per cent carpool**	**Speed (km/h)**	
Peak, private	3.750	41.4	31	26	
Peak, public	1.946	21.5		23	
Off-peak, private	2.426	26.8	27	50	
Off-peak, public	0.927	10.2		44	
Tax revenue (mio Euro/day)					
Private	0.469				
Public	−0.032				
External costs (mio Euro/day)	0.413				

NOTES

1. The dataset for Brussels is an extension and an update of the dataset used in the TRENEN I URBAN application for Brussels 2005. For more complete descriptions of data, we refer to Proost and Van Dender (1998) and Ochelen and Proost (1996).
2. There is also a market for non-motorised transport.
3. A more elaborate discussion of these scenarios can be found in Chapter 3 of this volume.
4. The resource cost of parking per km is derived from an average per trip cost of 1.9 Euros per trip (Halcrow Fox, 1996). As trip distances for the conversion to per kilometre cost we used complete journey distance (round trip), not just the distance driven on the Brussels' territory.
5. On a per trip basis, the situation is reversed.
6. The consumer surplus is part of the global welfare measure. It is a monetary measure of the net benefit which consumers get from consumption, given their preferences, income and prices.
7. This is only the case when parking charges are not improved. With improved parking charges, inhabitants not paying for parking in the reference situation will experience a welfare loss from optimal pricing
8. This has been compensated by introducing higher purchase and circulation taxes on diesel cars.
9. Direct estimates of the cost–benefit ratio are not available for Brussels. The MVA Study for London (MVA Consultancy, 1995) shows clear positive net revenues for various road pricing systems. This result probably holds for Brussels, given that the optimal congestion charges in Brussels are at least as high as the optimal London charges (compare Chapter 14 in this volume).

REFERENCES

Calthrop, E., Proost, S. and Van Dender, K. (2000), 'Parking policies and pricing', *Urban Studies*, **37**(1) 63–76.

EC doc II/576/95-EN (1995), *A Welfare Cost Assessment of Various Measures to Reduce Pollutant Emissions from Passenger Road Vehicles for the year 2010*, Final Report, 12 October 1995.

Halcrow Fox (1996), 'Pricing and financing of urban transport', Transport Research APAS – urban transport VII-28, Brussels, Luxembourg: ECSE-EC-EACC.

IRIS – Région de Bruxelles-Capitale (1993), *Plan Régional des Déplacements, Plan IRIS, Constat et Scenarion Tendanciel.*

MVA Consultancy (1995), *The London Congestion Charging Research Programme – Principal Findings*, Government Office for London, HMSO.

Ochelen, S. and Proost, S. (1996), *TRENEN-URBAN: Model Documentation Prototype Version 2.2*, Leuven: CES.

Proost, S. and Van Dender, K. (1998), *New Model Developments: Urban – Software and Documentation*, deliverable 8a of the TRENEN II STRAN project, Leuven: CES.

12. Urban transport pricing in Amsterdam: policy simulations for 2005

Jeroen C.J.M. van den Bergh and Erik T. Verhoef

12.1 INTRODUCTION

This chapter presents the results of urban transport pricing and technology regulation policy simulations that have been performed with the urban model for the city of Amsterdam in The Netherlands for the year 2005. This section presents some background information on the city and its transport.

12.1.1 General Information on Amsterdam[1]

Amsterdam is the capital city of The Netherlands. On 1 January 1996 it had about 718 000 inhabitants, including 353 000 households, composed of 165 000 single-person households, 85 000 couples, 28 400 single-parent families and 52 400 two-parent families. 143 378 people are younger than 19 years, 479 342 are between 19 and 65 and 95 371 are older than 65. Furthermore, 275 000 inhabitants are employed, 83 300 are unemployed and 168 806 people are studying (including all types of education). The city population reached a peak of 870 000 in 1960, and has stabilised somewhat since the 1990s.

The surface area of Amsterdam is equal to 20 158 hectares, its population density 4555 inhabitants per km^2, and its housing density 2213 houses per km^2. Most of the area is entirely flat and situated below sea level. A little over 5 per cent of the surface area (1116.26 ha) is infrastructure, including: 333.25 ha rail, 751.42 ha normal roads and 31.58 ha other. The city is divided into 19 districts that have a large degree of political autonomy and 98 neighbourhoods. Variation is large between these, in terms of, among other things, population density, demographic and ethnic structure, institutes for education and employment. This is a reason for much mobility

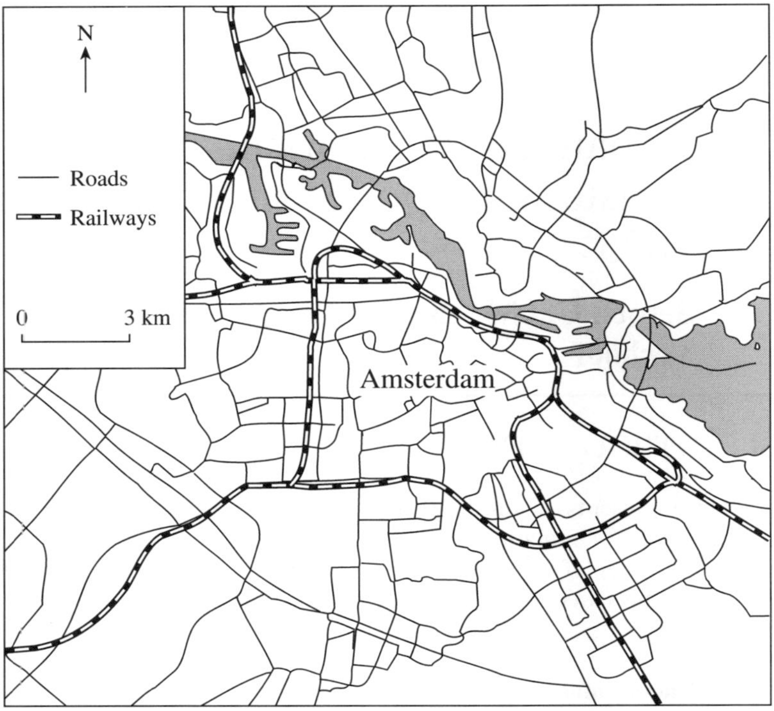

Figure 12.1 Map of Amsterdam

between the neighbourhoods. Peculiar topological features of Amsterdam are a dense network of waterways, including a systematic structured system of canals in the centre. As a result, the city has many bridges, some of them causing bottlenecks in the transport by road and tram. Figure 12.1 shows the geographical structure of Amsterdam.

Amsterdam is part of the province of Noord-Holland. Together with surrounding cities and villages it forms a region in which certain decisions and plans are coordinated. The region Amsterdam ('greater Amsterdam') has 1.4 million inhabitants, and 562000 employed people. Amsterdam is by far the largest city in the region and the province, which causes much commuting in the morning and late afternoon. The average net income per capita in Amsterdam is 1275 Euros per month (or 14600 Euros per year), which is a bit less than in the rest of the region.

The local economy is dominated by commercial services (over 45000 employed people), health care (over 45000 employed people), finance, trade and retail (each more than 25000), and education and local government (each more than 20 000). In 1996 transport offered employment to 15 835 people. Other sectors (more than 10 000 people) are publishing, construction, hotels and restaurants, and politics/culture/sport. Tourism is important for Amsterdam as indicated by the following indicators (for 1995): more than 4 million overnight stays; almost 2 million visitors, and over 10 million Euro revenues of taxes levied on tourists. Evidently, this creates some pressure on transport, mainly in the centre, and to the airport and train stations.

12.1.2 Transport

North of the Amsterdam centre lies a natural barrier, namely a waterway ('het IJ'). Three tunnels and one bridge connect Amsterdam with its district 'Amsterdam Noord' and the northern part of the province. An outer highway ring is connected with three main highways, in the directions south-west (Haarlem, Leiden, Den Haag and Rotterdam), east and south-east (Utrecht, Arnhem, Groningen, Nijmegen, Den Bosch, Eindhoven, Maastricht), and north-west (Zaandam, Alkmaar, Den Helder). Rail infrastructure is situated near the highways in all these directions. To the south, the highway and trains connect to Schiphol international airport (total arriving and departing passengers in 1995 about 25 million), about 20 minutes from Amsterdam centre (outside peak). In the western part Amsterdam has a harbour (31 million tons of goods 1995).

Amsterdam has many narrow, single direction roads in the centre, and only a few multi-lane roads. Many of the wider roads have special lanes for buses, trams and taxis, on which other transport is prohibited (with the exception of emergency traffic). As a result, average speeds outside the rush hours are quite low in comparison with many other capital cities. The following vehicles are owned by people and firms in Amsterdam: 210 342 personal cars, 20 311 small trucks, 1836 trucks, 409 buses, 7702 motorcycles and over 1200 other vehicles. Compared with other cities biking is very developed in Amsterdam, as in the rest of the Netherlands.

Public transport includes trains, trams, buses and subways. Two subways connect the centre of Amsterdam with districts in the south-east direction, and high-speed trams allow passengers to circle around Amsterdam: from the centre eastward to the south (the city of Amstelveen), and westwards to various train stations. Buses are operated on 21 lines and trams on 17 lines. Of 237 million trips made with public transport (827 person-kilometres (pkm)), approximately 139 million were by tram (321 pkm), 55 million by bus (230 pkm), 1.7 by nightbus (12 pkm), and 50 by subway (264 pkm). Amsterdam has seven train stations, with Central Station by far the largest (in terms of departure about 22 million travellers on a total of about 35 million in 1995).

In 1995 the number of paid parking places was 38000, while there were 91000 parking licences. Paying hours in the centre are from Monday to Saturday from 7.00h to 23.00h, and on Sundays from 12.00h to 23.00h. Total revenues from parking were about 37 million Euros in 1995, of which 61 per cent were based on parking places and 18 per cent on licences.

Transport, traffic and infrastructure policies have been aimed at reducing the amount of road transport, notably cars, in the city centre. In 1994 a referendum was held in which the inhabitants decided in favour of traffic calming policies. Since then most roads in the city are one-directional, bicycle lanes are separated from the roads, and recently there has been a restrictive parking policy. The Amsterdam soccer ('Ajax') stadium in the south-east hosts a 'park & ride' where cars can be parked and a direct subway connection with the centre is available. Finally, as part of general spatial planning in the Netherlands, a so-called '*ABC* policy' aims to match the mobility needs of businesses and services with the accessibility of different locations. Locations are graded *A, B* or *C* according to their accessibility by public and private transport. *A* locations are identified as having high public and low private road transport accessibility, and suitable for activities characterised by a high employee density, or large numbers of visitors, and little freight transport. *C* locations are well accessible from the main road network, suitable for businesses with a low density of employees and few visitors, and strongly dependent on passenger and freight transport by road. *B* locations are accessible by both private and public transport. The *ABC* policy has implications for the amount of parking lots allowed per number of employees: one parking lot per 10 employees at *A* locations, and per 20 employees at *B* locations. The whole centre is treated as an *A* location. Of course, this will in the long run affect the location of firms, which is expected to improve spatial and transport system use.

In 1995 the city of Amsterdam had a budget of almost 6.7 billion Euros, of which transport and water infrastructure and management received 7.3 per cent. In 1995 expenditures were almost 270 million Euros, and revenues almost 190 million Euros. The way the money price is levied for use of public transport in the Netherlands is as follows. Except for rail services, a unitary card ('strippenkaart') is used to facilitate payment for bus, tram and subway services offered by different private local and regional public transport companies throughout the entire country. The money collected by cards sold is distributed among the public transport companies. The share of all expenditures that a private company receives is based on the intensity of use of the services supplied by that particular company. An important measure in this context is occupation rates. As a result, the profit of each company depends on the share of the total income. In fact, the degrees of freedom for management decisions are therefore rather limited. A company's profit is consequently mainly determined by the share of public transport services in total transport demand on the one hand, and the ability of cost reduction within a company on the other hand. Infrastructure of heavy rail (trains) and subways has been financed by the national government, while tram infrastructure has been financed by the municipality. In the past the municipal public transport department (GVB) has faced many budget deficits, as a result of which both state and municipal governments have granted ad hoc financial support.

12.1.3 Purpose of the Study

This study aims to examine improved transport policy options for the city of Amsterdam by applying a model that reflects the above described situation of Amsterdam transport as well as possible. Improved and optimal policies will reflect external costs related to congestion, air pollution, noise and accidents. Details of these externalities are discussed in the next section. The study will focus on particular problems and policy issues. This includes the impact that parking policy and parking resource costs will have on the choices made by car users, and indirectly on traffic volumes of the various private and public transport modes. Moreover, it can be examined in which way the cost of financing public transport will be affected by changes in the composition and level of subsidies and taxes on buses, trams and subways. For this purpose, a number of scenarios for 2005 have been calculated. In addition to reference and full optimum scenarios, a 'congestion or cordon pricing' package is examined. The latter scenario is very close to a particular road pricing scheme that was originally planned for Amsterdam as from the year 2001 (Verhoef, Lijesen and Hoen, 1998).

Section 12.2 explains the construction of the reference situation that has been the basis for model calibration. Section 12.3 describes Amsterdam's transport problems in 2005 under this reference situation. Section 12.4 offers a detailed description and explanation of the optimal policy. Section 12.5 presents the results of cordon pricing. Section 12.6 compares all policy options. Section 12.7 presents conclusions.

12.2 CONSTRUCTING A REFERENCE CASE FOR 2005

12.2.1 The Structure of the Transport Market

The data on transport flows are based on the network model GENMOD, which has been developed by the Department of Infrastructure and

Transport of the municipality of Amsterdam.[2] The transport described by the model includes transport with origins and destinations in the city centre, within the ring road (A10 highway), as well as transport from and to surrounding zones with either the origin or the destination in the city centre within the ring road. This covers transport on main roads (highways) and on secondary roads (see Figure 12.1).

Car trips lead to a demand for parking space at the trip destination. Not all travellers have to pay for this space, because firms and other organisations provide free parking, or because street parking is free. For Europe, it is estimated that 70 per cent of all trips to urban centres leads to free parking. Since the resource cost of a parking space is clearly positive, provision of free parking space implies a distortion of the urban transport market. This is reflected by the model, which divides inhabitants and commuters (343 828 and 148 184 individuals) into those who do and those who do not have access to free parking. For Amsterdam, the division into four consumer groups used is:

- inhabitants (insiders), non-payers (IN): 240 000 individuals,
- inhabitants, payers (IP): 100 000 individuals,
- commuters (outsiders), non-payers (ON): 100 000 individuals,
- commuters, payers (OP): 50 000 individuals.

The model will be calibrated for 2005 based on the assumption of unchanged policies. For the demand side the same peak/off-peak distribution is used in 2005 as in 1995. The peak period amounts to 2 hours and the off-peak period to 17 hours.

The model includes the following transport modes: private transport by car; public transport separated into aggregate variables for bus and tram, and subway; and transport by bicycle. The utility or choice tree is shown in Figure 12.2. The distribution among different car types and among different public transport modes is assumed to be the same as in 1995. Constant real prices are assumed with regard to consumer prices paid for other than transport goods. Elasticities of substitution are derived to produce price elasticities for 1995, based on the 1990 reference situation. On the supply side gasoline cars use unleaded petrol; resource costs of standard 2005 vehicles are equal to the 1995 costs; resource costs of improved technologies are based on values used for the Brussels case study (Chapter 11 in this volume). Data on prices, costs, allocation or distribution between subcategories (like cars: pooled, alone, gasoline, diesel, and so on) are based on a mix of information on national and Amsterdam levels. Other data are based on translating Brussels' proportions to Amsterdam levels, or on general data sets on EU level (external costs specified for particular cities).

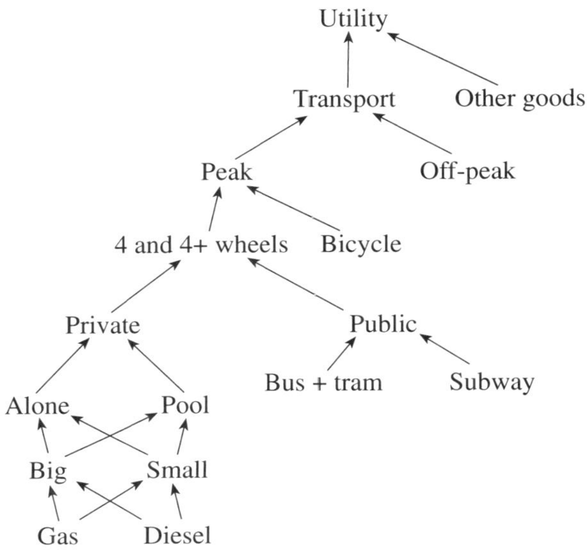

Figure 12.2 *Utility or choice tree in Amsterdam model*

12.2.2 Assumptions on Traffic Growth and Composition

The data on total volumes of transport for each mode have been calculated on the basis of the tables in Appendix A, which are based on predictions of the already mentioned GENMOD network model. The data apply to the evening peak period 16.00h–18.00h during a working day. The results are spatially desegregated into four zones, based on a zonal aggregation of a basic system of 592 zones in the traffic model GENMOD. The data include average trip length, total km travel led and average trip duration per mode, for public transport, bicycles and car, between and within the four aggregate zones. For our purpose only the trips starting or ending in zone I are relevant. As a result of this approach, the estimates of traffic volumes for 2005 can be considered conservative.

12.2.3 Assumptions on Road Capacity and Public Transport Capacity

The calibration assumes that there are no major road or public transport network capacity extensions until 2005. Public transport may include, however, the use of extra carriages and vehicles. The congestion function used for Amsterdam is shown in Figure 12.3.

The congestion function is a non-linear functional relationship between

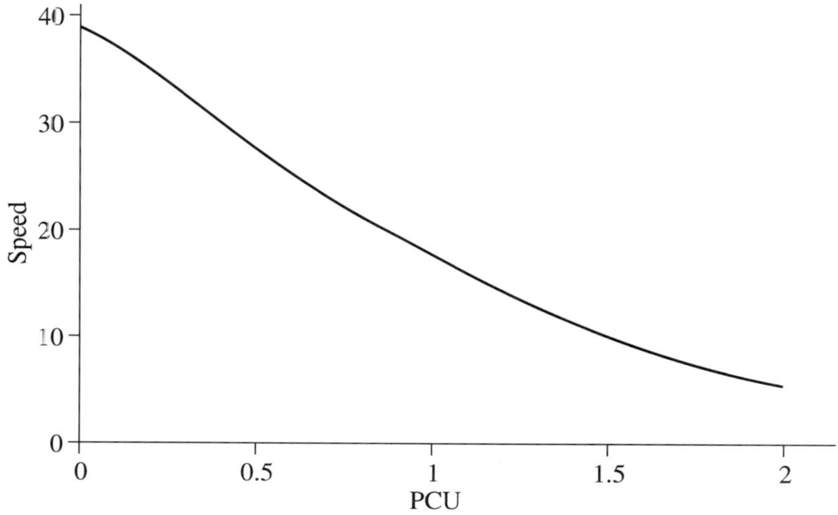

Notes: Speed in km/h; PCU in million passenger car units per hour

Figure 12.3 Speed–flow (congestion) function for Amsterdam, 2005

traffic volume and the time necessary to travel. It is used to model time losses due to congestion. The general formulation is the following:

$$S = \frac{1}{speed} = a + be^{g(PersonalCarUnits)} \tag{12.1}$$

The form of this function is explained in Chapter 10. The parameter values are the following: $a = 0.94004061$, $b = 0.55995939$, $g = 1.45429005$. The following information was used to estimate these parameters. Congestion relevant public transport equals 737 819 kilometres giving 40 990 pcu km. This is based on a correction factor 2/36 to cover the occupation rate 36 persons/bus in peak, and on a congestion effect of a bus being double that of a car. Congestion relevant car transport equals 1 409 082 kilometres giving 1 178 162 pcu km. This is based on an average car occupation equal to 1.196 (=0.14*2.4+0.86*1; where 14 per cent of the cars is pooled with an average occupation of 2.4 person/car). Subsequently, three 'observations' are needed to estimate the congestion function:

(1) the average speed is 26.1 km/h at a traffic volume equal to 40 990 (buses) + 1 178 162 (cars) = 1 219 152 pcu (in km),
(2) the average speed is 40 km/h at a traffic volume equal to zero,

(3) the average speed is 37 km/h at a traffic volume equal to 75 per cent of that under case (1).

This information is based on guestimates and calculations with the GENMOD network model.

12.2.4 Assumptions on Resource Costs and Taxes

Most data pertain to 1995 or 1996, and are used as approximates (for instance modal split) for 2005. For precise parameter estimates the year has been indicated. For the determination of all prices an exchange rate of fl2.19/Euros (exchange rate fixed in August 1997) is used. The main sources of information are the Central Statistical Office (CBS), Hague Consultancy Group (HCG), the Public Transport Company of Amsterdam (GVB), the Ministry of Finance, and the Department of Infrastructure and Transport of the municipality of Amsterdam. The GENMOD network model for Amsterdam has allowed calculation of peak flow data between four aggregate zones. This has made it possible to develop both a network and a one-link or standard TRENEN model. Tables 12.1a to 12.1g summarise other important data on resource costs and taxes.

The money price for PT is based on the average fare paid on public transport. Fare levels are measured by receipts per passenger-km for PT services. Within Amsterdam the average fare equals 2.5 strips of the Strippenkaart, that is, 0.9132 Euro.

We were bound to use information from the Rotterdam public transportation service since the Public Transport Company of Amsterdam could not

Table 12.1a Consumer price in Euros per vehicle-km (including all non-fuel cost: acquisition cost (with VAT and excise), insurance, reparations)

	Gasoline	Diesel
Small	0.2053	0.2565
Big	0.3341	0.3315

Source: Consumentenbond (1995)

Table 12.1b Price per litre fuel in Euros (including VAT and excise)

Gas	0.8539	Diesel	0.6027

Source: Consumentenbond (1995)

Table 12.1c Money price public transport (per period and mode) per passenger-km in Euros

	Bus	Subway
Peak	0.9132	0.9132
Off-peak	0.9132	0.9132

Source: Gemeentelijk Vervoersbedrijf, based on personal contact

Table 12.1d Resource vehicle costs, net of tax, in Euros per car-km (including all non-fuel costs: vehicle price (acquisition cost excluding VAT and excise), traffic tax, insurance, reparations)

	Gasoline	Diesel	Gasoline with catalytic converter	Diesel with catalytic converter
Small	0.1705	0.21	0.1705	0.21
Big	0.545	0.269	0.545	0.269

Source: Consumentenbond (1995)

Table 12.1e Resource costs in Euros per litre fuel (excluding VAT and excise)

Gas	0.2135	Diesel	0.1507

Source: Consumentenbond (1995)

provide information about these parameters. The fixed cost of public transport is 0.241 million Euros per day (source: Gemeentelijk Vervoersbedrijf).

12.2.5 Assumptions on External Costs

The method for estimating the external costs is explained in Chapter 7 of this volume. Four main types of externalities of urban transport are considered: congestion, air pollution, noise and accidents. Various estimates indicate that during peak hours congestion can make up for 60 to 70 per cent of total marginal external costs of cars; accidents for about 20 per cent; air pollution for 10 per cent and noise probably for less then 1 per cent.

Marginal external congestion costs indicate the value of the time loss which an extra km made causes to all other travellers. Multiplying this by

Table 12.1f Total resource cost in Euros per vehicle-km

	Bus	Subway
Peak	3.62	3.02
Off-peak	3.12	2.51

Source: Rotterdamse Electrische Tramweg maatschappij

Table 12.1g The proportions in which the vehicle fleet types are used

Vehicle classification	Cubic Capacity	Proportion (%)
Small Gasoline	800–1400	44.3
Large Gasoline	1400–2000	44.7
Small Diesel	1300–1800	5.45
Large Diesel	1800–2100	5.55

Source: CBS (1995b)

the total number of travellers gives the total marginal external congestion cost. The latter becomes significant during peak hours. Congestion externalities in the model depend on the congestion function (see Figure 12.3) and the value of time, which is 7.301 Euros per passenger per hour for car users during the peak period, and 6.177 Euros outside the peak period. For public transport these values are 5.62 Euros and 3.93 Euros for peak and off-peak periods, respectively. The value of time for walking and biking per hour is 2.803 Euros (source: HCG, 1990).

Marginal external air pollution costs are the cost of health damage and mortality caused by harmful pollutants emitted by engines. The data for air pollution related externalities are based on ExterneE-Transport figures. They include various local pollutants (nitrogen oxides, sulphur oxides, volatile organic compounds, carbon monoxide, lead and small particulate matter), and global pollutants (CO_2 and CO). These may cause ozone concentrations and acid deposits, and extra global warming, which have an impact on health and vegetation, and future climate, environment and generation. Accident-related externalities include the costs of an increased accident risk and the direct economic costs related to average accident risk. In 1995 17000 accidents occurred in Amsterdam, with 29 people being killed and 3300 people being injured. These numbers have been decreasing over the years; in 1975 there were 67 people killed and 4850 injured. Other categories of externalities are the costs of traffic noise and road damage. Both type of externalities are relatively less important.

12.2.6 Assumptions on Behaviour

The average occupancy rate in pooled cars is 2.4. To be able to assign car demand to solo car use and carpooling the proportion of carpoolers is required. The proportion of carpooling in the total car demand is 14 per cent (source: CBS, 1995a). Tables 12.1h to 12.1j show other demand-related data.

Table 12.1h Average occupancy rate in persons per vehicle in public transport

	Bus	Subway
Peak	36	33
Off-peak	28	26

Sources: Gemeentelijk Vervoersbedrijf and Noord Zuid Hollandse Vervoersmaatschappij (NZH)

Table 12.1i The demand in passenger-km per representative individual per day

	Bus	Subway
Insiders peak	2.6	5.4
Insiders off-peak	2.4	5.2
Outsiders peak	2.6	5.4
Outsiders off-peak	2.4	5.2

Source: Gemeentelijk Vervoersbedrijf

Table 12.1j (Cross-) price elasticities (in terms of money prices)

	Peak car	Off-peak car	Peak public transport	Off-peak public transport
Peak car	−0.35		0.023	0
Off-peak car		−0.60	0	0.025
(Peak public transport)	0.009	0	(−0.55)	
Peak bus			−0.23	
(Off-peak public transport)	0	0.01		(−0.683)
Off-peak bus				−0.28

Source: de Wit and van Gent (1986)

The average occupancy rate per vehicle in public transport is shown in Table 12.1h. This is the so-called dynamic occupancy rate, that is, the average occupation rate along the route supplied by public transport.

Table 12.1j shows price elasticities. In this case we were forced to translate the price elasticities based on fuel prices into elasticities on the generalised price level. For this purpose the values found in the referred studies were multiplied with the factor 0.178, which represents the share of fuel in the aggregate generalised price. Additionally, for buses a factor of 0.4133 was required to yield the correct elasticity that takes into account the share of bus usage given the total supply of transport services by bus, tram and metro.

12.3 THE AMSTERDAM TRANSPORT PRICING PROBLEMS IN 2005

This section presents the reference situation use to calibrate the model for Amsterdam. It will provide a link between the transport situation sketched in Section 12.2 and the model. The description of the characteristics of the case study will cover prices and taxes, as well as a comparison of taxes with marginal external costs.

Central to the model is the notion of generalised price or cost. This consists of resource costs, taxes and time costs. Each of these may differ among the different transport modes. The sum of the resource costs and the taxes is called the money price. The sum of the money price and the value (cost) of time spent to drive a kilometre is the generalised price. Apart from the generalised cost to the consumer, there are the marginal external costs related to each kilometre that has been driven. Marginal external costs can be regarded as real costs to society that are not included in the generalised price. Table 12.2 shows the values of each of these categories of marginal costs for the reference situation for Amsterdam.

Under the reference scenario in 2005 a trip into the centre of Amsterdam during peak hours by car from outside the larger ring of the city ('commuters') is associated with a money cost of about 0.26 Euro per km. This result holds for the case where the driver does not have to pay for parking space at his destination, for example when his employer provides free parking space. The generalised price is much higher, namely 0.85 Euro/km. This includes a time cost equal to 0.59 Euro/km. The situation described is inefficient, because the resource cost of parking is not charged to the drivers, and prices are below social costs. The discrepancy between prices and social costs leads to an inefficiently high demand for transport by car. Since the discrepancies vary according to the different transport modes and time periods, the modal distribution and the time distribution of transport demand will be suboptimal.

According to Table 12.2 the time cost, that is, the difference between generalised price and money price, equals 69 per cent of the total trip cost during, and 45 per cent of the total trip cost outside the peak period. Other price components only differ between peak and off-peak, as a result of speed differences that cause differences in fuel consumption. The money price of the kilometre in row 1 is significantly lower than the resource cost, because inhabitants do not pay for parking. This difference does not exist for drivers who have to pay for parking (compare row 3). Note that, as a result of the high parking costs in Amsterdam, the difference between the money prices for payers and non-payers is quite large. Furthermore, the resource cost per kilometre is higher for an inhabitant than for a commuter. The reason for this difference is that parking costs are converted from a per trip basis to a per kilometre basis, and average total trip distances are higher for commuters than for inhabitants. The difference in per kilometre costs (money price) between payers and non-payers is large. The cost of a kilometre driven is higher for a diesel car than for a petrol car, due to taxes on diesel vehicles being higher, which more than compensate for the lower per kilometre resource costs of diesel vehicles. The tax rate in generalised price terms is ca. 7 per cent in peak hours, and 15 per cent in off-peak (Table 12.4c). Taxes on private car use are far below marginal external costs in both the peak and off-peak periods, so that they do not reflect marginal external costs.

For public transport the money price is equal in peak and off-peak. Resource costs differ on a per passenger-kilometre basis because of differences in occupancy rates (36 persons/bus during peak, and 28 during off-peak). The consequence is that peak period bus driving almost covers the marginal resource cost of the bus. Note that, both during the peak and off-peak period, the net taxes on public transport are negative, so that the marginal cost of bus transport is not covered. Furthermore, the share of time costs in the total travel time is higher for public than for private transport. This is due to the fact that public transport involves walking and waiting.

The composition of traffic and the speeds in the reference situation are given in the lower second part of Table 12.2. Kilometres made during the peak represent 43 per cent of the total. Public transport during peak and off-peak accounts for about 24 per cent of total traffic. Carpooling is about the same in both periods, with an average occupancy rate equal to 2.4 persons per car. The speed of the cars during the peak is quite low, to some extent due to the presence of many narrow one-direction roads in Amsterdam which do not allow high speeds.

Table 12.2 Characterisation of the reference situation (Amsterdam, 2005)

Prices and costs (Euro/pkm)	Resource cost	Tax	Money price	Marginal external cost (per vkm)[3]	Generalised price
Peak					
car, solo, small, petrol, free parking					
inhabitants	0.7957	0.0791	0.2648	1.48621	0.84776
commuters	0.2957	0.0791	0.2648	1.48621	0.84776
car, solo, small, petrol, paid parking					
inhabitants	0.7957	0.0791	0.8748	1.48621	1.45776
commuters	0.2957	0.0791	0.3748	1.48621	0.95776
car, solo, small, diesel, free parking					
inhabitants	0.82779	0.07079	0.28857	1.48404	0.87154
bus/tram (inhabitants)	0.10056	−0.00924	0.09132	0.101969	1.1491
Off-peak					
car, solo, small, petrol, free parking					
inhabitants	0.79342	0.07247	0.25589	0.23228	0.46796
bus/tram (inhabitants)	0.11143	−0.02011	0.09132	0.153396	0.70841
Volume and composition of traffic	mio pkm	share (%)	% carpool	speed km/h	
Peak, private	2.470587	29.06	13.94	13.22	
Peak, public	1.176775	13.84		6.33	
Off-peak, private	3.966089	46.66	14.11	34.64	
Off-peak, public	0.88697	10.43		16.59	
Tax revenue (mio Euro/day)					
private	0.75005				
public	−0.01984				
External costs (mio Euro/day)	1.24507				

12.4 THE OPTIMAL POLICY (FO) AS A BENCHMARK

12.4.1 Major Assumptions

This section defines the optimal policy and explains its results, comparing these with the ones under the reference situation. The full optimum (FO) case includes perfect or first-best regulation settings of policy instruments so as to 'internalise' (or better: optimise) the previously discussed externalities of urban transport. Its implementation requires an advanced road-pricing system that determines taxes on the basis of congestion conditions in space and time, polluting and other characteristics of vehicles, and on accident externalities. Although this may seem unrealistic in the short run, it is certainly feasible in the long run, given progress in information technology. This FO counterfactual equilibrium should therefore be regarded as a benchmark equilibrium, which represents the maximal welfare gain to be expected from a reform in urban transport pricing and technology regulation.

The optimal policy charges all trips at their social cost. Given the space and time dependence of marginal external costs, the policy requires electronic road pricing systems. Since resource costs are fixed per kilometre, taxes are used to arrive at these optimal prices. In the optimal policy, taxes may be almost ideally adjusted to the level of external costs: they can vary according to the time of day, the vehicle type, the fuel type and the user type (inhabitants versus commuters). The implementation of such a pricing policy requires a highly sophisticated tolling mechanism, that also allows taxation to depend on vehicle emissions. Note that taxes are optimised in public transport as well as in private transport, and that the optimal taxes are not only determined by marginal external costs, but also by inefficiencies of the labour market. The only restriction on the flexibility of taxes is that the toll has to be equal for payers and non-payers for parking. This is not really a problem as it has been assumed that parking is charged at its resource cost to all car users. Hence, there is no need to use the tax instrument to correct the inefficiencies in parking charges. The reason for this assumption is that an electronic road pricing system cannot observe whether drivers will or will not have to pay for parking at their destination. Moreover, it will be assumed that no regulation of technology has taken place, so that all vehicles will have the same emission characteristics as in the reference situation. Discussion of scenarios where parking charges have not been improved, and where technology has been regulated, will be discussed in Section 12.5.

12.4.2 Optimal Pricing Policy

Optimal volumes

Tables 12.3 and 12.4 summarise the results of the optimal pricing policy, assuming that emission technology has not been regulated and that the resource cost of parking has been charged to all drivers. Table 12A.10 in Appendix 12A.2 gives more detailed results. The simultaneous introduction of improved parking charges and optimal pricing with respect to external costs leads to a welfare gain of 0.96 per cent relative to the generalised income of the reference situation. External costs of air pollution, noise and accidents decrease with about 0.05 million Euros per day, or a decrease of 12.5 per cent. The change in congestion conditions is reflected in the average travel speeds in the peak: 13.2 km/h under the reference scenario, and 19.8 km/h under the optimal policy. This increase will result in a decrease of time costs of trips. Off-peak speeds do not change significantly, because congestion in the reference situation is not problematic during the off-peak hours: speeds are 34.6 km/h versus 35.5 km/h, respectively. The increase in travel speeds is related to the change in traffic level, and in modal and time distribution of traffic. Overall, daily traffic drops with 0.566 million passenger car units, that is, a 6.7 per cent decrease. The share of peak traffic remains more or less constant (42.9 per cent in reference situation and 42.2 per cent in the optimum), but there is an important modal shift from private transport to public transport. The share of public transport in total transport during the day rises from 24.3 per cent to 37.0 per cent, more or less equally distributed over the peak and off-peak.

Optimal taxes

The results in the tables are represented in per vehicle-kilometre terms. Given an average car trip length of about 4 km for insiders and 15 km for outsiders (see Tables 12A.1–12A.3 in Appendix 12A.1), approximate optimal taxes per trip for Amsterdam are the following: during the peak period, 3.6 Euros for an average inhabitant (insider), and 13 Euros for an average commuter (outsider). The optimal taxes outside the peak period are 0.5 Euro for the average inhabitant and 1.4 Euros for the average commuter. This is much higher than the originally proposed cordon charges proposed in the Randstad area, which are in the order of 2.5 Euros per trip (average length 20 km, inbound and morning peak only) (see Verhoef, Lijesen and Hoen, 1998). The latter charges, however, were not based on optimum computations.

In Table 12.4a optimal taxes are compared with reference taxes. Taxes increase for private transport, but more significantly for the peak period due to the high level of externalities, notably congestion-related ones. In the case of public transport subsidies in the peak are changed into taxes, and

Table 12.3 Key results of optimal policy compared with reference situation (Amsterdam, 2005) (optimal policy without technology regulation and with parking charges improved)

	Welfare level	Per cent welfare gain	Per cent maximal welfare gain	Traffic level (mio/ pkm)	Per cent peak, private traffic	Per cent peak, public traffic	Per cent off-peak, private traffic	Per cent off-peak, public traffic	External cost (mio Euro/day)
RF	74.50	–	–	8.500	29.06	13.84	46.66	10.43	0.402
FO	75.46	0.96	88.4	7.934	22.27	19.89	40.71	17.13	0.350

Note: The maximal welfare gain results when both technology and parking charges are improved

Table 12.4a Taxes in reference situation and optimal pricing (Euro/passenger km, % change w.r.t. reference situation, Amsterdam, 2005)

	Euro/pkm				% change			
	IN	IP	ON	OP	IN	IP	ON	OP
RF								
peak, car*	0.079	0.079	0.079	0.079	0	0	0	0
peak, bus	−0.009	−0.009	−0.009	−0.009	0	0	0	0
off-peak, car*	0.072	0.072	0.072	0.072	0	0	0	0
off-peak, bus	−0.020	−0.020	−0.020	−0.020	0	0	0	0
FO								
peak, car*	0.912	0.912	0.842	0.842	1054	1054	966	966
peak, bus	0.047	0.047	0.040	0.040	−622	−622	−544	−544
off-peak, car*	0.133	0.133	0.095	0.095	85	85	32	32
off-peak, bus	−0.021	−0.021	−0.015	−0.015	−5	−5	25	25

Notes:
* small petrol car driven alone
IN inhabitants nonpayers for parking, IP inhabitants payers, ON commuters nonpayers, OP commuters payers

Table 12.4b Generalised prices in reference situation and optimal pricing (Euro/passenger km, % change w.r.t. reference, Amsterdam, 2005)

	Euro/pkm				% change			
	IN	IP	ON	OP	IN	IP	ON	OP
RF								
peak, car*	0.848	1.458	0.848	0.958	0	0	0	0
peak, bus	1.149	1.149	1.040	1.040	0	0	0	0
off-peak, car*	0.468	1.078	0.468	1.078	0	0	0	0
off-peak, bus	0.708	0.708	0.561	0.561	0	0	0	0
FO								
peak, car*	2.096	2.096	1.526	1.526	147	44	80	59
peak, bus	0.904	0.904	0.796	0.796	−21	−38	−6	−16
off-peak, car*	1.133	1.133	0.596	0.596	142	5	27	−45
off-peak, bus	0.670	0.670	0.554	0.554	−5	−5	−1	−1

Note: * small petrol car driven alone

Table 12.4c Composition of generalised prices in reference and optimal pricing for a small petrol car driven alone by an inhabitant not paying for parking (Amsterdam, 2005)

	Peak		Off-peak	
	RF	FO	RF	FO
Time cost/GP	0.69	0.19	0.45	0.18
MP/GP	0.31	0.81	0.55	0.82
Tax/GP	0.09	0.44	0.15	0.12
Resource cost/GP	0.94	0.38	0.62	0.26
Tax/MP	0.30	0.47	0.28	0.14

subsidies in the off-peak are increased. The first finding is due to the discrepancy between resource costs per passenger-kilometre and prices per passenger-kilometre in the reference situation. The second finding is a bit unexpected, and is caused by the Mohring effect: when public transport demand increases, the frequency of public transport services is assumed to optimally respond. Consequently, a demand increase gives rise to decreasing waiting times at public transport stops. In order to obtain this positive externality off-peak public transport use needs to be subsidised. Note that the optimal taxes are also differentiated between different groups of travellers, that is, between inhabitants and commuters.

Optimal generalised prices

Taxes influence the generalised price of transport, which will in turn influence travel decisions made by consumers. Table 12.4b compares generalised prices in the reference situation and in the full optimum. Whereas generalised prices of private transport increase, those of public transport decrease. Tables 12.4a and 12.4b show that the changes in generalised prices – whether positive or negative – are much smaller than the associated tax changes. The reason is that tax increases, which cause money price increases, are partly offset by gains in travel speeds, which lead to lower time costs. The net generalised price increase during peak hours is most significant; it more than doubles for inhabitants that do not pay for parking. For public transport, an additional cause of decreasing time costs is the already mentioned Mohring effect.

Table 12.4c supplies additional information on the changes in price structure between reference situation and optimal pricing. For the peak period in particular this price structure is remarkably similar to the one that has been presented for Brussels. The share of time costs in the generalised price decreases strongly, which results from the increase in the money price and the decrease in the time cost levels. Tax rates in terms of generalised prices increase, and are higher in the peak than in the off-peak, while the relation is opposite in the reference situation. Monetary tax rates are more or less equal in peak and off-peak periods in the reference situation, but the peak monetary tax rate is higher in peak hours under optimal pricing. Since external costs are internalised in the generalised price, resource costs become smaller as a share of the generalised price. Finally, the monetary prices relative to the generalised prices are almost equal in the optimal situation. Note that under the optimal pricing policy taxes exceed marginal external costs. This is due to the efficiency of the global taxation system: net revenues are assumed to be used for the reduction of distortionary labour taxes.

12.5 ANALYSIS OF CORDON PRICING

The idea of this scenario is to implement a simple cordon around Amsterdam, in which a time differentiated cordon toll can be determined optimally. The cordon pricing scenario is more precisely defined by the following conditions: public transport prices are equal to reference levels; for insiders, private transport prices are equal to reference levels; for outsiders, private transport prices are optimised, with the constraint that the toll is equal for payers and non-payers. Detailed results for this scenario are reported in Table 12A.11 in Appendix 12A.2. As shown by Table 12.5, the inhabitants (insiders IN and IP) benefit from cordon pricing, whereas the commuters (outsiders ON and OP) lose, relative to the optimal pricing scenario. The reason is that imposing taxes on commuters will lead to an increase in the generalised prices for this group, so that their demand for traffic will decrease. If nothing else would change, then overall welfare would increase, as the policy brings prices in line with marginal external costs for some part of the system at least. For inhabitants an entirely different picture emerges. Although they are not subject to changing money prices of transport (relative to the reference situation), their generalised cost of transport decreases. This is caused by reduced time costs of transport due to reduced traffic from commuters. Although this seems to increase welfare, inhabitants raise their demand for traffic, giving rise to a negative welfare effect. As this is imperfectly taken into account by optimal cordon taxes a second-best outcome results.

As shown by Table 12.5 introducing optimal transport prices will lead to an increase in the consumer surpluses for all groups, except for inhabitants who did not pay for parking in the reference situation. For this group, the per kilometre increase of private transport prices is so high that it offsets all other gains from the optimal policy. This illustrates that the introduction of optimal pricing, combined with optimal tax revenue use, does not

Table 12.5 Percentage changes in consumer surpluses for two scenarios (Amsterdam, 2005) (with respect to reference situation)

	IN	IP	ON	OP
Optimal pricing	−3.82	2.62	0.79	3.13
Cordon pricing	−2.99	2.84	−1.24	1.29

necessarily lead to welfare gains for all consumers. Table 12.5 also raises the question whether the initial welfare level of non-paying inhabitants was not artificially high because of the parking subsidy.

12.6 COMPARISON OF ALL POLICY OPTIONS

Tables 12.6a–d summarise the main results of the scenarios which have been discussed in the previous sections. The results pertain to reference situation (RF), optimal pricing (FO) and cordon pricing (CO), each for the case with and without technology regulation and improved parking charges. Some remarks are in order. First, the traffic volume under the CO scenario for reference parking charges is higher than in the reference situation. Under the CO scenario less commuter traffic reduces the time costs for public transport, so that the public transport volume more than offsets the reduction in private transport during the peak. The Mohring effect may contribute to this.

Some general remarks that follow from comparison between the three main types of transport policies, irrespective of whether parking charges and technology have been changed, are as follows. Both in terms of welfare gain and external cost reduction, the FO scenario scores better than the CO scenario. The decrease in external congestion costs is for the greater part realised by a reduction of traffic by car and a shift to public transport, these effects being most clear for the peak period. In addition, there is a shift of traffic from the peak to the off-peak period. In particular, this leads to more public transport outside the peak. These findings are consistent with a trend already followed by public transport providers in the Netherlands, notably the Dutch railways, namely to stimulate off-peak travel by price differentiation.

A few other general points can be made. The search for welfare-improving transport policies seems to be dominated by the congestion externalities. Partial policies are less effective in this sense. In other words, the policies affecting a larger portion of transport users perform better in terms of overall efficiency. FO aimed at all users performs better than CO aimed at commuters only. The latter policy will involve 'leakage' or offsetting effects, due to lower generalised prices for other travellers, notably private car users.

Table 12.6a Key results of counterfactual equilibria (Amsterdam, 2005), reference parking charges, reference technology

	Per cent welfare gain	Per cent maximal welfare gain	Traffic level (mio/pkm)	Per cent peak, private traffic	Per cent peak, public traffic	Per cent off-peak, private traffic	Per cent off-peak, public traffic	External cost (mio Euro/day)
RF	0	0	8.500	29.06	13.84	46.66	10.43	0.402
CO	0.23	17.8	8.541	28.56	14.60	46.46	10.38	0.395
FO	1.136	88.1	7.860	22.44	20.06	40.00	17.51	0.345

Table 12.6b Key results of counterfactual equilibria (Amsterdam, 2005), reference parking charges, regulation of technology

	Per cent welfare gain	Per cent maximal welfare gain	Traffic level (mio/pkm)	Per cent peak, private traffic	Per cent peak, public traffic	Per cent off-peak, private traffic	Per cent off-peak, public traffic	External cost (mio Euro/day)
RF	0	0	8.500	29.06	13.84	46.66	10.43	0.402
CO	0.24	18.6	8.542	28.56	14.60	46.46	10.38	0.388
FO	1.143	88.7	7.861	22.44	20.05	40.02	17.49	0.340

Table 12.6c Key results of counterfactual equilibria (Amsterdam, 2005), improved parking charges, reference technology

	Per cent welfare gain	Per cent maximal welfare gain	Traffic level (mio/pkm)	Per cent peak, private traffic	Per cent peak, public traffic	Per cent off-peak, private traffic	Per cent off-peak, public traffic	External cost (mio Euro/day)
RF	0	0	8.500	29.06	13.84	46.66	10.43	0.402
CO	0.98	76.0	8.044	27.71	16.92	40.15	15.22	0.363
FO	1.287	99.8	7.934	22.27	19.89	40.71	17.13	0.350

Table 12.6d Key results of counterfactual equilibria (Amsterdam, 2005), improved parking charges, regulation of technology

	Per cent welfare gain	Per cent maximal welfare gain	Traffic level (mio/pkm)	Per cent peak, private traffic	Per cent peak, public traffic	Per cent off-peak, private traffic	Per cent off-peak, public traffic	External cost (mio Euro/day)
RF	0	0	8.500	29.06	13.84	46.66	10.43	0.402
CO	0.99	76.8	8.044	27.71	16.92	40.16	15.22	0.358
FO	1.294	100	7.934	22.28	19.88	40.73	17.11	0.345

Evidently, such partial policies are neither attractive from a perspective of distribution of welfare (or of welfare improvements).

The use of less polluting technology, imposed by government regulation, leads to a small welfare gain of less than 1 per cent of the maximal possible gain (compare tables 12.6a and 12.6b). FO already achieves more than 88 per cent of the maximal attainable welfare gain. Improving the parking charges system such that all passenger car users pay for the resource cost of parking at the trip destination, is capable of attaining a higher welfare gain than improving car engine technology.

A complete analysis of policy instruments has to take into account the implementation costs of the policy instruments. Fuel price increases, technology regulation and improved parking charges do not require large investments in equipment, but cordon pricing and optimal pricing do, although several studies show that the benefits outweigh these (see Small, 1992). The political and administrative feasibility, and the public acceptance of the instruments are harder to judge (see Verhoef, 1996). Improved parking charges are not beneficial to the majority of transport users at present and will thus find little support, although the model simulations clearly show that letting all private car users pay for parking at the urban centre destination will achieve most of the attainable welfare gains from transport policy. Road pricing is not popular either, but the results of this case study show that they are beneficial to most transport users. The results of this study could perhaps be used to promote desirable elements of urban transport policy in Amsterdam and other cities.

12.7 CONCLUSIONS

The case study for Amsterdam presents some useful insights on the design of transport policies oriented towards internalisation of transport related externalities. The foremost important empirical insight is that pricing instruments should focus on the congestion externalities, since these dominate the total external costs of urban transport in Amsterdam. The largest welfare gains are therefore to be expected from policies that internalise such external congestion costs. Moreover, transport policies should concentrate on affecting a large portion of transport users, since policies that cover only part of the transport users may have undesirable outcomes in terms of both efficiency and distribution. The use of less polluting technology, imposed by government regulation, leads to a small extra welfare gain of less than 1 per cent of the maximal possible gain for Amsterdam. Better parking charges as such lead to a welfare gain of almost 60 per cent of the maximal welfare gain of urban transport policy. An optimal road pricing system combined with improved parking charges can lead to a welfare gain of over 88 per cent of the maximal attainable gain. Finally, it should be noted that optimal policy taxes are above marginal externality costs due to the inefficiency of the global tax system. Free parking in particular leads to a significant distortion of the optimal functioning of transport markets.

Current transport policy plans include the introduction of cordon charges in the Randstad area, which are in the order of 2.5 Euros per incoming trip during the morning peak. These suggestions are not directly linked to optimum computations as is the case in the present study. Although there is a slow extension of charged parking areas in the centre of Amsterdam, there are currently no concrete plans to charge for private parking supply, so that the inefficiency caused by an incomplete coverage of resource costs by individual road users will remain. There are also no concrete proposals for significant changes in the pricing of public transport, based on external cost considerations. Current trends of privatisation and improved cost management, however, may lead to at least a reduction of implicit subsidies.

ACKNOWLEDGEMENT

The model in this study has been developed in the TRENEN II STRAN project (contract no. ST-96-SC-116), which was funded by the European Commission under the Transport RTD Programme of the 4th framework Programme.

We are grateful to Frans Bal for assistance in gathering the data, to Kurt Van Dender for support of the model implementation for Amsterdam, and to Bruno De Borger and Stef Proost for helpful comments on the text.

APPENDIX 12A.1 GENMOD NETWORK MODEL PREDICTIONS

For an explanation see Section 12.2.2.

Table 12A.1 Average trip length 1995 TRENEN zones in kms: public transport

	I	II	III	IV
I	5.4	33.6	42.2	64.2
II	28.1	20.9	43.7	92.8
III	39.5	50.7	41.6	139.1
IV	55.9	94.6	135.9	116.4

Table 12A.2 *Average trip length 1995 TRENEN zones in kms: bicycle*

	I	II	III	IV
I	3.4	9.4	8.5	8.5
II	8.6	4.3	9.3	–
III	7.4	8.3	5.8	8.3
IV	10.3	–	8.6	5.7

Table 12A.3 *Average trip length 1995 TRENEN zones in kms: car*

	I	II	III	IV
I	6.1	29.1	27.9	43.9
II	26.6	17.1	40.5	89.8
III	26.0	46.4	50.1	106.3
IV	44.4	92.4	94.6	114.8

Table 12A.4 *Kilometrage 1995 TRENEN zones: public transport*

	I	II	III	IV
I	524934	396236	525014	678799
II	62643	383547	62584	77727
III	345166	113176	5229993	1873726
IV	278442	145321	1203330	23173746

Table 12A.5 *Kilometrage 1995 TRENEN zones: bicycle*

	I	II	III	IV
I	368721	11092	9581	5339
II	3830	112396	2376	–
III	6230	1440	106722	967
IV	3935	–	688	85076

Table 12A.6 *Kilometrage 1995 TRENEN zones: car*

	I	II	III	IV
I	842847	508681	606946	864502
II	193600	1786044	183829	355472
III	400134	278550	23130859	4170108
IV	498616	449116	1551821330	103086316

Table 12A.7 Average trip duration 1995 TRENEN zones in minutes: public transport

	I	II	III	IV
I	26	66	78	90
II	62	46	87	120
III	71	88	71	172
IV	82	124	170	137

Table 12A.8 Average trip duration 1995 TRENEN zones in minutes: bicycle

	I	II	III	IV
I	22	51	45	43
II	46	28	57	–
III	41	54	33	46
IV	51	–	46	33

Table 12A.9 Average trip duration 1995 TRENEN zones in minutes: car

	I	II	III	IV
I	14	32	31	39
II	29	24	40	68
III	30	44	46	80
IV	39	70	73	80

APPENDIX 12A.2 DETAILED RESULTS OF COUNTERFACTUAL SCENARIOS

Table 12A.10 Characterisation of the full optimum (FO) with improved parking charges and standard emission technologies (Amsterdam, 2005)

Prices and costs (Euro/pkm)	Resource cost	Tax	Money price	Marginal external cost (per vkm)[3]	Generalised price
Peak					
car, solo, small, petrol, free parking					
inhabitants	0.7957	0.912	1.70769	0.79957	2.09649
commuters	0.2957	0.84194	1.13763	0.79957	1.52643
car, solo, small, petrol, paid parking					
inhabitants	0.7957	0.912	1.70769	0.79957	2.09649
commuters	0.2957	0.84194	1.13763	0.79957	1.52643
car, solo, small, diesel, free parking					
inhabitants	0.82779	0.94182	1.76961	0.82895	2.15841
bus/tram (inhabitants)	0.10056	0.04699	0.14754	0.046754	0.90372
Off-peak					
car, solo, small, petrol, free parking					
inhabitants	0.29342	0.13323	0.92666	0.08389	1.13341
bus/tram (inhabitants)	0.11143	−0.02138	0.09004	0.046154	0.67038
Volume and composition of traffic	**mio pkm**	**share (%)**	**% carpool**	**speed km/h**	
Peak, private	1.766917	22.27	17.51	19.83	
Peak, public	1.577975	19.89		9.50	
Off-peak, private	3.229508	40 71	11.96	35.53	
Off-peak, public	1.35923	17.13		17.02	
Tax revenue (mio Euro/day)					
private	1.97788				
public	0.00246				
External costs (mio Euro/day)	0.34998				

Table 12A.11 Characterisation of the cordon pricing (CO) with reference to parking charges and standard emission technologies (Amsterdam, 2005)

Prices and costs (Euro/pkm)	Resource cost	Tax	Money price	Marginal external cost (per vkm)	Generalised price
Peak					
car, solo, small, petrol, free parking					
inhabitants	0.7957	0.0791	0.2648	1.2386	0.78311
commuters	0.2957	0.9231	1.1088	1.2386	1.62711
car, solo, small, petrol, paid parking					
inhabitants	0.7957	0.0791	0.8748	1.2386	1.39311
commuters	0.2957	0.9231	1.2188	1.2386	1.73711
car, solo, small, diesel, free parking					
inhabitants	0.82779	0.07078	0.28857	1.26797	0.80689
bus/tram (inhabitants)	0.10056	−0.00924	0.09132	0.068658	1.05119
Off-peak					
car, solo, small, petrol, free parking					
inhabitants	0.29342	0.07247	0.25589	0.08815	0.46744
bus/tram (inhabitants)	0.11143	−0.02011	0.09132	0.046387	0.70882
Volume and composition of traffic	**mio pkm**	**share (%)**	**% carpool**	**speed km/h**	
Peak, private	2.439381	28.56	19.57	14.87	
Peak, public	1.247352	14.60		7.12	
Off-peak, private	3.967965	46.46	14.35	34.73	
Off-peak, public	0.886668	10.38		16.63	
Tax revenue (mio Euro/day)					
private	1.148				
public	−0.02106				
External costs (mio Euro/day)	0.39509				

NOTES

1. This is largely based on O&S (1996).
2. The complete Dutch name of this department is: Dienst Infrastructuur, Verkeer en Vervoer, Afdeling Strategie en Beleid, Onderzoek, Gemeente Amsterdam.
3. The marginal external cost in Table 12.3 differs from that in Table 12.2. The reason for this difference is that in Table 12.2 no account was taken of the effect of parking charges for payers. Hence, the estimates in this table are based on higher demands, with higher external costs.

REFERENCES

CBS (1995a), *Mobiliteit Nederlandse Bevolking*, Heerlen: Centraal Bureau voor de Statistiek.

CBS (1995b), *Statistiek van de Motorvoertuigen*, Heerlen: Centraal Bureau voor de Statistiek.

Consumentenbond (1995), *Consumentengids oktober 1995*, Den Haag: Consumentenbond.

HCG (1990), *The Netherlands 'Value of Time' Study: Final Report*, The Hague: Hague Consultancy Group.

O&S (1996), *Jaarboek Amsterdam in Cijfers*, Amsterdam: Het Amsterdamse Bureau voor Onderzoek en Statistiek.

Small, K.A. (1992), *Urban Transportation Economics*, Chur: Harwood.

Verhoef, E.T. (1996). *The Economics of Regulating Road Transport*, Cheltenham: Edward Elgar.

Verhoef, E.T., Lijesen, M. and Hoen, A. (1998), 'The economic effects of road pricing in the Randstad area', Discussion paper TI 98-078/3, Amsterdam-Rotterdam: Tinbergen Institute.

Wit, J. de and van Gent, H. (1986), *Vervoers- en Verkeerseconomie*, Leiden: Stenfert Kroese.

13. Improved transport pricing in Dublin

Edna Gibbons and Margaret O'Mahony

13.1 BACKGROUND

Growth rates for Ireland in recent years have exceeded the EU average and as a result there has been significant employment growth in the 1990s. The Dublin Region has reflected national economic trends as the city is an integral part of the region's economy. Thousands of people living in the greater Dublin area commute daily into the city to work. Many of the transport services based in the city serve regional and also national and international markets. The current and future transport requirements of the city cannot be underestimated.

The population of Dublin city increased by 0.7 per cent between 1991 and 1996 from 478 389 to 481 854 (Central Statistics Office, 1996). Recent inner city residential development has played a major role in stemming the trend of population decline in the city. However, such development is counterbalanced by very rapid growth in the greater Dublin area. The outward spread of the city has contributed to the increasing transport problems currently evident in Dublin. While there is a need to concentrate on transport issues within the city centre, the transportation requirements of the peripheral areas must also be taken into account.

The private car is the most popular mode of transport within the city with a forecasted increase in car ownership rates in line with forecasted economic growth. During the period 1991 to 1996 the number of licensed vehicles in Dublin city and county grew, on average, by 3.9 per cent per annum. Between 1994 and 1996, there was a 6.1 per cent growth per annum in the number of licensed vehicles in Dublin city and county, with the number of licensed private cars exceeding 300 000 in 1996 (DOE, 1991–1996).

It is widely recognised that in the peak period the road network into the city centre is operating at capacity. Since there are no plans to increase road capacity within the city centre, further car-based growth is not possible or desirable. An integral part of maintaining and developing the city as a viable place both to live and work will be the reduction in private vehicular traffic. Public transport will need to become a more attractive option to the journey-maker, particularly those who commute to work, in order to achieve the desired modal transfer from the private car.

The Dublin Transportation Initiative (DTI) Strategy is the result of a major transportation study carried out over four years (1991–1994) in the city of Dublin and its hinterland. The DTI was a new and innovative approach to transportation planning in the Greater Dublin area in that it sought solutions to traffic problems which were not focussed entirely on increased provision of road infrastructure. The significant elements of the strategy include an enhanced role for public transport, traffic management and the provision and promotion of other sustainable modes.

Currently, public transport within Dublin city comprises the bus service provided by Dublin Bus and rail service provided by Iarnrod Eireann. There are various problems associated with public transport provision ranging from lack of priority within the city centre to poor interchange facilities to overcrowding on certain routes and a limited catchment area for the rail service. The DTI strategy seeks to increase the quantity and quality of the bus and rail network particularly in the morning and evening peak periods.

An improved bus service is being addressed through the implementation of a network of Quality Bus Corridors (QBC) and the allocation of funds towards upgrading the bus fleet. The QBC facilitates the provision of a faster, more frequent and more reliable bus service. The aim of the DTI Strategy in terms of suburban rail is to maximise the capacity of the rail network by the provision of additional rolling stock and line improvements. The option of a light rail transit system for the city has undergone intense public enquiry and it remains to be seen whether the government will proceed with implementation. It is intended to provide high quality facilities for pedestrians and cyclists which will not only address concerns about the issue of safety but also encourage motorists to transfer to more sustainable forms of urban transport. The DTI recognised that the control and pricing of city centre parking is a critical element in restraining car commuting in the urban area. Dublin Corporation is in the process of implementing a parking strategy for the city centre. So far the number of free on-street parking spaces has been substantially reduced and enforcement of parking regulations has been stepped up with the introduction of a wheel-clamping and tow-away service for illegally parked cars.

The first stage in the implementation of the model was the collection of a data set specific to Dublin. The fact that the various elements of the DTI strategy, as mentioned above, have not been fully implemented at this stage is reflected in the data. The next section in this chapter briefly outlines some of the data required for the implementation of the model and the output from the reference equilibrium which results. Leading on from reference equilibrium, the results produced when the model is allowed to optimise without constraint (full optimum scenario) are examined. A comparison between the reference and full optimum scenarios indicates the direction of the deviations which the model will make from the reference equilibrium. Both the reference and full optimum scenarios can be used as benchmark scenarios against which alternative pricing policy scenarios can be measured. This chapter concludes with the analysis of a series of sensitivity tests which were carried out on various parameter inputs to the model.

13.2 THE REFERENCE SITUATION FOR 2005

The network model of Dublin was developed during the DTI as part of the technical analysis for the study. The transport network of Dublin was replicated in the computer model with all significant road links, bus routes and rail lines present. Predictions for future mode and route choice are provided by the network model as well as forecasts for future public transport usage and the number of vehicles on each road. Data and results from the network model for Dublin played an integral role in the construction of the reference solution with unchanged transport policies.

It was necessary to derive the consumer prices, costs and volumes of transport by mode and period for 2005. Transport volumes were extracted from the 2006 forecasts in the DTI model and a constant real price was assumed as regards consumer prices paid for goods and resource costs of standard vehicles. Following a definition of the user groups in the model, the volume and consumer price data for private transport, the volumes and prices for public transport, the speed-flow relationship and the external cost data are discussed.

The model distinguishes between four types of consumers on the basis of two characteristics: inhabitants versus commuters and those who pay for their parking spot at the destination and those who do not. Inhabitants of Dublin were defined as residents within a close proximity of the city centre, whereas residents of the peripheral area of Dublin were classified as commuters. The zoning system in the network model of Dublin was used to categorise the consumer type according to inhabitant and consumer. Trips originating in the zones which lay more or less within the canal ring of Dublin were classified as inhabitant trips. The DTI zone map is replicated in Figure 13.1, with trips generated by inhabitants represented by the shaded zones. The 367 zone trip matrices of the network model were compressed into two zone matrices – one zone representing total trips generated by inhabitants, the other zone representing total trips generated by commuters.

Figure 13.1 DTI zone map of the Dublin region

13.2.1 Private Transport

Peak and off-peak hourly travel demand was extracted from the DTI model. In the model an average weekday is considered to be of 13 hours duration containing 2 hours representing an am peak hour and pm peak hour. The remaining 11 hours are considered to be the off-peak period. It was assumed that travel demand in both peak hours is equal to the demand in the modelled morning peak hour. Similarly, demand during all off-peak hours was assumed to be equal to that in the modelled off-peak hour.

The model requires further classification of travel demands for the car mode by car size, occupancy rate and fuel type. This data was not directly available and so was derived from data available from a number of sources. A breakdown of the Irish private vehicle fleet by cubic capacity and fuel type was obtained in the Irish Bulletin of Vehicle and Driver Statistics (Department of the Environment, 1996). To account for the demand for car travel in solo or pooled vehicles it is assumed that 20 per cent of all vehicles are pooled. The average occupancy rate for private vehicles used in the DTI Study was 1.37 persons per vehicle and this figure is adapted for use in the TRENEN model. The values of time employed in the TRENEN model (Table 13.1) were also based on those used in the DTI study.

Table 13.1 Values of time used in DTI study (Steer Davies Gleave, 1995)

	Peak		Off-Peak	
	IR£/hr	EUR/hr	IR£/hr	EUR/hr
Private vehicle	3.06	4.181	3.72	5.083
Public transport	1.20	1.640	3.72	5.083
Slow modes	2.40	3.279	7.44	10.165

Annual acquisition costs for the four types of vehicle classified in the TRENEN model were calculated based on the method presented in Mayeres (1993). The 'Recommended New Passenger Car Price List – January 1997' published by the Society of the Irish Motor Industry (1997) provided the starting data for the calculations. The costs shown were derived from prices for a sample of 37 vehicles. In the calculations it is assumed that the actual purchase price is typically 8 per cent lower than the recommended retail price (Revenue Commissioners, 1996). A return on savings, based on the rate of return of a five year government bond, of 5.68 per cent was provided by the National Treasury Management Agency (1997). It is assumed that a new car stays with the original owner for five years. In the sixth year it is sold at a price that is 20 per cent of the original catalogue price exclusive of taxes. The process was carried out both including and excluding VAT and Vehicle Registration Tax (VRT) (at a rate of 21 per cent and 23.2 per cent respectively) for the purposes of carrying the figures forward to the consumer price and resource cost calculations. An annual average vehicle mileage of 10692 miles (17107 km) per annum has been used (taken from the CSO 1994–95 Household Budget Survey for one-car households) in order to translate car costs into costs per vehicle-kilometre.

The fuel prices were based on 1995 end of year prices from the 'Statistical Report of the Revenue Commissioners – 1995'. The resource costs of fuel are the fuel prices exclusive of VAT and excise. The calculation of operating costs incorporated all other non-fuel costs for the privately owned vehicle. These were assumed to include motor taxation, insurance and general maintenance costs. To obtain the costs per vehicle-kilometre, the annual costs were divided by the average distance travelled in one year by a passenger car. The data was taken from a report on motoring costs published by the Automobile Association (1996).

The insurance values are average rates for third party, fire and theft policies. No allowance is made for no-claims discount. However, an average claims cost is subtracted from the insurance premium. The claims bill per registered vehicle is given as IR£509 (Deloitte and Touche, 1996). Also included in the insurance premium is a government tax of 2 per cent. Other costs such as oil, tyres, servicing, repairs and replacements are assumed to include a VAT rate of 12.5 per cent. Parking at a rate of IR£1300 per annum (Automobile Association, 1996) is incorporated into the TRENEN model where the issue of 'payers' and 'non-payers' (of parking) is considered. Given that the annual average distance travelled is 17107 km, the annual parking cost translates into a cost of approximately 7.5 pence per km (although this will vary for inhabitants and consumers due to the difference in average trip lengths). As in the case of vehicle acquisition costs, the operating costs were calculated including and excluding tax. The private transport consumer price is the sum of the annual acquisition cost and the other operating costs including taxes.

13.2.2 Public Transport

Within the TRENEN model public transport comprises bus and rail services. Taxis and private-hire buses have not been included due to the difficulty in obtaining the sufficient levels of data required by the model. The money price for public transport corresponds to the average fare paid. Fare levels are measured by receipts per passenger-kilometre for bus, DART and other Dublin suburban rail services (based on information supplied by Coras Iompar Eireann (CIE), Iarnrod Eireann and Dublin Bus). It is of the order of 0.1147 EUR per passenger-kilometre for bus and 0.0563 EUR per passenger-kilometre for rail.

A distinction has been made between fixed and variable costs. The fixed costs are independent of the volume of transport services produced. The variable costs are constant per passenger-kilometre and differ between the peak and off-peak period. The fixed cost of public transport was based on figures extracted from the Annual Reports of CIE, Dublin Bus and Irish Rail for 1995. Fixed costs refer to non-operating costs incurred only during the current year. This figure includes items such as additions made to tangible assets and infrastructure costs. It was calculated as 0.0855mEUR per day.

To estimate the variable costs it has been assumed that the average occupancy rate is constant for peak period and off-peak period. Average bus occupancies in the peak and off-peak periods were estimated at 37 and 20 persons respectively, based on information from Dublin Bus. The average occupancy rates for rail transport were based on average figures for the urban railway line, DART. The capacity of the DART is approximately 180 per carriage. During the peak period there are six carriages per train while during the off-peak period there are four carriages per train. This rail service has proved very popular since its implementation in 1984 and during the peak period the average occupancy is 1080 persons per train. During the off-peak period the occupancy rate averages around 120 per train.

In the peak period the costs related to capacity (number of buses and carriages) are included. These costs are not included in the off-peak period. The resource costs for Dublin Bus were based on the operating costs taken from the Annual Report of Dublin Bus (CIE, 1995). To differentiate between peak and off-peak periods, costs relating to non-use-related depreciation and exceptional operating costs (costs relating to the implementation of a one person bus operation) were assigned totally to the peak period. The resource costs for rail are based on the operating costs for DART and for Other Dublin Suburban Rail Services taken from the CIE Annual Report (1995). The resource costs for bus and rail are summarised in Table 13.2.

Table 13.2 Resource costs for bus and rail

	Peak EUR/vehicle-kilometre	Off-peak EUR/vehicle-kilometre
Bus	3.9997	2.4945
Rail	7.8598	7.6333

13.2.3 Speed–Flow Relationship

The speed–flow relationship defines the travel characteristics for the city and allows travel times to be calculated. To derive the speed–flow relationship for Dublin the DTI model was used to calculate average traffic delays and flows resulting from varying levels of demand. The model runs were straightforward assignment runs where the demand matrix was assigned to the relevant network. The demand variations were simulated by factoring the matrix within the range of 0.6 to 1.4 in steps of 0.2. The average free-flow speed was calculated by subtracting the value for over-capacity queues from the total travel time. Dividing total travel distance by the new travel time yielded the average free-flow speed. The values derived produced averages of 40kph for the peak hour and 41kph for the off-peak hour. An exponential function was fitted through the data points to produce the relationship between unit travel time and total travel distance for both peak and off-peak periods. Readers should refer to Chapter 10 for more detail.

The next stage in the process was to assign a mathematical function to the speed–flow relationship, the format of which had been determined from work by O'Mahony, Kirwan and McGrath (1997). Two relationships were derived for the peak and off-peak periods respectively. An intermediate level was established from averaging of the peak and off-peak period relationships. This all-day speed–flow function is as follows:

$$T = 1.41846 + 0.07492\exp^{1.18338X}$$

where T is time taken to travel 1 km in minutes and
X is in travel distance in million pcu.kms.

Once the travel times are known and combined with the estimates of value of time, generalised prices can be calculated. The generalised prices in the reference equilibrium are shown in Table 13.3.

13.2.4 The External Costs

The reference equilibrium as summarised in Table 13.3 shows that taxes on car use are much smaller than marginal external costs. This is particularly the case in the peak period where taxes cover only one quarter of the marginal external cost.

A second major inefficiency in the pricing of car use is unpaid parking. This means that for 70 per cent of the car users even the resource costs are not paid. The importance of the parking cost as an element in a trip can be seen in Table 13.3 by comparing money price for car users with free parking with the money price for car users who pay their parking costs. Parking costs are a relatively smaller share of the total trip costs for commuters because they make longer trips. The discrepancy between marginal external costs and taxes paid is relatively higher for diesel cars that pay less tax and cause higher external healthcare damage.

Turning to public transport, it can be seen that off-peak buses pay the resource cost and almost the full external cost. This means that no changes in the pricing policy are required. The resource costs of peak bus users are subsidised by approximately 55 per cent and external costs are obviously not covered.

Table 13.3 Resource costs, prices, taxes and external costs in the reference situation

Prices and costs (EUR/pkm)	Resource cost	Tax	Money price	Marginal external cost (per vkm)	Generalised price
Peak					
Car, solo, small, petrol, free parking					
inhabitants	0.393	0.121	0.340	0.496	0.553
commuters	0.311	0.121	0.340	0.496	0.553
Car, solo, small, petrol, paid parking					
inhabitants	0.393	0.121	0.515	0.496	0.728
commuters	0.311	0.121	0.433	0.496	0.646
Car, solo, small, diesel, free parking					
inhabitants	0.374	0.096	0.295	0.524	0.508
Bus (inhabitants)	0.108	−0.059	0.049	0.026	0.206
Off-peak					
Car, solo, small, petrol, free parking					
inhabitants	0.390	0.116	0.331	0.086	0.474
Bus (inhabitants)	0.124	0.006	0.130	0.007	0.571

13.3 THE FULL OPTIMUM SCENARIO

The full optimum scenario determines the optimal combinations of policies that maximise the net benefits to society. It implies that the authorities have perfect pricing instruments available which can be used to charge consumers on a precise basis for the full marginal social cost of transport. It also assumes that vehicle emissions can be regulated through the mandatory requirement of improved technology. Such a scenario would be difficult to implement effectively in reality since it implies highly differentiated charging for different consumers. However, it is used as a benchmark in order to compare other policy scenarios and the reference case.

Four variations of the full optimum scenario were run using different combinations of reference and improved parking charges and standard and improved technology. The naming convention adapted for the different options is shown in Table 13.4.

Table 13.4 Naming convention for option tests

FO1	Optimal pricing, reference parking, standard technology
FO2	Optimal pricing, reference parking, improved technology
FO3	Optimal pricing, improved parking, standard technology
FO4	Optimal pricing, improved parking, improved technology

The model which achieved the highest overall welfare gain combined the reference parking charge and improved technology. This can be seen in Table 13.5 where the key results from the full optimum scenario are highlighted. Compared with the reference situation the full optimum, FO2, returns a welfare gain of 0.47 per cent and a reduction in total external cost (excluding congestion) of 16 per cent. There is a decline of 14 per cent in the overall transport level (second column of Table 13.5). Demand for private transport across all consumer types reduces in the full optimum scenario, with the share of private transport in the peak period dropping from 23.78 per cent in the reference scenario to 22.58 per cent in FO4.

Demand for the bus mode of public transport decreases in the peak period and increases slightly for commuters in the off-peak period. Demand for the rail mode of public transport decreases in both peak and off-peak periods for inhabitants and for commuters. These reductions can be attributed to the increase in taxes which public transport users face in the full optimum scenario. The share of private transport drops in the off-peak period as well as in the peak period, whereas the share of public transport only drops in the peak period and shows an increase of 16 per cent in the off-peak period.

Table 13.5 Key results from the full optimum pricing scenario

	% Welfare gain	External cost (excluding congestion)	% Peak private	% Peak public	% Off-peak private	% Off-peak public
REF		1.00886	23.78	7.26	53.42	15.54
FO1	0.46	0.86462	22.60	5.92	53.47	18.01
FO2	0.47	0.84987	22.61	5.91	53.51	17.97
FO3	0.44	0.86172	22.57	5.92	53.38	18.13
FO4	0.45	0.84698	22.58	5.91	53.42	18.09

Table 13.6 Taxes in reference and full optimum scenarios (EUR/pass.km)

	Inhabitant parking non-payer	Inhabitant parking payer	Commuter parking non-payer	Commuter parking payer
REF				
Peak, car	0.122	0.122	0.122	0.122
Peak, bus	−0.059	−0.059	−0.059	−0.059
Off-peak, car	0.116	0.116	0.116	0.116
Off-peak, bus	0.006	0.006	0.006	0.006
FO2				
Peak, car	0.583	0.583	0.458	0.458
Peak, bus	0.152	0.152	0.079	0.079
Off-peak, car	0.383	0.383	0.283	0.283
Off-peak, bus	0.176	0.176	0.107	0.107

In the full optimum scenario there is a significant increase in taxes across all modes of transport. The increases in taxes for each consumer driving a small petrol car driven alone and on buses are shown in Table 13.6.

Public transport no longer receives a subsidy in the peak period in the full optimum scenario. An inhabitant using the bus in the peak period receives a subsidy of 0.38 EUR/trip in the reference scenario but in the full optimum scenario this consumer is charged a tax of 0.99 EUR/trip. In the off-peak period the tax on buses rises from 0.04 EUR/trip to 1.07 EUR/trip for an inhabitant and from 0.05 EUR/trip to 0.91 EUR/trip for a commuter. Overall, however, the taxes imposed on public transport are still considerably lower than those on private transport due to the high occupancy rates of these vehicles.

It is worth noting that the costs of providing the infrastructure or in-vehicle units necessary to implement a road pricing policy have not been included in the TRENEN model. The impact of including these costs on the overall model results would depend on how the costs were treated within the model. If the car user had to pay for, say, the in-vehicle unit then this cost would be added onto the resource cost of the vehicle. On the other hand, if the government paid for the in-vehicle unit then the way in which the cost is treated in the model depends on the ownership status of the in-vehicle unit. If the unit was owned by the car user, but paid for by the government, it would be considered a subsidy to the car user. If the government charged the car user for the cost of road pricing infrastructure this would increase the taxes paid by the car user, possibly causing a slight reduction in external costs.

13.4 SENSITIVITY TESTS

Sensitivity tests were carried out on the model to examine the robustness of the results. The model was run for each of the sensitivity tests under the reference and full optimum policy scenarios. The objective of running the model under the reference scenario was to test the accuracy of the model. It was hoped that the results output from the full optimum scenario would provide an insight on the workings of the model. Six tests were carried out as described in Table 13.7.

Table 13.7 Sensitivity tests for the 2005 TRENEN model

Test 1	Values of time for private and public transport are halved
Test 2	Values of time for private and public transport are doubled
Test 3	Substitution elasticity between peak and off-peak transport increased from 0.8 to 1.2
Test 4	Substitution elasticity between peak and off-peak transport decreased from 0.8 to 0.4
Test 5	Substitution elasticity between motorised and non-motorised modes of transport increased from 0.3 to 0.8
Test 6	Substitution elasticity between private and public transport in the peak period increased from 1.05 to 1.5

13.4.1 Reference Scenario

The transport demands (extracted from the DTI network model) are the same for the calibration of the various sensitivity tests. Since transport demands are constrained to their reference level in the reference scenario, it is expected that the results from each test will produce the same overall levels of demand for the different transport modes. However, the results from this scenario show that small differences in demand are actually generated by the model. The differences which occur give an indication of the numerical accuracy of the model.

The passenger-kilometres demanded over the total population of Dublin are shown in Table 13.8. The largest percentage change from the original 2005 reference scenario is for public transport in the peak period. This occurs in Test 4 where demand is lower than in the original scenario by 0.09 per cent. In Tests 1 to 4, differences in the range of −0.08 per cent to 0.08 per cent are observed for peak private transport. Differences in the off-peak period are smaller than those in the peak period, with the largest differences of 0.05 per cent and −0.05 per cent occurring for public transport in Tests 1 and 2 respectively.

Table 13.8 Reference passenger-kilometres demanded over total population ($\times 10^6$)

	REF	Test 1	Test 2	Test 3	Test 4	Test 5	Test 6
Peak private	5.9366	5.9317	5.9411	5.9399	5.9323	5.9372	5.9366
Peak public	1.8131	1.8132	1.8126	1.8143	1.8114	1.8133	1.8126
Off-peak private	13.3339	13.3304	13.3387	13.3306	13.3380	13.3343	13.3339
Off-peak public	3.8777	3.8797	3.8759	3.8766	3.8791	3.8778	3.8777

Table 13.9 shows the percentage market shares for private and public transport in the peak and off-peak periods in each of the sensitivity tests. The largest difference occurs once again for public transport in the peak period. In Tests 1 and 3, the market share increases by 0.14 per cent. In the off-peak period, the share of public transport drops by 0.13 per cent in Test 2. The share of private transport in Test 3 increases by 0.08 per cent in the peak period.

Table 13.9 Percentage reference market share of transport quantities demanded

	REF	Test 1	Test 2	Test 3	Test 4	Test 5	Test 6
% Peak private	23.78	23.77	23.79	23.80	23.77	23.78	23.78
% Peak public	7.26	7.27	7.26	7.27	7.26	7.26	7.26
% Off-peak private	53.42	53.42	53.42	53.40	53.44	53.42	53.42
% Off-peak public	15.54	15.55	15.52	15.53	15.54	15.53	15.54

Overall, the differences in the test results and the original reference scenario are small and thus confirm the numerical precision of the model calibration. However, it is assumed that changes in the test results, under the full optimum scenario, which are smaller than the differences noted in the reference scenario calibration are not significant.

13.4.2 Full Optimum Scenario

The full optimum policy scenario was run for each of the sensitivity tests described in Table 13.7. The full optimum scenario allows all policy instruments to be used to internalise the externalities and the results from this scenario therefore show the greatest changes from the results produced in the reference scenario.

The transport demands in the full optimum scenario for the original and various sensitivity tests are presented in Table 13.10. The greatest reduction in demand (with respect to the reference scenario results) for private transport in the peak period occurs in Test 2 (reducing by 21 per cent) where the value of time for private and public transport has been doubled. Earlier results have shown that congestion imposes a considerable time cost on the consumer and Test 2 implies that the value of that time cost increases. On the other hand, the decrease in demand for public transport in the peak period is considerably less in Test 2 than in any of the other tests and the 9 per cent increase in demand for public transport in the off-peak period is significant. In Test 1, where the value of time is halved, the largest reduction in demand for public transport occurs in both peak and off-peak periods. The values of time are over 50 per cent lower for public transport than private transport in the peak period but equal in the off-peak period. From the results produced in Tests 1 and 2, it would appear that the value of time has an important impact in the model in determining the demand for a particular mode of travel.

The significant changes in demand for Test 2 are reflected in the percentage changes in market shares as shown in Table 13.11. The share of peak private transport drops by 8 per cent while the share of off-peak public transport increases by over 26 per cent. In Test 1, the largest decrease in the share of peak public transport occurs along with the smallest increase in the share of off-peak public transport (mirroring the effects on demand in Table 13.10). The share of peak private transport decreases by the least amount and in the off-peak increases the most. The consumer in Test 1 is less affected by congestion costs (since the values of time lost are halved) and the preference to travel by private transport dominates. The increase in ease of substitution between peak and off-peak period in Test 3 is reflected in the market shares, with larger decreases in the peak share and

Table 13.10 Full optimum passenger-kilometres demanded over total population ($\times 10^6$)

	FO	Test 1	Test 2	Test 3	Test 4	Test 5	Test 6
Peak private demand	4.82	4.97	4.69	4.73	4.95	4.81	4.84
Peak public demand	1.26	1.00	1.52	1.21	1.33	1.25	1.18
Off-peak private demand	11.42	11.72	11.03	11.52	11.27	11.44	11.42
Off-peak public demand	3.84	3.42	4.23	3.88	3.78	3.85	3.84

Table 13.11 Percentage full optimum market share of transport quantities demanded

	FO	Test 1	Test 2	Test 3	Test 4	Test 5	Test 6
% Peak private share	22.60	23.56	21.86	22.16	23.22	22.53	22.74
% Peak public share	5.92	4.77	7.11	5.69	6.24	5.88	5.56
% Off-peak private share	53.47	55.45	51.35	53.95	52.81	53.56	53.63
% Off-peak public share	18.01	16.22	19.68	18.21	17.73	18.03	18.06

larger increases in the off-peak share than those in the original full optimum scenario.

The variation in taxes and money prices which occur in each of the sensitivity tests are highlighted in Tables 13.12 and 13.13 respectively. Taxes and prices reach their highest level in Test 2. The tax rises from 1.02 EUR/trip for an inhabitant driving a small petrol car alone in the peak period to 7.05 EUR/trip in Test 2. An increase or decrease in the elasticity of substitution between peak and off-peak transport (Tests 3 and 4) affect the value of tax more noticeably in the peak period. Where the elasticity of substitution has been decreased, taxes are higher since people cannot easily transfer between periods of travel.

Table 13.14 provides a summary of the overall results produced during the sensitivity tests. The largest welfare gain, of 0.51 per cent, occurs in Test 1. This may be attributed to the reduction in marginal external congestion costs. The tax revenue generated by private transport in Test 1 is also affected by the reduction in external congestion costs, since the tax required to internalise the marginal social cost has been also reduced. This observation is reversed for Test 2, with higher marginal social costs leading to higher levels of tax revenue. The slight increase in demand for slow modes of transport in Test 5 is most clearly observed in the lower levels of tax revenue for public and private transport since the slow modes are tax free. The results from Test 6 deviate by the least amount from the original full optimum results which means that the level to which consumers will

Table 13.12 Comparison of taxes in sensitivity tests

Prices and costs (EUR/pkm)	Ref	Original FO	Test 1 FO	Test 2 FO	Test 3 FO	Test 4 FO	Test 5 FO	Test 6 FO
Peak								
Car, solo, small, petrol, free parking								
inhabitants	0.121	0.583	0.450	0.840	0.564	0.612	0.542	0.585
commuters	0.121	0.458	0.333	0.700	0.436	0.497	0.434	0.459
Car, solo, small, petrol, paid parking								
inhabitants	0.121	0.583	0.450	0.840	0.564	0.612	0.542	0.585
commuters	0.121	0.458	0.333	0.700	0.436	0.497	0.434	0.459
Car, solo, small, diesel, free parking								
inhabitants	0.096	0.608	0.475	0.866	0.590	0.637	0.567	0.610
Bus (inhabitants)	−0.059	0.151	0.132	0.192	0.150	0.155	0.136	0.151
Off-peak								
Car, solo, small, petrol, free parking								
inhabitants	0.116	0.383	0.344	0.463	0.384	0.381	0.342	0.383
Bus (inhabitants)	0.006	0.176	0.148	0.234	0.176	0.174	0.137	0.176

Table 13.13 Comparison of money price in sensitivity tests

Prices and costs (EUR/pkm)	Ref	Original FO	Test 1 FO	Test 2 FO	Test 3 FO	Test 4 FO	Test 5 FO	Test 6 FO
Peak								
Car, solo, small, petrol, free parking								
inhabitants	0.340	0.801	0.669	1.059	0.783	0.831	0.761	0.803
commuters	0.340	0.676	0.551	0.918	0.654	0.716	0.652	0.677
Car, solo, small, petrol, paid parking								
inhabitants	0.515	0.976	0.844	1.234	0.958	1.006	0.936	0.978
commuters	0.433	0.769	0.644	1.011	0.747	0.809	0.746	0.771
Car, solo, small, diesel, free parking								
inhabitants	0.295	0.807	0.674	1.065	0.789	0.837	0.766	0.809
Bus (inhabitants)	0.048	0.259	0.240	0.300	0.258	0.263	0.244	0.259
Off-peak								
Car, solo, small, petrol,								
inhabitants	0.331	0.598	0.559	0.679	0.600	0.596	0.558	0.598
Bus (inhabitants)	0.130	0.300	0.273	0.359	0.301	0.299	0.262	0.300

Table 13.14 Percentage change in overall results w.r.t. reference scenario

	FO	Test 1	Test 2	Test 3	Test 4	Test 5	Test 6
% Welfare	0.46	0.51	0.40	0.47	0.45	0.42	0.46
% Total external cost	−14.30	−14.33	−14.67	−14.26	−14.38	−14.24	−14.38
% Tax revenue private	139	103	211	135	145	113	140
% Tax revenue public	658	502	957	663	647	505	653

substitute between private and public transport in the peak period is limited.

13.5 POLICY IMPLEMENTATION IN DUBLIN

Policy implementation in Dublin to date has largely been regulatory in nature. In 1995, the Dublin Transportation Office (DTO) was set up to coordinate and monitor the implementation of the DTI strategy. The pace of implementation of the DTI strategy has been much slower than anticipated due to a variety of factors which include greater opposition than anticipated to projects during the public consultation phase, insufficient funding for some elements of the strategy and financial and operational constraints on the delivery of public transport services in Dublin. A Short-Term Action Plan was published by the DTO in 1998 to accelerate those elements of the DTI strategy which can be completed by 2000. The action plan outlines public transport enhancement, traffic management and the provision and promotion of cycling facilities and other sustainable modes as the areas in which a significant impact can be achieved.

The Office of Director of Traffic was established as part of Dublin Corporation in 1997 to improve and coordinate traffic policy and management. This includes better use of existing assets by:

- encouraging improved use of existing roadspace
- development of the traffic control system
- control of roadworks in the city centre
- strategic routes analysis to identify problems and propose solutions

Since this office has been established, the number of taxis on the road has been increased by the issuing of new licences and taxis are permitted to use bus lanes. Parking policy measures recently introduced include an increase in long-term parking fees, removal of free on-street parking and the introduction of a wheel-clamping and tow-away service as part of a strict parking enforcement regime.

In the current market the social cost of transport activity exceeds the private cost and as a result the low transport prices have induced high excess demands for transport activities. Economic policy measures have important advantages over the regulatory approaches to environmental protection. When they are introduced in the form of taxes this allows for the opportunity to reduce other taxes which have negatively distorting effects. Unlike regulatory policy the form of response to an economic policy measure is left to the user since individuals are not directly prevented from transport activity. Economic measures are sometimes deemed less efficient than other instruments because their physical results are less certain. It is difficult to link charges directly to the users due to classification problems and unless charges reflect the cost to the individual user it would be difficult for an economic policy to gain public acceptance.

However, there is considerable scope for improvement with regard to bringing prices in line with social costs as current taxes fall well below the full external costs of the different transport modes. The tax on vehicle purchase and the annual motor tax are not well related to the external cost generated by vehicles, and although fuel taxes differ according to fuel type they do not always favour those which are least harmful to the environment.

The Irish government has recently commissioned a review of the potential for road-use pricing as an additional transport demand measure to be integrated with the public transport, parking and other restrictive measures identified in the DTI short-term action plan. The findings of this project are not yet available but it is likely that the consultants will recommend more detailed investigation of road-use pricing as a means of curbing the rising levels of car travel demand in Dublin.

REFERENCES

Automobile Association – Technical Services (1996), *Motoring Costs – May 1996.*

Central Statistics Office (1996), *Census of Population 1996 – Preliminary Results*, Government Publications.

Coras Iompair Eireann (CIE) (1996), *Group and Subsidiaries Annual Reports 1995.*

Deloitte & Touche (1996), *Report on the Economic Evaluation of Insurance Costs in Ireland*, Department of Enterprise and Employment.

Department of the Environment (DOE) – Vehicle Registration Unit (1996), *Irish Bulletin of Vehicle and Driver Statistics 1995*, Department of the Environment.

Dublin Bus Annual Report (1995), Dublin, Ireland: Dublin Bus.

Dublin Transportation Office Short-term Action Plan (1998), Dublin 2, Ireland: Dublin Transportation Office.

Mayeres, I. (1993), *The Private Car User Costs*, Catholic University Leuven: Centre for Economic Studies.

O'Mahony, M.M., Kirwan, K. and McGrath, S. (1997), 'Modelling the internalisation of external costs of transport', *Transportation Research Record*, 1576, 93–98. Washington DC: Transportation Research Board, US National Research Council.

Revenue Commissioners (1996), *Statistical Report of the Revenue Commissioners – Year ended 31st December, 1995*, Government Publications.

Steer Davies Gleave (1995), *Transport Modelling in DTI Phase 2 – Final Report*, Department of the Environment.

The Society of the Irish Motor Industry (1997), *Recommended New Passenger Car Price List: Issue 1 – January 1997.*

14. What is wrong with transport prices in London

John Peirson, Duncan Sharp and Roger Vickerman

14.1 BACKGROUND TO THE CASE STUDY

In common with most large cities around the world, London is facing a major problem from traffic congestion. Overall traffic flows continue to increase while average peak time traffic speeds are around 25 km/hour overall, although can be as low as 16 km/hour in Central London (Department of Transport, 1996). Many areas (particularly Central and Inner London) have for some time experienced all-day peaks, with little discernible difference between daytime peak and off-peak traffic speeds and flows. Inevitably, this level of congestion leads to high external costs in the form of lost time in the movement of both people and goods, together with health and physical damage costs due to high pollution levels, noise and accidents.

The prospect of an integrated transport policy, coordinated by the government or a local authority (LA), to deal with the problem of road congestion has been made more difficult since the privatisation of the buses and railways. Eleven separate companies now operate train services in and around London, and it will inevitably be more difficult to coordinate them into offering an integrated service than when a single operator provided all of London's heavy rail services. The government now has very little control over the running of the railways except through the Railway Regulator, which does not have a coordinating role. Although bus services are provided by private operators, the planning of bus routes is still centrally controlled by London Transport thereby giving greater scope for buses to be effectively coordinated with London Underground services. Again, though, it is difficult to see London Transport's services being easily coordinated with those offered by the various rail operating companies.

This situation is now likely to be changed again under the provisions of a new White Paper on Transport (DETR, 1998). This proposes greater integration as a key priority and there are further proposals for the reorganisation of regional government, especially for London with the creation of an elected Mayor for London. There may thus be some prospect of a more integrated transport policy for the London region.

In addition, both the underground and heavy rail networks face problems with their infrastructure. The underground has suffered a lack of infrastructure investment for many years and is now facing increasingly costly repairs just to keep it running safely in its present form. The heavy rail infrastructure is also suffering from a lack of investment which together with its age means that many lines have relatively low speed limits which obviously affect journey times and limit total capacity.

The Greater London region is situated in the south-east of the United Kingdom. It is a large area with a diameter of approximately 40 kilometres and is cut into roughly equal halves by the River Thames, which runs west to east. It can be broadly divided into three areas: Central London (an area roughly bounded by a line connecting the main rail termini), Inner London and Outer London, the latter covering by far the largest geographical area and being bounded by the M25 orbital motorway. The resident population (over 5 years old) is around 6 570 000 (DETR, 1997a), and the average population density is high relative to most other European cities at 4360 per square kilometre (European Commission, 1994).

It should be noted that London has not been controlled by a unitary authority since 1984. Instead it is governed by 33 separate local authorities. This has made the implementation of city-wide transport policies more difficult although a London Transport authority has remained in existence to effect some coordination of public transport, including the franchising of unprofitable bus routes.

This chapter considers the application of the urban model to the London region. The model is an aggregate model which looks at total traffic levels within the area and does not aim to model traffic on individual links. It also considers only passenger travel. Although this is the major source of traffic within the London region this is a limitation, but some development of models allowing for freight transport have been developed for interregional traffic. We build up first a reference case which examines the likely transport and traffic situation in London for the year 2005. This is based on existing evidence on the structure of travel demands in the London region in 1995 and projects these forward to 2005 on the assumption that the policy environment remains unchanged.

From the reference case we then make a series of alternative policy tests. The first test is to move to a full optimum in which all travel is undertaken at prices which cover full marginal social costs. We then test alternative policy packages which represent partial approximations to charging full marginal social costs: a cordon pricing case in which only traffic crossing a certain cordon is charged, and two cases in which fuel prices are increased in line with predicted EU policies, in the second of which we allow for car users to be charged in addition to the full resource cost of parking. In each of these cases we examine the impact on traffic flows by the major modes, total welfare impacts, tax/charging revenues and the impacts on external costs.

14.2 THE REFERENCE CASE

The reference case is a forward projection of the base situation to 2005, assuming no changes in policy. It is constructed from a wide range of different sources of information on both traffic flows and the internal and external costs of transport. In this section, we discuss the nature of the transport market, current patterns of travel and ways of representing the consumer choice structure. We then generate a reference situation for the year 2005 and make allowance for planned increases in capacity before discussing the construction of the resource cost and external cost data and the assumed elasticities of travel demand.

14.2.1 The Structure of the Transport Market

The area considered is that of Greater London (the 32 London Boroughs and the City of London, plus some additional areas within the M25 London Orbital Motorway, see Figures 14.1 and 14.2). This is by far the largest area for application of the urban model. Figure 14.1 shows the local authority structure of the Greater London area and identifies the three main areas of Outer, Inner and Central London as defined by traffic cordons. Figure 14.2 illustrates the major road network inside the M25 Orbital Motorway.

The size of the area poses certain problems for the development and application of the urban model. The most serious of these are caused by the complexity of travel patterns in such an area. There is a high volume of traffic which does not have origins or destinations in the Central London area and there is a significant volume of traffic which originates or has destinations outside the Greater London area. The 1991 *London Area Transport Survey* (London Research Centre/Department of Transport, 1994) identified 20.6 million trips in the area on a typical weekday (07.00 to 21.00), of which 16.6 million were non-walk trips and 13.7 million were made by residents of the area. Of these trips 3 million were to and from the Central Area (roughly the Cities of London and Westminster and small adjacent parts of Camden, Islington, Hackney, Southwark and Lambeth).

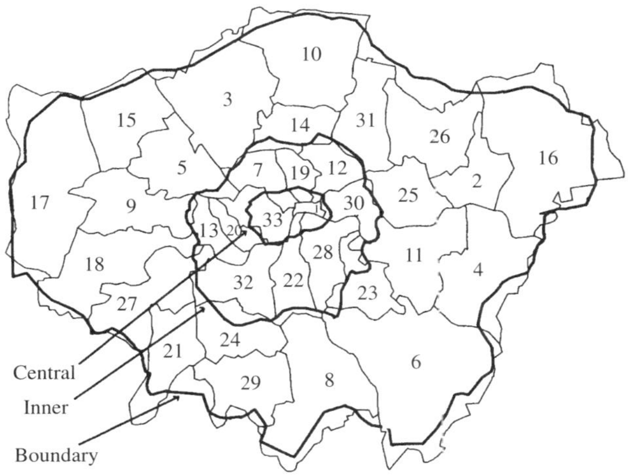

1 City of London
2 Barking & Dagenham
3 Barnet
4 Bexley
5 Brent
6 Bromley
7 Camden
8 Croydon
9 Ealing
10 Enfield
11 Greenwich
12 Hackney
13 Hammersmith & Fulham
14 Haringey
15 Harrow
16 Havering
17 Hillingdon
18 Hounslow
19 Islington
20 Kensington & Chelsea
21 Kingston upon Thames
22 Lambeth
23 Lewisham
24 Merton
25 Newham
26 Redbridge
27 Richmond upon Thames
28 Southwark
29 Sutton
30 Tower Hamlets
31 Waltham Forest
32 Wandsworth
33 Westminster

Figure 14.1 Greater London (Department of Transport, 1996)

A large part of this travel occurs within the peak periods. Peak travel time in London is defined as 07:00h to 10:00h in the morning, and 16:00h to 19:00h in the evening. All other periods are considered to be off-peak, and the period 02:00h to 05:00h is not included. Traffic levels in these peaks are typically about twice of those at other times of the day. Nevertheless, as we shall see, congestion is not confined to these periods and road congestion is endemic throughout the region for most of the working day. Indeed, the nature of congestion is substantially different in London from the other cities studied.

In order to construct the model, four groups of representative consumers were identified classified according to two criteria: place of residence and availability of free parking at the typical destination. The view taken here was that those resident in the area would have a different pattern of travel than those commuting in over longer distances, which could affect each trip made. Clearly the constraint on parking space in congested inner city areas is a factor which helps to determine choice of mode, but for some people the availability of a free or highly subsidised parking space, especially at the workplace, can be a major influence on mode choice. The evidence is that parking is typically charged for at rates well below the true resource costs of the space, the subsidy often being paid by the employer.

Since each of these groups will face different sets of costs and probably

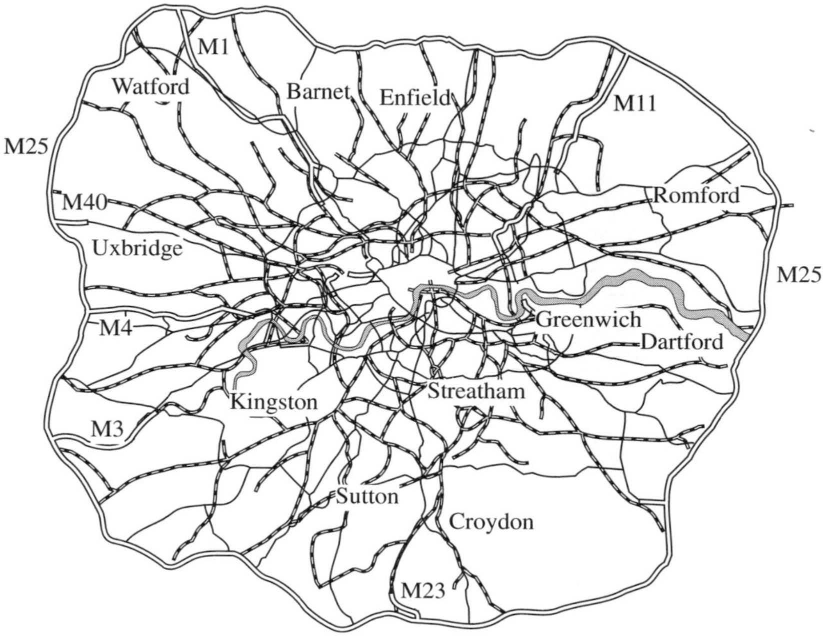

Figure 14.2 The main London road and rail networks (London Research Centre, 1991)

display different elasticities, it is important to model them separately. However, we also need to aggregate the total trip demands of each group, thus an estimate has had to be made of the numbers in each of these categories as follows:

Residents, free parking;
Residents, paid parking;
Non-residents, fee parking;
Non-residents, paid parking;

The size of the London area means that the number of residents tends to dominate the commuters from outside Greater London more than is the case in the other case studies.

The travel choice model allows for the choice between peak and off-peak travel, and within each of these there is a basic choice, first between rail and road and within road between private and public transport. Private transport allows for a choice of solo driving or carpooling and of type of fuel. Public transport involves a choice between bus and underground (metro), which is treated as more equivalent to bus than rail in terms of its demand characteristics. This application is slightly different from the other case studies which allowed an initial choice between motorised and non-motorised, but did not distinguish the rail mode differentially. The role of rail, especially for longer distance commuting trips in London, is so important that it was necessary to sacrifice the separate identification of walking and cycling trips as discussed later.

Roads

Greater London has an extensive road network of about 2122 kilometres (Department of Transport, 1996). There are several motorways feeding into the region from the north, west, south and south-west together with many more trunk roads feeding in from all points of the compass. There is a partial inner ring road around the Central Area and a further partial intermediate ring known as the North and South Circular Roads (which includes the whole of Inner London and a little more) and the Greater London region is bounded by the M25 orbital motorway. The Outer London area has the highest concentration of motorway, dual carriageway and trunk roads, while the proportion of single carriageway roads becomes greater towards the central area. This is reflected in the average speeds of the three areas – the average daytime off-peak speed in Central London is 17 km/hour, for Inner London it is 25.6 km/hour, and for Outer London it is 36.9 km/hour.

On a typical weekday, around 8 million car trips are made either wholly or partially within the London area. This represents roughly half the total number of non-walk trips made each weekday, making the car by far the most popular form of motorised transport. The majority of trips are relatively short, with 75 per cent of trips being under 10 km and the overall average about 13 km in length (data from Department of Transport).

Over the course of a typical weekday, around 25 per cent of all car trips are made between home and work. This figure rises to nearly 50 per cent during the morning peak. During the daytime inter-peak period, some 26 per cent of car trips are made in the course of employer's business (data from Department of Transport).

There are a total of 2 401 420 cars registered in the Greater London region (DETR,1997b). The vast majority (93.9 per cent) are petrol driven (there is traditionally much less price advantage, if any, to diesel fuel in the UK than in most other EU countries), and slightly more than half (57.7 per cent) have an engine size of less than 1600cc. London-based vehicles account for about 86 per cent of the total number of weekday trips.

Over 900000 cars enter London each day, of which 25 per cent pass through London to another destination (77 per cent of these are on the M25 orbital motorway). Over 60 per cent of those entering do not penetrate further than the Outer London area, and only 4 per cent get as far as Central London (LRC, 1994). This reflects the problems already referred to and again distinguishes London from the other case studies.

At present, motorists are not charged for using specific parts of the road network, except for a small number of tolled bridges and tunnels, only one of which is in the London area (the crossing of the Thames Estuary at Dartford). Car users pay duty and VAT on fuel (0.45 Euro/litre unleaded petrol/diesel, 1995 prices) and pay an annual vehicle tax of about 160 Euros (1995 prices) which is not differentiated by location or type of vehicle.

Rail

London has both extensive heavy rail and underground networks which were mostly built in the nineteenth century. As a consequence, the opportunities for their development in line with the changes that have occurred in London during the twentieth century have been somewhat limited, and the underground (in particular) is now experiencing problems of infrastructure decay. Only two new lines have been built in the past 30 years, one of these is still not completed. Although there have been plans, no new heavy rail route has been constructed within London, unlike the situation in a number of other European cities.

Both the underground and rail networks are characterised by very different areas of concentration. The underground network serves virtually all of Greater London to the north of the River Thames, but offers only a very limited coverage south of the river. Heavy rail, on the other hand, offers a dense network south of the River Thames but has a more limited service to the north which is based largely on the mainline routes heading out of London. Hence, a rail user travelling locally in the southern half of London is likely to use a heavy rail train, whereas the traveller in the northern half is more likely to be on an underground train. There is only one major conventional rail route across Central London. Thus it is important to consider both underground and conventional rail services as these are both complementary and competing services for different consumers.

Demand patterns show clear differences between the peak and off-peak periods. Over two-thirds of all daily underground and heavy rail trips are made during the morning and evening peak periods. Commuting between home and work is the single most important purpose for both types of rail travel, with around 50 per cent of all weekday rail trips being made for this reason. Shopping trips represent 5 per cent of the daily trips, and education trips a further 6 per cent.

Since the 1993 Railways Act, the British heavy rail network has been split up and sold to the private sector. Heavy rail services in London and the Southeast used to be run by a single operator (part of the state-owned British Rail) known as Network South East, but now this area is served by 11 private train operating companies. Each of these provides passenger services on specific franchised routes in and around London. These companies only operate the trains – ownership and maintenance of the rail infrastructure, trains, stations, and so on falls to other companies from which these services are leased by the train operating companies.

The London Underground is still within the public domain and is responsible to London Transport (also responsible for the control of London's bus service network). There are proposals that London Underground will also be placed in the private sector, although in what form is unclear at present.

The pricing structure for both rail and underground services can be complicated, depending on the exact requirements of the individual traveller, and does not always follow a clear peak/off-peak structure. This presents problems for modelling the corect price of any journey. Standard fare prices are typically set for travel in the morning peak (07:00h–10:00h) and are based on a combination of distance travelled and nature of the market (typically upgraded lines have higher fares for a given distance), but passengers can obtain (often quite generously) discounted fares at other times.

However, all travellers have the option to purchase a 'Travelcard' which allows unlimited travel on trains, underground and buses for a given period of time. Travelcard prices are based on a zone system – London is divided up into six travel zones (zone 1 = Central London, zone 6 = outskirts of Outer London), and the traveller must decide on which zones he/she wishes to travel within/between and buy the appropriate Travelcard that covers these zones. A Travelcard may be purchased that allows travel for a period of one day (not valid for the morning peak), or for longer periods of weeks, months or years.

Travellers commuting from outside London have three options – they can buy an ordinary return fare (with a Travelcard if they need to change mode in the course of their journey), buy a station to station season ticket (for example Canterbury to London Victoria) which allows unlimited travel between two elected stations for an optional number of weeks or months, or thirdly buy a Travelcard with an extension to a station outside of zones 1–6 which effectively gives the traveller unlimited travel within London and between London and one elected station outside of the city. Since the ordinary fare price for a given journey is around twice as much when travelling in the morning peak, most commuters travelling at this time opt for some form of season ticket which is generally priced at approximately the off-peak rate if travel occurs on five days per week. Indeed, commuters regularly travelling in the morning peak for three or more days per week will generally save sufficient money on a season ticket to make it worthwhile.

To further complicate matters, various concessions are available to those with disabilities, those between the ages of 16 and 25 years old, those at school, or those who have reached retirement age. Indeed, there are nearly one million London residents over retirement age who are entitled to free underground travel and reduced price rail travel, although free underground travel is not permitted before 10:00h.

A detailed procedure was developed to calculate relevant prices for journeys. This allowed for the distribution of trips throughout the day and data from operators on the incidence of Travelcard use at different times.

Buses

Since 1985, private companies have progressively taken over the operation of bus service routes in Greater London to the extent that now all bus services are operated by private companies. However, unlike the rest of the UK, bus services in London are in the main still centrally planned. London Transport is responsible for planning routes, procuring services (either for individual routes or groups of routes in an area) from private bus operators (through a system of tendered bids) and ensuring that these operators fulfil their contracts.

Bus demand in London shows marked spatial variations. Inner London residents tend to use buses most frequently, making an average of 0.48 bus trips per person per day, whereas the corresponding figure for Outer London residents is 0.34. Bus trip lengths tend to be short in length, with over 80 per cent of trips being less than 5 km (LRC, 1994). Interestingly, the total number of bus trips is fairly evenly distributed throughout the day, with no noticeable difference between the peak and off-peak periods. The number of trips that occur during the inter-peak period is approximately the same as the number occurring during the combined morning and evening peak periods. Average trip lengths, however, are longer during the peak periods reflecting the fact that work journeys tend to be longer than others.

The trip purpose of bus users shows significant differences when compared to rail users. Only around 25 per cent of the daily trip total is for work purposes (although this rises to 42 per cent in the morning peak), whereas shopping trips account for 31 per cent and education trips 15 per cent.

A further difference between buses and the rail-based modes is in the income level of passengers. Households with higher annual incomes tend to make more rail trips than those from lower income households.

However, in the case of bus passengers, the opposite is true, and the most frequent travellers are those with the lowest incomes.

The various types of Travelcard are valid for bus travel in the same way as described above for underground and rail use, as well as concessions for those who have reached retirement age. In addition, travellers may purchase ordinary fares on the bus, or purchase a one day or period bus only pass. As with rail a detailed analysis was undertaken of travel patterns in order to develop representative prices for use in the subsequent modelling.

Choice structures of the utility function

The tree structure implied by the choices available is shown in Figure 14.3. The preferences of the consumer are modelled by using nested CES-type utility functions. The homothetic nature of the CES implies that, at each level, quantity and price indices can be constructed as a weighted sum of lower-level quantities and prices. The nested utility structure used for the simulation exercises is represented in Figure 14.3. At the highest level total utility depends on two aggregate goods, passenger transport and other goods. These other goods can be further subdivided to allow for those which generate demands for freight transport and those which do not, but we concentrate here on the direct passenger transport impacts.

At the first level of the utility tree, the transport subutility component contains transport demands in two periods of the day (peak and off-peak) as arguments. Subsequently we only develop the structure in detail for the peak but the off-peak is exactly analogous. At the second level, there is the choice between rail and road modes as discussed previously. At the third level 'road' transport demand includes 'private' and 'public' demands. At the fourth level, public transport can be disaggregated into bus and underground (metro). At level five, private transport can involve either 'carpooling', to reflect the differential costs of multiple occupancy, or 'driving solo'. Finally, two car sizes are considered, big and small and then two possible fuels, gasoline and diesel and two possible types of technology, clean and non-clean technology.

One important difference between the London application of the model and the other case studies is the need to incorporate rail as a separate and independent mode. This led to some software problems with the choice structures and this led to the need to omit walking and cycling. Walking is not unimportant in London, it accounts for about 20 per cent of all identifiable journeys, and walking is a component of most public transport journeys. However, the greater size of London and the longer average journey length makes walking a less significant contributor to total transport demand. Its omission is unfortunate, but is not so serious as it would be in a much smaller city. Cycling is rather less important

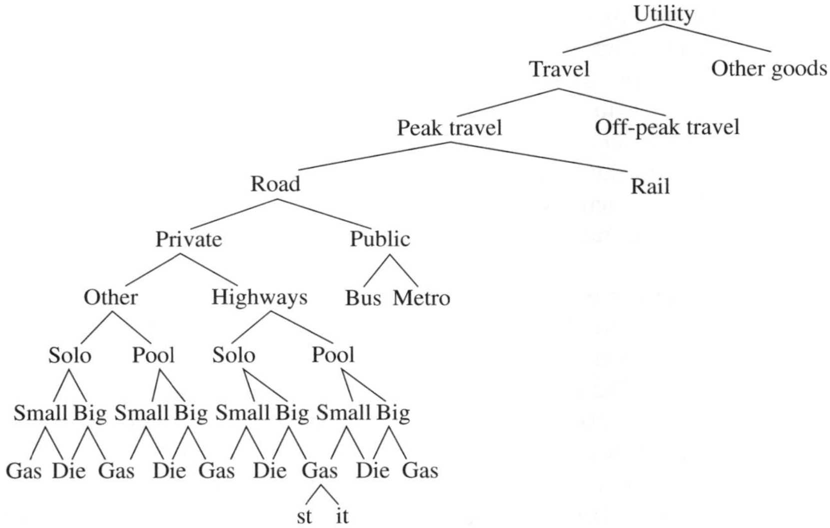

Figure 14.3 Nested CES utility function

(about 1.5 per cent of total trips) and its omission is not seen to be a major problem.

The model structure in Figure 14.3 allows calibration of a general equilibrium model in which all equilibrium prices and quantities are endogenous. It is possible therefore to make changes to any one, or a set, of policy variables, and observe the impact on traffic volumes for each mode and total traffic and the consequent welfare implications of these changes.

14.2.2 Assumptions on Traffic Growth and Composition

In order to make comparable assessments of different policy options we have to project the reference case forward to 2005. This means applying a set of growth factors to the traffic situation observed in 1991, our base year. It is not simply a case of applying a growth factor, since we have to recognise that in the absence of any change in capacity, congestion would increase and this would automatically lead to some readjustment of both modal split and peak–off-peak split of traffic. The growth has been based on the National Road Traffic Forecast supplied by the Department of Transport (see DETR, 1997b for the latest forecasts) which are based on assumptions of economic growth and income growth, and hence car ownership. In order to make the model comparable to other case studies and subject to the constraints imposed by the CES structure of the utility function we have used a common set of elasticity assumptions for the responses of the model.

14.2.3 Assumptions on Road Capacity and Public Transport Capacity

We have also to make allowance for any planned changes in the capacity of the transport system between 1995 and 2005. The basic assumption has been that there is no significant change in aggregate capacity of either the road system or the public transport system. This is a reasonable assumption since there are no plans for significant development of the road network in London. Any plans for improving the utilisation of existing capacity are effectively incorporated in the policy tests.

We also assume that there will be no major expansion of the public transport network, effectively the underground and rail systems. There is one new underground line to be completed during the period in question, the Jubilee Line Extension. Although this is a substantial investment, it represents only a marginal addition to the extensive underground system and ignoring it is not a serious omission. No major expansion of the heavy rail network is scheduled except for the completion of the Heathrow Express direct rail service from Heathrow Airport. Again this has only marginal impacts on the total capacity and its use by the bulk of London's traffic.

14.2.4 Assumptions on Resource Costs and Taxes

Estimating the resource costs of transport is not a simple exercise. Such costs include both capital and operating costs of each mode of transport, each of these has to be estimated net of any relevant taxes or subsidies. It is also difficult just to use market prices for these resources as these do not always reflect the true resource costs due to market imperfections.

We have assumed that the infrastructure is fixed, as discussed above, such that capital and depreciation costs are related solely to the stock of vehicles which is assumed to be able to adjust fully to meet changes in demand. For public transport marginal capacity costs are allocated to the peak period. Operating costs depend principally on vehicle size, fuel used and operating characteristics (mainly speed). We make assumptions about the proportions of vehicles of different sizes based on evidence on vehicle stocks and use available data on fuel costs (mainly distinguishing between petrol and diesel). Public transport data has been assembled from detailed information obtained from a sample of train operators and from London Transport. This has enabled us to estimate as good a data set for both average and marginal costs as we believe is possible, although confidentiality has prevented this from being as detailed as we would have liked. The main criterion, however, has been to use data which is as consistent as possible between modes.

Speed–flow relationships are estimated from observed data to which an exponential function is fitted as shown in Figure 14.4. This is expressed in monetary terms by the use of standard values of time. This standard speed–flow relationship is consistent with that used in all urban case studies but, as we shall discuss later, does produce an extremely flat relationship for London. This is reasonable given the extent of off-peak congestion in London, but has the effect of implying relatively low marginal congestion costs since additional traffic has very little impact on overall speed–flow patterns given the very high levels of congestion and low overall speeds.

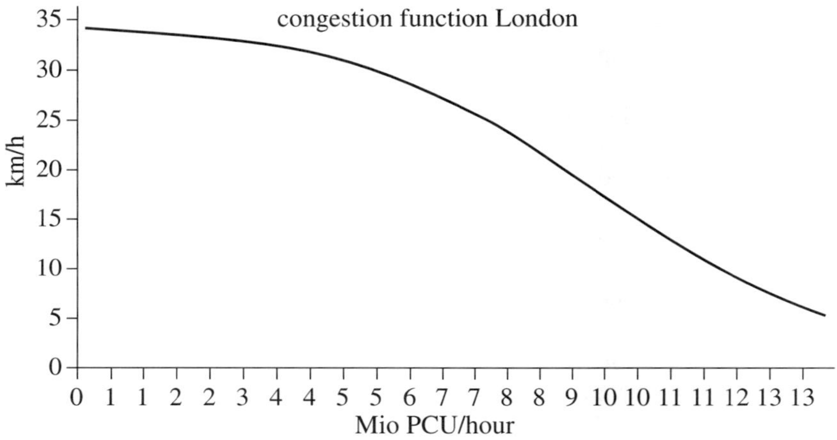

Figure 14.4 Speed–flow relationship for London

For car users there are two other critical factors. One is the number of people using the car, the other is the cost of parking. We identify from observed data the split between solo drivers and multiple occupancy of cars; this is used to apportion costs. Parking costs are estimated from evidence on the resource costs of parking space. Reliable data is not available on the proportion of car trips for which the full resource cost of parking is actually paid. We have used the arbitrary assumption that only 30 per cent of trips actually pay the full resource costs. Many of the rest probably pay something towards the cost of parking rather than receive totally free parking, but we have assumed that this is not the case in order to use the simple four-way classification.

The resource costs are all expressed in terms of Euro/passenger kilometre. These show costs of between 0.3 and 0.8 Euro/pkm for solo car users and around 0.1 Euro/pkm for bus users.

14.2.5 Assumptions on External Costs

Marginal external costs are real costs to society which are not included in the price paid, or other costs directly incurred, by users. These costs fall both on other users of the particular transport system, such that a marginal decision by one user has impacts on the real costs faced by all users in the system, and on non-users through the damage done to the environment (for a more detailed description of the methodology, see deliverable D7 of the TRENEN II STRAN project).

We identify four main categories of such costs:

- Marginal external congestion costs. This is the value of the time loss which a traveller causes to all other travellers, when he decides to consume an extra kilometre of travel. For drivers of private vehicles, this extra kilometre will lead to a marginal slowing down of all other traffic on the network. For public transport the impact is more complex since it typically does not cause an extra vehicle, but will lead to longer stops at bus stops or stations and thus both increases the time taken by other travellers and, for buses, will have impacts on other road users. In the decision to travel the extra kilometre, the traveller takes into account his own time loss, but not the time loss caused to others. The decrease in speed and increase in journey times is small but, when multiplied by the total number of travellers, the marginal external congestion cost becomes significant, especially during peak hours. The congestion impacts are measured using the speed–flow function shown in Figure 14.4. Given the volumes of traffic in London, this function is actually remarkably flat over the relevant range.
- Marginal external air pollution costs. This is the cost of health damage and mortality caused by harmful pollutants emitted by engines. We have used data on these costs which are consistent with results of the ExternE consortium (JOULE II Programme of the EU).
- Marginal external accident costs. Some accident costs are included in travellers' own resource costs. Drivers have to pay insurance premia and their behaviour is such that some costs are absorbed in, for example, longer journey times by obeying speed limits. However, not all costs of accidents are taken account of when the decision to travel or not is taken. These include both the impact on others of reckless

behaviour and accidental impacts on pedestrians, property owners and so on.

- Marginal external noise costs. Traffic generates noise, which has negative well-being and health effects particularly on non-users. These costs are not charged to drivers.

The marginal external costs, that attributable to the additional trip, amount to about 0.3 Euro/pkm for solo car drivers in the peak and about 0.1 Euro/pkm in the off-peak. On average, for car drivers, about 50 per cent of the peak marginal external costs, but only about 10 per cent of off-peak marginal external costs, are accounted for by congestion. Most of the remainder is accounted for by air pollution costs, but it is difficult to give representative figures since there is a close interrelationship between flow and congestion on the one hand and air pollution, noise and accident costs on the other.

14.2.6 Assumptions on Elasticities

A key element in the operation of the model is the assumption made about the elasticities with respect to changes in price. These elasticities concern the potential shifts between modes, time of day and whether to travel at all. The evidence on elasticities is mixed. Most empirical evidence relates to specific situations, and is very time and location specific. We reviewed a substantial amount of available evidence on elasticities to ensure consistency with other traffic models for London, and with the traffic projections used for 2005. There are also some difficulties in assuming that elasticities are symmetrical between increases and decreases in price or time, and whether consumers will perceive any direct charging, for example for road space, in the same way as they do the (often hidden) direct costs of using the private car.

For practical reasons a set of standard elasticities was adopted for the model which need to respect the properties of the specified CES utility function. These imply greater elasticities for lower level choices in the utility function.

14.3 THE LONDON TRANSPORT PRICING PROBLEM IN 2005

The reference case is based on the assessments of the current resource costs of transport by the different modes in London and the actual prices charged, projected forward to 2005 as discussed above.

The total marginal cost to the consumer (the generalised price) of travelling one kilometre using some mode consists of the resource costs (the cost of material inputs required to produce that kilometre with that mode), taxes and time costs. The sum of resource costs and taxes is called the money price. The sum of the money price and the value of time spent driving the kilometre (time cost) is the generalised price. In addition to these costs to the consumer, there are marginal external costs. The marginal external costs are real costs to society which are not included in the generalised price.

The resource costs of using a private car may also differ between some users according to whether they can park without paying the full resource costs of parking at the destination. We have allowed for differing assumptions about this in the calculation of the reference situation.

The following marginal external costs have been distinguished (as discussed above).

- congestion costs
- air pollution
- external accident
- noise costs

As we can see from Figure 14.5 (see Appendix Table 14A.1 for the full details) there are some substantial differences between the estimates of current generalised prices and the full costs of the car mode as represented by the addition of marginal external costs and, particularly, parking resource costs. The current level of taxes typically contributes only between one-third and one-half of the marginal external costs in the peak.

Note that those who have to pay the resource costs of parking will typically pay a total price which is roughly equivalent to the full costs, but these are in a minority. Those who live within the Greater London area will typically also make a larger tax contribution per pkm in the peak than those commuting in from outside. Much of this is due to lower annual distances driven by residents, thus increasing the burden of fixed costs such as the flat fee annual vehicle excise duty.

Public transport users in London, where prices are set more according to commercial considerations than in most European cities, are typically paying at least the full social costs of their trips.

The results of this have two key effects on London traffic. One is that off-peak traffic is a much larger share of total traffic than in other cities studied. The peak accounts for some 60 per cent of all traffic in Brussels, but only 45 per cent in London. This leads to off-peak speeds being much lower in London, with much less differential (only around 5 km/h) between peak

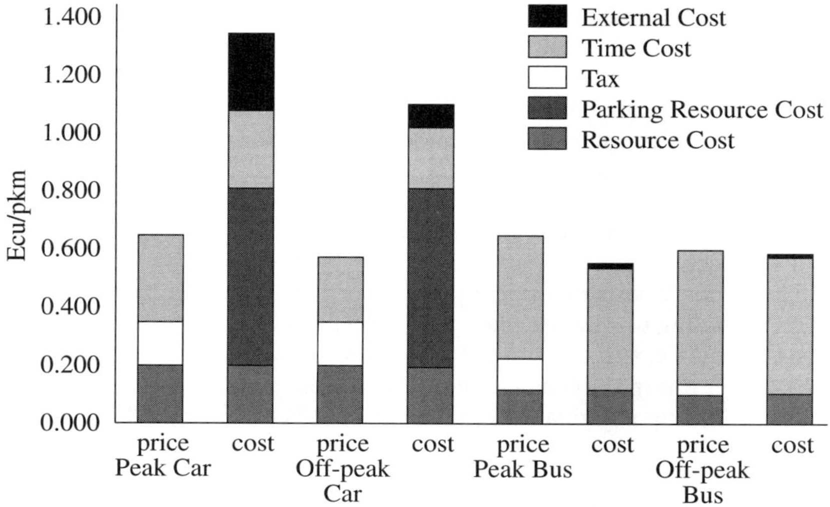

Figure 14.5 Reference prices and costs for London

and off-peak. This helps explain the rather flat congestion function identified above.

The second effect is on the distribution between public and private transport, especially in the peak, where private transport retains a larger share of peak transport than in the other cases. This is in part a pricing effect, although the larger and more diverse area of London leads to a larger share of trips not having destinations in the central area. Although public transport retains a high share of trips to Central London, many more trips for both work and non-work activities have destinations in other centres in both Inner and Outer London, which are not so well served by public transport, especially for non-radial journeys.

The reference scenario (Appendix Table 14A.1) is thus characterised by high parking resource costs, prices which do not reflect the full resource plus marginal external costs, and serious congestion in both the peak and off-peak periods. The seriousness of congestion in London limits the scope for using pricing to switch traffic between peak and off-peak periods. Since levels of congestion are very high and speeds low the marginal cost of the additional user is low, relative to the average cost. Pricing according to this marginal cost would not therefore lead to much reallocation of traffic. There are also large external costs and serious problems in financing the transport infrastructure and the subsidies to many transport users.

14.4 ALTERNATIVE POLICY SCENARIOS

We now turn to examining a set of alternative policy scenarios to be compared with the reference situation. These scenarios or policy packages are common to all the case studies. Four basic packages have been defined:

- the full optimum situation in which the model is allowed to calibrate the full equilibrium prices and quantities for each mode and the impacts on mode usage, total traffic and total welfare is calculated. This provides a benchmark against which other more practical policy packages can be evaluated.
- cordon or congestion pricing, in which it is assumed that only traffic passing through the outer cordon to enter the case study area will be charged at a basic rate. This is a representation of some simple area charging schemes. In practice this would probably only apply in the peak period and thus is a crude form of congestion pricing, but one which does not distinguish how much travel is undertaken and only charges those entering the designated area from outside. Parking is assumed charged at the reference scenario costs. The appropriate charge is calibrated by the model. Public transport prices are simply set at their marginal resource costs
- uniform pricing (using reference charges for parking), in which it is assumed that fuel prices are increased in line with current EU proposals to the proposed reference level for excise duties of 0.5 Euro/litre for petrol and 0.393 Euro/litre for diesel, to which local VAT rates are applied in addition. No specific charges are assumed in urban areas and parking costs are left at the calculated reference levels.
- uniform pricing (full resource cost charging for parking) in which the same fuel price increases are assumed but now the full resource costs for parking are applied to all users.

These alternative policy packages are relatively simple, but do represent examples of the sort of policy interventions which are feasible. Some experimenting has also been undertaken with alternatives which allow for different approaches to parking costs in each package and which also make alternative assumptions about the introduction of new emission technologies which would give both resource and external cost savings.

14.4.1 A Full Optimum Policy

The full optimum policy (see Appendix Table 14A.2) sets prices to reflect full marginal external costs and the elimination of other market imperfections (for example in the supply of public transport) by the use of taxes. This is assumed to be possible in an infinitely variable way such that taxes will vary according to vehicle type, fuel type, time of day and user (for example between residents and commuters). This is not because it is believed that such a policy is immediately implementable, but because it will give us a reference benchmark against which all other policies can be assessed. A full optimum will generate the maximum welfare and thus other policies can be assessed in terms of their relative achievement of this maximum which can be compared with the costs of implementation.

We assess the results in terms of a number of indicators, welfare change (a monetary measure of the net benefits assuming all tax revenues are used for improving consumer welfare), traffic volume changes, the split of traffic between time of day and mode, and the impact on external costs.

The basis result from the implementation of full optimum compared with the reference case, shown in Table 14.1, is that high taxes are imposed on road users, but traffic levels and external costs fall, there are large reductions in the use of cars in both the peak and off-peak periods. Tax revenues from both private and public transport users rise.

Traffic changes and external cost changes are substantial in this with a 15 per cent fall in total traffic and a significant 32.5 per cent fall in external costs. Welfare increases are rather smaller having allowed for the increased cost of travel, but are nevertheless a significant increase. Perhaps of greatest significance in London is the substantial shift in off-peak traffic from private to public reflecting the very high levels of congestion in both periods in the reference case. There is, however, relatively little shifting of the proportion of traffic between peak and off-peak such that the fall in total traffic is spread fairly evenly between both peak and off-peak periods. Speeds do not increase by much in the off-peak but increase by around 4 km/h in the peak such that average speeds are similar throughout the day.

Prices of transport rise substantially. For a resident driving a small car and not paying for parking the price (Euro/pkm) would rise from 0.63 to 1.53. For bus users in the peak the rise would be more modest from 0.64 to 0.68 (that is, from slightly more than the car driver pays to around 40 per cent).

A full optimum implies a substantial increase in the tax revenue from transport, which would rise from around 14 million Euro per day to nearly 50 million. This is accounted for in the total change in welfare.

14.4.2 A Cordon Pricing Policy

Cordon pricing is implemented as a partial congestion pricing policy in which non-residents are charged for entry into the Greater London area.

Table 14.1 Comparison of full optimum with reference case

	Welfare level	Per cent welfare gain	Traffic level (mio/ pkm)	Per cent change in traffic level	Per cent total traffic, peak private	Per cent total traffic, peak public	Per cent total traffic, off-peak private	Per cent total traffic, off-peak public	Other external costs (mio Euro/day)
RF	1413.669	0	126.42	0	33.96	12.89	41.12	12.04	9.07865
FO	1429.791	+1.14	107.05	−15.3	26.50	19.92	28.11	25.47	6.12841

This will thus have little effect on inhabitants, but commuters are more heavily taxed. The details are given in Appendix Table 14A.3 and summarised in Table 14.2.

As would be expected with such a crude policy the gain in welfare is only small compared with the reference situation, traffic levels fall by only just over 3 per cent and the impact on external costs is only a relatively small reduction of 4 per cent. This can be seen as a simple result from the implementation of much higher charges for non-residents, the user of a small car not paying full parking costs would see the price (Euro/pkm) rise from 0.58 to 1.19 if non-resident but fall slightly from 0.63 to 0.62 if resident. As might be expected from such small changes in the prices faced by the majority of users there is only a marginal change in the mode split and virtually none in the time of day split of traffic. Tax revenues from private car users do rise by about 60 per cent.

Obviously a crude cordon pricing is less effective in a large city such as London where a large proportion of total journeys are entirely within the area. In London, cordon pricing gains only 13 per cent of the gain possible from a full optimum (in Brussels it can capture as much as 54 per cent). In practice a more sophisticated cordoning using more than one cordon with Central London attracting a very high charge would be needed. This does again give us a base line for looking at the relative effects of policy types from which refinements can be sought.

14.4.3 Uniform Pricing Policies

A policy of charging uniform prices which do not distinguish between types of user or time of day but simply changing fuel prices in line with EU predicted policy is one of the easiest policy scenarios to implement and thus provides an interesting contrast with both the full optimum and with more specific versions of a cordon pricing policy. This is shown in detail in Appendix Tables 14A.4 and 14A.5. We have shown separately here the detailed analysis of implementing improved parking policies as part of a uniform pricing strategy (UP2) and this given in Table 14A.5.

The basic results are summarised in Table 14.3, again with comparison to the reference situation. Looking first at the introduction of a simple uniform pricing policy without any adjustment to reflect the resource cost of parking, we see that this has very little impact on traffic levels, on traffic distribution between modes or time of day and only reduces the external cost of transport by a mere 1.42 per cent. Prices change very little and total tax revenues change very little (by less than 2 million Euro/day). Thus even quite substantial changes in fuel prices will have very little impact on the traffic situation in a large densely populated city, principally because they

Table 14.2 Comparison of cordon pricing with reference case

	Welfare level	Per cent welfare gain	Traffic level (mio/ pkm)	Per cent change in traffic level	Per cent total traffic, peak private	Per cent total traffic, peak public	Per cent total traffic, off-peak private	Per cent total traffic, off-peak public	Other external costs (mio Euro/day)
RF	1413.669	0	126.42	0	33.96	12.89	41.12	12.04	9.07865
CO	1415.445	+0.13	122.19	−3.3	32.36	14.15	39.41	14.08	8.71297

Table 14.3 Comparison of uniform pricing with reference case

	Welfare level	Per cent welfare gain	Traffic level (mio/ pkm)	Per cent change in traffic level	Per cent total traffic, peak private	Per cent total traffic, peak public	Per cent total traffic, off-peak private	Per cent total traffic, off-peak public	Other external costs (mio Euro/day)
RF	1413.669	0	126.42	0	33.96	12.89	41.12	12.04	9.07865
UP1	1414.742	+0.08	125.11	−1.0	33.74	13.19	40.55	12.51	8.94948
UP2	1425.628	+0.85	113.57	−10.2	30.40	16.69	32.86	20.06	7.27554

fail to differentiate adequately between different users, different times of the day and capture all the sources of external costs.

The refinement of uniform pricing polices to allow for the estimated resource costs of parking demonstrates two effects. First, it shows the benefits from more sophisticated pricing policies which aim to charge the identifiable additional costs of sources of imperfection in transport markets to those incurring them. Second, it demonstrates the large distortion in resource allocation which is caused by the absence of accurate full charging for parking. With these adjustments traffic levels do fall by a more significant 10 per cent and there is some impact on mode split. External costs fall by a more appreciable 19.9 per cent compared with the reference case. However, tax revenues would fall in this situation since most of the change in traffic levels is caused by the direct charging for parking and not by taxes imposed on road users.

14.4.4 Other Policy Elements

In addition to these policy scenarios discussed in detail above we have looked at the impact of changing parking charges in each of the basic cases and of introducing improved technology. These are summarised in Table 14.4 as changes in welfare from the base cases of reference parking charges and standard technology within each scenario. Generally there is not much impact on the overall welfare effects of the different scenarios from the introduction of new more fuel efficient technologies in policy scenarios short of the full optimum. However, improved parking charges reflecting the full resource costs of parking do make a substantial impact on improving the results from the uniform pricing and cordon pricing scenarios. In fact with improved parking charges more than 70 per cent of the full optimum improvement can be obtained. Regardless of the overall policy option, it is thus clear that there is a substantial impact from the introduction of improved parking charges.

Table 14.4 Welfare changes from varying technology and parking charges

Scenario	% dW Ref PC St Tech	% dW Ref PC Imp Tech	% dW New PC St Tech	% dW New PC Imp Tech
REF	0	+0.006		
UP	0	+0.006	+1.014	+1.018
CO	0	−0.007	+0.776	+0.780
FO	0	+0.004	−0.011	−0.008

14.5 A COMPARISON OF POLICY OPTIONS

In this section we make some simple comparisons between the main options discussed in Section 14.4. These are summarised in Table 14.5 which draws together material from Tables 14.1 to 14.3 above.

As expected the overall welfare effect is best from full optimum pricing, but a uniform pricing scenario which includes the full resource costs of parking (especially to residents of the inner area) generates a substantial proportion (74 per cent) of the maximum benefits available. As suggested in Table 14.5 even greater gains could also be made from a cordon charge which also charged residents appropriately for parking. Neither of these would be so useful in generating tax revenues. These policies achieve this gain from a reduction in total traffic levels and a switch between modes, but rather less between times of day, reflecting the extent to which congestion in London is already an all day phenomenon. It is very clear that a single pricing measure, such as fuel prices or cordon pricing, cannot generate a major reduction in traffic levels or contribute to a substantial increase in overall welfare, indeed in some modified scenario runs of the model the uniform pricing scenario has generated some reductions in welfare from the reference case since it fails both to reduce external costs and to generate sufficient tax revenue to compensate for the increased costs incurred by road users.

It should be stressed, however, that these tests are made on simple assumptions concerning possible policy packages in order to provide contrasting scenarios.

14.6 POLICY RECOMMENDATIONS

The above discussion has highlighted five major issues relating to the characteristics of traffic patterns in London and the impacts of alternative policy scenarios:

- Current traffic levels are unsustainable leading to excessive congestion, which lasts throughout the day, and to excessive levels of external cost, none of which are reflected in the prices paid by users of any mode of transport.
- Introduction of full welfare maximising optimum prices which aim to achieve an optimal distribution of resources both within transport and between transport and other goods could lead to substantial benefits which would add significantly to overall welfare. It should be noted that the welfare gains here allow for the increased expenditure

Table 14.5 Key results of counterfactual equilibria (case, 2005)

	Per cent welfare gain	Per cent maximal welfare gain	Traffic level (mio/pkm)	Per cent total traffic, peak private	Per cent total traffic, peak public	Per cent total traffic, off-peak private	Per cent total traffic, off-peak public	External cost (mio Euro/day)
RF	0	0	126.4208	26.50	12.89	41.12	12.04	9.07865
CO	+0.13	11.4	122.1877	32.36	14.15	39.41	14.08	8.71297
UP1	+0.08	7.0	125.1072	33.74	13.19	40.55	12.51	8.94948
UP2	+0.85	74.6	113.5717	30.40	16.69	32.86	20.06	7.27554
FO	+1.14	100	107.0465	26.50	19.92	28.11	25.47	6.12841

on transport and thus a reduction in expenditure on other activities. This explains why such gains are lower than the suggested gains in GDP which have been suggested by commercial interests from the reduction in congestion alone. The latter do not allow for the impact on welfare in general, only from certain classes of user and hence tend to overestimate gains.

- Current attempts to increase fuel prices as a partial measure to address, in particular, the environmental external impact of transport, only go a very small way towards improving the traffic situation, and in some cases may actually be welfare reducing.
- Simple cordon pricing policies to introduce a form of congestion pricing on access into congested city areas can achieve some benefit, but much would depend on where the cordon(s) were situated. External cordon pricing can cause important redistributive effects between residents and non-residents in favour of the former.
- One of the main distortions currently in operation is the failure to charge full resource costs of parking. It appears vital that in any policy package some attempt is made to address this issue through the removal of benefits deriving from free or subsidised parking to those entering inner cities.

From this we would identify that the following major components of any set of improved policies would be needed:

- effective charging for the resource costs of parking;
- cordon charging around the central and inner areas, especially charging which is sensitive to time of day variations in traffic, if more sophisticated pricing mechanisms cannot be introduced;
- recognition of the overall welfare effects, implying the need to ensure that tax revenues are allocated in a welfare enhancing manner and that benefits accruing to individual groups are not weighted excessively.

We have to recognise some key limitations of the analysis undertaken above:

- Many of the resource costs are only estimated, mainly because of the difficulty of identifying these more accurately, a situation which has become worse with the increasing private provision of public transport;
- Despite continuing improvements in the valuation of the external costs of transport, there is still much to be done to obtain valid

transferable values for use in such studies. This includes the key value, that of time, which is implied in any congestion charging policy;

- The model has concentrated on passenger traffic and has not allowed for freight and other commercial traffic. This approach can be defended on the grounds that passenger traffic essentially defines the peak;
- The model does not identify a network explicitly and hence does not allow for improving efficiency in the use of the network by, for example, traffic management measures using real time information on congestion and so on.

APPENDIX TABLES

Table 14A.1 Characterisation of the reference situation (case, 2005)

Prices and costs (Euro/pkm)	Resource cost	Tax	Money price	Marginal external cost (per vkm)	Generalised price
Peak					
Car, solo, small, petrol, free parking					
inhabitants	0.80713	0.15641	0.35154	0.29348	0.63187
commuters	0.32113	0.10241	0.29754	0.29348	0.57787
Car, solo, small, petrol, paid parking					
inhabitants	0.80713	0.15641	0.96354	0.29348	1.24387
commuters	0.32113	0.10241	0.42354	0.29348	0.70387
Car, solo, small, diesel, free parking					
inhabitants	0.78885	0.12496	0.30181	0.43835	0.58215
Bus/tram (inhabitants)	0.11692	0.0996	0.21652	0.011582	0.64183
Off-peak					
car, solo, small, petrol, free parking					
inhabitants	0.80534	0.15368	0.34702	0.1092	0.57149
bus (inhabitants)	0.105	0.02581	0.13081	0.010858	0.59903
Volume and composition of traffic	mio pkm	share (%)	% carpool	speed (km/h)	
Peak, private	42.92734	33.96	23.53	27.50	
Peak, public	16.29327	12.89		24.49	
Off-peak, private	51.9806	41.12	32.69	32.73	
Off-peak, public	15.21959	12.04		29.15	
Tax revenue (mio Euro/day)					
Private	11.88196				
Public	2.5235				
External costs (mio Euro/day)	9.07865				
Welfare level	1413.669				
Total traffic level	126.4208				

Table 14A.2 Characterisation of the full optimum situation (case, 2005)

Prices and costs (Euro/pkm)	Resource cost	Tax	Money price	Marginal external cost (per vkm)[1]	Generalised price
Peak					
Car, solo, small, petrol, free parking					
inhabitants	0.80713	1.08995	1.28508	0.15034	1.5299
commuters	0.32113	0.57586	0.77099	0.15034	1.01581
Car, solo, small, petrol, paid parking					
inhabitants	0.80713	1.08995	1.89708	0.15034	2.1419
commuters	0.32113	0.57586	0.89699	0.15034	1.14181
Car, solo, small, diesel, free parking					
inhabitants	0.78885	1.24523	1.42209	0.29521	1.6669
Bus/tram (inhabitants)	0.11692	0.17798	0.29491	0.004412	0.68305
Off-peak					
Car, solo, small, petrol, free parking					
inhabitants	0.80534	1.00105	1.1944	0.09789	1.41406
Bus (inhabitants)	0.105	0.14846	0.25346	0.008486	0.68456
Volume and composition of traffic	**mio pkm**	**share (%)**	**% carpool**	**speed (km/h)**	
Peak, private	28.36832	26.50	25.11	31.49	
Peak, public	21.32304	19.92		28.04	
Off-peak, private	30.0867	28.11	36.11	33.45	
Off-peak, public	27.26844	25.47		29.78	
Tax revenue (mio Euro/day)					
Private	43.46567				
Public	6.29469				
External costs (mio Euro/day)	6.12841				
Welfare level	1429.791				
Total traffic level	107.0465				

Note:

1. The marginal external cost in Table 14A.2 differs from that in Table 14A.1. The reason is that in Table 14A.1 no account was taken of the effect of parking charges for payers. Hence the estimates there are based on higher demands, with higher external costs.

Table 14A.3 Characterisation of the cordon pricing situation (case, 2005)

Prices and costs (Euro/pkm)	Resource cost	Tax	Money price	Marginal external cost (per vkm)[1]	Generalised price
Peak					
Car, solo, small, petrol, free parking					
inhabitants	0.80713	0.15641	0.35154	0.24426	0.6183
commuters	0.32113	0.73225	0.92738	0.24426	1.19414
Car, solo, small, petrol, paid parking					
inhabitants	0.80713	0.15641	0.96354	0.24426	1.2303
commuters	0.32113	0.73225	1.05338	0.24426	1.32014
Car, solo, small, diesel, free parking					
inhabitants	0.78885	0.12496	0.30182	0.38912	0.56858
Bus(inhabitants)	0.11692	0.0996	0.21652	0.009114	0.63109
Off-peak					
Car, solo, small, petrol, free parking					
inhabitants	0.80534	0.15368	0.34702	0.1066	0.57019
Bus (inhabitants)	0.105	0.02581	0.13081	0.010299	0.59907
Volume and composition of traffic	mio pkm	share (%)	% carpool	speed (km/h)	
Peak, private	39.53842	32.36	24.17	28.90	
Peak, public	17.28428	14.15		25.73	
Off-peak, private	48.15611	39.41	33.83	32.92	
Off-peak, public	17.20891	14.08		29.32	
Tax revenue (mio Euro/day)					
Private	18.94793				
Public	2.74776				
External costs (mio Euro/day)	8.71297				
Welfare level	1415.445				
Total traffic level	122.1877				

Note:
1. The marginal external cost in Table 14A.3 differs from that in Table 14A.1. The reason is that in Table 14A.1 no account was taken of the effect of parking charges for payers. Hence the estimates there are based on higher demands, with higher external costs.

Table 14A.4 Characterisation of the uniform pricing (1) situation (case, 2005)

Prices and costs (Euro/pkm)	Resource cost	Tax	Money price	Marginal external cost (per vkm)[1]	Generalised price
Peak					
Car, solo, small, petrol, free parking					
inhabitants	0.80713	0.17302	0.36815	0.28153	0.64301
commuters	0.32113	0.17302	0.36815	0.28153	0.64301
Car, solo, small, petrol, paid parking					
inhabitants	0.80713	0.17302	0.98015	0.28153	1.25501
commuters	0.32113	0.17302	0.49415	0.28153	0.76901
Car, solo, small, diesel, free parking					
inhabitants	0.78885	0.12817	0.30503	0.4264	0.57989
Bus (inhabitants)	0.11692	0.0996	0.21652	0.010982	0.63753
Off-peak					
Car, solo, small, petrol, free parking					
inhabitants	0.80534	0.16655	0.35989	0.1082	0.5837
Bus (inhabitants)	0.105	0.02581	0.13081	0.010643	0.59846
Volume and composition of traffic	**mio pkm**	**share (%)**	**% carpool**	**speed (km/h)**	
Peak, private	42.21452	33.74	23.83	28.05	
Peak, public	16.50138	13.19		24.97	
Off-peak, private	50.73445	40.55	33.41	32.83	
Off-peak, public	15.6569	12.51		29.23	
Tax revenue (mio Euro/day)					
Private	13.73158				
Public	2.57021				
External costs (mio Euro/day)	8.94948				
Welfare level	1414.742				
Total traffic level	125.1072				

Note:
1. The marginal external cost in Table 14A.4 differs from that in Table 14A.1. The reason is that in Table 14A.1 no account was taken of the effect of parking charges for payers. Hence the estimates there are based on higher demands, with higher external costs.

Table 14A.5 Characterisation of the uniform pricing (2) situation (case, 2005)

Prices and costs (Euro/pkm)	Resource cost	Tax	Money price	Marginal external cost (per vkm)[1]	Generalised price
Peak					
Car, solo, small, petrol, free parking					
inhabitants	0.80713	0.17302	0.98015	0.19309	1.23499
commuters	0.32113	0.17302	0.49415	0.19309	0.74899
Car, solo, small, petrol, paid parking					
inhabitants	0.80713	0.17302	0.98015	0.19309	1.23499
commuters	0.32113	0.17302	0.49415	0.19309	0.74899
Car, solo, small, diesel, free parking					
inhabitants	0.78885	0.12817	0.91703	0.33796	1.17187
Bus (inhabitants)	0.11692	0.0996	0.21652	0.00655	0.62177
Off-peak					
Car, solo, small, petrol, free parking					
inhabitants	0.80534	0.16655	0.97189	0.1012	1.19273
Bus (inhabitants)	0.105	0.02581	0.13081	0.009154	0.59585
Volume and composition of traffic	**mio pkm**	**share (%)**	**% carpool**	**speed (km/h)**	
Peak, private	34.52158	30.40	25.20	30.25	
Peak, public	18.95049	16.69		26.94	
Off-peak, private	37.31985	32.86	37.05	33.27	
Off-peak, publc	22.77981	20.06		29.62	
Tax revenue (mio Euro/day)					
Private	10.50787				
Public	3.20578				
External costs (mio Euro/day)	7.27554				
Welfare level	1425.628				
Total traffic level	113.5717				

Note:
1. The marginal external cost in Table 14A.5 differs from that in Table 14A.1. The reason is that in Table 14A.1 no account was taken of the effect of parking charges for payers. Hence the estimates there are based on higher demands, with higher external costs.

REFERENCES

Department of the Environment, Transport and the Regions (DETR) (1997a), *Transport Statistics Great Britain*, London: HMSO.
Department of the Environment, Transport and the Regions (DETR) (1997b), *National Road Traffic Forecasts 1997*, London: DETR.
Department of the Environment, Transport and the Regions (DETR) (1998), *A New Deal for Transport: Better for Everyone*, Cm3950, London: HMSO.
Department of Transport (1996), *London Traffic Monitoring Report: 1996 Edition*, London: HMSO.
European Commission (1994), 'Competition and Cohesion: Trends in the Regions', Fifth Period Report on the Social and Economic Situation and Development of the Regions in the Community, Brussels: European Commission.
London Research Centre (LRC) (1994), *Travel in London, London Area Traffic Survey 1991*, London: HMSO.

15. Evaluating pricing policies for interregional transport in Belgium

Bruno De Borger

15.1 INTRODUCTION

The purpose of this chapter is to study the welfare implications of various transport pricing and regulatory policies in Belgium for the reference year 2005. An integrated transport policy is highly desirable: although a large number of specific measures have been implemented (promotion of car-pooling, public transport subsidies, investment in infrastructure, and so on), congestion and accident rates on the Belgian road system remain substantial. High congestion is common during peak hours on the major highways linking the most important urban centres (Brussels, Antwerp, Ghent) as well as on a large number of other secondary routes. Moreover, some sections of the network are congested even during the off-peak period. Accident rates have been stabilising in recent years, but the external costs associated with accidents remain high.

Since the Belgian economy is a small, open economy in the heart of Europe characterised by very intense trade flows with other member states of the European Union, it seemed useful to take account of at least some of the international dimensions of transport flows in the design of pricing policies in Belgium. The international component creates a number of complications that were captured in the modelling exercises in the simplest possible way. For example, since a non-negligible share of all (especially freight) flows on Belgian territory consists of international transport and pure transit, a substantial fraction of external congestion, accident and pollution costs in Belgium is generated by foreign transport firms. Moreover, it is well known that some transport externalities generate international spillovers; emissions of particular pollutants in Belgium spill over to other regions (acid rain, global warming, and so on) and therefore generate external costs abroad. Vice versa, some external costs in Belgium are due to emissions in other countries. Finally, the prevalence of international transport flows and pure transit implies the possibility for countries to shift the burden of transport taxes to foreigners. Generally speaking, individual countries are likely to ignore or underestimate the implications of their policies on the welfare of foreigners, so that an international setting introduces the potential for tax exporting and tax competition between countries.

In order to capture some of the above complications all empirical results reported in this chapter were derived using a two-region model of a hypothetical federation consisting of Belgium and 'the rest of Europe', taken as a single entity. This second region was defined as the aggregate of all other members of the European Community (EC12) as of 1991.[1] In 1992, this region covered 2 365 306 km^2 and had 343 million inhabitants. The model used in the empirical analysis is the two-region version of the interregional model, as described in Chapter 5 of this book. Although the focus of the current chapter is mainly on Belgian transport policies, application of the model allows us to illustrate the interrelation between international transport flows and pricing policies. Moreover, it allows us to report on the implications of strategic behaviour by individual countries if policies are not federally coordinated.

It is important to note that, as explained in previous chapters, the model focuses on a quite detailed transport sector (in terms of travel modes, period of travel, car types, and so on), but it does so at the cost of an extremely limited level of sectoral and spatial desegregation. Freight transport is aggregated by mode, but it is not further disaggregated according to the type of commodity transported. Similarly, no spatial disaggregation is captured by the model. Apart from the fact that the model includes two regions and different types of roads within each region, it uses a simple one-link representation of the network for each mode.

The structure of this chapter is as follows. In Section 15.2, we describe the assumptions and procedures underlying the construction of the reference situation for 2005. This reference case corresponds to the expected situation of the Belgian and European (non-urban) transport market in 2005. It was constructed using observations on traffic flows and prices for 1991 by extrapolating recent trends up to 2005. In Section 15.3, we discuss the expected transport problems in the two regions that naturally follow from the discussion of the reference case. In the rest of the chapter we use the model of Chapter 5 to analyse various transport policies. In Section 15.4 we present the results of a 'Full Optimum', that is, a set of optimal policies for Belgium and the rest of Europe on the assumption that perfect pricing as well as regulatory instruments were available. Using the full optimum as a benchmark, we then turn to the application of the model to two sets of policies derived from recent proposals at the EU level. These policies only use existing pricing instruments and can be implemented in the short run, so that they can be considered to be realistic policy scenarios. In Section 15.5 we consider the results of a 'Uniform Pricing' scenario in which the model simulates the introduction of minimum levels of excise taxes on fuels in combination with an exogenously imposed toll on highways. Section 15.6 develops a 'Congestion Pricing' scenario. It is assumed that the authorities are interested in implementing optimal peak and off-peak tolls on highways while public transport is priced at resource cost, eliminating all variable subsidies. A brief comparison of the various scenarios is given in Section 15.7. Finally, in Section 15.8 we illustrate the strategic aspects of transport policies in an international context, and the possible distortions that arise when these policies are decentralised. Section 15.9 concludes with a review of policy implications drawn from the analysis.

15.2 CONSTRUCTING A REFERENCE CASE FOR 2005

In the reference situation we consider the expected prices, transport flows and vehicle regulations in 2005, assuming unchanged policy. It is constructed using information from a large number of sources, so that only a brief description can be provided here. More details can be found in De Borger and Swysen (1996), Courcelle (1997) and De Borger et al. (1999). Although the reference case had to be constructed both for Belgium and the rest of Europe, our description mainly focuses on the Belgian case; the procedures for the second region are analogous.

15.2.1 The Structure of the Transport Market

The study areas considered consist of Belgium and the 'rest of Europe', as previously defined. In each region both passenger and freight transport flows are considered. With respect to the former, we capture private car transport and public transport by train and by bus. Since the focus is on interregional transport, walking and cycling are not taken into account. Air and sea transport are ignored as well. With respect to freight transport, the model captures road traffic, rail transport and inland waterway transport; again, air transport and overseas shipping are excluded. In the remainder of this subsection we provide some general information on the structure of the transport market in terms of infrastructure, vehicle stock, supply of public transport, current pricing procedures and the demand side of the market.

Belgium has a very dense road network. In 1991 it was estimated that there were 5.48 kilometres of motorway per 100 square kilometre of surface, and as much as 465 kilometres of road per 100 square kilometres. The density of the road network reflects high population densities and the proximity of several large urban centres. For example, the distance between Antwerp and Brussels is only 50 kilometres, and a third medium-sized city (Mechelen) is situated in between the two urban areas. Similarly, Antwerp and Ghent as well as Brussels and Ghent are less than a 100 kilometres apart. With the exception of some user fees for very specific network components (for example, the Liefkenshoektunnel near Antwerp), the use of the road network by cars is free of charge.[2] Although recently the idea of some form of road pricing has been considered, no formal plans exist for its implementation. The absence of congestion charges combined with a high demand on a dense and complex network implies that congestion is a serious problem. Highways near the urban centres (especially Brussels) and some interurban links (for example, Antwerp–Brussels, Ghent–Brussels) are severely congested at peak times. More generally, during peak hours a large fraction of the network of highways and other major roads is subject to congestion, even in the absence of accidents or other traffic obstructions. Moreover, periods of reduced speed frequently occur, even at off-peak times of the day.

The car stock was estimated at approximately 3.86 million units as of 1991. In the model used for the purpose of this chapter, the private car stock and the associated transport flows are desegregated according to the size of the car used and according to the type of fuel consumed. Two car sizes (small and large) and two fuel types (diesel and gasoline) are distinguished. The distinction between small and large was based on motor power; the cut-off point was situated at 60 kw for gasoline and 50 kw for diesel cars. It was estimated that in 1991 the market share of small and large diesel cars in the car stock was approximately 17 per cent and 11 per cent, respectively, whereas small and large gasoline cars accounted for 44 per cent and 25 per cent. Note that LPG has a very small market share in Belgium and was therefore ignored.

Taxation of car ownership and car use consists mainly of an annual vehicle tax (differentiated according to car size and fuel used) and a fuel tax (differentiated according to fuel type). Note that neither fixed taxes nor fuel taxes are able to price car use according to the external costs (mainly congestion) generated. A remarkable characteristic of the Belgian tax system is that ownership of diesel cars is more heavily taxed than ownership of gasoline cars, but that the fuel tax on diesel is much lower than on gasoline. This tax structure largely explains the structure of the car stock (see above) and of the demand for car kilometres (see below).

The supply of public passenger transport includes both bus and rail services. Rail services are operated by the national railway company NMBS-SNCF which, despite privatisation of some (mainly non-transport-related) services, is one of the few remaining public enterprises in Belgium.

Although track length has been substantially reduced over the past decades, the company continues to operate a very dense rail network of some 4000 kilometres. Demand for passenger rail services is heavily concentrated both in time (peak demand largely dominates off-peak demand) and in space (incoming flows into the urban centres in the morning peak, outgoing flows in the evening peak). Note that for investment in infrastructure the company is heavily dependent on the federal government. Insufficient investment in the past two decades and, more recently, the concentration of financial inputs on the construction of the high-speed rail infrastructure (TGV) are seen by many as serious obstacles to the increase of the railroad's domestic market share.

Public bus services are now operated by separate regional public authorities for Flanders, Wallonia and Brussels. Since these companies have substantial autonomy, policies and scheduling procedures differ between the regions. Many individual bus lines are subcontracted to local private operators. Bus schedules still suffer from a lack of coordination between regional bus operators on the one hand and between bus operators and the rail company on the other hand. Better coordination in the future may stimulate multimodal trips on the public transport system. Unfortunately, recent restructuring of the rail network and frequent changes in timetables makes the envisaged coordination a difficult exercise.

The pricing structure for both rail and bus transport is complex: regular fares are highly non-linear with distance travelled, and a large number of options are available, including travelcards, fixed-period passes, special reductions for large families and families with young children, for students, for elderly people, and so on. The result is that a large fraction of passengers is actually subsidised. Public transport has been used as an instrument of social policy: prices are only loosely related to production costs, and many routes are served at unprofitable frequencies. For some categories of travellers free bus services have been introduced in at least one city (Hasselt), and a system whereby cities and municipalities contract with the bus company for free service for their inhabitants is under discussion.

As for the demand side, we distinguish two time periods: the peak period covers five hours (from 7.00 to 9.00 am and from 4.00 to 7.00 pm), the off-peak period was defined as covering 17 hours (from 4.00 to 7.00 am, from 9.00 am to 4.00 pm, and from 7.00 pm to 2.00 am). Traffic between 2.00 and 4.00 am was found to be negligible, and was therefore ignored. In Belgium, in 1991 the total demand (including urban transport) for passenger transport amounted to about 181 million passenger-kilometres per day, of which about 49 per cent was peak period demand. Total freight demand amounted to 112 million ton-kilometres per day. More than 70 per cent of all freight flows can be situated in the off-peak period.

Private car transport is by far the dominant mode in passenger transport, capturing more than 90 per cent in both peak and off-peak periods. Public transport has an overall market share of about 7.7 per cent in the peak, and of 9.2 per cent in the off-peak. In both periods, rail is more important than bus: 39 per cent of the public transport demand for passenger-kilometres goes to the bus mode, whereas rail captures 61 per cent.

The market shares of diesel and gasoline cars in the total demand for passenger-kilometres are quite different from their respective shares in the car stock, simply because average distances differ a lot. Indeed, it is well known that diesel cars are more intensively used. For example, survey results suggest average annual distances by small diesel and gasoline cars of 22 344 and 13 833 kilometres, respectively. Although the share of diesel cars in the stock was only some 28 per cent, the share of diesel cars in the total number of passenger-kilometres amounted to approximately 39 per cent in 1991.

The market for freight transport consists of road, rail and inland waterways. Only one truck type was considered and, very close to actual observation, it was assumed that all trucks used diesel. In 1991, it was estimated that road occupied a market share in Belgium of about 67 per cent, rail 20 per cent, and inland waterways 13 per cent. Again, peak and off-peak traffic is distinguished, but the distinction seems only relevant for road transport. More than 70 per cent of all ton-kilometres are produced during off-peak hours.

It is important to stress that, since the model considers Belgian transport policies in an international framework, total freight flows on the Belgian transport system were divided into domestic flows (freight flows on Belgian territory by Belgian trucking firms) and international (transit) flows (for example, flows on Belgian roads by foreign firms). It was estimated (see Courcelle, 1997, for details) that freight flows on Belgian highways consist of more than 25 per cent of foreign trucks. Similarly, about 33 per cent of all freight flows generated by Belgian production activities are flows on foreign territory. Of course, given the relatively small size of the Belgian economy in comparison with the rest of Europe, the share of Belgian freight flows abroad in the total flows abroad is negligible.

The best way to appreciate the structure of the transport market as it will be used in the model is to consider Figures 15.1 and 15.2. In order to allow for a large variety of different transport services consumer preferences in each region *i* have been modelled using nested CES-type utility functions (see Keller, 1976). The nested utility structure used for the optimisation exercises is represented in Figure 15.1. At the highest level (level zero) utility is specified as a function of two aggregate goods, namely passenger transport and an aggregate consumption good. Passenger transport is then

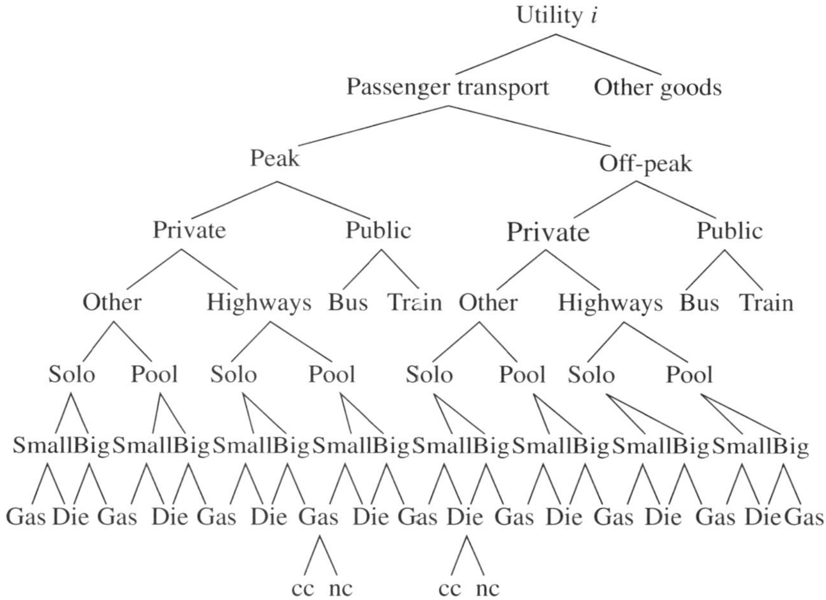

Figure 15.1 The nested CES utility function for passenger transport

systematically further desegregated. First, the transport subutility component contains transport demands in two periods of the day (peak and off-peak) as arguments. At a second level, both peak and off-peak passenger transport are desegregated in private and public transport demand. The public transport subaggregate further captures both the demand for bus and train services. For private car transport, the distinction is made between highways and other major roads, and between carpooling and driving alone. Towards the bottom of the utility tree two car sizes are being considered, large and small. Finally, there are two possible fuel types, gasoline and diesel, and two possible types of technology for each fuel type, cc and nc, the precise meaning of which will be explained below.

In each region, the aggregate consumption good that enters the utility of the representative consumer is assumed to be produced by an aggregate private sector. Cost minimising behaviour by producers in a given region *i* not only generates a derived demand for domestic freight transport but also implies some freight flows abroad, that is, transport in the other region associated with region *i*'s production activities. To model a large number of freight transport alternatives we again use a tree structure based on a CES specification, this time for the production and cost functions of the

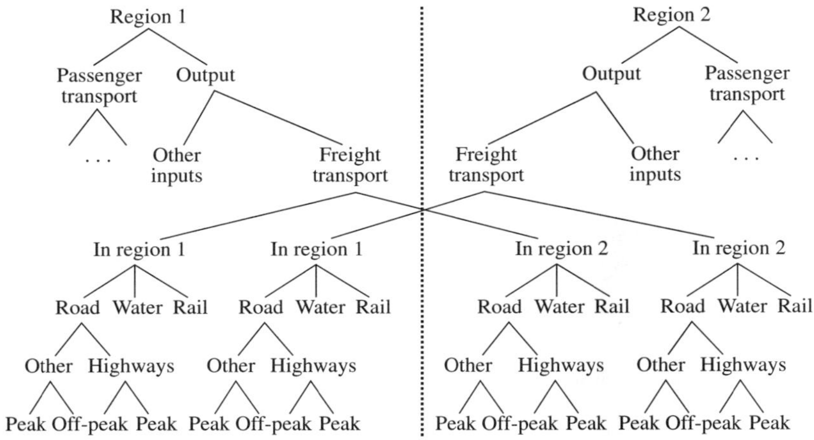

Figure 15.2 The nested CES production function for freight transport

producers of the aggregate good in each region. In order to clearly indicate the linkages between the two regions through the demand for freight transport, we present the nested structure in Figure 15.2 for the federation as a whole. In each region, utility maximisation generates the demand for passenger transport and the demand for the aggregate consumer good (output). From the former, the utility tree presented in Figure 15.1 branches off. As explained in Chapter 5 it is then assumed that the demand for the aggregate consumer good generates demands for freight transport and an aggregate other input, treated as numeraire. Freight flows associated with production in *i* are disaggregated in domestic flows and 'international' transport in the other region *j*. The idea is that some transport abroad is associated with domestic production, for example to ship foreign intermediate inputs to the domestic firms. Moreover, the modelling procedure implies that there is some (possibly very small) substitution possibility between domestic and international flows; perfect complementarity can be modelled as an extreme case. In each region, three relevant modes (road, rail and inland waterways) are distinguished at level three. Further down the tree, road transport is divided in the flows on highways and the flows on other major roads, and for road transport the distinction is made between peak and off-peak demand.

15.2.2 Assumptions on Traffic Growth and Composition

To arrive at predictions for the traffic levels for 2005 to be used in the reference case, assuming unchanged transport policy, we applied recent historical trends to the relevant time series. The exact procedure used is carefully described in De Borger and Swysen (1996) and Courcelle (1997) for Belgium, and in Courcelle (1997) for the rest of Europe. Application of the procedure yielded increases of 29 per cent in total passenger-kilometres at the level of the rest of Europe between 1991 and 2005, and a 23 per cent increase in freight flows measured in ton-kilometres. Higher initial congestion levels and smaller recent growth rates implied somewhat smaller figures for Belgium; they amounted to 19 per cent and 14 per cent, respectively. More details on transport flows in the reference situation are given in Section 15.3 below.

15.2.3 Assumptions on Transport Capacity

It is assumed for all modes that transport capacity remains fixed at its current level. For the road network, no substantial infrastructural adjustments are planned; therefore, capacity of the road network is treated as fixed. We consider two types of road: highways and 'other roads'. One speed–flow relation for each type of road was constructed by applying the functional form given in Kirwan, O'Mahony and O'Sullivan (1995) using Belgian data for Belgium, and average European data for the rest of Europe. With respect to public transport capacity it is assumed that capacity and supply are passively adapted to changes in demand. No major changes in the rail and waterway network were taken into account.

15.2.4 The Supply Side: Assumptions on Resource Costs, Taxes and Prices

Three strong assumptions underlie the construction of the reference situation for 2005. First, it is assumed that no substantial changes take place between now and 2005 in neither overall tax policies towards the transport sector nor in real public transport prices. Second, it is assumed that in the absence of taxes, transport services will be supplied at producer prices equalling the marginal resource cost. Consumer prices then consist of the marginal resource cost plus the indirect tax per unit. For private car transport the marginal resource costs consist of vehicle costs, expenditures on fuel, maintenance, and so on.[3] For freight transport and public passenger transport, resource costs include expenditures on labour, energy, materials and rolling stock. Infrastructural costs are excluded. Third, all prices, resource costs and taxes are expressed per passenger- or ton-kilometre, although they may in principle be the result of multipart tariffs. For example, the fixed annual tax on car ownership and the variable taxes on car use were aggregated and transformed into a uniform tax per passenger-kilometre.

The relevant price, cost and tax information for Belgium and the rest of Europe has been computed for the various transport services considered, using a large number of sources. For the rest of Europe account has been taken of road tolls for the countries where these have been introduced. We refer to Courcelle (1997) for details. To get an idea of the calculated prices and resource costs, consider some figures obtained for Belgium. For example, the resource cost of one passenger-kilometre by a small diesel car in the peak period was calculated to be 0.142 Euro; the corresponding figure for a passenger-kilometre produced in the same period by a small gasoline car was 0.175 Euro. Unit taxes per passenger-kilometre were calculated to be 0.080 and 0.052 Euro for small gasoline and diesel cars in the peak, respectively. This results in 'prices' of 0.194 Euro and 0.255 Euro per passenger-kilometre for diesel and gasoline.

Public transport prices were computed using statistical information from the respective public transport firms. Note that there is no peak–off-peak price discrimination in the reference situation. However, marginal resource costs of public transport do differ between peak and off-peak. For bus transport, off-peak marginal resource cost was approximated by the average variable cost. The latter consists of expenditures on labour, energy (insofar as related to rolling stock operations) and materials, including maintenance costs. In order to approximate the long-run marginal cost, we added marginal costs associated to rolling stock to arrive at peak marginal costs. In other words, the marginal cost of rolling stock was completely allocated to the peak period. For rail transport, the procedure to calculate prices and costs was slightly different. Indeed, Belgian rail transport price data are much more reliable than economic cost data. We therefore started from prices and tax (or, more typically, subsidy) information to arrive at appropriate cost figures. Prices were derived from the national railroad company's accounts for Belgium and from the international railroad organisation Union International des Chemins de Fer (UIC) for the rest of Europe.

Again, some figures for Belgium illustrate the calculated prices. Prices of bus and rail services per passenger-kilometre were calculated to amount to 0.03 and 0.046 Euro, respectively. Application of the above-described procedure resulted in marginal resource costs of 0.042 and 0.106 per passenger-kilometre for bus and rail services in the peak period, respectively; the figures for the off-peak amounted to 0.026 and 0.054 Euro. These figures imply subsidies for public transport by bus and by train in the peak period. In the off-peak period, there is a subsidy for rail transport but a small tax for public bus services. Note that the results obtained for the rest of Europe, derived as a weighted average of the relevant variables in the various countries, were qualitatively slightly different. All peak and off-peak public transport was found to be subsidised.

It is important to note that the method used to approximate the marginal cost of public transport services implies that costs differ strongly between peak and off-peak period, but that marginal resource cost is independent of traffic levels within a given period. Obviously, these are very strong assumptions that should, however, be interpreted with consideration of the aggregate nature of the numerical optimisation model and the implicit assumption of passive adaptation of public transport supply. Although, on individual lines, Mohring effects (Mohring, 1972; Jansson, 1984) may yield very small marginal costs of extra passengers, this will not necessarily be the case at the network level where some lines incur high rates of capacity utilisation even in the off-peak period. Given the current highly concentrated spatial demand structure, demand increases at the network level do have non-negligible effects on long-run operating costs.

With respect to road transport, the lack of reliable data and the heterogeneity of loads in terms of commodity groups, distances travelled, and so on, made us start from observations on costs and taxes in order to arrive at estimates of average prices per ton/kilometre. Again, Courcelle (1997) has all the details. We approximated long-run marginal costs by including costs of rolling stock next to the cost of fuel, labour, tyres and maintenance. Taxes include, among others, vehicle and fuel taxes and, as indicated before, they were transformed to an average figure per ton-kilometre. Note that the distinction between domestic and international (transit) freight flows by road necessitated an estimate of the proportion of the fuel used by foreign truckers on Belgian roads that was bought outside Belgium. In the model, this proportion was specified as a logit function of relative fuel prices in Belgium and the rest of Europe.

Rail costs were approximated by starting from revenue out of freight flows, dividing by the number of ton-kilometres produced to arrive at a price per unit, and correcting for taxes or subsidies so as to end up with an estimate of the relevant resource cost. For Belgium, we arrived at a price of 0.039 Euro per ton-kilometre and a subsidy (negative tax) of 0.003 per ton-kilometre. Finally, the prices of waterway transport were weighted averages of official rates over various commodity groups and different lengths of trajectory. Since reliable cost information is scarce, costs were approximated by eliminating all tax elements from the observed prices. For Belgium, we arrived at a resource cost per ton-kilometre of 0.025 Euro and a price of 0.029 Euro.

A last set of assumptions concerning the supply of transport services is related to the treatment of different emission technologies in vehicles. This is relevant because the model also allows an analysis of the effects of introducing new technologies. In Figure 15.1 standard and improves technologies were represented by cc and nc, respectively. Two observations are relevant here. First, for the determination of standard vehicle technologies in 2005, we refer to recent EC regulations (directive 91/441/EEC): we assume that, by the year 2005, Belgium will have fully implemented these standards. This implies that in 2005, all gasoline cars will be equipped with 3-way catalytic converters and that diesel cars have improved engine technology (that is direct injection, turbo-supercharger, charge cooling and exhaust gas recirculation) and are equipped with an oxidation catalyst. Trucks and buses are also equipped with improved engines and improved tyres. Second, it is assumed that, without any pollution regulations and without any taxes or subsidies, there are no incentives for suppliers of transport services to implement cleaner technologies. Indeed, the required investment expenditures (for example, to install particulate filters in diesel cars) increase the private resource costs of transport services, whereas the benefits consist of reductions in external, and not in private, costs. Without government intervention, suppliers will therefore have no incentive to select cleaner technologies. As a consequence, we chose to analyse the potential desirability of the introduction of new emission technologies under the assumption that the government is willing to subsidise the installation of cleaner technologies if the latter are welfare improving.

15.2.5 Assumptions on External Costs

The following external costs caused by transport are considered in our model: congestion, air pollution, accident costs and road depreciation. It should be noted at the outset that for some applications considered in this chapter, the distinction between local and global external costs was quite relevant. For example, local marginal pollution costs in a given region would ignore the spillovers to other regions; global external costs would include them. Similarly, local external congestion costs only include time losses to domestic truckers, whereas global congestion costs do include time losses to foreign truckers.

Zero congestion was assumed for rail and waterway transport. Road congestion was captured via the use of generalised prices in demand functions for both passenger and freight transport. Generalised prices per passenger- or ton-kilometre include the relevant monetary expenditures, as well as the monetary value of the time needed to travel one kilometre. The latter is calculated using an endogenously determined speed–flow relationship that represents traffic speed as a function of the number of passenger car units (PCU). It has been assumed that large and small cars have the same impact on congestion and are equal to one PCU while buses and trucks equal two PCUs. A separate speed–flow relation was calibrated for highways and other roads using the functional form given in Kirwan, O'Mahony and

O'Sullivan (1995). The marginal external congestion cost per kilometre then represents the extra time loss of all other road users induced by one extra vehicle-kilometre, and is the product of three elements: the extra time loss per vehicle, the number of vehicles on the network and the value of the time lost. The monetary value of travel time per kilometre is simply the value of time per hour multiplied by the inverse of the speed in kilometres per hour.

All externalities other than congestion were assumed to have a constant cost per kilometre. Details about the procedures used are provided in Mayeres, Ochelen and Proost (1996) and in Chapter 7 of this book. We considered six air pollutants: SO_2, NO_X, HC, CO, CO_2 and PM. The level of pollution in each region is a function of the level of deposition of each pollutant in the region. Deposition of each pollutant in a region is related to the level of emissions in both regions by an 'emission-deposition' matrix. Accident costs were supposed constant per vehicle-km; they take into account both material and physical damages. Finally, consistent with Newbery (1988), road depreciation was fully attributed to trucks.

To get some idea of the composition and overall value for marginal external costs consider the information captured in Table 15.1. This presents the results of the calculations for a number of relevant submarkets for Belgium. The relative magnitudes of the various components is similar for the rest of Europe. As for cars, note that the reported figures are weighted averages for 'small' cars for the two road types (highways, other roads) considered.

Table 15.1 Marginal external costs in the reference situation (Euro/passenger-kilometre for passenger modes; Euro/ton/kilometre for freight modes)

	Congestion	Accidents	Air pollution	Total
Peak gasoline car	0.921	0.046	0.007	0.973
Peak diesel car	0.921	0.046	0.015	0.985
Peak bus	0.049	0.002	0.008	0.059
Peak train	0.000	0.000	0.001	0.001
Off-peak gasoline car	0.009	0.046	0.006	0.061
Off-peak diesel car	0.009	0.046	0.016	0.070
Off-peak bus	0.001	0.003	0.021	0.025
Off-peak train	0.000	0.000	0.003	0.003
Peak truck	0.163	0.004	0.011	0.178
Off-peak truck	0.001	0.004	0.008	0.013
Rail freight	0.000	0.000	0.003	0.003
Waterways	0.000	0.000	0.003	0.003

Calculated marginal external costs for 2005 indicate that, as road transport is concerned, congestion is by far the dominant external cost in the peak period. This holds both for car and truck transport. In the off-peak period, however, marginal external congestion costs are dominated by marginal external accident costs. In both cases marginal external congestion costs per passenger-kilometre are much smaller for public transport by bus as compared to car. The calculated marginal external pollution costs are quantitatively somewhat less important. The reason is that the standard technologies for cars as assumed for 2005 will be far less polluting than in the 1990s. The marginal external cost of pollution of a private gasoline car will be comparable to those of public bus transport and represent less than 0.01 Euro per passenger-kilometre.

15.2.6 Assumptions on Behaviour

Price elasticities are based on literature surveys (Oum, Waters and Jong, 1992, Goodwin, 1992). They are discussed in more detail in De Borger et al. (1997). To get a feeling for the elasticities used, we report in Tables 15.2a and 15.2b some aggregate elasticities for passenger and domestic freight transport for Belgium, respectively. They are aggregate in the sense that they reflect price sensitivities at aggregate levels in the utility and cost trees that were used to distinguish different transport markets. Note that for international and transit transport (not reported in the table) we assumed much higher price sensitivities for Belgium than for the rest of Europe.

Table 15.2a Price elasticities passenger transport

		Peak		Off-peak	
		Private	Public	Private	Public
Peak	Private	−0.329	0.068	0.068	0.068
	Public	0.002	−0.183	0.002	0.002
Off-peak	Private	0.073	0.073	−0.489	0.073
	Public	0.003	0.003	0.003	−0.265

Table 15.2.b Price elasticities freight transport

	Road	Rail	Water
Road	−0.499	0.017	0.017
Rail	0.004	−1.455	0.004
Water	0.001	0.001	−1.323

Indeed, depending on the pricing instruments used, international flows and especially pure transit can easily avoid high prices in Belgium (by fuelling abroad, by selecting alternative routes, and so on).

15.3 THE INEFFICIENCY OF CURRENT TRANSPORT PRICING POLICIES: THE REFERENCE CASE FOR 2005

A comparison of prices, taxes and marginal external costs in the reference year 2005 identifies some obvious inefficiencies of current transport pricing and regulation policies. In Table 15.3 we put together some relevant information on the reference situation for a number of submarkets. Several observations are worth mentioning. First, all transport modes show important imbalances between the level of taxes and the marginal external costs. For almost all transport modes and all alternatives (except some of the off-peak services), taxes are below the marginal external costs. Moreover, note that marginal external costs vary significantly according to the characteristics of the transport modes. For example, marginal external costs of road traffic strongly differ between peak and off-peak periods, mainly due to differences in congestion levels. No similar differentiation is observed in the corresponding taxes. Second, note that in both regions public rail transport during the peak period is heavily subsidised. Third, if we compare monetary prices for (private and public) passenger transport in the two regions, we see that they are marginally higher in the rest of Europe, reflecting current tax differences. On the other hand, prices for freight transport are on average somewhat higher in Belgium.

The modal shares in the reference situation are the following. First, with respect to passenger transport, private transport accounts for 87 per cent in Belgium, and for 78 per cent in the rest of Europe. Road traffic is also the dominant mode for domestic freight transport: it accounts for some 70 per cent of all freight flows in Belgium and for some 80 per cent of total flows in the rest of Europe. Railways and waterways account each for some 15 per cent in Belgium, and for about 10 per cent in the aggregate European region. For international freight transport, road captures 57 per cent of the market for Belgium and 49 per cent for the rest of Europe.

Two important findings are not explicitly represented in the table. First, as mentioned earlier, there are differences in tax treatment between gasoline and diesel. In Belgium, for example, diesel is taxed at a lower rate per passenger-kilometre than gasoline. Second, by far the largest fraction of marginal external costs are local costs. We found (see De Borger, Courcelle

Table 15.3 Characterisation of the reference situation[a]

			Price (Euro/pass-km); (Euro/ton-km)	Tax (Euro/pass-km); (Euro/ton-km)	Marginal external cost (Euro/pass-km); (Euro/ton-km)
Passenger	Peak	Car, solo, small, diesel	0.193 (0.227)	0.051 (0.064)	0.985 (1.121)
		Train	0.046 (0.054)	−0.060 (−0.059)	0.001 (0.001)
	Off-peak	Car, solo, small, diesel,	0.201 (0.236)	0.056 (0.070)	0.070 (0.060)
		Train	0.046 (0.054)	−0.008 (−0.021)	0.003 (0.003)
Domestic freight		Peak road	0.059 (0.062)	0.009 (0.012)	0.178 (0.208)
		Off-peak road	0.059 (0.062)	0.009 (0.012)	0.013 (0.017)
		Railways	0.039 (0.052)	−0.003 (−0.014)	0.003 (0.004)
		Waterways	0.029 (0.030)	0.004 (0.005)	0.003 (0.005)
Volume and composition of traffic			Volume (Million pkm or tkm/day)	Market share (%)	Speed (km/h)
Passenger		Peak, private	93.68 (3121.64)	42.86 (38.38)	36 (35)
		Peak, public	12.98 (775.11)	5.94 (9.65)	28 (27)
		Off-peak, private	96.42 (3212.86)	44.12 (40)	110 (107.5)
		Off-peak, public	15.46 (923.89)	7.07 (11.50)	85 (83)
Domestic freight		Road	47.31 (3017.78)	69.17 (78.98)	Peak 23 (23)
		Railways	10.86 (406.29)	15.88 (10.63)	55 (55)
		Waterways	10.22 (397.04)	14.95(10.39)	10 (10)
Transit freight		Road	14.26 (23.59)	57.08 (49.36)	idem as domestic
		Railways	7.43 (6.47)	29.75(13.55)	idem as domestic
		Waterways	3.29 (17.74)	13.18 (37.10)	idem as domestic
Tax revenue (mio Euro/day)					
Passenger			14.84 (457.85)		
Freight			0.38 (34.29)		
External costs other than congestion (mio Euro/day)			9.75 (256.84)		

Note: [a] Figures are given for Belgium and, between brackets, for the rest of Europe. All figures for road transport refer to use of highways. External costs are global external costs.

and Swysen, 1999, for more details) that spillovers from Belgium to the rest of Europe were only important for road freight transport. This is largely due to congestion, because important time losses are imposed on foreign truckers.

The abovementioned observations allow us to clearly summarise the transport problem in Belgium in 2005 and the possibility of using pricing policies to improve welfare. First, given the significant differences in congestion between peak and off-peak, pricing instruments are needed that allow differentiation according to the period of the day. Second, if good policy instruments are available, public transport pricing will be drastically affected; current subsidies on variable costs are expected to be eliminated or to become much less important. Third, to the extent that fuel taxes are a component of the tax instrument mix, they should be closely related to the relative external pollution costs of gasoline versus diesel. Fourth, in small open economies spillovers of external costs may be nontrivial due to large shares of foreign truckers on domestic roads. This has two implications. Small open economies may have an incentive to ignore the effect of their policies on the level of externalities experienced by foreigners. In addition, they may be inclined, depending on the instruments available, to shift the burden of externality taxes to other regions. This raises the question as to what extent tax harmonisation is desirable at the European level in order to prevent countries engaging in tax exporting behaviour.

15.4 OPTIMAL PRICING POLICY: THE FULL FEDERAL OPTIMUM (FO)

In this section we present the results of a 'full federal optimum' pricing policy which has been determined using the interregional model described in Chapter 5. Belgium is explicitly treated as part of a two-region federation, and the numerical optimisation model is used to determine the optimal combination of policy instruments that will maximise the overall welfare of the federation. Perfect pricing instruments to tax the different transport modes in the different regions are available by assumption (this includes, among others, the possibility to discriminate between peak and off-peak traffic, between traffic on highways and on other roads, and so on), and it is assumed that the use of clean technologies can be subsidised. This scenario may, of course, not be realised in the short run because it requires new pricing technologies such as electronic road pricing. However, since it yields the highest possible welfare, it provides an interesting benchmark with which to compare other policies.

15.4.1 Optimal Prices, Taxes and Marginal External Costs

Table 15.4 contains some details for a number of submarkets. In each region, taxes on all transport modes are set at the (global) marginal external cost. This implies that optimal taxes are now largely differentiated according to the type of road and the period of the day. It is important to note that optimal prices are not fully harmonised between the two regions due to differences in external costs at the optimum. As expected, at the optimum public transport subsidies are eliminated and replaced by taxes reflecting marginal external costs. Moreover, the substantial differences between diesel and gasoline are eliminated as well.

In comparison with the reference situation, optimal pricing in the peak period requires an increase of almost all passenger and freight transport prices. These price increases can be substantial. Note, for instance, the increase of the money price per passenger-kilometre for a small diesel car on highways in the peak period in Belgium (rest of Europe) by 158 per cent (156 per cent). Prices of road freight transport on highways also sharply increase in the peak period (by 98 per cent and 115 per cent for Belgium and the rest of Europe, respectively). Price increases are more severe on highways as compared to other main roads. The difference can be explained by differences in marginal external congestion costs in the reference situation; moreover, highways and other main roads are treated in the model as imperfect substitutes. Concerning the off-peak period, several car prices decrease in the optimum because, in the reference situation, users paid more than the marginal social cost they imposed.

Note that the increase in transport prices in the optimum implies in both countries small increases (for example, less than 1.5 per cent for Belgium) in the consumer price of the non-transport good. These changes are limited despite the large increases in money prices of freight transport services because generalised prices increase by far less than money prices (due to reductions in congestion) and because of the fairly small share of transport costs in overall production costs.

Optimal pricing is quite successful in reducing external costs. In the peak period, marginal external costs are substantially below their reference levels. For example, the marginal external cost of an extra passenger-kilometre in a small diesel car on highways in the peak period in Belgium decreases from 0.985 Euro/pkm (in the reference situation) to 0.355 Euro/pkm (in the full federal optimum).

Table 15.4 Taxes and marginal external costs in the full federal optimum[a]

Prices and costs (Euro/pass-km); (Euro/ton-km)			Tax	Marginal external cost	Money price	% money price increase relative to reference situation
Passenger	Peak	Car, solo, small, diesel, highways	0.355 (0.418)	0.355 (0.417)	0.499 (0.583)	158.36 (156.34)
		Car, solo, small, diesel, other roads	0.120 (0.111)	0.120 (0.111)	0.265 (0.277)	35.85 (20.93)
		Car, solo, small, gasoline, highways	0.349 (0.412)	0.349 (0.412)	0.524 (0.614)	105.18 (112.65)
		Train	0.001 (0.001)	0.001 (0.001)	0.108 (0.115)	132.03 (112.15)
	Off-peak	Car, solo, small, diesel, highways	0.068 (0.060)	0.068 (0.060)	0.215 (0.228)	7.13 (−3.47)
		Car, solo, small, gasoline, highways	0.059 (0.051)	0.059 (0.051)	0.237 (0.256)	−10.79 (−14.59)
		Train	0.003 (0.003)	0.003 (0.003)	0.057 (0.079)	23.58 (44.87)
Freight		Road, peak, highways	0.067 (0.084)	0.067 (0.084)	0.117 (0.134)	98.03 (115.19)
		Road, off-peak, highways	0.013 (0.018)	0.013 (0.018)	0.063 (0.068)	7.33 (8.61)
		Railways	0.003 (0.004)	0.003 (0.004)	0.045 (0.070)	15.79 (33.46)
		Waterways	0.004 (0.005)	0.004 (0.005)	0.029 (0.030)	1.28 (−0.70)

Note: [a] Figures are for Belgium and, between brackets, for the rest of Europe

15.4.2 Demand and Modal Composition

The key results are presented in Tables 15.5a and 15.5b. In the tables 'RF' refers to the reference situation and 'FO' to the full federal optimum. As before, figures for the rest of Europe are reported between brackets. As indicated in column 3 of Table 15.5a, the optimal prices would have a rather small negative impact on the *total* demand for passenger transport. Both in Belgium and in the rest of Europe, total freight transport flows would go down as well. In view of the large price increases, the decline in transport flows is quite moderate (less than 6 per cent in many cases), however. This is due to the importance of the time cost in total generalised cost: monetary costs substantially rise, but this is to some extent offset by reductions in congestion.

As suggested by Table 15.5b, the composition of demands is obviously somewhat affected. There is an important shift of private transport demand from the peak to the off-peak period. The share of public transport in the peak period increases for both regions, but decreases in the off-peak period.

15.4.3 Choice of Technology and Welfare Components

The results summarised in Table 15.5c further suggest that it is not welfare improving to subsidise the installation of the improved technologies previously discussed on gasoline cars. On the other hand, better technologies for diesel cars do improve welfare. This means that, for gasoline cars, the decrease of the hypothetical federation's tax revenue associated with the subsidies would not be compensated by the reduction of the external pollution costs, while the opposite holds for diesel cars. These findings should be interpreted in terms of the implementation costs of the new technologies and the externality-reducing power of these technologies.

With one exception we observe a reduction of all external costs for both regions. As reflected by the increase of speeds on both kinds of roads in the peak period, congestion levels decrease drastically. Federal welfare obviously increases as compared to the reference. This gain of welfare amounts to 45 billion Euros per year. Note also that, due to the implementation of new technologies for diesel cars, passenger pollution costs associated with diesel use largely decrease.

Summarising, it may be stated that the welfare optimum implies substantially higher road transport prices in the peak period, reduced congestion and pollution, higher public transport fares, price differentiation according to peak and off-peak periods for all road traffic, elimination of the price differentials between diesel and gasoline, and introduction of cleaner technologies in gasoline cars.

Table 15.5a Key results of the full federal optimum: total demands

	Private passenger transport volume (mio pkm/day)	Public passenger transport volume (mio pkm/day)	Total passenger transport volume (mio pkm/day)	Domestic freight transport volume (mio tkm/day)	Transit freight transport volume (mio tkm/day)	Total freight transport volume (mio tkm/day)
RF	190.10 (6334.50)	28.44 (1698.99)	218.54 (8033.50)	68.39 (3821.11)	24.99 (47.81)	93.38 (3868.92)
FO	185.46 (6401.73)	26.84 (1560.58)	212.30 (7962.31)	65.98 (3659.79)	23.90 (45.23)	89.89 (3705.62)

Table 15.5b Key results of the full federal optimum: composition of demands

	% peak car traffic	% peak public traffic	% off-peak car traffic	% off-peak public traffic	% road in dom. freight traffic	% rail in dom. freight traffic	% water in dom. freight traffic	% road in transit freight traffic	% rail in transit freight traffic	% water in transit freight traffic
RF	42.86	5.94	44.12	7.07	50.66	11.63	10.95	15.28	7.96	3.53
	(38.86)	(9.65)	(40)	(11.50)	(78.00)	(10.50)	(10.26)	(0.62)	(0.17)	(0.46)
FO	38.90	6.81	48.46	5.84	51.02	10.62	11.77	16.45	6.15	4.00
	(34.48)	(11.81)	(45.92)	(7.79)	(79.17)	(8.09)	(11.51)	(0.60)	(0.15)	(0.49)

Table 15.5c Technology choice and welfare components of the full federal optimum

	Technology choice	
	RF	FO
Gasoline	Standard (Standard)	Standard (Standard)
Diesel	Standard (Standard)	Improved (Improved)
	Welfare components (mio Euro/day)	
	RF	FO
Utility	526.61 (15243.11)	526.37 (15359.81)
Pollution passengers	1.65 (62.81)	1.40 (55.93)
Pollution freight	0.53 (26.33)	0.51 (25.29)
Accidents	7.56 (166.82)	7.36 (167.48)
Road depreciation	0.018 (0.880)	0.018 (0.855)
Total external cost excluding congestion	9.75 (256.84)	9.28 (249.56)
Speed car (km/h)		
Peak, highway	36 (35)	67 (66)
Off-peak, highway	110 (107.5)	109 (106)
Peak, other roads	57 (58)	60 (61)
Off-peak, other roads	72 (74)	72 (74)
Welfare level of the federation	15503.13	15627.33
% welfare gain relative to the reference situation	0	0.80

Table 15.5d Percentage increase of fuel prices w.r.t. reference situation

	Belgium	Rest of Europe
Gasoline price	11	3
Diesel price	32	11

15.5 UNIFORM PRICING

In view of recent European Union (EU) proposals on transport policy, the interregional model was used to analyse the effects of two specific policy packages. They may be considered stylised versions of some of these proposals. In this section we look at a first example, a 'Uniform Pricing' scenario. This is a policy package that amounts to increasing the cost of road transport (both for freight and private passenger transport) using available policy instruments such as increases in fuel prices, implementation of a vignette to be paid on an annual basis for the use of highways, etc. These instruments aim at uniformity at the EU level and their implementation costs are likely to be smaller than the costs brought about by the use of more complex pricing instruments.

More specifically, we use the model to simulate the joint effect of the following policy measures:

(a) a fuel price increase (in comparison with the reference). We assume that the levels of excise for gasoline and diesel will correspond to the target minimum levels proposed by the EU for 2002. The levels of excise are uniform for all European countries and fixed at 0.5 Euro/l and 0.393 Euro/l for gasoline and diesel, respectively. The specific rate of VAT of each country is then applied to the sum of the resource cost and the level of excise to obtain the relevant fuel prices in Belgium and the rest of Europe. Increases in fuel prices with respect to the reference situation are outlined in Table 15.5d;
(b) a toll (Eurovignette) imposed on users of highways. The idea is to charge each truck and car an annual fee of 1000 Euros and 100 Euros respectively, for the use of highways. As our model does not distinguish fixed and variable taxes associated with vehicles, this idea is simulated by translating the toll to an extra tax per kilometre on highways.

Two variants of the uniform pricing scenario have been implemented. We first simulate the impact of the pricing measures as defined above; the results are denoted UP. We then repeat the analysis on the assumption that, in addition to price adjustments, cleaner technologies can be implemented (referred to as UPCT; see Appendix 15A.1).

Some key results for the uniform pricing scenario (UP) are presented in Table 15.6 (price information) and in Appendix 15A.1 (demand effects, technology choice and welfare implications).

The price effects of the UP scenario can be summarised as follows (note that not all submarkets are shown in Table 15.6; for more details, see Appendix 15A.1). Users of diesel cars in Belgium will incur price increases of about 6 to 7 per cent (other roads) and 13 to 14 per cent (highways). Gasoline car use becomes only marginally more expensive; price increases range from 1 per cent to 4 per cent for other roads and highways, respectively. Overall, the average price increase is 6.5 per cent. As shown in Table 15.6, price increases for passenger car use are even less important in the rest of Europe. The prices per ton-kilometre carried by road in Belgium

Table 15.6 Prices and price increases in the 'uniform pricing' (UP) scenario

			Price (Euro/pkm or Euro/tkm)	% increase of prices relative to the reference situation
Passenger	Peak	Car, solo, small, diesel	0.218 (0.251)	12.80 (10.20)
		Train	0.046 (0.054)	0 (0)
	Off-peak	Car, solo, small, diesel	0.228 (0.261)	13.45 (10.24)
		Train	0.046 (0.054)	0 (0)
Domestic freight		Peak road	0.064 (0.064)	8.36 (3.39)
		Off-peak road	0.064 (0.064)	8.36 (3.39)
		Railways	0.039 (0.052)	0 (0)
		Waterways	0.029 (0.030)	0 (0)
Transit freight		Peak road	0.064 (0.064)	3.54 (4.92)
		Off-peak road	0.064 (0.064)	3.38 (4.76)

increase by some 3 per cent and 8 per cent for transit and domestic freight transport, respectively. Transit transport suffers less because it is able to a large extent to avoid the fuel tax increase. In the rest of Europe, road freight price increases are limited to 3–5 per cent.

Total demands for passenger and freight transport decrease slightly as a result of the imposed price increases (see Appendix 15A.1). For passenger transport, demand slightly shifts from private to public transport. It is hardly surprising that, given the moderate price increases, the welfare gain of this scenario appears to be very limited. The welfare gain with respect to the reference situation amounts to as little as 8.48 per cent of the welfare gain that would be obtained when perfect pricing and regulatory instruments were available (full federal optimum). Allowing possible implementation of new technologies as an additional policy instrument (scenario UPCT) only marginally increases the welfare gain up to 8.93 per cent of the gain under the full optimum. The difference in welfare gain between UP and UPCT is due to the decrease of pollution costs of cars. The new technology has, however, no impact on congestion.

This inevitably leads to the conclusion that the combination of moderate fuel price increases and a general (that is, not time-differentiated) highway toll is a policy package with positive but fairly limited welfare implications. It hardly affects congestion and other external costs, does not substantially change the modal split, and price increases are nowhere near the levels required for optimal pricing. The policy package is highly inefficient because fuel prices do not allow differentiation according to congestion levels; similarly, tolls can only be efficient if they are time-differentiated.

15.6 CONGESTION PRICING

In the previous section, we simulated the implications of a policy package consisting of exogenously determined fuel price increases and uniform highway tolls. It has been shown that the welfare improvements associated with such policies were limited. The current section considers an alternative policy package that should in principle more significantly affect interregional congestion. It is based on a time-differentiated use of highway tolls. Although the implementation of this policy package is more difficult than in the case of 'uniform pricing', it only requires pricing technologies that are usually available. This contrasts sharply with the full optimum which requires a sophisticated system of electronic road pricing. The 'congestion pricing' scenario consists of a combination of two policy instruments:

(a) An optimal highway toll per passenger-kilometre (for cars) and per ton-kilometre (for trucks). The toll can be differentiated according to time of day (peak versus off-peak).
(b) Optimal public transport prices. Prices depend on the specific public transport mode used and are differentiated between peak and off-peak.

Price differentiation according to time of day allows for prices being tuned to the appropriate marginal external costs. The two policy instruments (highway toll, public transport prices) are determined so as to maximise welfare. This implies that public transport subsidies may be eliminated if prices are set at the corresponding resource cost. Note that the toll is imposed on highways only; the use of other roads remains free. Moreover, since congestion is tackled by time differentiated tolls it is assumed that fuel prices remain at their reference levels. Finally, we again consider two variants of this scenario: in the first case (referred to as CP) we use the instruments described above, in a second application (denoted CPCT), we repeat the analysis with one extra instrument, namely the possibility to subsidise new technologies.

Turning to results, first consider the optimal tolls to be charged on highways in Belgium and the rest of Europe. The optimisation exercise implied the optimal toll values reported in Table 15.7, expressed per vehicle-kilometre (vkm). For the private car, peak tolls in Belgium and the rest of Europe are in the range of 0.28 to 0.32 Euro per vehicle-kilometre.

Applying these figures and comparing prices with those in the reference case we found that for Belgium these tolls imply money price increases per passenger-kilometre in the peak period in the range of 70 per cent to 146 per cent, depending on the type of car and the type of fuel used. For the rest of Europe the corresponding price increases are between 69 per cent and 142 per cent. Interestingly enough, the table shows that the optimal highway toll for passenger cars in the off-peak period turned out to be zero in Belgium as well as in the rest of Europe.[4] The reason for this is that fuel prices were kept at their reference values in the optimisation exercise. The relatively high levels of current fuel prices imply that any additional charge for off-peak highway use is unnecessary. The fairly moderate congestion levels in the off-peak are more than captured by existing fuel prices so as to make off-peak tolls welfare reducing. As a consequence, prices in the off-peak period on other major roads remain the same as in the reference situation.

Table 15.7 Optimal toll on highways (Euro/vkm)

		Belgium	Rest of Europe
Peak	Car	0.28	0.32
	Truck	0.69	0.81
Off-peak	Car	0	0
	Truck	0.08	0.06

As for freight transport, optimal peak-period highway tolls are 0.69 and 0.81 Euro per tkm in Belgium and the rest of Europe, respectively. The off-peak tolls for this category are much smaller although, in contrast to tolls for cars, they are positive: 0.08 and 0.06 Euro in the two respective regions. In other words, the current fuel taxes imposed on trucks are insufficient to cover the marginal external cost even in the off-peak period. Note that applying the reported tolls yields overall price increases for truck use of 104 per cent in the peak period in Belgium and of 116 per cent in the rest of Europe. In the off-peak prices rise by 11 per cent and 18 per cent respectively.

Public transport prices are expected to increase substantially relative to the reference case. This is borne out by the results. The congestion pricing scenario yields welfare-optimal public transport prices which are adjusted to marginal social costs. Information on optimal public transport prices is summarised in Table 15.8.

As a consequence of the elimination of subsidies on variable cost, prices for rail transport increase in both the peak and the off-peak period in the

Table 15.8 Congestion pricing (CP): public transport prices

		Price (Euro/pkm)	% change relative to the reference situation
Peak	Bus	0.041 (0.063)	38.98 (17.76)
	Train	0.106 (0.114)	129.25 (109.43)
Off-peak	Bus	0.026 (0.054)	−11.86 (0.93)
	Train	0.055 (0.076)	18.08 (39.52)

two regions. The price increase in the peak is much larger than in the off-peak: in the peak prices more than double, in the off-peak increases are limited to 20–40 per cent. Differences between the two periods are not related to external cost differences; they are simply due to differences in resource costs. For the economic reasons previously mentioned, the marginal capital cost of rolling stock was entirely allocated to the peak period. For bus transport, optimal prices per pkm increase for both regions in the peak period (by approximately 39 per cent in Belgium and 17 per cent in the rest of Europe). The price in the off-peak period remains almost unchanged in the rest of Europe, and it actually decreases in Belgium. These findings are due to current prices in the reference case. Since no peak-load pricing techniques are currently used by the Belgian bus companies, prices in the off-peak exceed the relevant marginal social cost.

More detailed results with respect to demand, modal shifts, and welfare implications are presented in Appendix 15A.2. First, total demands slightly decline as compared to the reference. Differences are small, however. As the road toll was restricted to highways in the peak period, a transition takes place from private to public modes and there is substitution between time periods and between different types of roads. This leads to a typical second-best outcome. In comparison with the full optimum, overall traffic reductions are limited because all prices were optimally adjusted in the full optimum, implying a more substantial overall price increase. Second, there is an important increase in the market share of public transport in the peak period. Highway traffic is substantially reduced (even more significantly than in the full optimum!), whereas peak public transport raises its market share from 6 per cent to almost 8 per cent in Belgium, and from somewhat below 10 per cent to 14.5 per cent in the rest of Europe. Public transport is more successful under congestion pricing than at the full optimum. Note that off-peak traffic and road traffic on other roads are not substantially affected by the congestion pricing scenario. Third, as for private passenger transport, there is a shift from the peak to the off-peak period on both highways and other roads. For highways, the explanation is straightforward because the use of highways remains free in the off-peak. For other roads, the explanation is different. The toll induces a small fraction of the users of the highway system in the peak period to shift towards other roads, resulting in increased congestion there. The associated speed reduction induces a further shift from peak use of other roads towards off-peak traffic or to other modes like bus and train. Fourth, the induced shifts for freight transport are in the same directions as for passenger transport: road transport loses market share to the other modes, whereas both rail and inland waterways gain. Overall changes for off-peak traffic and for road traffic on other roads are rather limited. Fifth, note that the results are only very marginally affected by allowing cleaner technologies as an extra instrument. The reason is that congestion is the dominant marginal cost and better technologies do not have any additional impact on congestion.

The results in Appendix 15A.2 suggest that the welfare gains of the 'congestion pricing' scenario are substantial. In the CP and CPCT versions, respectively, the federation will obtain 82.79 per cent and 83.15 per cent of the welfare it could obtain in the 'full federal optimum'. In other words, optimal time-differentiated highway tolls are a fairly efficient way of tackling the congestion problem in an interregional setting.

Summarising, the results in this section illustrate the fact that optimal time-differentiated highway tolls and public transport prices may be reasonable policy instruments to approximate the long-term full optimum. Highway tolls can be implemented with existing technologies and the implementation costs are likely to be much smaller than those required to implement the full optimum.

15.7 A COMPARISON OF DIFFERENT POLICIES

In Table 15.9 we compare the welfare implications of the different versions (without and with technology choice) of the uniform pricing and the congestion scenarios. The difference in welfare performance is obvious. In terms of impact on overall welfare, the congestion scenario clearly outperforms the uniform pricing instruments. The latter have been shown inadequate to internalise the external costs for at least three reasons. First, the resulting price increases are not sufficient to internalise external costs of those modes and alternatives which cause important external costs. Second, the uniformity of the instruments used does not allow a differentiation of the taxes according to the characteristics of the different modes and alternatives. Third, this policy package does not cover all transport modes and alternatives: for instance, no tax reform has been foreseen for public transport and for freight transport by railways and waterways.

Table 15.9 Comparison of welfare effects of the different scenarios

	Welfare components (In million Euro/day)					
	RF	UP	UPCT	CP	CPCT	FO
Utility	526.61	526.97	526.83	528.63	528.49	526.37
	(15243.11)	(15250.8)	(15245.52)	(15343.09)	(15337.77)	(15359.81)
Pollution pass	1.65	1.63	1.44	1.68	1.49	1.40
	(62.81)	(62.85)	(57.09)	(66.95)	(61.30)	(55.93)
Pollution freight	0.526	0.52	0.52	0.52	0.52	0.51
	(26.33)	(26.10)	(26.10)	(26.02)	(26.01)	(25.29)
Accidents	7.56	7.43	7.42	7.38	7.37	7.36
	(166.82)	(164.73)	(164.68)	(162.34)	(162.29)	(167.48)
Road depreciation	0.018	0.017	0.017	0.017	0.017	0.018
	(0.880)	(0.87)	(0.869)	(0.87)	(0.86)	(0.858)
Total external cost	9.75	9.59	9.40	9.59	9.40	9.28
	(256.84)	(254.55)	(248.74)	(256.17)	(250.46)	(249.56)
Speed cars (km/h)	36 (35)	38 (37)	38 (37)	66 (64)	66 (64)	67 (66)
Peak highways	110 (107.5)	110 (108)	110 (108)	110 (107)	110 (107)	109 (106)
Off-peak highways	57 (58)	57 (58)	57 (58)	58 (60)	58 (60)	60 (61)
Peak other roads	72 (74)	72 (74)	72 (74)	72 (74)	72 (74)	72 (74)
Off-peak other roads						
Welfare level	15503.13	15513.67	15514.22	15605.96	15606.40	15627.33
% welfare gain relative to RF	0	0.068	0.071	0.66	0.67	0.80
% welfare gain relative to FO	0	8.48	8.93	82.79	83.15	100
Technology choice						
Gasoline	Standard	Standard	Standard	Standard	Standard	Standard
	(Standard)	(Standard)	(Standard)	(Standard)	(Standard)	(Standard)
Diesel	Standard	Standard	Improved	Standard	Improved	Improved
	(Standard)	(Standard)	(Improved)	(Standard)	(Improved)	(Improved)

Notes: RF: reference situation; UP: uniform pricing scenario with standard technologies; UPCT: uniform pricing scenario with optimal choice of technology; CP: congestion pricing with standard technologies; CPCT: congestion pricing with optimal choice of technologies; FO: full optimum

As a result, uniform pricing as studied under this scenario attains only 8.48 per cent (8.93 per cent if new technologies are subsidised) of the welfare gain that could be obtained, relative to the reference situation, in the full optimum.

Consistent with the information in Table 15.9 the congestion pricing scenario was shown to be much more efficient. There are three reasons for this finding. First, this scenario involves optimal, and not exogenously imposed, transport prices for an important subset of traffic flows. Second, it captures improved pricing by public transport operators. Third, and most importantly, it allows a differentiation of highway pricing according to the period of the day. This is extremely important because of the difference of congestion levels between periods. Even though other main roads remained free of tolls, and no specific pricing measures were directed at rail and inland waterway freight transport, the congestion pricing scenario makes it possible to realise 82.79 per cent of the maximal welfare gain in the full optimum (83.15 per cent if, in addition, better technologies can be introduced that reduce pollution costs).

A final observation should be made. Although uniform pricing was shown to be quite inefficient, it does perform better than the congestion scenario in reducing some external costs other than congestion. For example, it is more effective in reducing pollution caused by passenger transport, where the congestion scenario does not perform well at all. However, the congestion scenario does much better in terms of reducing congestion and accidents.

15.8 ILLUSTRATING STRATEGIC BEHAVIOUR

In the exercises discussed above, we were concerned with the welfare of a hypothetical federation consisting of Belgium and the rest of Europe. For example, in analysing the full federal optimum as well as the congestion scenario the implicit assumption was that the different countries would cooperate in the sense of coordinating their policies so as to maximise federal welfare. In this section we analyse transport pricing policies in individual countries in the case of non-cooperative behaviour. The results illustrate the implications of strategic behaviour by individual countries and provide an indication of the welfare cost of non-coordination. It is assumed that each region is interested in its own welfare, and that it is fully aware of the international dimensions of transport flows and the associated externalities.

To study the role of strategic behaviour in a non-cooperative framework, we used the two-region version of the interregional model to determine the Nash equilibrium values for the policy variables in the two regions. The

Nash equilibrium is defined such that in each region the policy variables (prices, taxes and choice of emission technology) are chosen so as to maximise regional welfare, conditional on the values for the policy instruments in the other region. The Nash outcome may be substantially different from the full optimum because each region has an incentive to tax foreign traffic on its territory (tax exporting), but is at the same time likely to underestimate or completely ignore the impact that its pricing policies have on the other region. For example, Belgium has an incentive to tax foreign truckers for their contribution to congestion on Belgian roads, but is likely to ignore the time losses suffered by foreign truckers on Belgian roads and the implications of Belgian taxes on foreign truckers.

Importantly, the strategic interaction between Belgium and the rest of Europe is used in this section as an example to analyse pricing policies under various assumptions. Of course, this does not imply that in reality Belgium is indeed playing a strategic game against the rest of Europe, which itself acts as one entity. In fact, a more elaborate model would be desirable in which the policies of the different member states would be taken into account. The two-country version used here merely provides an interesting illustration of the potential implications of strategic behaviour between countries of unequal size.

In principle, Nash equilibria can be determined under different restrictions on the policy instruments. In this section we present only one possible scenario: we focus on the case where regions, for legal or technical reasons, cannot discriminate prices between domestic and foreign freight traffic on their territory.[5] For example, we assume that Belgium cannot charge different taxes to Belgian truckers and foreign truckers operating on Belgian roads. Whether or not road pricing, fuel taxes or annual highway tolls are used, it is assumed that the implemented pricing schemes apply equally well to domestic and foreign traffic. This seems to be a reasonable assumption, since an implementation of substantial price discrimination between domestic and foreign traffic would not only violate the underlying principles of European Union policies, but would also be difficult from a technical point of view.

The theoretical background for this particular case is provided in De Borger, Courcelle and Swysen (1999). Three important characteristics of the Nash equilibrium conditions should be mentioned. First, it has been shown that optimal prices for freight transport in each region will strongly depend on the share of foreign flows in total transport flows. Since each region will have an incentive to shift the burden of the imposed taxes to some extent to foreigners, prices for freight transport will tend to be higher, *ceteris paribus*, the larger the share of international traffic on the domestic transport network. Second, each country will base its decisions on local external costs, ignoring the impact which domestically generated externalities have on foreigners. Third, the assumption of zero discrimination between domestic and international transport does require equal taxes on domestic and international freight transport flows in each region, but does not require uniform taxes across regions. Indeed, differences in external costs and in the share of international flows between countries may lead to substantial tax differences.

We do not report the results for passenger transport except for the statement that the Nash equilibrium prices are quite close to their values at the full optimum. This is not surprising for the following reason. In the Nash scenario, in both regions and for all passenger transport flows, taxes are set at the local rather than at the global marginal external cost, since each region ignores the cost imposed on foreigners.[6] However, given that the vast majority of external costs were previously found to be local costs, the implications in terms of price increases relative to the reference case are very similar to those for the full federal optimum.

The most relevant differences obviously refer to the treatment of freight transport. Each region now trades off the possibility of tax exporting on transit flows on their territory and prices that reflect the social costs for domestic freight transport. The outcome of this trade-off is very different depending on the share of international transport flows in the two regions. This is clearly borne out by a summary of the results for a number of relevant markets, presented in Table 15.10. First consider Belgium. Optimal taxes exceed marginal external costs by a wide margin for all freight flows. This is due to the fact that the share of international freight transport from the rest of Europe on Belgian roads is large. This being the case, the increase in tax revenue obtained from international flows more than compensates for the excess burden associated with domestic freight flows facing prices that do not reflect true social costs. For the rest of Europe the situation is quite different. Taxes are set only very slightly above the local marginal costs. The reason is that the share of freight transport carried out by Belgian firms in the rest of Europe, compared to overall flows in this region, is very small. In the rest of Europe increased tax revenues on Belgian truckers due to taxes exceeding marginal cost are quickly dominated by the welfare losses imposed on domestic freight flows.

The implications for demands, modal shares and welfare effects are reported in Appendix 15A.3. With respect to passenger transport, results are again very similar to those in the full optimum. Due to tax exporting behaviour by the two governments, total demand for freight transport is below its value in the full federal optimum. The reason is obvious: freight transport prices are raised above marginal social cost, unlike in the full optimum. The choice of technology is the same as in the full optimum. Not

Table 15.10 Taxes and local marginal external costs in the Nash equilibrium, no price discrimination

		Tax (Euro/pkm or Euro/tkm)	Local marginal external cost (Euro/pkm or Euro/tkm)	% increase of prices relative to the reference situation[a]	% increase of prices relative to the full optimum[a]
Domestic and transit freight	Peak road	0.127	0.063	200.44	98.73
		(0.087)	(0.084)	(119.72)	(115.22)
	Off-peak road	0.047	0.011	64.49	7.38
		(0.019)	(0.018)	(11.05)	(8.58)
	Railways	0.033	0.003	91.76	15.81
		(0.005)	(0.004)	(36.40)	(33.48)
	Waterways	0.127	0.004	43.97	1.21
		(0.087)	(0.005)	(4.50)	(−0.87)

Note: [a] Price increases are relative to the reference for domestic transport. Although figures for transit are in the same order of magnitude, numerically they differ slightly. Figures between brackets are for the rest of Europe.

surprisingly, both regions experience higher overall welfare as compared to the reference situation. Remarkably, however, Belgium is even better off in the Nash equilibrium than in the full federal optimum. The reason for this is that Belgium benefits from increased tax revenues associated with its tax exporting behaviour, and at the same time it only marginally suffers from tax exporting by the rest of Europe. Indeed, given the share of Belgian freight flows abroad, taxes in the rest of Europe only marginally exceed external costs. The rest of Europe, on the other hand, suffers a welfare loss compared to the full optimum.

The Nash equilibrium reported in this section illustrated that uncoordinated pricing policies by individual governments involve a loss in welfare as compared to the federal optimum. Individual regions will fail to capture the fraction of the relevant external costs that is imposed on foreigners in their decisions; more importantly, they have an incentive to engage in tax exporting behaviour. Within the framework of the model used in this chapter, this has a large impact on freight transport pricing. Indeed, the resulting prices exceed marginal external costs by a wide margin in countries in which total transport flows on the domestic road, waterway and rail network consist to a large extent of international flows.

15.9 POLICY CONCLUSIONS

The purpose of the empirical applications was to gain some insights in the effects of transport policies. Three types of case studies have been presented. We first presented the full optimum in which optimal taxes and prices were determined on the assumption that perfect pricing instruments were available allowing perfect differentiation of prices for all transport alternatives according to the relevant external costs. Of course, this ideal of perfect marginal external cost pricing is not feasible in the short run. It would require very sophisticated pricing technologies that allow prices to be differentiated according to the period of the day and to the precise pollution characteristics of different types of vehicles. In a second type of case study we therefore considered two more realistic recent EU policy proposals that do not require insurmountable technical obstacles and that can in principle be implemented reasonably soon. The 'uniform pricing' scenario consisted of a combination of an exogenously determined fuel price increase and an annual fee for the use of the highway system. The 'congestion pricing' scenario looked at the effects of an optimal time-differentiated highway toll and optimal public transport prices. Finally, a third type of case study addressed the issue of strategic behaviour by individual countries in an international setting if policies are not properly coordinated.

There are several lessons to be learnt from the reported exercises. First, pricing all transport modes and alternatives at marginal social cost would entail drastic price changes and demand shifts across modes and periods of the day. Since current pricing policies fail to capture the full marginal external cost the optimal policy would imply substantial price increases for many transport services, especially road transport in the peak period. As a consequence, the marginal external costs are reduced considerably due to lower traffic levels at the optimum, implying much lower congestion and pollution.

Second, it has been demonstrated that the combination of moderate fuel price increases and an annual highway fee turns out to be rather inefficient. Although it represents an improvement compared to the status quo, the welfare improvement is small in comparison with other potential policies. More specifically, the welfare gain is limited to less than 9 per cent of the gain that can potentially be realised by perfect pricing. The reason for this is that fuel prices and licence fees do not differentiate between periods of the day, and that the suggested price increases appear not to be large enough to internalise external costs in the peak period. Third, a policy aiming at price differentiation between peak and off-peak periods yields much better welfare results. The scenario representing a combination of optimal time-differentiated highway tolls and public transport prices has been shown to be a quite efficient policy. Such policies involve optimal, and not arbitrarily determined, transport prices, and they allow a differentiation of highway pricing according to the period of the day so as to capture differences of congestion levels between periods. Even though other main roads remained free of tolls and no specific pricing measures were taken for rail and inland waterway freight transport, the policy analysed allows one to capture more than 80 per cent of the maximal welfare gain to be realised in the full optimum.

Finally, it has been demonstrated that transport policies should be carefully coordinated at the European level. The need for policy coordination at the European level was emphasised by the analysis of optimal transport pricing in an international setting. The Nash equilibrium that describes the results of non-cooperative behaviour by individual countries illustrated that pricing policies implemented by individual governments will fail to pursue the best policies from the viewpoint of the federation as a whole. Not only do individual regions fail to capture the fraction of the relevant external costs that is imposed on foreigners in their decisions. More importantly, depending on the importance of international flows on the domestic transport networks and the price responsiveness of international flows to local prices, they have an incentive to engage in tax exporting behaviour. Within the framework of the model used in this chapter this was shown to have a great impact on freight transport pricing. Indeed, the resulting prices exceeded marginal external costs by a wide margin in those countries that experience a lot of international transport flows on their road, rail and waterway networks.

APPENDIX 15A.1: KEY RESULTS FOR THE UNIFORM PRICING SCENARIO: DEMANDS AND MODAL COMPOSITION

The purpose of this appendix is to provide more detailed information on the numerical results obtained for the uniform pricing scenario. Two versions of this scenario are considered, namely uniform pricing with standard technologies (UP), and uniform pricing with optimal choice of technologies (UPCT). Table 15A.1 contains information on overall traffic volumes under uniform pricing, and it compares the results with traffic volumes in the reference situation (RF) and the full optimum (FO). Tables 15A.2a and b look at demand composition and, finally, in Table 15A.3 welfare effects are summarised. As usual, figures are reported for Belgium and, between brackets, for the rest of Europe.

Table 15A.1 Uniform pricing scenario: total demands

	Passenger traffic level (mio pkm/day)	Domestic freight Traffic level (mio tkm/day)	Transit freight Traffic level (mio tkm/day)
RF	218.54 (8033.50)	68.39 (3821.11)	24.99 (47.81)
UP	217.03 (8025.22)	67.07 (3791.44)	24.91 (47.77)
UPCT	216.98 (8022.74)	67.05 (3790.17)	24.90 (47.76)
FO	212.30 (7962.31)	65.98 (3659.79)	23.91 (45.82)

Table 15A.2a Uniform pricing scenario: demand composition passengers

	% car transport, highways		% car transport, other roads		% public transport	
	Peak	Off-peak	Peak	Off-peak	Peak	Off-peak
RF	15.00	15.44	27.86	28.68	5.94	7.07
	(13.60)	(14.00)	(25.26)	(26.00)	(9.63)	(11.50)
UP	14.84	14.77	27.87	28.62	6.42	7.48
	(13.37)	(13.45)	(25.18)	(25.91)	(10.22)	(11.87)
FO	12.37	16.96	26.53	31.50	6.81	5.84
	(10.58)	(15.97)	(23.90)	(29.95)	(11.81)	(7.79)

Table 15A.2b Uniform pricing scenario: demand composition freight

	% road freight transport, highways		% road freight transport, other roads		% rail freight transport	% inland waterway freight transport
	Peak	Off-peak	Peak	Off-peak		
RF	6.63	28.97	5.65	24.69	19.59	14.48
	(7.35)	(32.10)	(7.3)	(31.87)	(10.67)	(10.72)
UP	6.94	27.97	5.6	24.23	20.25	15.00
	(7.65)	(31.56)	(7.3)	(31.72)	(10.87)	(10.92)
FO	6.4	30.09	5.28	25.72	16.76	15.77
	(6.59)	(33.36)	(6.68)	(33.14)	(8.24)	(12.00)

Table 15A.3 Uniform pricing scenario: welfare effects

	Welfare components (mio Euro/day)			
	RF	UP	UPCT	FO
Utility	526.61 (15243.11)	526.97 (15250.85)	526.83 (15245.52)	526.37 (15359.81)
Pollution pass	1.65 (62.81)	1.63 (62.85)	1.44 (57.09)	1.40 (55.93)
Pollution freight	0.526 (26.33)	0.52 (26.10)	0.52 (26.10)	0.51 (25.29)
Accidents	7.56 (166.82)	7.43 (164.73)	7.42 (164.68)	7.36 (167.48)
Road depreciation	0.018 (0.880)	0.017 (0.87)	0.017 (0.869)	0.018 (0.858)
Total external cost	9.75 (256.84)	9.59 (254.55)	9.40 (248.74)	9.28 (249.56)
Speed car (km/h)				
Peak, highways	36 (35)	38 (37)	38 (37)	67 (66)
Off-peak, highways	110 (107.5)	110 (108)	110 (108)	109 (106)
Peak, other roads	57 (58)	57 (58)	57 (58)	60 (61)
Off-peak, other roads	72 (74)	72 (74)	72 (74)	72 (74)
Welfare level	15503.13	15513.67	15514.22	15627.33
% welfare gain relative to RF	0	0.068	0.071	0.80
% welfare gain relative to maximal welfare gain at FO	0	8.48	8.93	100
Technology choice				
Gasoline	Standard (Standard)	Standard (Standard)	Standard (Standard)	Standard (Standard)
Diesel	Standard (Standard)	Standard (Standard)	Improved (Improved)	Improved (Improved)

APPENDIX 15A.2: KEY RESULTS FOR THE CONGESTION PRICING SCENARIO: DEMANDS AND MODAL COMPOSITION

This appendix provides more detailed results for the congestion pricing scenario. Two versions are considered: congestion pricing with standard technologies (CP) and congestion pricing with optimal technology choice (CPCT). The structure and interpretation of the tables is the same as in Appendix 15A.1.

Table 15A.4 Congestion pricing scenario: total demands

	Passenger traffic volume (mio pkm/day)	Domestic freight Traffic volume (mio tkm/day)	Transit freight Traffic volume (mio tkm/day)
RF	218.54 (8033.50)	68.39 (3821.11)	24.99 (47.81)
CP	218.06 (8145.25)	67.78 (3803.63)	24.94 (47.88)
CPCT	218.00 (8142.58)	67.76 (3802.34)	24.93 (47.88)
FO	212.30 (7962.31)	65.98 (3659.79)	23.91 (45.82)

Table 15A.5a Congestion pricing scenario: demand composition passengers

	% car transport, highways		% car transport, other roads		% public transport	
	Peak	Off-peak	Peak	Off-peak	Peak	Off-peak
RF	15.00	15.44	27.86	28.68	5.94	7.07
	(13.60)	(14.00)	(25.26)	(26.00)	(9.63)	(11.50)
CP	12.05	15.94	27.53	29.60	7.88	7.01
	(10.31)	(14.30)	(23.95)	(26.56)	(14.47)	(10.42)
FO	12.37	16.96	26.53	31.50	6.81	5.84
	(10.58)	(15.97)	(23.90)	(29.95)	(11.81)	(7.79)

Table 15A.5b Congestion pricing scenario: demand composition freight

	% road freight transport, highways		% road freight transport, other roads		% rail freight transport	% inland waterway freight transport
	Peak	Off-peak	Peak	Off-peak		
RF	6.63	28.97	5.65	24.69	19.59	14.48
	(7.35)	(32.10)	(7.3)	(31.87)	(10.67)	(10.72)
CP	6.06	28.3	5.64	24.47	20.44	15.10
	(6.24)	(32.40)	(7.40)	(31.65)	(11.13)	(11.19)
FO	6.4	30.09	5.28	25.72	16.76	15.77
	(6.59)	(33.36)	(6.68)	(33.14)	(8.24)	(12.00)

Table 15A.6 Congestion pricing scenario: welfare effects

	Welfare components (mio Euro/day)			
	RF	CP	CPCT	FO
Utility	526.61	528.63	528.49	526.37
	(15243.11)	(15343.09)	(15337.77)	(15359.81)
Pollution passengers	1.65	1.68	1.49	1.40
	(62.81)	(66.95)	(61.30)	(55.93)
Pollution freight	0.526	0.52	0.52	0.51
	(26.33)	(26.02)	(26.01)	(25.29)
Accidents	7.56	7.38	7.37	7.36
	(166.82)	(162.34)	(162.29)	(167.48)
Road depreciation	0.018	0.017	0.017	0.018
	(0.880)	(0.87)	(0.86)	(0.858)
Total external cost	9.75	9.59	9.40	9.28
	(256.84)	(256.17)	(250.46)	(249.56)
Speed car (km/h)				
Peak, highways	36 (35)	66(64)	66(64)	67(66)
Off-peak, highways	110 (107.5)	110 (107)	110 (107)	109(106)
Peak, other roads	57 (58)	58(60)	58(60)	60 (61)
Off-peak, other roads	72 (74)	72(74)	72(74)	72 (74)
Welfare level	15503.13	15605.96	15606.40	15627.33
% welfare gain relative to RF	0	0.66	0.67	0.80
% welfare gain relative to maximal welfare gain at the FO	0	82.79	83.15	100
Technology choice				
Gasoline	Standard	Standard	Standard	Standard
	(Standard)	(Standard)	(Standard)	(Standard)
Diesel	Standard	Standard	Improved	Improved
	(Standard)	(Standard)	(Improved)	(Improved)

APPENDIX 15A.3: KEY RESULTS OF THE NASH EQUILIBRIUM: DEMANDS AND MODAL COMPOSITION[7]

In this appendix we present results of the Nash equilibrium scenario, again, a comparison with the reference situation (RF) and with the full optimum (FO) is provided. Structure and interpretation of the tables is the same as in Appendices 15A.1 and 15A.2.

Table 15A.7 Nash equilibrium scenario: total demands

	Passenger traffic volume (mio pkm/day)	Domestic freight Traffic volume (mio tkm/day)	Transit freight Traffic volume (mio tkm/day)
RF	218.54 (8033.50)	68.39 (3821.11)	24.99 (47.81)
NASH	213.86 (7966.11)	52.09 (3615.73)	16.70 (47.49)
FO	213.00 (7966.09)	66.26 (3660.12)	23.45 (46.16)

Table 15A.8a Nash equilibrium scenario: demand composition passengers

	% car transport, highways		% car transport, other roads		% public transport	
	Peak	Off-peak	Peak	Off-peak	Peak	Off-peak
RF	15.00	15.44	27.86	28.68	5.94	7.07
	(13.60)	(14.00)	(25.2)	(26.00)	(9.6)	(11.50)
NASH	12.39	16.97	26.47	31.45	6.84	5.88
	(10.57)	(15.96)	(23.89)	(29.93)	(11.4)	(7.81)
FO	12.36	16.98	26.52	31.54	6.79	5.81
	(10.57)	(15.95)	(23.89)	(29.93)	(11.84)	(7.82)

Table 15A.8b Nash equilibrium scenario: demand composition freight

	% road freight transport, highways		% road freight transport, other roads		% rail freight transport	% inland waterway freight transport
	Peak	Off-peak	Peak	Off-peak		
RF	6.63	28.97	5.65	24.69	19.59	14.48
	(7.35)	(32.10)	(7.3)	(31.87)	(10.67)	(10.72)
NASH	6.43	30.25	5.68	27.68	13.83	16.12
	(6.61)	(33.48)	(6.73)	(33.34)	(8.19)	(11.65)
FO	6.37	29.96	5.26	25.67	16.87	15.89
	(6.58)	(33.36)	(6.68)	(33.13)	(8.23)	(12.01)

Table 15A.9 Nash equilibrium scenario: technology choice and welfare components

	Welfare components (mio Euro/day)		
	RF	NASH	FO
Utility	524.68 (15246.10)	526.42 (15359.24)	526.34 (15360.14)
Pollution pass	1.65 (62.81)	1.41 (56.01)	1.40 (56.01)
Pollution freight	0.526 (26.33)	0.42 (25.02)	0.51 (25.30)
Accidents	7.56 (166.82)	7.34 (167.34)	7.38 (167.46)
Road depreciation	0.018 (0.880)	0.014 (0.85)	0.017 (0.86)
Total external cost	9.75 (256.84)	9.19 (249.22)	9.31 (249.62)
Speed car (km/h)			
Peak, highway	36 (35)	67(66)	67(66)
Off-peak, highway	110 (107.5)	110 (106)	109(106)
Peak, other roads	57 (58)	60(61)	60 (61)
Off-peak, other roads	72 (74)	72(74)	72 (74)
Welfare Belgium	514.32	517.23	517.03
Welfare Rest of Europe	14959.26	15110.03	15110.52
Welfare federation	15503.58	15627.26	15627.55
% federal welfare gain relative to RF	0	0.80	0.80
% federal welfare gain relative to maximal welfare gain at FO	0	99.41	100
Technology choice			
Gasoline	Standard (Standard)	Standard (Standard)	Standard (Standard)
Diesel	Standard (Standard)	Improved (Improved)	Improved (Improved)

NOTES

1. Namely: Belgium, Denmark, Germany, Greece, France, Ireland, Italy, Luxemburg, Netherlands, Portugal, Spain, and United Kingdom.
2. For heavy vehicles a Eurovignette has been implemented.
3. A detailed data appendix is available in which the calculation of costs and prices is carefully explained.

4. The zero tolls in the off-peak are the result of the optimisation. We realistically assumed that the toll should be nonnegative.
5. Other possibilities are both theoretically and empirically analysed in De Borger, Courcelle and Swysen (1999).
6. We assume in our study that both pollution and congestion costs have local as well as global effects (road depreciation and accidents are assumed entirely local). Local pollution costs refer to the share of pollutants emitted in a region which are deposited in the same region. Global pollution costs include local pollution costs plus the pollution cost exported to the other region. The local congestion cost is defined as the time lost by domestic traffic, while the global congestion cost also includes the time lost by international traffic.
7. To ease the interpretation of results, it is assumed in the Nash equilibria that all taxes collected on transport occurring in a region are received by this same region. The reference situation and the full federal optimum have been re-computed using the same assumption in order to compare the Nash equilibria. This can explain small differences between results for the reference situation and the full federal optimum presented in this section and those presented in the rest of the report.

REFERENCES

Courcelle, C. (1997), *TRENEN-II Interregional database*, University of Antwerp, UFSIA.

De Borger, B. and Swysen, D. (1996), *TRENEN-Interregional model documentation*, University of Antwerp, UFSIA.

De Borger, B., Ochelen, S., Proost, S. and Swysen, D. (1997), 'Alternative transport pricing and regulation policies: a welfare analysis for Belgium in 2005', *Transportation Research D*, 177–98.

De Borger B., Courcelle, C. and Swysen, D. (1999), 'Optimal pricing of transport externalities in a federal system', working paper, University of Antwerp, UFSIA.

Goodwin, P.B. (1992), 'A review of new demand elasticites with special reference to short and long run effects of price changes', *Journal of Transport Economics and Policy*, **26**, 155–69.

Jansson, J.O. (1984), Transport system of optimisation and pricing, New York: Wiley.

Keller, W.J. (1976), 'A nested CES-type utility function and its demand and price index functions', *European Economic Review*, **7**, 175–86.

Kirwan, K.J., O'Mahony M. M. and O'Sullivan, D. (1995), 'Speed-flow relationships for use in an urban transport policy assessment model', Working Paper, Trinity College, Dublin.

Mayeres I., Ochelen, S. and Proost, S. (1996), 'The marginal external costs of urban transport', *Transportation Research D*, **1**(2) 111–30.

Mohring, H. (1972), 'Optimisation and scale economies in urban bus transportation', *American Economic Review*, **62**, 591–604.

Newbery, D. (1988), 'Road user charges in Britain', *Economic Journal*, **98**, 161–76.

Oum, T.H., Waters, W.G. and Jong, J.S. (1992), 'Concepts of price elasticities of transport demand and recent empirical estimates', *Journal of Transport Economics and Policy*, **26**, 139–54.

16. Reform of interregional transport pricing policies in Ireland

Quinten Heaney, Margaret O'Mahony and Edna Gibbons

16.1 INTRODUCTION

This chapter reports on the results of applying the interregional model to study different pricing policies that reflect the external costs of the various transport services in Ireland. As Ireland is an island with no through traffic the one-country version of the model was used to calculate optimal policies. The structure of this chapter is the following. Section 16.1 describes the Irish transport problem. The next two sections explain the construction of the reference situation to be expected for 2005 and the main economic characteristics of the Irish transport market in this reference case, respectively. Sections 16.4 and 16.5 report the results of two pricing scenarios, a full optimal transport pricing policy and a scenario which does not allow price discrimination between peak and off-peak periods. Differences between the scenarios are discussed in Section 16.6. Finally, Section 16.7 concludes.

16.2 THE TRANSPORT PROBLEM IN IRELAND

Ireland is an island on the west of Europe, covering an area of 70 283 square kilometres, and has a population of 3.621 million people. The country suffered economically in the 1980s and early 1990s but is currently enjoying a period of economic prosperity. The general increase in disposable income amongst the population has induced a large increase in car ownership, particularly in the last few years, resulting in a noticeable increase in traffic congestion on urban and interregional routes.

Dublin is the capital city and largest sea port. It is located on the east coast of Ireland and currently has a population of 1.2 million. Other significant urban areas are Cork in the south, Galway and Limerick in the west and Waterford in the south-east. Road congestion on the main routes is mainly associated with bottlenecks during peak periods at the villages located on the major corridors. The variation and lack of reliability of travel times is probably one of the most costly features of the bottlenecks. Some villages and towns have been bypassed with additional new infrastructure in recent times; however, in some cases bottlenecks at other points have become more evident in the short term as a result of these improvements. The higher throughput from the new sections implies that the rate at which vehicles are arriving at a bottleneck further along the route is higher than was previously the case.

Private car traffic is by far the dominant mode for passenger transport in Ireland, and it is rising fast. In 1995 and 1996, interregional road travel in Ireland increased at an annual rate of almost 8 per cent (NRA 1995, 1996). This growth occurred simultaneously with a number of major improvements in the Irish road network. Indeed, an increasing number of kilometres of motorway have been built in Ireland in recent years, mainly short sections to relieve bottlenecks close to Dublin on the most important interregional corridors. Despite these investments, the number of highway kilometres is still quite small compared to the rest of Europe.

Iarnrod Eireann (Irish Rail), a subsidiary of the umbrella organisation known as Coras Iompair Eireann (CIE), runs all passenger rail network services. Bus Eireann (Irish Bus) and Dublin Bus, respectively the main interregional and Dublin bus companies, are also subsidiaries of CIE. Bus Eireann runs services on many interregional routes, but increasingly private bus operators offer competitive services.

The majority of freight in Ireland travels by road. The road haulage industry is characterised by a large number of small firms with 75 per cent of licensed operators owning only one or two vehicles. Rail freight holds only a nominal proportion of the freight market.

In Ireland current pricing policies are not aimed at optimal taxation of the external costs of transport. For example, the private car user does not pay the full cost that the use of the car imposes on others and on the environment. Moreover, public transport services are heavily subsidised by the government, although maintaining demand for interregional public passenger transport is difficult due to slow sections of the network and, consequently, long travel times. By analysing various policies, this chapter will provide information on the outcome of appropriately pricing all external costs of transport. Successful implication of such policies could result in a more efficient pricing system.

16.3 CONSTRUCTING THE REFERENCE CASE

The meaning of the reference situation has been sufficiently explained in previous chapters. In this section we briefly describe the construction of this baseline scenario for the Irish case in the year 2005.

16.3.1 The Transport Market in the Model

The transport modes included for the Irish case study are passenger cars, scheduled bus services, freight and passenger rail, and road freight. Transport between Ireland and the rest of the world is by air or sea; these modes are not dealt with in this study. Similarly, the problem of transit freight traffic is not an issue in Ireland and is not addressed here. All results reported in this chapter have been derived using the one-country version of the TRENEN model.

The nature of the Irish interregional network means that congestion is localised and typically associated with towns on the main routes. The interregional road system is modelled as one link in the TRENEN model. Traffic delay statistics are therefore aggregated over the whole network to give a representative average figure. It is necessary to know what the average speed of the traffic will be for a given total level of demand. In this study the speed–flow function developed by O'Mahony, Kirwan and McGrath (1997), and explained in more detail in Chapter 9, was used.

It is necessary to distinguish between two time periods (peak and off-peak) when calculating an average speed. A peak period interregional journey is difficult to quantify in that part of a journey may occur during the peak period and the other part during the off-peak. It is therefore necessary to calculate an overall average journey time for interregional routes and to adjust it using expansion factors, supplied by the National Road Authority (NRA, 1996) to obtain peak and off-peak period speeds.

16.3.2 Transport Flows and Modal Shares

The NRA (see NRA, 1995) provides information on the demand for travel on interregional roads in 1995. The 1995 figure was extrapolated to 2005 using historical trends. The NRA also estimated an average vehicle occupancy rate of 1.85 person/vehicle, a figure calculated from survey data. Details on the car fleet (diesel versus gasoline, small versus large cars, and so on) were obtained from the Department of the Environment (DOE, 1995) and from the Central Statistics Office (CSO, 1994, 1995).

Levels and modal composition of passenger and freight traffic in Ireland are shown in Table 16.1. This confirms that the most popular mode of transport for interregional passenger travel is the car. The number of passenger-kilometres travelled by private car per day is 23.680 million in the whole peak period and 35.520 million in the off-peak period. Peak car travel has a share of 36.50 per cent; the share of off-peak car travel amounts to 54.75 per cent. Public transport has a very small market share. Passenger rail carries 4.27 per cent of the total passenger-kilometres travelled per day, whereas buses account for 4.49 per cent.

Table 16.1 Transport flows and modal shares, reference situation (2005)

Volume and composition of traffic			(million pass. or ton-km)	Share (%)	Speed (km/h)
Passenger	Peak	Private car	23.680	36.50	54.6
		Train	0.997	1.54	70.0
		Bus	1.274	1.96	42.0
	Off-peak	Private car	35.520	54.75	82.8
		Train	1.496	2.31	70.0
		Bus	1.911	2.95	63.7
Freight		Peak road	2.931	17.64	35.5
		Off-peak road	12.025	72.36	53.8
		Rail	1.662	10.00	55.0

The majority of freight (90 per cent) is carried on the road network, compared with only 10 per cent on the rail network. The short distances in a small country such as Ireland make rail freight transport less competitive. Most freight is shipped during off-peak hours.

16.3.3 Costs and Taxes

The consumer price of private transport includes the annual acquisition cost, transformed into a per kilometre figure, fuel costs and other operating costs (all including taxes). The fuel costs per car kilometre are calculated by multiplying the fuel consumption per kilometre by the average price per litre of the fuel considered.

The calibration programme of the model requires a money price for public transport, which corresponds to the average fare paid for public transport. Data on total receipts from scheduled passenger bus services including private bus services, Bus Eireann services and urban services (CSO, 1997) were used for this purpose. Demand for interregional services was calculated using data from the sources mentioned above.

The resource costs for rail services are based on the operating costs for mainline rail services taken from the CIE Annual Report (1995). The capital costs of the rolling stock and the infrastructure costs are applied to the peak period only.

The resource costs for bus services are based on the operating costs for Bus Eireann services taken from the CIE Annual Report (1995). It was not possible to obtain data on the operating costs of private bus operators. For the purposes of the empirical application it is assumed that the resource cost for Bus Eireann is representative of the resource cost of all bus services.

The CIE Annual Report (1995) was used to calculate the demand and prices of rail freight. Road freight transport costs were obtained from Globetrotter, an Irish freight company, using data from surveys of the haulage industry. This was supplemented by road freight activity levels (CSO, 1994).

16.4 PRICES, TAXES, AND MARGINAL EXTERNAL COSTS IN THE REFERENCE SITUATION: IRELAND 2005

If one considers the relation between prices, taxes and marginal external costs for the Irish reference situation, as reported in Table 16.2, it is apparent that most transport services are taxed substantially below their corresponding marginal external costs. Car users in the peak period pay one-half to one-third of their marginal external costs. In the worst case of a small (engine size) diesel car, the user pays only 0.086 EUR/pass.km as compared with the marginal external cost of 0.319 EUR/pass-km.

Interestingly, off-peak car users pay more than their marginal social costs. A large petrol car user pays a tax of 0.161 EUR/pass-km whereas use of this car in that particular period imposes a marginal external cost of only 0.093 EUR/pass-km. The main reason for the significant difference in marginal external costs between the two periods is the difference in congestion.

It can be seen in Table 16.2 that the prices and taxes for private cars are very similar in the peak and off-peak whilst the marginal external costs are drastically different. This highlights the inefficiency that is inherent in the current taxation system. It is necessary to use time differentiating instruments so as to solve this problem.

It should be noted that all public transport in Ireland is subsidised; peak period train services receive the largest subsidy at 0.133 EUR/pass-km (Table 16.2). The marginal external cost of passenger rail transport is very low at only 0.002 EUR/pass.km. When the results for rail freight are examined it can be seen that subsidisation is at a level of 0.122 EUR/pass-km and its marginal external cost is 0.004 EUR/ton-km.

Table 16.2 Prices, taxes and marginal external costs in the reference situation (2005)

Prices and costs (EUR/pass-km)				Price	Tax	Marginal External cost
Passenger	Peak	Private	small, petrol	0.319	0.112	0.310
			large, petrol	0.468	0.162	0.312
			small, diesel	0.274	0.086	0.319
			large, diesel	0.326	0.106	0.326
		Train		0.066	−0.133	0.002
		Bus		0.086	−0.041	0.092
	Off-peak	Private	small, petrol	0.324	0.115	0.092
			large, petrol	0.466	0.161	0.093
			small, diesel	0.277	0.088	0.101
			large, diesel	0.325	0.105	0.105
		Train		0.066	−0.030	0.002
		Bus		0.086	−0.039	0.055
Freight Transport		Peak road		0.074	0.012	0.110
		Off-peak road		0.074	0.012	0.037
		Railways		0.036	−0.122	0.004
Tax revenue (mEUR/day)						
	Passenger		4.5787			
	Freight		−0.0275			
External Costs (mEUR/day)			2.998			

Road freight transport currently pays one-tenth of its marginal social costs in the peak period. In the off-peak period it pays one-third of its marginal external costs. It can be inferred from these results that road freight imposes large unpaid costs in terms of externalities. Road freight is the major contributor to road damage and also imposes costs in terms of accidents, pollution and time delay.

16.5 OPTIMAL PRICING POLICY: THE FULL OPTIMUM

The full optimal policy (FO) scenario considers the case where the government faces no restrictions on price instruments. It assumes that price differentiation between peak and off-peak is possible for all modes; in other words, apart from fuel and vehicle taxes, the government can use time differentiating road tolls. Moreover, the government can subsidise improved technologies for diesel and gasoline cars if this turns out to be welfare improving. The definition of the technological improvements is identical to that in other exercises considered in this book.

Table 16.3 reports some important results with respect to the calculated optimal taxes. The table compares the optimal tax with the corresponding marginal external cost, and it indicates the percentage price increase in the full optimum as compared with the prices in the reference situation. In the peak period, for both passenger and freight transport, prices rise: taxes increase so that each individual is paying for his or her marginal external costs. The price rise is proportionally larger for small cars, because the tax paid in the reference was much less than the marginal external cost than for large cars. Small petrol cars optimally would have to face a price rise of 38.2 per cent, and small diesel cars an increase of 56.8 per cent. Corresponding figures for large petrol and diesel cars are 15.5 per cent and 43.5 per cent, respectively. This results in a smaller price difference between small and large cars. Also note that in the reference situation diesel car users paid considerably less than their marginal external costs as compared with petrol car users. It is therefore noted in the FO that the diesel car price rises proportionally more than the petrol car price. This results in a smaller price difference between diesel and petrol cars in the FO.

The reason prices tend to converge is that the marginal external cost for the different car types are not that different. The main element of external costs associated with car use is the contribution to congestion. In the model this contribution is assumed to be exactly the same for different types of cars. In addition, the differences in pollution costs are quite small and accident costs are assumed to be the same for all car types (see Chapter 7).

Table 16.3 Taxes and marginal external cost in full optimum (EUR/passenger-km; EUR/ton-km) for 2005

				Tax	Marginal external cost	% increase of prices w.r.t. reference
Passenger	Peak	Private	small, petrol	0.234	0.233	38.15
			large, petrol	0.235	0.234	15.52
			small, diesel	0.240	0.239	56.80
			large, diesel	0.245	0.244	43.50
		Train		0.002	0.002	202.52
		Bus		0.082	0.082	142.70
	Off-peak	Private	small, petrol	0.097	0.096	−5.79
			large, petrol	0.097	0.097	−13.58
			small, diesel	0.103	0.102	5.96
			large, diesel	0.106	0.105	0.89
		Train		0.002	0.002	47.47
		Bus		0.056	0.056	110.07
Freight Transport	Peak road			0.085	0.085	98.39
	Off-peak road			0.039	0.039	36.00
	Railways			0.004	0.004	347.45

In the off-peak period, the small and large petrol car prices decrease by 5.79 per cent and 13.58 per cent compared with the reference situation. In the reference situation, the taxes paid were greater than the external costs imposed so that the results in the FO strive to rectify this situation. The diesel car prices increase by a very small amount because the taxes paid in the reference situation did not quite cover the external costs imposed. The relative change in prices makes the diesel/petrol and the large/small price difference smaller. This trend is similar to that which occurred in the peak period.

Road freight prices rise substantially in both periods, with the largest effect occurring in the peak when congestion is highest. Finally, note that all public transport prices increase substantially as well, since in the reference situation public transport was heavily subsidised. The largest increase is in peak train prices where 203 per cent and 347 per cent price rises are observed for passenger and freight transport, respectively.

The prices imposed on the different passenger transport modes create a shift in demand away from the peak period to the off-peak period. This is illustrated in Table 16.4. The increase in off-peak car traffic is quite noticeable; it increases from 54.75 per cent to 59.28 per cent. Note the large decrease in demand for public transport, mainly for the peak period. The largest relative decrease occurs for peak train travel (due to the 203 per cent price rise): its modal share drops from 1.54 per cent to 0.80 per cent. Moreover, the drastic price changes for freight transport also result in a shift in demand from the peak to the off-peak. Note that, since rail freight was heavily subsidised in the reference situation and therefore experienced a large price rise, this change almost wipes out rail freight transport: its share of the freight transport market decreases from 10 per cent to 1.31 per cent.

Table 16.4 Modal shares in the reference (RF) and the full optimum (FO)

Market share (%)	Peak traffic			Off-peak traffic			Road freight	Rail freight
	Car	Bus	Train	Car	Bus	Train		
RF	36.50	1.96	1.54	54.75	2.95	2.31	90.00	10.00
FO	33.97	1.61	0.80	59.28	1.95	2.38	98.69	1.31

Some other key results obtained in the full optimum are shown in Tables 16.5, 16.6 and 16.7. It follows from Table 16.5 that total passenger traffic levels decrease from 64.88 million pass-km/day to 63.36 million pass-km/day. In total, external costs per day decrease by 3 per cent. Importantly, the

Table 16.5 Some other key results of the optimal policy

	Welfare level (mio EUR/day)	% welfare gain	Passenger traffic level (mio pkm/day)	Freight traffic level (mio tkm/day)	External cost (mio EUR/day)
RF	162.33	0	64.88	16.62	3.00
FO	162.80	0.29	63.36	15.38	2.90

Table 16.6 Technology choice and welfare components

	RF	FO
Technology choice		
Petrol	Standard	Standard
Diesel	Standard	Improved
Welfare components		
Utility	165.33	165.70
Pollution from passenger transport	0.51	0.43
Pollution from freight transport	0.23	0.22
Accidents	2.22	2.21
Road depreciation	0.04	0.04
Total external cost excluding congestion (mio EUR/day)	3.00	2.90

Table 16.7 Speeds and tax revenues

	RF	FO
Speed car		
Peak	54.6	61.2
Off-peak	82.8	81.6
Tax revenue (mio EUR/day)		
Passenger	4.58	5.92
Freight	−0.03	0.70

overall welfare gain compared to the reference situation is 0.47 million EUR per day, which amounts to a 0.29 per cent rise.

Table 16.6 reports on the optimal technology choice and it provides more details on the components of the overall welfare gain. As in many previous applications of the model reported earlier in the book, subsidised technological improvements are only justified for diesel cars. For gasoline cars, the pollution reduction does not outweigh the cost of the subsidies to the government. Further note from Table 16.6 that pollution externalities decrease considerably. Accident costs also slightly decrease due to the overall reduction in transport demand shown before.

Table 16.7 shows that tax revenues for the FO would increase by a large amount, notably so from freight transport. The government would no longer subsidise public transport and collect substantial extra tax revenues, leading to an increase of some 0.70 million EUR/day. Finally, note that the shift in demand away from the peak period increases the average speed for road traffic in the peak from 54.6 km/hr to 61.2 km/hr. The off-peak period speed decreases marginally from 82.8 km/hr to 81.6 km/hr.

16.6 OPTIMAL PRICING WITHOUT TIME DIFFERENTIATING TOLL

The common case studies (defined in Chapter 3 of this volume) were examined for the Irish case as well. Results are reported in the comparative overview given in Chapter 17. In addition to the common case studies, a number of other policies were studied for the Irish case. One of these policies is presented here. This case study is a simple policy in which the government cannot use a time-differentiated road toll to specifically tax peak road traffic. Moreover, public transport prices are kept at their reference levels. In others words, only fuel and vehicle costs are assumed to be taxable. The government is also allowed to subsidise new technologies if this is welfare improving. Of course, in general this policy has a reduced ability to manage congestion because of the absence of tolls. The scenario is referred to for the remainder of the chapter as FV.

Optimal tax results of this scenario are shown in Table 16.8. Since tax differentiation of road passenger and freight traffic between the peak and off-peak periods is not possible, we find optimal taxes situated in between marginal external costs for the two periods. The consequence is that car use is underpriced in the peak, where congestion implies high external costs, and it is excessively taxed in the off-peak. For example, a small petrol car user pays a tax of 0.139 EUR/pass-km tax; marginal external costs amount to 0.298 EUR/pass-km and 0.092 EUR/pass-km in the peak and off-peak periods, respectively.

Additional results are reported in Tables 16.9, 16.10 and 16.11. Table 16.9 shows that there is a small decrease in overall passenger transport levels from 64.88 million pass-km/day in the reference situation to 63.78 million pass-km/day. The market shares, shown in Table 16.10, show correspondingly small changes. There is a small shift towards public transport from private transport. Road freight increases its market share from 90 per

Table 16.8 Taxes and marginal external costs for policies (2005)

Prices and costs (EUR/pass-km); (EUR/ton-km)				Tax	Marginal External Cost	% increase of prices compared with reference
Passenger	Peak	Private	small, petrol	0.139	0.298	8.62
			large, petrol	0.138	0.300	−5.28
			small, diesel	0.147	0.305	22.77
			large, diesel	0.150	0.310	14.13
		Train		−0.133	0.002	0.00
		Bus		−0.041	0.090	0.00
	Off-peak	Private	small, petrol	0.139	0.092	7.41
			large, petrol	0.138	0.092	−4.96
			small, diesel	0.147	0.098	21.78
			large, diesel	0.150	0.101	14.28
		Train		−0.030	0.002	0.00
		Bus		−0.039	0.055	0.00
Freight		Peak road		−0.015	0.105	−36.37
		Off-peak road		−0.015	0.037	−36.37
		Railways		−0.122	0.004	0.00

Table 16.9 Key results of policy without time-differentiated policy (2005)

	Welfare (mEUR/day)	Welfare gain (%)	Passenger traffic level (m pass-km/day)	Freight traffic level (mton/km/day)	External cost (m EUR/day)
RF	162.33	0.00	64.88	16.62	3.00
FV	162.43	0.06	63.78	17.17	2.95

Table 16.10 Market share for each mode type

Market share (%)	Peak traffic			Off-peak traffic			Road freight	Rail freight
	Car	Bus	Train	Car	Bus	Train		
RF	36.50	1.96	1.54	54.75	2.95	2.3	90.00	10.00
FV	36.56	2.04	1.57	54.46	3.02	2.35	93.83	6.17

Table 16.11 Technology choice and welfare components

	Reference	Fuel and vehicle pricing without tolls
Technology choice		
Petrol	Standard	Standard
Diesel	Standard	Improved
Welfare components		
Utility	165.33	165.38
Pollution from passenger transport	0.51	0.47
Pollution from freight transport	0.23	0.24
Accidents	2.22	2.19
Road depreciation	0.04	0.04
Total external cost excluding congestion (m EUR/day)	3.00	2.95

cent to 93.83 per cent. The overall welfare gain achieved by the FV scenario is only 0.06 per cent (Table 16.9). This is much smaller than in the full optimum due to the inability to tax differentiate between periods and the absence of pricing policies towards public transport in the FV scenario. The reduction in external costs (excluding congestion) is achieved mainly by the reduction in pollution from passenger transport from 0.51 to 0.47 million EUR/day (Table 16.11). Pollution due to road freight can be seen to increase due to the increase in its market share. Finally, note that technology choice is the same as in the case of the full optimum.

16.7 COMPARISON OF SCENARIOS

In the reference situation the prices for private car users were found to be very inefficient. In the peak period the taxes paid are considerably less than the imposed external cost, whilst in the off-peak the taxes are generally greater than the relevant external cost. The FO scenario, through the use of time-differentiated tolls, optimises prices so that the taxes paid do cover the external costs. This has the effect of reducing peak demand and encouraging off-peak travel whilst also reducing the overall demand for private car use. The FV scenario does not use time-differentiated tolls and so peak car users cannot be targeted as efficiently as in the FO scenario. This results in off-peak car users paying a tax that is considerably more than the imposed external costs whereas peak car users do not cover their external costs. Finally, note that in the reference situation there is a subsidy to the public transport user. The FO scenario removes this and imposes a tax so that the public transport user pays for the external cost that is imposed.

Some summary figures useful for the comparison between scenarios are presented in Table 16.12. Private car use in the peak is most discouraged in the full optimum. The modal share of public transport is considerably reduced in this period. In the FV scenario on the other hand, public transport prices were kept at their reference levels. This raises the public transport market share due to price increases for car users and associated substitution effects.

The external cost in the reference situation is 3.00 million EUR/day. The FO scenario and the FV scenario reduce this to 2.90 million EUR/day and 2.95 million EUR/day respectively. The FO achieves a 0.29 per cent gain in welfare over the reference, compared to only 0.06 per cent for the FV scenario. Again, the reason is that it is achieved without time-differentiated tolls.

16.8 CONCLUSIONS

It is apparent that the greatest welfare gain is achieved when peak private car users are targeted with time-differentiated tolls. This has the effect of reducing peak private car demand and so reduces congestion. A notable feature of the results is that the welfare gain achieved for the Irish interregional transport network is small due to the apparent relatively low level of congestion on Irish roads. Of course interregional road congestion is dependent on the design level of service and predicted traffic levels. The current level of service used for road design in Ireland is Level of Service (LOS) D.[1] This should be borne in mind when comparing interregional congestion levels in Ireland with other countries.

Table 16.12 Key results of policies (2005)

	Welfare gain (%)	Traffic level (mpass km/day)	Peak private demand (%)	Peak public demand (%)	Off-peak private demand (%)	Off-peak public demand (%)	External cost (mEUR/day)
RF	0.00	64.88	36.50	3.50	54.75	5.25	3.00
FV	0.06	63.78	36.56	3.60	54.46	5.39	2.95
FO	0.29	63.36	33.97	2.41	59.28	4.33	2.90

The removal of subsidies from public transport in the FO scenario has the effect of reducing its market share. In the FV scenario the public transport prices are maintained at the reference level and so the public transport market share is increased at the expense of the private car. Before any policy relating to public transport could be implemented it would be necessary to decide what objective is required. Which is more important, the efficient pricing of transport or the provision of an affordable public service?

The model highlights the inefficiencies of the current pricing structure. As one might expect, in an ideal situation the users to be targeted would be those adding to peak period congestion. Although in percentage terms the level of welfare gain is small, the charge per person per transport user per year would be about 500 EUR. The use of the revenue generated is beyond the scope of the TRENEN project. However, if used for reduced labour taxes or for transport its impact should be at least noticeable.

Integration of the more peripheral regions in Ireland with the urban areas of Ireland and in turn the main continent in Europe is a high priority government agenda item. Due to the relatively low perceived interregional congestion problem compared with urban and suburban areas, it is unlikely that taxation of interregional transport, particularly related to congestion, is unlikely to be that high on the government's agenda. Urban transport congestion is the most likely area to which such interventions will be made. The Irish government has recently commissioned a scoping study (Oscar Faber et al., 1999) to evaluate the potential impact if road use pricing were to be introduced in Dublin. Its conclusions suggest that road use pricing would indeed help to reduce private transport demand if it was introduced as a traffic demand management measure to complement the existing measures. It recommended, however, that further work would be needed to examine the practical feasibility of its introduction to the city.

NOTE

1. Level of Service (LOS) is a measure of the operational characteristics of the road. LOS D indicates traffic flow that is approaching unstable conditions, where passing demand is high, while passing capacity approaches 0, and where 5–10 vehicle platoons are common although speeds of 50 mph can still be maintained.

REFERENCES

Coras Iompair Eireann CIE (1995), *Coras Iompair Eireann Group and Subsidiaries' Annual Reports 1995*.
Central Statistics Office (1994), *Road Freight Transport Survey 1994*.
Central Statistics Office (1995), *Household Budget Survey 1994–95*.

Central Statistics Office (1997), *Statistical Bulletin March 1997*.
Department of the Environment (DOE) (1995), 'Irish Bulletin of Vehicle and Driver Statistics', in *Traffic Station Counts and Road Travel for 1995*, National Roads Authority.
O'Mahony, M.M., Kirwan, K.J. and McGrath, S. (1997), *Modelling the Internalisation of External Costs of Transport*, Transportation Research Record, 1576, 93–98, Washington DC: Transportation Research Board, US National Research Council.
National Roads Authority (1995), *Traffic Station Counts and Road Travel for 1995*.
National Roads Authority (1996), *Traffic Station Counts and Road Travel for 1996*.
Oscar Faber, Goodbody, TSRG and TORG (1999), *Technology Options. Dublin Road Pricing Study*, Dublin, Ireland: Department of the Environment.

17. How large is the gap between present and efficient transport prices in Europe?

Stef Proost, Kurt Van Dender, Christoph Courcelle, Bruno De Borger, John Peirson, Duncan Sharp, Roger Vickerman, Edna Gibbons, Margaret O'Mahony, Quinten Heaney, Jeroen C.J.M. van den Bergh and Erik T. Verhoef

17.1 INTRODUCTION

The present policy mix in European transport markets contains measures ranging from traffic safety and environmental performance regulation of vehicles to public transport subsidies, excises on fuel and taxes on the ownership and use of vehicles. The recent Green Paper of the European Commission on Fair and Efficient Pricing concluded that this mix of instruments yields unsatisfactory results, including excessive congestion, an excessive accident rate and excessive pollution. The Green Paper pleaded for a more fundamental role of pricing policies to control the negative side effects of transport activities.

In this concluding chapter we analyse the gap between present transport prices and efficient transport prices with the help of the six case-studies that were discussed in the other chapters of this volume. The process of determining efficient prices involves two consecutive steps. First, one has to find out to what extent current prices deviate from the corresponding social marginal costs. This requires the computation of resource costs, external costs and current taxes on all transport markets. The second step is to compute what is the most appropriate correction of transport taxes.

The case studies focus on the pricing of both urban and interurban transport. Long-range international transport flows have not been studied; for example, airline and shipping problems are not treated. All other modes have been considered. Case study results are presented for four urban areas (Amsterdam, Brusselss, Dublin, London) and for non-urban transport in two countries: Belgium and Ireland. For each of these areas we constructed a reference equilibrium with unchanged policies for 2005. Moreover, we calculated the different types of external costs, resource costs and tax levels for all transport services in the reference equilibrium. This gives information on the deviation between expected taxes and marginal external costs for 2005. To measure the gap between expected prices in the reference case and efficient prices we next computed the full optimum prices. The full optimum price computation assumes that perfect pricing instruments are available allowing us to discriminate, without implementation costs, between peak and off-peak time, between types of cars, and so on. This scenario should therefore be considered as a benchmark giving information on appropriate directions and magnitude of price changes.

The same modelling tool has been used for all the case studies. The model represents the transport market of a given zone by modelling the demand and supply of all modes of transport with their interactions. The major limits of the models used are their degree of aggregation and their static character. Our model represents transport demand behaviour for a given region via a few representative consumers or firms. The transport network properties of a given region are aggregated into one speed–flow relationship per mode. The model used is static: it models the transport markets in a given period, considering the road and rail network as fixed and assuming that the car, truck, bus and rail carriage stocks are optimally adjusted. The model therefore is well suited to discuss optimal short-run pricing of infrastructure but not to study optimal investment decisions in infrastructure. The case studies therefore all focus on the year 2005.

Using the same model structure for each of the case study areas has several advantages. First, not only does this approach yield results that can be easily compared, it also allows us to trade off the effects of pricing reform in urban and interurban transport markets. A second advantage of the models used is their economic consistency: all modes of transport are treated simultaneously and the same principles are applied to each of them. A simultaneous treatment of all modes is necessary as there may exist strong substitution possibilities. In the presence of strong substitution between modes combined with imperfect policy instruments, spillover effects to other markets become crucial in the evaluation of policy reform.

The structure of this chapter is the following. Section 17.2 briefly presents the characteristics of the various study areas. Section 17.3 is devoted to an analysis of the reference equilibrium: to what extent do current pricing policies imply prices that deviate from social marginal costs?

Section 17.4 studies the optimal pricing scenario. Implementation issues are discussed in Section 17.5. Finally, Section 17.6 presents conclusions.

17.2 DESCRIPTION OF THE STUDY AREAS

Table 17.1 summarises the characteristics of the four urban areas and the two regions studied in this chapter. It is clear that in all cities and regions peak period congestion is a severe problem. In London, off-peak congestion is high as well. The cities and areas studied differ substantially in size and traffic flows and composition. Coverage of Northern and Southern Europe would probably show even larger differences.

17.3 REFERENCE EQUILIBRIUM

17.3.1 Structure of Generalised Prices and Costs

The starting point for the model is the construction of a reference case for each city and region. A crucial element in constructing reference scenarios is the determination of prices and marginal social costs for all relevant transport services. First, prices in the reference case are to be interpreted as generalised prices that include the value of travel time experienced by the user. For example, for car traffic the generalised price per kilometre is calculated as the sum of the corresponding resource cost (for fuel, maintenance, and so on), the time cost of the traveller (the monetary evaluation of the time spent in traffic) and any taxes that are being paid, expressed on a per kilometre basis. For public transport the generalised price consists of the money price plus the value of travel time; if public transport is subsidised the money price may well be below the corresponding marginal resource cost. It is clear that because of differences in congestion the generalised price per kilometre may be quite different for the peak and off-peak periods. Second, the marginal social cost associated with a particular transport service consists of the marginal resource cost, the time cost experienced by the traveller, and the marginal external cost. The latter includes the marginal external cost of congestion, pollution, noise, accident risks and road damage. Note that the gap between generalised price and marginal social cost for each mode and transport service gives an indication of the most important inefficiency of current transport pricing policies.

The resource costs of transport are those associated with the (internal) production of transport; it is a private cost to the provider or user. It

Table 17.1 Characteristics of the areas studied (expected for 2005)

Location		Amsterdam	Brussels	Dublin	London	Belgium	Ireland
I. Population (Mio potential transport users)		0.492 (actual users)	1.585	1.26	7.499	9.988	3.654
II. Passenger transport							
II.b Passenger-km/mode/year (Mio pkm/year)	Private	1287	1151	3854	18981	69386	21607
	Public	412	443	1138	6302	10381	2072
III. Freight transport in Country							
III.a Total ton-km/year		n-m	n-m	n-m	n-m	34078	6066
III.b Ton-km/mode/year							
Road (Mio tkm/year)		n-m	n-m	n-m	n-m	22471	5459
Railways (Mio tkm/year)		n-m	n-m	n-m	n-m	6676	607
Waterways (Mio tkm/year)		n-m	n-m	n-m	n-m	4931	n-m
IV. Number PCU per hour							
peak (Mio PCU/hour)	Highways	–	–	–	–	5.739	3.342
	Other	–	–	–	–	10.335	–
	Urban	1.260	0.643	2.602	6.32	–	–
Off-peak (Mio PCU/hour)	Highways	–	–	–	–	1.967	1.615
	Other	–	–	–	–	3.312	–
	Urban	0.235	0.148	1.077	2.88	–	–
V. Perceived severity of problem		Peak congestion; strict parking policy in place	Peak congestion	Peak congestion	Peak and off-peak congestion	Peak congestion	Peak congestion

Note: n-m = not modeled in this case study

depends on three main elements: the capital costs of the infrastructure and the vehicles, the choice of fuel and the speed of traffic (which depends on traffic flow). This latter factor is particularly relevant in determining time costs and fuel usage. The resource costs are therefore derived from a detailed analysis of the capital and depreciation costs and the direct operating costs of each mode, varying according to size of vehicle and fuel type. Road infrastructure is taken as fixed, but the stock of cars, buses, trucks and rail carriages is assumed to be fully adjustable to changes in demand. Similarly, rail and waterway infrastructure are assumed to be fixed, but the number of rail carriages and inland navigation ships can be completely adapted to demand. The marginal capacity costs of rail carriages and buses are allocated to the peak period, consistent with the peak-load pricing principle.

One element which requires some discussion is that of parking costs since this is an important element in the different policy scenarios for the urban areas considered. Typically, large groups of the population do not have to pay the full resource costs of parking. We assume that a parking spot is only needed for urban trips at the final destination. In the reference cases, it is assumed that only 30 per cent of cars actually pay the resource cost of parking, the remainder parks for free (except for Amsterdam where the assumption is that 70 per cent are payers).

As previously indicated, the generalised price is obtained by adding to the resource costs (obviously excluding parking resource costs for non-paying car travellers) the current level of taxes payable in the form of vehicle and fuel taxes, and an estimate of the time costs experienced by travellers. The latter is based on appropriate values of time and estimates of the speed–flow relationship for each mode and time period. The marginal social cost includes the private resource cost of the mode (and the resource cost of parking where relevant) and the time cost as above, to which the marginal external cost of the mode is added. The marginal external cost consists of marginal congestion costs, as given by the speed–flow relationship, and of the various other marginal external costs. The key element is the congestion cost which is driven by the relevant speed–flow relationship, as estimated for each case study on the basis of 'fitting' a congestion function to observed data and results of detailed network models. The functional form of the speed–flow relationship is identical for all case studies and is based on O'Mahony et al. (1997).

To get a feeling for the congestion functions used, they are graphically reproduced in Figure 17.1 for the urban cases and in Figure 17.2 for the interurban cases (congestion functions are presented for both highways and other main roads in the case of Belgium). Both the position and the shape of the congestion functions highly depend on the characteristics of

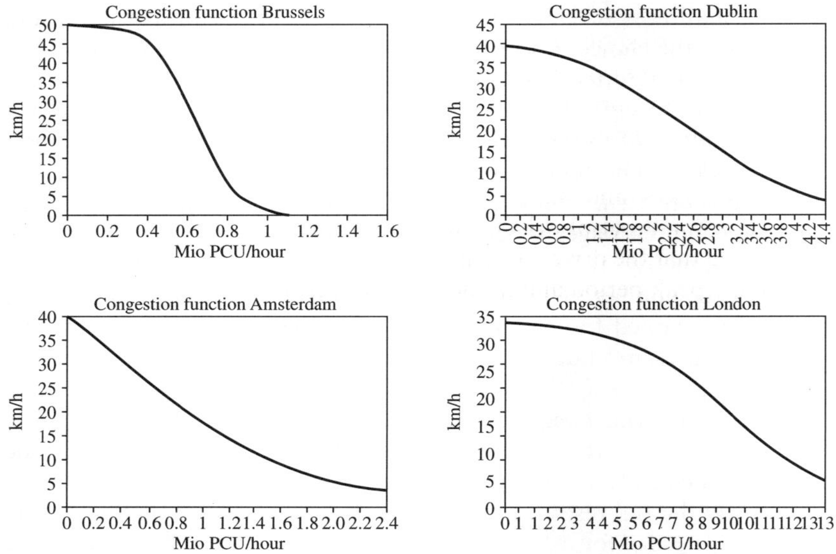

Figure 17.1 Speed–flow relationships for a car in the urban model (PCU: Passenger Car Units)

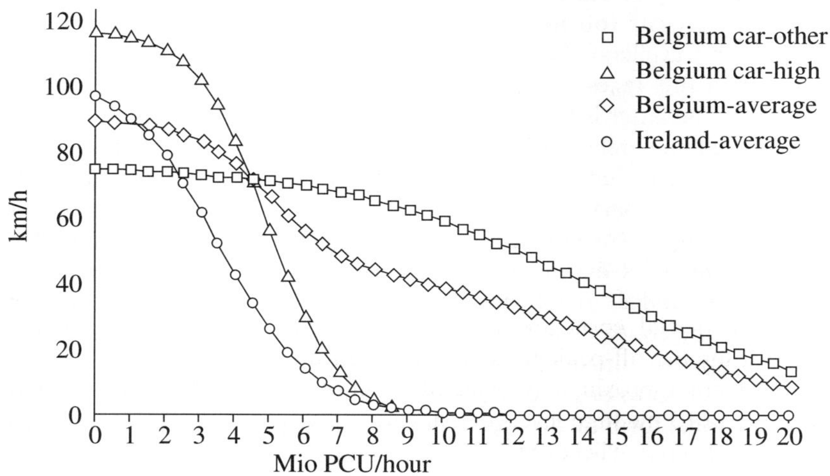

Figure 17.2 Speed–flow relationships for a car in the interregional model

the road network. The current congestion levels (and associated speeds) as well as the corresponding marginal external congestion costs additionally depend on local or regional traffic flows.

To give an example of the comparison of generalised prices and marginal social costs in the reference situation, consider the example for London in Figure 17.3. The figure gives the different components of the calculated reference prices and marginal social costs for four types of transport service: a small petrol driven single occupancy car in peak and off-peak (assuming that the driver benefits from free parking), and also the use of a bus in the peak period and in the off-peak period.

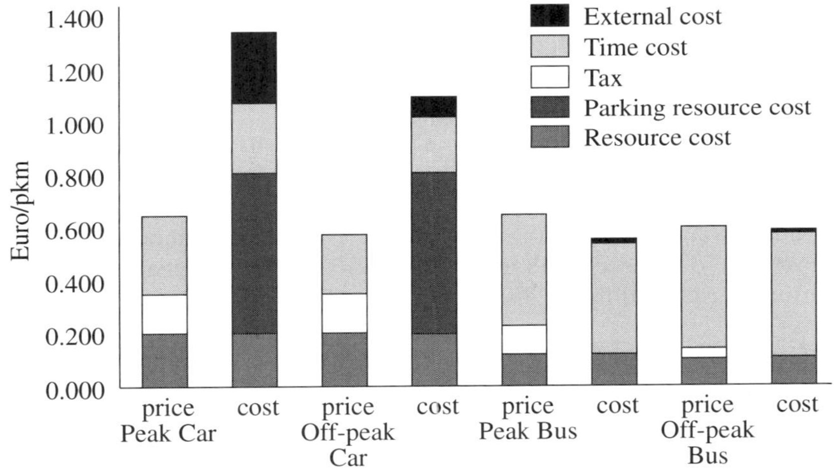

Figure 17.3 Reference prices and costs for London

Each pair of columns in Figure 17.3 represents generalised price and marginal social costs per passenger-kilometre (pkm) for one of the four cases. With respect to the car mode the figure shows that peak prices and marginal social costs are substantially higher than the corresponding figures for the off-peak period. Moreover, marginal social costs in both periods are approximately twice the level of generalised prices. A part of this is due to the high levels of parking resource costs which are not paid for in the case where free parking is available, the remainder can be explained by external (congestion) cost differences. Note that when parking was to be paid for at resource cost this element would also appear in the price paid and the shortfall of price from cost would be correspondingly less. It is also clear that, at least for the London case, marginal external cost exceeds the tax paid (expressed on a per passenger-km (pkm) basis) in the peak period, but that the opposite holds in the off-peak. Again, congestion is mainly responsible for this finding.

For bus transport, the prices are slightly higher than the marginal social cost. Taxes substantially exceed marginal external costs. Bus prices per pkm are similar to those for car, but marginal social costs are smaller, especially in the peak.

Figure 17.3 shows clearly that the external congestion cost dominates in the peak period. Other important external costs are accidents and air pollution. The methodology for the estimation of the marginal external costs is described in Chapter 7 of this volume.

17.3.2 Comparison of the Reference Scenario between Case Studies

The same procedure was followed in each of the study areas to estimate generalised prices and marginal social costs.

Some interesting results for the reference scenarios in the different cities and regions are given in Figures 17.4 to 17.10. Information is provided for each of the same four transport services discussed in connection with the London example underlying Figure 17.3. The figures demonstrate some substantial differences both in the estimated level of marginal social costs between cases, and in the disparity between generalised prices and social costs.

Consider estimated peak car costs in Figure 17.4. The figure shows that marginal social costs in Amsterdam and Brussels are almost twice those in

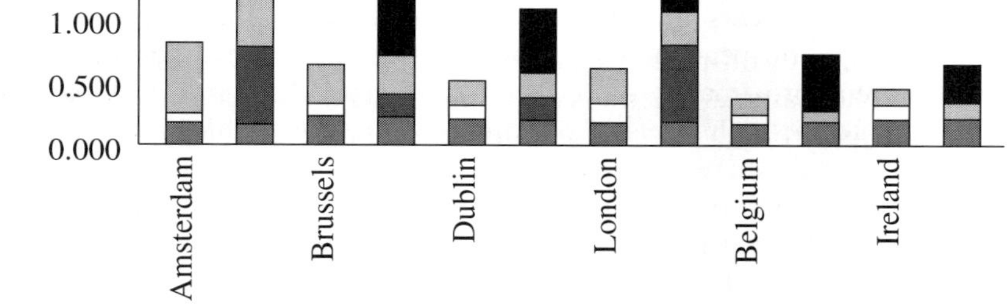

Figure 17.4 Peak car reference prices and costs

London or Dublin, mainly due to congestion cost differences. Estimates of generalised prices are reasonably close together, although their composition is quite different. For example, tax levels are much higher in London and time costs are much higher in Amsterdam. In the two regions (Belgium and Ireland) considered, peak car prices and marginal social costs are much lower than in the urban cases analysed; this is mainly due to higher average speeds in the interurban environment. The generalised price is slightly higher in Ireland than in Belgium, but the opposite holds for the marginal social cost, mainly due to external cost differences.

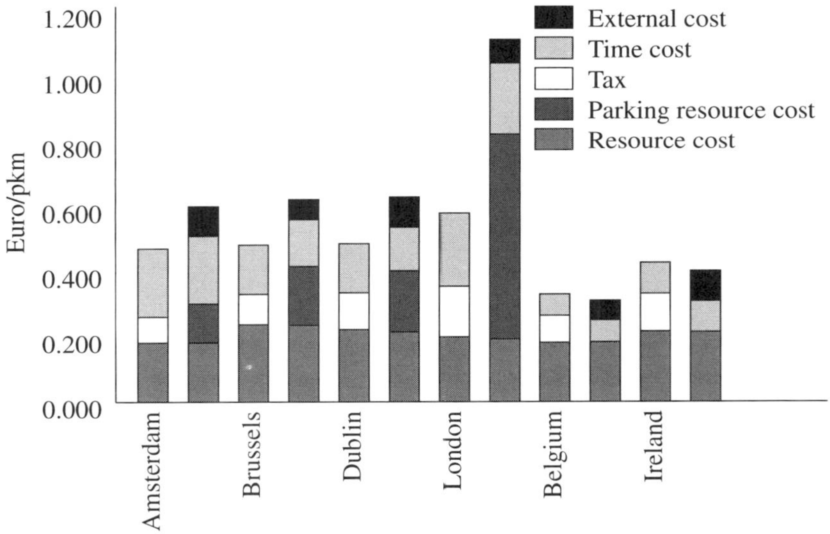

Figure 17.5 Off-peak car reference prices and costs

Turning to off-peak car costs and prices (see Figure 17.5) we observe a more consistent pattern across the different cities with the exception of substantially higher costs in London, due to the much higher resource costs of parking. Generally off-peak prices are also higher in London due to higher tax levels. The marginal external cost estimates do not differ so much in the off-peak, where congestion is less of a problem. For the interregional cases, off-peak marginal social costs as well as prices remain lower than in the urban situations. External costs are much lower than in the peak, and they are higher in Ireland than in Belgium. Note also that taxes in both countries slightly exceed the corresponding marginal external cost, at least for the off-peak period.

Bus costs and prices in the reference case are affected principally by the extent to which bus services are subsidised. The cost of public transport was assumed to consist of a fixed component (independent of the number of passengers) and a variable component. The marginal social cost of public transport only captures the variable cost component. Per vehicle-kilometre, the marginal social cost is greater in the peak than in the off-peak period because it includes the capital costs of vehicles and carriages. However, occupancy rates are higher in peak periods, so that the per passenger-kilometre cost can be lower in the peak. We interpret subsidies consistently as a situation where variable costs are not covered by revenues.

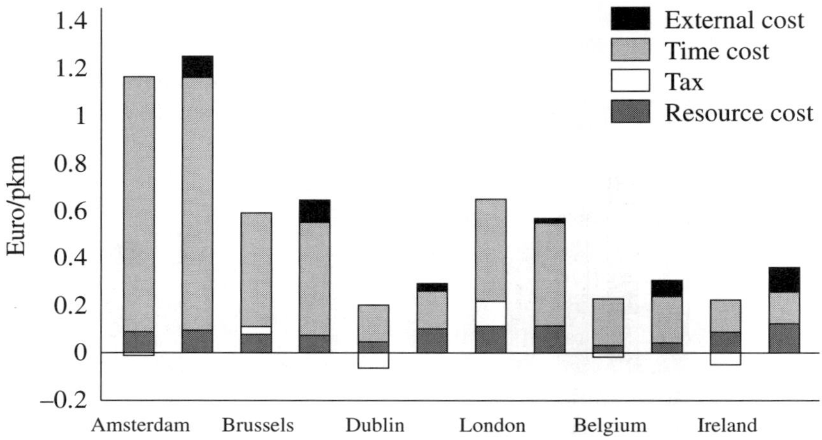

Figure 17.6 Peak bus reference prices and costs

With these ideas in mind, consider Figures 17.6 and 17.7. Note that subsidies are identified in both Amsterdam and Dublin in the peak period, whereas both in Amsterdam and especially in Brussels off-peak public transport is subsidised. These negative taxes are set against the resource costs in each case. Generally there is a closer fit between generalised prices and marginal social cost for bus transport than for car traffic in both the peak and off-peak periods in all of the urban areas. In London, where support to public transport is much lower, prices tend to exceed social marginal costs. In the other cities, prices are generally smaller than social costs, although for Dublin (in the peak) and Brussels (in the off-peak) this is only due to the level of subsidy. Per passenger-kilometre, external costs are generally much less significant for buses than for cars. Finally, in the two regions considered, subsidies are identified in the peak period; in the off-peak, Irish bus use is subsidised but in Belgium bus

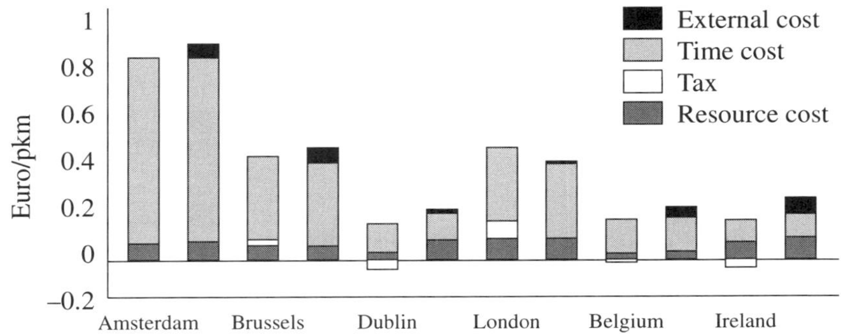

Figure 17.7 Off-peak bus reference prices and costs

users pay slightly more than the resource cost, resulting in small taxes. A similar analysis can be made for other public transport modes (underground, rail, tram).

Finally, consider Figures 17.8, 17.9 and 17.10 in which information related to non-urban freight transport is presented for Belgium and Ireland. Road transport is characterised by fairly similar generalised prices and marginal social costs in the two countries. Prices are way below marginal social costs. For rail freight transport, resource costs and subsidies in Ireland are much larger than in Belgium. However, generalised prices in the two countries are similar. External costs by rail are quite small.

This analysis of the reference case shows clearly the potential for better adjustment of prices to marginal social costs.

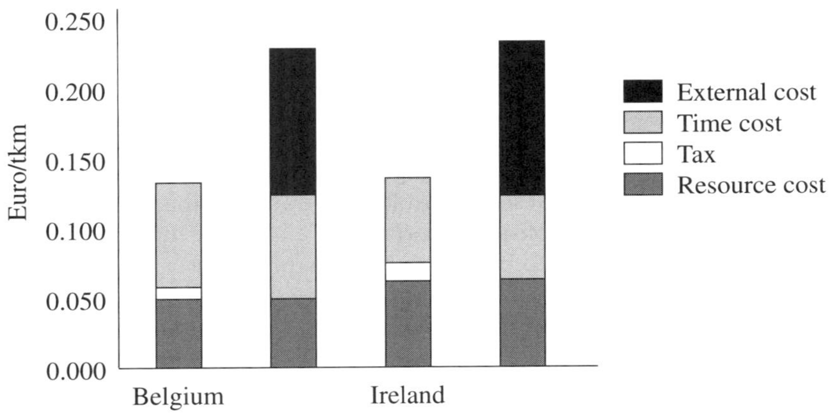

Figure 17.8 Peak truck reference prices and costs

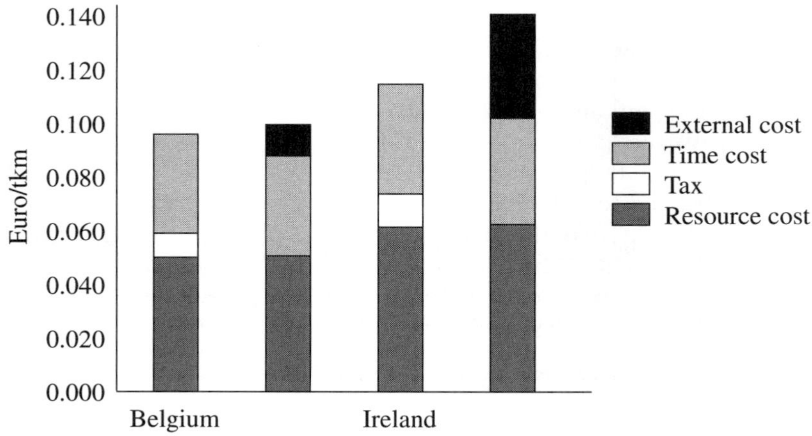

Figure 17.9 Off-peak truck reference prices and costs

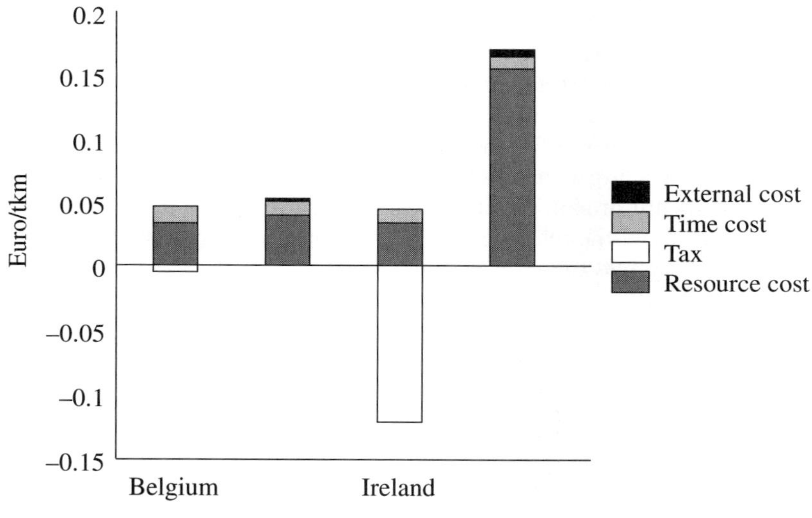

Figure 17.10 Rail reference prices and costs

17.4 THE FULL OPTIMUM SCENARIO

The full optimum scenario for the various cities and regions was calculated by maximising economic welfare under the assumption that perfect pricing instruments are available. This implies, amongst others, the existence of a pricing technology that allows price differentiation between peak and off-peak road traffic according to the differences in external costs generated. Moreover, in the urban model it implies the possibility to discriminate between inhabitants and commuters, and to operate a system of charges so as to make drivers pay the resource cost of parking. In the interregional model it implies the possibility to differentiate between domestic and transit traffic, and to differentiate between the use of highways and other main roads. Finally, in both models it implies the possibility of introducing improved vehicle emission technologies. Although refined discriminatory charges may prove very costly to implement, the full optimum yields an interesting estimate of the maximum gross benefit from improved pricing in the transport sector.

In the remainder of this section we present some summary results. We discuss the optimal prices in the different cities and regions, we look at the correspondingly optimal traffic volumes, we describe the main welfare effects relative to the reference equilibrium, and we briefly discuss the impact on travel speeds. We limit the presentation and discussion of results to a few relevant submarkets.

17.4.1 Passenger Transport

We first focus on passenger transport prices in the different cities that were studied. In Table 17.2 we present three pieces of information for a few submarkets (for example, a small gasoline car used in the peak period, off-peak bus transport, and so on) in all cities: the percentage increase in the full optimum price relative to the reference situation, the optimal tax (Euro/pkm), and the marginal external cost (Euro/km) at the optimum. To calculate percentage price increases we took into account the fact that only a fraction of car users pay the resource cost of parking in the reference case. In other words, the reference prices used to determine the percentage changes were a weighted average of prices for those that paid for parking and those that did not.

Several implications of the results are worth noting. One finding is that optimal pricing requires very large percentage increases in the price of car use in the peak period in all cities studied. Figures vary from 73 per cent (London) to over 280 per cent (Amsterdam) for inhabitants and from 74 per cent (Dublin) to 282 per cent (Amsterdam) for commuters. The large price increases come from two sources: high congestion in the peak implies high marginal externality taxes, and all car users pay the resource cost of parking in the full optimum. Another important finding is that the optimal price adjustment is much lower than the marginal external cost measured in the reference equilibrium. For Brussels, the marginal external cost in the

Table 17.2 Prices (% change w.r.t. reference), taxes and costs (Euro per passenger-km) for the urban case studies in the full optimum scenario

	Urban Model*											
	Amsterdam			Brussels			Dublin			London		
	Money Price (%)	Tax	MEC	Money Price (%)	Tax	MEC	Money Price (%)	Tax	MEC	Money Price (%)	Tax	MEC
Peak car petrol												
Inhabitants	147	0.91	0.80	155	0.60	0.46	116	0.45	0.24	152	0.54	0.11
Commuters	233	0.84	0.80	138	0.56	0.46	91	0.39	0.24	128	0.44	0.11
Off-peak car petrol												
Inhabitants	179	0.13	0.08	61	0.20	0.05	67	0.25	0.076	135	0.44	0.06
Peak car diesel												
Inhabitants	146	0.93	0.82	134	0.61	0.49	143	0.47	0.27	176	0.55	0.13
Peak bus												
Inhabitants	63	0.05	0.05	38	0.08	0.02	424	0.15	0.012	23	0.15	0.00
Off-peak bus												
Inhabitants	−1	−0.02	0.05	210	0.10	0.01	124	0.17	0.00	71	0.12	0.00

Note: * Improved emission technologies

reference equilibrium is larger than 1.5 Euro per vehicle-kilometre for a small gasoline car. The optimum tax is only 0.6 Euro per vehicle-kilometre. This is due to the external congestion costs that depend directly on the volume of traffic. The efficient volume of traffic is much lower than in the reference and this implies a much lower congestion tax. Also note that, in all cities, peak car users optimally pay somewhat more than the corresponding marginal external cost. This can be explained by the non-zero shadow cost of public funds used in urban models, which means that 1 Euro of government tax revenue is valued at slightly more than 1 Euro of consumer benefits. The consequence is that deviations between taxes and marginal external costs tend to be higher for non-elastic goods. Accounting for parking costs also introduces a remarkable difference between inhabitants and commuters. Inhabitants face at the optimum a higher tax per kilometre than commuters. Since commuters can spread out the parking fees over a larger average distance travelled, the impact of parking fees on the tax per kilometre is much smaller than for inhabitants.

The prices of off-peak car use all increase as well, although typically by much less than in the peak (ranging from 37 per cent in Brussels to 220 per cent in Amsterdam). This is due to fully charging parking costs and external costs. Again, all off-peak taxes exceed marginal external costs, and the extra tax is relatively higher than in peak periods. Also note that diesel is generally slightly higher taxed than gasoline in order to reflect differences in external pollution costs. The recent ExternE estimates have been used as a basis for the estimation of the air pollution costs. They show that external costs of diesel and gasoline vary strongly in function of population density, and that they are indeed higher for diesel.

Public transport prices rise in all cities and in both the peak and off-peak periods: existing subsidies are eliminated and replaced by taxes that reflect marginal external costs and a variety of own and cross-price elasticities. In Brussels and Dublin, off-peak public transport prices exceed those in the peak due to large differences in peak and off-peak occupancy rates.

Turning to the results in Table 17.3 for the interregional models applied to Belgium and Ireland, the following observations can be made. First, all prices equal marginal social costs, since a zero shadow cost of public funds was assumed in these analyses. Second, peak car prices rise by 38 per cent to 45 per cent for gasoline and by 57 per cent to 79 per cent for diesel; these differences are due to higher external costs and lower initial taxes on diesel. Off-peak car prices slightly decrease, by some 6 per cent in Ireland and 10 per cent in Belgium. The reason is that the existing tax system already implies taxes that exceed the marginal external cost at the optimum.

Bus prices rise in both the peak and off-peak periods. The larger increase in the peak can be explained by the higher external cost in this period and

*Table 17.3 Prices (% change w.r.t. reference), taxes and costs (Euro per passenger-km) for the interregional case studies in the full optimum scenario**

	Belgium			Ireland		
	Money Price (%)	Tax	MEC	Money Price (%)	Tax	MEC
Peak car small petrol Inhabitants	45	0.195	0.195	38	0.234	0.233
Off-peak car small petrol Inhabitants	−10	0.056	0.056	−6	0.097	0.096
Peak car small diesel Inhabitants	79	0.202	0.202	57	0.240	0.239
Peak bus Inhabitants	127	0.027	0.028	143	0.082	0.082
Off-peak bus Inhabitants	47	0.018	0.020	110	0.056	0.056

Note: * improved emission technologies

the lower initial tax in the existing tax system. Optimal bus taxes are much larger in Ireland than in Belgium, reflecting differences in external costs.

The drastic price increases of many transport services imply some obvious changes in transport volumes. The relevant changes are summarised in Table 17.4. Not surprisingly, all peak car traffic declines. The reduction is limited to some 9–12 per cent in the interregional model, but ranges from 19 per cent (Dublin) to 33 per cent (London) in the urban areas considered. The response of off-peak car traffic volumes to optimal price changes is quite different in the urban and regional environments. A decline is observed in all cities (ranging from 8 per cent in Brussels to 41 per cent in London), whereas both in Belgium and Ireland interregional off-peak car volumes rise, by 7 per cent and 6 per cent respectively. The reason is that off-peak car use in the interregional environment becomes cheaper at the full optimal price levels.

Public transport volumes in the peak period increase everywhere, with the exception of Ireland. The reason for the latter finding is the strong public transport price increase because of high initial Irish subsidy levels. In the off-peak period no consistent picture emerges due to differences in optimal price adjustments: Amsterdam and London experience a strong increase in public transport use, Belgium (including Brussels) and Ireland face a reduction of some 20 per cent.

Table 17.4 Total volume and composition of traffic (% change w.r.t. reference)

	Urban model *				Interregional model*	
	Amsterdam	Brussels	Dublin	London	Belgium	Ireland
Peak private	−28	−22	−19	−33	−12	−9
Peak public	34	28	−30	32	11	−33
Off-peak private	−19	−8	−14	−41	7	6
Off-peak public	53	−22	0	84	−20	−19
Total volume	−6.66	−8.25	−14.32	−13.73	−2.86	−2.35

Note: * improved emission technologies

Optimal pricing induces reductions in total transport volumes of some 7 per cent to 14 per cent in the urban areas considered, and much smaller effects (2–3 per cent) in regional transport. The largest impact is to be expected in Dublin and London.

Finally, consider the implications of optimal pricing for the speed of passenger transport flows. These are summarised in Table 17.5. All average speeds in the peak period substantially increase, reflecting congestion reductions. In the off-peak the impact is small.

Table 17.5 Speeds (% change w.r.t. reference)

	Urban model *				Interregional model*	
	Amsterdam	Brussels	Dublin	London	Belgium	Ireland
Peak private	50	70	32	13	5	12
Peak public	50	70	32	14	86	12
Off-peak private	3	0	3	2	0	−1
Off-peak public	3	0	3	2	0	−1

Note: * improved vehicle emission technologies

17.4.2 Freight Transport

Freight transport is explicitly included in the interregional models only. Therefore, results are limited to the Belgian and Irish interregional case studies. Results are in Table 17.6.

Table 17.6 Prices (% change w.r.t. reference), taxes and costs (Euro per ton-km)

	Belgium			Ireland		
	Money Price (%)	Tax	MEC	Money Price (%)	Tax	MEC
Freight (domestic)						
Peak road	63	0.046	0.046	100	0.085	0.085
Off-peak road	7	0.013	0.013	36	0.039	0.038
Railways	15	0.003	0.003	353	0.004	0.004
Waterways	0	0.004	0.004	–	–	–

At the full optimum, road transport is substantially more expensive as compared to the reference situation. In the peak period the price per ton-kilometre increases by 63 per cent (Belgium) and 100 per cent (Ireland) respectively. Off-peak road freight transport prices rise as well, by 7 to 36 per cent. Prices of rail freight services at the optimum reflect marginal social costs, which implies price increases of 15 per cent and 353 per cent for Belgium and Ireland, respectively. The figure for Ireland is to be interpreted in view of extremely high subsidies in the reference case. No notable price change is in effect for inland waterways, which are only relevant in Belgium.

The implications for freight traffic volumes are summarised in Table 17.7. As far as Belgium is concerned, domestic freight traffic flows by road decline by 5 per cent in the peak, and by some 3 per cent overall. Rail loses

Table 17.7 Volumes, composition of traffic and speeds (% change w.r.t. reference)

	Belgium	Ireland
Domestic freight		
Road	−3	1.50
Railways	−12	−87.85
Waterways	3	n-m
Transit freight		
Road	4	n-m
Railways	−26	n-m
Waterways	9	n-m
Total volume	−3.73	−7.44

Note: n-m = not modelled

traffic as well, some 12 per cent. The main beneficiary of optimal prices is waterway transport; flows increase by 3 per cent. The picture for transit freight is slightly different: road traffic gains, rail loses substantially (26 per cent), waterways gain (some 9 per cent). Total freight flows decline by 3.73 per cent as a consequence of optimal pricing policies.

The enormous rail price increases in Ireland yield a different picture. Total road traffic volume actually increases as a consequence of the relative price reduction in comparison with rail services. Rail loses substantially. Overall there is a marked reduction in freight flows by some 7.5 per cent.

17.4.3 Welfare Gains

A summary of the welfare implications of optimal pricing policies is given in Table 17.8. Welfare gains are presented as a percentage of total income. They are gross gains, since specific implementation costs of new pricing systems are not taken into account. First note that households are better off in all cities and regions considered. The reduction in congestion and pollution combined with the reimbursement of tax payments outweighs the utility loss due to the price increases of transport services. The largest percentage gains are observed in Brussels and Amsterdam, the welfare gains in Ireland are proportionally smaller. Second, optimal pricing induces large tax revenue increases. For passenger transport increases are much more limited in interregional transport than in the urban areas considered: they range from 25 per cent in Belgium to over 170 per cent in Amsterdam and Brussels.

In all urban case studies improvements in technology are found to be welfare-improving. In the interregional environment this is the case for diesel cars, but not for petrol cars. For diesel cars used in interurban transport the reduction in pollution compensates for the increase in resource cost.

In all cities and regions, external congestion costs as well as other external costs decline. Non-urban reductions in external costs other than congestion are much smaller; they amount to 3 per cent and 5 per cent in Ireland and Belgium respectively. This can be explained by the much smaller external air pollution and noise costs in non-urban areas due to lower population densities. For this reason it seems no longer optimal to select improved car emission technologies for petrol cars in non-urban areas.

17.5 IMPLEMENTATION OF NEW PRICING POLICIES

The case studies have shown that the pricing policies for transport are potentially welfare improving. The two major elements of the new policies are the

Table 17.8 *Welfare (% gain w.r.t. the reference situation), total external costs and tax revenues (% change w.r.t. reference)*

	Urban model				Interregional model	
	Amsterdam	Brussels	Dublin	London	Belgium	Ireland
Welfare gain	1.29	1.22	0.47	1.04	0.80	0.29
Tax revenue						
Passenger	171	185	123	108	25	29
Freight	–	–	–	–	233	[a]
Technologies						
Small gasoline	Improved	Improved	Improved	Improved	Standard	Standard
Big gasoline	Improved	Improved	Improved	Improved	Standard	Standard
Small diesel	Improved	Improved	Improved	Improved	Improved	Improved
Big diesel	Improved	Improved	Improved	Improved	Improved	Improved
External costs (other than congestion)	−14	−13	−16	−35	−5	−3

Note: [a] % change not calculable because of negative value in the reference situation. Tax revenue increases from −0.027 (in the reference to 0.696 in the full optimum) overall higher price levels and their degree of differentiation over time and space. A general increase of the price levels of transport and appropriate differentiation brings them in line with the corresponding social costs. Of course, the translation of simulation results of highly simplified models to policymaking raises many new issues. We discuss five of them: the reliability of the results, the costs of implementation, the use of tax revenues, the division of authority and the relation with environmental and safety policies.

17.5.1 Reliability of Results

The main contribution of using highly simplified models is to advance a direction of reform that is logical and internally consistent. Of course, using simple models to simulate important changes comes at a cost and is always somewhat risky. Therefore, the results need confirmation in several ways. More sensitivity tests and use of the models on a larger part of the European Community are needed as well as verifications on the basis of more detailed models and experiments. Network models can provide the necessary spatial desegregation; dynamic models are well suited to study in more detail the optimal transition to better pricing instruments.

17.5.2 Implementation Costs of Road Pricing

In the simulation results, no account has been taken of the transaction costs of new pricing technologies such as road pricing. The implementation costs consist of the costs of extra equipment in the vehicles, sensor equipment along the roads and operating costs. The latter may include important enforcement and monitoring costs. We have not studied the practical implementation and it is therefore difficult to advance cost estimates for the different cities and countries. Previous studies have shown that the cost of the simpler pricing systems (for example, one or two city cordons) cost about 30 to 50 Euros per car per year. This amounts to some 20 to 30 per cent of the gross benefits of congestion pricing. Moreover, the cost of these systems decreases every year due to learning effects and technological evolution. A reliable and cheap road pricing technology with technical specifications that are harmonised all over Europe is a prerequisite for the pricing reforms studied in this chapter.

17.5.3 Use of Externality Tax Revenues

The pricing reforms studied can be an important source of net tax revenue. For public transport the case is different from country to country. In some cities and countries, the marginal resource costs of public transport are not covered by the fares and this subsidy is no longer justified for efficiency reasons when the other modes can be priced correctly. In other countries, an important extension of public transport is justified and this could, given the decreasing marginal social cost of public transport, require higher subsidies.

In the analysis it has been assumed that the net revenue from the transport sector is used in an efficient way in the rest of the economy. More specifically, the implicit assumption has been that these revenues are used to decrease other existing distortionary taxes (for example, taxes on labour). When this efficient use of tax revenue is guaranteed, optimal taxes in the transport sector should in general be higher than the marginal social costs. Of course, if the increased tax revenue is used inefficiently by spending it on non-justified projects in the transport sector or in other sectors, the optimal level of taxes in the transport sector could very well be much smaller than those proposed here.

In general, two ways of using the extra revenue are advocated. The first is an investment in road infrastructure and in public transport. Investments in road infrastructure (beyond adaptation of the network to road pricing) are not necessarily justified by the mere fact that there are funds available. Road pricing will decrease the use of existing roads to the most efficient level and can be seen as a short-term substitute for road extension projects. It is the new, lower level of road use that should be considered as the basis for investment appraisal. Investments in public transport infrastructure are probably needed in most cities and regions. There is, however, no relation between the net revenue from optimal pricing in the transport sector and the needs for subsidies to public transport. Every project has to be judged on its own merits given the transport demand levels that can be expected with new pricing. An important second type of claim on the increased tax revenues on the transport sector is based on an income distribution argument. An attempt can be made to compensate all victims and in particular low income groups. Although it is technically speaking impossible and inefficient to compensate all victims, all households will be compensated by a reduction of labour taxes and by improved transport quality (higher speeds in peak periods). The poor households may need a specific compensation because of equity concerns. The best way to do this is via specific income supplements rather than via reduced transport prices. As a consequence distributional arguments do not provide a compelling reason not to account for external costs in pricing structures.

17.5.4 Who Decides Best on New Prices?

The most important requirement of more efficient pricing systems is that they should be adapted to local transport conditions. This requires that the levels of taxes on road use should not be fully harmonised at a European level, but need to be varied, both between urban and non-urban areas and between different cities. One implication of optimal pricing is that the role of fuel taxes and registration taxes decreases, because road pricing systems take over their revenue and regulating function. This requires that the authority on pricing decisions will have to move at least partly from the European level to the national and local levels. This raises two issues. First, what is the appropriate reallocation of transport tax revenues over levels of government? As there will be a shift of tax resources to the more local levels, this requires compensations for the other governmental levels if there is no parallel shift in public expenditure responsibilities. The second problem is related to the incentive of local governments to implement correct pricing levels. Local governments have superior information on local transport conditions but may abuse the new instrument to engage in tax practices where non-residents pay more than the marginal external costs. This can only partly be avoided by requiring non-discriminatory road pricing as the local governments may systematically charge more on routes or modes that are used more frequently by non-residents.

17.5.5 Safety and Pollution Policies

This study addresses several types of externalities simultaneously. The case studies have mainly been focused on the congestion externality. The major policy instrument studied has been the price of different transport modes at different times of the day. As the congestion problem is directly linked to the flow of transport this is the most successful instrument. Accident externalities and air pollution externalities have been reduced simultaneously but other complementary instruments should be used to reduce them. In the case studies, the imposed introduction of cleaner vehicles has been studied briefly. This needs to be complemented by instruments that address the present variance in car emissions as a function of make, age, fuel quality and maintenance. The same holds for the noise and road damage externalities. Furthermore, the accident externalities need to be addressed with specific instruments that pay attention to the driver's behaviour (insurance and liability incentives) and to the potential of infrastructure and road safety policies.

CONCLUSIONS

In this chapter a common modelling methodology has been used to estimate the gap between present and efficient prices for passenger and freight transport in six zones in Europe. Starting from observations on current prices and volumes, reference equilibria were constructed for the six transport markets. Combining current taxes with external costs estimates and unpaid resource costs produced estimates of the current inefficiencies in the pricing policies of transport in Europe. Peak private passenger and peak private freight transport were found to have marginal external costs which are considerably larger than the current tax levels and parking was found to be an important unpaid resource cost in urban areas. In the off-peak period, taxes on private transport are sometimes too high and sometimes too low. For public transport the picture is more complex with, depending on the case study, too low and too high subsidies on variable costs. Efficient prices need to be computed such that the price level corresponds to the marginal social cost at the efficient level of traffic. This means that optimal taxes are much lower than the marginal external costs measured in the reference equilibrium. Nevertheless, important increases in the money prices of peak private transport are required (between 35 per cent and 233 per cent) leading to decreases in volumes between 10 and 33 per cent. This requires spatial and time differentiated road pricing. Also public transport prices will need to be revised in certain zones. A reduction of the important subsidies on the variable costs of off-peak public transport is one of the priorities.

Important welfare gains can be achieved when this type of reform can be implemented. Of course, the analysis in this book remains a simple modelling exercise that needs to be confirmed by case studies in the rest of the EU and by the use of more detailed models and experiments.

BIBLIOGRAPHY

Bickel, P., Schmid, S., Krewitt, W. and Friedrich, R. (eds) (1997), *External Costs of Transport in ExternE*, Final Report.

De Borger, B., Mayeres, I., Proost, S. and Wouters, S. (1996), 'Optimal pricing of urban passenger transport, A simulation exercise for Belgium', *Journal of Transport Economics and Policy*, January, 31–54.

Glaister, S. and Lewis, D. (1978), 'An integrated fares policy for transport in London', *Journal of Public Economics*, 341–55.

Mayeres, I., Ochelen, S. and Proost, S. (1996), 'The marginal external cost of urban transport', *Transportation Research D*, **1**(2), 111–30.

Mohring, H. (1972), 'Optimisation and scale economies in urban bus transport', *American Economic Review*, 591–604.

Ochelen, S., Proost, S. and Van Dender, K. (1998), 'Optimal pricing for urban road transport externalities'.

O'Mahony, M., Kirwan, K. and McGrath, S. (1997), 'Modelling the internalisation of external costs of transport', *Transportation Research Record*, 1576, 93–8.

Index